CHICAGO
QUARTERLY
REVIEW

Volume 24
Winter 2017
The South Asian American Issue

Cover Illustration and design by Laura Williams

The Chicago Quarterly Review is published by The Chicago Quarterly Review 501(c)3 in Evanston, Illinois. Unsolicited submissions are welcome through our submissions manager at Submittable. To find out more about us, please visit www.chicagoquarterlyreview.com.

TABLE OF CONTENTS

NONFICTION

POETRY

ART

Editor's Note

Once, after having read an Indian-American friend's manuscript, I pointed out that Indira Gandhi was not the president of India but prime minister. He asked, "Are you sure?" That was a fair question. He had grown up in the U.S. I had grown up in Pakistan and that kind of knowledge was a natural part of me. The problem, though, was not lack of knowledge. No one person can be Omniscience. Dislocation, physical or emotional, allows on the one hand one to see things objectively and impartially, yet on the other it disorients the view as well. But, as Ibn al-Arabi said to Averroes, knowledge alone is not sufficient, as one needs imagination, humility, nuance, and experience to understand how one arrives at certain knowledge. The world needs a Rashomon Effect. I didn't know that Indian immigrants in the U.S. had been producing literature, as Roshni Rustomji-Kerns points out, since the early 1900s, some published in Ghadar Party pamphlets. The American Library Association's website confirms that Dhan Gopal Mukerji won the Newbery Medal for his *Gay Neck, the Story of a Pigeon* in 1928. He had already published poems and a play based on Laila and Majnun in San Francisco around 1916. How many South Asian writers writing in English in the U.S. would know their American literary history? It's no one's fault. An animal so huge, it is difficult for the South Asian writer to know all its body parts and how they relate to each other.

The South Asian writers included in this volume are alert to the fractured nature of their lineage and identity and to complicate matters further, we have competing master narratives. Our identities are always shifting a bit, are in a state of flux, and although our identities are often not a result of our conscious choices, they are determined by the point at which we, as individuals and as a group, are marginalized (by external forces) in the U.S. Despite being on the left, generally speaking, on most issues, we are not completely free of unchecked biases, our unexamined loyalties to the myths drilled into our and our parents' mind before we left our ancestral lands. Some of us might be more given to side with the political posturing by the leaders of our country of "origin" and readily find blemish in the beauty of others. We are not angels by any measure, but as Oscar Wilde hinted, some of us are looking at the star! Just as I had once erred in assuming that all

Hindus were vegetarians, there are assumptions held by some Indians about Pakistanis too. How much do Pakistanis know about Sri Lankan authors? Or Sri Lankans about Bengali poets except Tagore? As Cool Hand Luke said before getting shot in the neck, "What we've got here is a failure to communicate." Yet we, the unruly South Asian bunch, also like to talk, argue, holler, and listen and learn as well.

Luke might have been speaking not just for his fellow prisoners, but for many of us who are prisoners of history caught between the desire to escape and yet be caught. The failure to communicate is part of our identity, is embedded in our colonial history, served to us in the form of an era of discontinuity, a painful disconnect with our roots. We are the reed Rumi speaks of, our sound a mixture of longing and love of what we have lost, a yearning for union. But we also want to be the scream of Munch as we react to the barbarity displayed by our civilized world. The South Asian writers are a fractured bunch, severed from each other by history, language, culture, but—surprisingly—brought together, in a perplexing mosaic, by the same.

In the U.S., we form an extended family. We read each other's work. We compliment and critique. We keep an eye on what fellow SA authors are producing. We comment among ourselves about the risks our works take. We also seek each other out when times are hard and we plan our survival, our battles, seeking advice from other like-minded writers, artists, and intellectuals, asking for moral guidance from other minority or marginal writers.

It is incumbent upon every literary and artistic community to assess, from time to time, its progress, its "terra firma," and perhaps ask some hard questions. Where do they stand, how far have they come, and where might they be headed? Is it Tule Lake? Hotel Chelsea? White Castle? What is their relationship with the society and people whose voice and image they reflect? This burden of representing is more problematic, I suggest, for writers and artists from minority or marginal groups. Some might succumb to market forces, indulging in self-perpetuated orientalism. Others might crack under similar pressures to regurgitate an image of the *other* manufactured in a Tintin comic. Even the great poet Tagore admitted to have fallen prey to such a temptation:

> In my translations I timidly avoid all difficulties, which has the effect of making them smooth and thin. I know I am misrepresenting myself as a poet to the western

readers. But when I began this
career of falsifying my own coins
I did it in play. Now I am becoming
frightened of its enormity and I am
willing to make a confession of my
misdeeds and withdraw into my
original vocation as a mere Bengali poet.

-*Tagore, Letter to Edward Thompson, 1921*

I ought never to have intruded
into your realm of glory with my
offerings hastily giving them a
foreign shine and certain assumed
gestures familiar to you. I have done
thereby injustice to myself and the
shrine of Muse which proudly
claims flowers from its own climate
and culture.

-*Tagore, Letter to Sturge Moore, 1935*

Compared to Tagore, we are mere mortals, but the story doesn't
end there.

In the U.S., for those of us who write in English, whether as
immigrants or first generation, our claim to the language has been
contentious. We have been treated as outsiders like no other group,
both in terms of how we write and the topics we choose. In order to
get published, be accepted by the establishment, we too had to dilute
our text occasionally. Sometimes our English is too pretty and smells of
biryani. If we could change the *colour* of our text to *color*, or if we could
tweak our symbolism and metaphor to align with the western ear, or if
we could just stick to arranged marriages, elephants and monkeys, or
freshen up on poverty porn, our prose or poetry would be acceptable.
Not anymore! There was a time when the South Asian writer treaded
the linguistic register rather carefully. Rushdie's *Midnight's Children* shook
things up and made many of us his children. Not anymore! The new
South Asian American writer is a wild beast. When I sent out emails
to several contributors to find out who their influences were, none
mentioned Rushdie. That felt a bit cruel and sad. We owe him a great
deal. I certainly do. Along with Rulfo, Toomer, Toni Morrison, Adrienne
Rich, Henry Dumas . . .

The writers included here exhibit a deep level of self-confidence

[handwritten margin note: We must look to American lit at this when struggle we may connect t]

evident in their relaxed relationships with the topics they chose to write about. They seem unencumbered by the fear of how much and far they can stretch the text and syntax. As a sign of their confidence the formats they have chosen are all over the place. This also hints at the varied sources of their influences. Their concerns cut across religious, ethnic, gender, and national lines. They feel connected to the issues regarding race and U.S. imperial foreign policy. They claim the entire globe and act as witnesses to the good and bad our ruling elites do in our name. Their role models are writers from various ethnic and racial groups such as James Baldwin and Alice Walker. They mention Li-Young Lee, Audre Lorde, Ray Bremser, Sylvia Plath, Pablo Neruda and Faiz. One writer mentions Ginsberg, another Warsan Shire. And another Kamau Brathwaite and Haryette Mullen. Ramanujan, Hoskote, Purnendu Patri, and Mirabai and Kabir and more.

There have been a few attempts before to showcase the collective literary scream of South Asian writers in American publications, such as in the *Massachusetts Review* in the late '80s and *Weber: The Contemporary West* in the late '90s and 2016. There have been a handful of anthologies in the last twenty years, most notable among them Roshni Rustomji-Kerns's *Living in America: Poetry and Fiction by South Asian American Writers; Indivisible: An Anthology of Contemporary South Asian American Poetry* and *Our Feet Walk the Sky: Women of the South Asian Diaspora*. There has been one online effort by Soniah Kamal.

It is my feeling that this effort, at the behest of my friends at *Chicago Quarterly Review*, Elizabeth McKenzie and Syed Afzal Haider, pushes the boundaries like never before.

There were socioeconomic reasons why the South Asian writer felt reluctant to push the boundaries before. We were as a group different from other literary groups. There's a troubling socioeconomic reason for that. By and large, we are a very middle-class phenomenon. As a group, we have no ghetto experience, like those experienced by the Chinese, Vietnamese, Filipino, Latino immigrants, African Americans and Native Americans. Most of us came to this country equipped with a false sense of superiority, be it Muslim or Hindu, the two predominant groups, because we could speak English better than the natives. The literary establishment's patronizing attitude didn't help either. So our stories and poems mainly dealt with middle-class problems. Our hold on American reality was shaky, so we often resorted to explaining or fetishizing India or explaining Pakistan. From the establishment's point of view, we wrote safe material.

Though we remain a middle-class bunch, the younger generation of South Asian writers included in these pages show a remarkable transition. These young writers may not have experienced the harsh life of a poverty-stricken neighborhood personally, they have experienced wars, racism, sexism, and homophobia and have developed a deep sense of sisterhood with the many others who came before us and coexist around her. They have helped the previous generation of South Asian writers to break the shackles of self-censorship and be more involved with the country that their children call home. The pages of this issue crackle with hope and hiss with anger. Finally, as Roshni Rustomji-Kerns has written, literature produced by the modern South Asian American writers, walking in the footsteps of other marginalized writers, enriches and also subverts literary traditions and the grand narratives of American letters.

This is by no means a comprehensive roundup and the reader will miss some important names. There are some very fine writers whom I did not reach for one reason or another. This does not mean that I do not respect their work. Quite the contrary. Yet there are those, too, who did not respond or declined for reasons I understood well. This issue reflects my preferences and biases, but I hope any shortcomings a reader might anticipate is erased by the pleasure of what one finds in these pages.

–Moazzam Sheikh

The SONGS IN SAM'S HEAD
Neelanjana Banerjee

S am peels at the labels on his beer. He wants the bartender wearing the dirty cowboy hat to comment on his actions. If she says something, then he'll know what to say back. He'll smile and duck his head and tell her, "No ma'am, not me. I take out my frustrations in other ways."

The labels slide off the green bottles easy and Sam pastes them to the bar. Maybe she'll frown at the mess he's making, maybe she'll shake her head and say: "I'm gonna have to scrape all those off at three a.m. this morning, is that what you want?"

The bar is rectangular and the bartender moves around it quickly, dipping her head down to mix drinks and Sam likes her hat. It fits her small head just perfectly and it seems soft and worn, like she wore it ranching cattle, like she sweated in it and broke it in out in the sun. Her hair is curly underneath, so the hat sits up on her head. But he's just trying to focus on the hat so he stops looking at her tits. She's wearing a red tank top with silky black bra straps showing and there is a shadow of cleavage between her breasts. Sam imagines that he could fit two whole fingers in that dark space between her breasts. He goes back to peeling the labels.

Imagine that, Tanvir, Sam thinks. *Duto angol*, two whole fingers between her breasts. Sam laughs to himself imagining Tanvir slack-jawed in awe at the bar next to him, sipping on Johnny Walker, giddy with America. Sam would ask him how to say breasts in Bengali. He only knew the words his mother called them and that didn't seem right in this context. How do you say tits, Tanvir? How do you say: I want to tittie fuck the bartender?

Real American woman, Sahib Dada, Tanvir would say, approving. You have fun with real American woman then come back with me and marry yourself a nice Bengali girl.

I'll stick with the bartender, Sam says. You keep those fish head girls for yourself. Tanvir laughs, the sound whistling through the gap in his front teeth.

"You want another?" the bartender asks, suddenly in front of Sam. He nods, feeling his face burn. She uncaps a bottle and places it in front of Sam quickly, moving down the bar before he can make a comment. "Shit," he says under his breath. He goes back to peeling labels and looking around. It's seven p.m. on a Friday night, that lull when happy hour is fizzling out and the night crowd is coming in. There are a few old men sitting on the corner opposite Sam, wearing bolo ties and drinking beers. Sam imagines that they'll get up soon, get in their pickups and go back to their wives, spend the rest of the night in front of the television. Down the bar from him are a couple of nasty bar flies, a woman missing some teeth with a scratchy voice who keeps telling the same joke to the bartender, a joke about stealing peaches. "It's funny, huh?" the woman keeps saying. "It's a cute joke. It's funny, right, sweetie?"

The dusky tables in the corners are filling up and Sam eyes the girls coming in with their hair teased up around their head. His knee bounces, occasionally knocking against the wood paneling under the bar. He's only been back at the base three days and he's been waiting to hit the bars. After working the camps in Zakho and a few days in Riyadh, he flew to Germany and there everyone went out and drank for days. Sam remembers that time as just a bleary stupor, the bars full of soldiers so thirsty from the desert that they could barely even talk to each other. But since he's been back in America, he's had this feeling crawling up and down his legs, this excitement that he can't quite figure out. Even here, in the dusky lights of The Horseshoe, the second closest bar to the base, located in a strip mall next to the uniform tailor and a tanning salon—Sam feels like sipping on his beer is something new.

Next time the bartender comes over, he decides to tell her that he just got back from Desert Storm. Maybe he'd show her his military ID, tell her something interesting about the desert, about the time he traded a Bedouin boy five empty shells for a blue-tinged crystal that he kept for good luck, or about the scorpion baby he kept in a matchbox until it grew to be as big as his palm. Yeah, sure I'm proud, he'd tell her. I served my duty. I did my job.

You should sing her a song, Sahib Dada, Tanvir suggests, trilling off into a song that sounds familiar to Sam. There is nothing more beautiful than Rabindra Sangeet.

I don't know that shit, man, Sam says. But maybe I'll put some Johnny Cash on the jukebox. Sam takes a final swig of his beer and walks over to the jukebox. His jeans feel tight around the thighs and his sneakers feel light on his feet. He wonders how long it will take for everything to become normal again, routine. When he will stop measuring time forwards instead of backwards: *ten days ago today I was still in the desert. Forty-two days ago I was still breathing the foul tank air, rubbing on that shard of crystal, praying for it to end.* Sam stands at the jukebox flipping through the albums but the song Tanvir always sang flickers in his ears like a mosquito. Sam finds himself trying to hum the melody over the blare of Patsy Cline whining from the speakers.

Sam was trying to patch the holes in his boots with electrical tape he stole off the last construction convoy heading north to Zakho, when Sergeant Jeffries sent for him. Jeffries was a tall, pale man whose skin had not adjusted to the desert climate over the past nine months. It seemed to turn red, blister and then peel off in various stages and the men had begun calling him The Leper. Sam found him sitting in the command tent with his shirt off, a pungent-smelling paste covering his face and neck. His eyes were closed and Sam wondered if this was the only position he could sleep in.

"Sergeant?" Jeffries eyes shot open and Sam noticed that even his eyes were red-tinged as though the sun had begun eating away at his insides as well. "Sergeant, you asked for me, sir?"

"Right, Roy. Where are your people from again?" Jeffries grimaced while he stared at Sam through the cream on his face and began to slowly rub one of his shoulders against the thick canvas of his chair.

"My people, sir?"

"Yes, Roy. Where are you from?"

"Oh, I'm from Tulsa, sir."

"God damnit, Roy. Stop fucking around. I need to know what kind of language skills you have that we can use to get these fucking civilian workers off their asses. You speak Indian?" Jeffries was rubbing his shoulder more vigorously against the chair and Sam could hear the rough tear of his skin.

"Well, um, I can speak some … Indian," Sam replied, not interested in correcting Jeffries.

"Well, I need you to report to the loading dock at 0700 hours," Jeffries said.

"Are we moving north, sir?"

"Yes Roy, we're going to build refugee camps for the Kurds. That's our reward for winning this fucking war."

"Sir? My boots are slogging sand again. It's like walking with twenty extra pounds in each boot."

"Look, Roy, we ordered new boots back in January. What the fuck do you want me to do? Don't wear the fucking things, I don't give a fuck at this point." Jeffries reached back to his shoulder to attack the itching spot with his hand.

"Sorry, sir, I'll manage." Sam came to attention to salute and Jeffries, looking irritated, pulled his hand away to raise it to his head. Sam saw that it was bloody from relief.

The civilian workers that lasted out the war in Kuwait were a grimy bunch. Sam found the men hunched around a transport tractor that seemed like it had seen its share of close calls. These men wore sun-faded rags wrapped around their heads and disintegrating flip-flops on their feet. They had belts doubled around their thin waists. Most of them looked Asian to Sam, though he couldn't tell where they were from.

"These are the fuckers that are going to help us build shit?" Jimmy boomed into Sam's ear. A pudgy Filipino medic from California, Jimmy always managed to yell directly into Sam's ear. Sam didn't know him that well except he had, at one point, one of the biggest porn collections in their unit. Supposedly his brother ran a porn store somewhere in Orange County and kept Jimmy in a steady supply. That was before they started dumping stuff, before the war had begun and ended.

"What are you doing here?" Sam asked.

"Probably same as you, my Asian brother. I'm here to talk to the civilians. I didn't tell Jeffries I only know how to say 'Do you like it up the ass?' in Tagalog," Jimmy yelled, guffawing with laughter. "Nah, fer real though, look at these skinny-ass motherfuckers. But I guess these folks are the survivors, most of the workers were kicked out of Kuwait when the shit started to go down. These dudes not only survived, they're still working."

Jimmy walked up to two men squatting by the tires of the tractor and shot off a round of quick Tagalog. The men squinted up at him blankly and then looked at each other. Jimmy looked back at Sam. "I guess they don't like it up the ass," he screamed, laughing so hard that spit flew out of his mouth. Sam shook his head and walked around to the front of the truck to see if he could find someone to tell him what to do. The hood of the tractor was open and Sam saw two wiry brown legs sticking out of the bottom of the truck, the soles of the bare feet thick with calloused skin.

"Hello?" Sam called.

"Hullo?" A muffled voice answered from under the car. Then a small, dark-skinned man shimmied his way out from under the car. He was wearing an ill-fitting Coca-Cola t-shirt, black with oil stains, and a pair of torn trousers. His thick dark hair mushroomed from his head and his nose was both squashed and crooked. As soon as he saw Sam he smiled widely and the whiteness of his two rows of teeth was like a bolt of lightning.

"Indian?" the man asked, and suddenly Sam recognized his accent.

"Yeah, I'm Indian. You speak English?"

"Yes, boss. I speak," the man said, wobbling his head in a way that Sam remembered shopkeepers doing when his mother pressed them about cheating her with faulty scales back in Calcutta. "You are American soldier?" The man was beaming in such a way that Sam wasn't sure whether to feel proud or suspicious. He noticed the sizeable gap between the man's two front teeth.

"That's right. I'm here to translate for the workers. Are you in charge here?"

"I'm just driver. The truck needs fix." The man pointed to the truck. "Too much trouble on the road."

"Where are you coming from?"

"Mina Sa'ud. Supply ships at the port." The man stepped over to inspect the engine again. "The road has been worse since Iraq fall. So, you real American soldier, huh? What your name, boss?"

"I'm Sam. Well, my real name's Shambu. Shambu Roy." The man turned towards Sam and his smile grew so big Sam was worried that he might be wrong in the head.

"*Apne ki Bangali?*" the man asked incredulously. And it took a moment for the words to sink in: *Are you Bengali?*

Sam nodded his head, smiling back. "*Ha, ami Bangali.*"

The man laughed loudly and suddenly Sam realized that he wasn't so much of a man, that he was probably not too much older than Sam, perhaps twenty-five at the oldest. He thumped Sam on the back like an old friend and ran over to the driver side of the car, motioning Sam to stay where he is. He pulled a small package wrapped in pink plastic and rubber bands out of the glove compartment and went about unwrapping it. Finally, he produced a miniature bottle of whiskey, the kind you find in hotel rooms.

"Where did you get that?" Sam asked with amazement as the man pushed it into his hands.

"Drink, drink," the man said in Bengali, and Sam thought of his mother standing over him at the dinner table, making sure he drained his glass of milk. Sam took a small fiery sip and handed it back to the man, who also took a little sip, leaving just enough for another day. "In Mina, you can get many things on the docks. Listen, whatever you want you can get. What do you want, Sahib Dada? Next time I will get it for you. What do you want? Tell me. Just tell me and I'll bring it."

There's something about the way the Bengali sounded in this place, the fast way it rolled off the man's tongue, the lisping Bangladeshi accent, that filled up Sam's head. Suddenly there were words in his mind that he hadn't thought of for over a year. Sounds that he knew more completely than any other sound and here they were erupting from this stranger's mouth next to a truck full of bullet holes, in the middle of desert that Sam had been wandering for months. The sun was setting in the ferocious way it seemed to each day and the long rays of orange start to stream around the giant HETs that were used to haul tanks to the border.

"What's your name?" Sam asked the man.

"Tanvir," he replied, reaching over to thump Sam on the back again. "Sahib Dada! How amazing, a real American Brother."

The Horseshoe is filling up and Sam's ears pop, which means he's getting drunk. People crowd around the bar, pushing in to order their drinks. Another bartender comes on, a man with a ponytail and a droopy moustache. Damn Tanvir, Sam thinks. I didn't even get to tell you about the goofy-looking dudes that populate this country.

The bartender with the hat comes around again and Sam waves her down, drunk enough to open his mouth now. Her nose is slightly upturned and Sam wishes he could take a picture of it and send it to Tanvir.

"Hey, what's your name?" Sam asks.

"Do you want another drink?"

"Yeah, I'll have another. But what's your name?" The bartender reaches into the cooler under the bar and opens the beer, giving Sam a quick look down her shirt. She slaps the beer down in front of him and starts to clear the rest of his mess.

"It's quite a mess you've made here," she says, smiling tightly.

"Hey, I knew you were gonna say that," Sam says, throwing five dollars on the bar. "C'mon. Can't I just know your name?"

"It's Miranda," she sighs, giving him the tight little smile again. She turns to someone standing behind Sam and takes the order.

"Hey, Miranda. You know what?" Sam says, feeling brave.

"What's that?" She moves quickly along the bar, holding bottles by both hands.

"I just got back from Desert Storm."

"Is that right?" Miranda says. "You and every other guy in here, huh?"

"No, really. I was out there. I'm a soldier. You wanna see my ID?" Sam went for his wallet.

"No, I believe you. That's great." She wipes her hands on her jeans and moves on to the next order. She ends up in front of Sam again, squeezing lemons into a tall glass.

"I was in Desert Storm. Yeah, I'm proud of what I did," Sam says, smiling at her. "I did good things there."

The bartender rolls her eyes at him and puts down the drink.

"I don't know why you guys all think that I'm going to get excited when you tell me that you just came back from the desert. You think

I care? Maybe I think what happened over there was a crock of shit. Then what? You're proud of what you did? Well, I'm not. Sorry, but I'm tired of pretending so tell your war stories to someone else."

Sam laughs at what she says because that's what he does when he's embarrassed. She moves away to work the other side of the bar and Sam laughs some more. He tries to hum one of the songs that Tanvir always sang, one of the ones the freedom fighters in Bangladesh sang during the war, but he can't get it. Sam catches the attention of the other bartender and orders a shot of whiskey.

After they first met, Sam found out that Tanvir had driven tractors full of batteries and water along MSR Dodge, a two-lane road that ran north along the Kuwait/Iraq border, for months during the buildup and even during combat. While Sam was in full biological warfare gear inside an armored vehicle waiting for the word to go, Tanvir was racing jeeps past enemy lines in order to help the ground units advance their positions. He didn't even have a gas mask. Tractors he had driven had been shot at, driven through mine fields and even targeted by Iraqi bombers. He always managed to escape or, more often, accomplish his mission. The man was indestructible, it seemed. A war hero.

But really he was just a fisherman's son from a village in Faridpur who had too many sisters. He told Sam about how he waited around the Kuwaiti Embassy for weeks, sleeping on the streets of Dhaka's rich Gulshan neighborhood, trying to get recruited. And when it had happened, his whole family had come to the airport to see him off. He had just been working at a refinery for four months when the trouble started but he couldn't go back, not so soon. He heard that contract companies were hiring truck drivers to run supplies for the Allied forces and he signed up. Most of the other drivers he started with were dead, not so much from combat but from bad accidents and wrong turns along the desolate MSRs. But Tanvir laughed it off, claiming he had a good sense of direction and a good relationship with Allah.

In Zakho, Tanvir sang songs while he built latrines for the Kurdish refugee camps. He sang while they lowered him by rope to dig the deepest part of the wells. He worked three times faster than the others and had seemingly boundless energy. The other soldiers didn't associate with the civilians, but Sam found himself gravitating towards the workers more and more. He was put in charge of translating for other migrant workers from Bangladesh and India, all of them with similar stories as Tanvir. There were others from Indonesia, Sri Lanka, Sudan and the Philippines. It was the first time Sam held a position of power. It was the first time that he was doing work that he understood. It was the first time since the Gulf War started that Sam felt as though he were helping people.

"Doesn't the singing make you tired?" Sam called up to Tanvir one day, as he was helping batter down a roof on one of the shelters.

"No, the songs give me energy," Tanvir called down.

"What are you singing about? I can't understand," Sam confessed later, as they handed out blankets to an endless line of Kurdish families who were slowly coming into the safe zone from the mountains.

"Sahib Dada, how can you not know these songs? Rabindranath? Kazi Nazrul Islam? Even in America, you must have listened. I knew Bengalis in Kuwait. Rich Bengalis with fancy houses and TVs, and even they listen to these songs." Tanvir broke out in song again and a little girl smiled at the two men as she walked by. "My sisters love to sing. They were always singing in the house. We would go up on the roof at night and have singing parties, sometimes going until morning prayer started."

"When was that?"

"Four."

"Jesus Christ! Four in the morning? You got up to pray at four in the morning?"

"Everyone does. You are a Hindu, right?" Tanvir asked, seriously.

"I don't know. I guess," Sam shrugged.

"Are your parents Hindu?" Tanvir asked, confused.

"Yeah, my mom's really ... I don't know the word in Bengali. Religious. She prays a lot."

"Well, if your parents are Hindu, you must be too?" Tanvir said, laughing at Sam's recalcitrance. "I had a good Hindu friend in my village. I liked her very much."

"A girl?" Sam teased. "What kind of friend was that?"

Tanvir laughed. "Oh Sahib Dada, you don't know what you are missing. You come to my village and meet my sisters. My village has the most beautiful women in the country. We're known for it. You see these women, then you'll understand why I am singing all the time."

"No, you should come to America. I'll take you to one strip joint and you'll forget all about girls in Bangladesh. Trust me," Sam said. "Actually, you should come to America anyway. You'll make way more money for your family there."

"Really, Sahib Dada, you think I should come to America?"

"Sure, I'll help you out."

"I'll come then. We can work together maybe. I know in America it is easy to start your own business. Easy to succeed." Tanvir smiled his infectious smile and Sam didn't have the heart to tell him the truth.

It is so loud at The Horseshoe now that people have to yell to the bartenders, so people keep yelling their drink orders into Sam's ears.

He finally gets tired of sitting at the bar with people pushing into him from all directions and decides to get up, pick another song on the jukebox. He tries to walk over but there is a group of people blocking it, some big-haired girls standing around listening to a stocky guy with the leathery tan of someone who was in the field. Sam doesn't recognize him but the bartender was right, everybody in this bar was probably over there at some point. Sam is drunk now and he doesn't know where to go. He should probably leave, go get some air, but instead he just stands in the middle of the room feeling as though he is floating towards the ceiling because he is used to walking around with hot sand in his boots. One of the girls looks back at him and he tries to smile at her but someone pushes him from behind and he stumbles instead.

"Damn it, Tanvir," he mumbles. "Where are you?"

He moves over to lean against the wall next to the jukebox. He wants to just lean his head back and zone out, try and sober up, stop thinking about the desert.

"The worst part were the fucking Abduls, man," he hears the guy at the jukebox say. "The fucking sand niggers, man. Those guys in Vietnam had it easy with the fucking gooks. These people are such morons that they live in the desert. There were these crazy fucking homeless sand people called bodins or something. Man, you could give 'em a shoelace and they'd give you a piece of gold. I'm serious. A buddy of mine got a real freaking nugget of gold for some shoelaces."

Sam knows he should go outside. He knows that he's too drunk to be in this bar but he doesn't. He moves closer to the jukebox. He lets the man's words climb inside of his head, he hears a buzzing in his ears, a sloshing. He hears the desert winds lashing against tents. He hears the girls laughing too hard.

* * *

"Weren't you afraid?" Sam asked Tanvir one day as they were unloading a supply truck.

"Afraid of what?"

"Afraid of dying?"

"I'm not so afraid. I was just doing my job. I knew I couldn't die."

"So, you just know you're not going to die. That's crazy. You were risking your life and it wasn't even your country. It wasn't your war."

"You are here because it is your country?"

"No."

"Then?"

"I was afraid. I didn't want to be there."

"You, too, are just doing your job. I don't believe in all this country and belief. There are still places near my village that if you try and dig a well, all you will come up with are bones because they buried thousands of people there. Thousands of people because they wanted to speak this language we are speaking. What if we were there then instead of here, fighting in someone else's war. Would that have made any difference?"

* * *

Sam tries to remember how to laugh at the jokes the man by the jukebox is making. He knows that he has laughed with men like this. But all he can remember is trying to dig out of his trench in the sand during a sand storm, the way he couldn't breathe.

"Fucking Christ. You have no idea. They went about it all wrong. They should have dropped a huge fucking bomb on the whole area. Wiped the whole region out, just flattened it and then had some scientists go back and try and make it habitable again. Then we could just use the oil and have gotten rid of those useless motherfuckers," the man says. "You know what I'm saying? And god, now they have all the poorest people from other countries coming in to work and rebuild shit. Talk about the scum of the earth."

Sam wants to tell the bartender about Tanvir. That's what he should have told her. He should have told her that he knew a real war hero, one that wasn't there for the wrong reasons. He wanted to tell her that he was going to bring Tanvir here and then she could see for herself. She had it all wrong. Everyone had it all wrong.

* * *

It was barely six weeks in Zakho before Sam found out he was going home. He had been in the Middle East for nine months. The Kurds were returning to their villages and Tanvir was going back to Kuwait to work on rebuilding the city. He had heard that the construction contracts with the big American companies were good, that they offered benefits and housing. Before he left for Riyadh, Sam found Tanvir working on a truck.

"You remember India, Sahib Dada?" Tanvir asked, his head under the hood.

"I remember it. Sometimes," Sam said.

"You say, I should come to America but maybe you come to Bangladesh. My village has more ponds than you can count. Imagine that, we come from a place that has as much water as this place has sand. Can you imagine?"

"I can't imagine. Not from where we're standing." Sam looked across at the hurried shelters they had made. The sun was just coming up and the chill was still in the air. Tanvir had a scarf wrapped around his head the way Sam remembers old men doing in India. It made him laugh.

"Well, I'm going," Sam said, offering his hand to Tanvir.

"Don't you know, in Bengali you don't say anything about leaving. Instead you say, I'm coming again soon."

"That's right. I remember," Sam said. "*Ami ashchi.*"

* * *

Sam should leave. He should go outside and throw up in the parking lot but instead he pushes past the big-haired girls in order to find the bartender.

"Hey, dickwad, watch where you're going," the man says.

Sam stands again in the middle of the room and tries to listen. I'm not so afraid, Tanvir says. I'm not so afraid.

"Hey, do you speak English? I said watch out," the man says, coming up to Sam. "You'd think I've had enough with the assholes for the last four months. Hey, what's your problem?"

Sam turns around and the man stares at him, his eyes narrowing down into small blue points. The man's mouth keeps moving but Sam can't hear him anymore. He clenches his fist tight and listens to it swish through the air. ∎

THREADING THE GHAZAL
Tanu Mehrotra Wakefield

We braid our days with snippets of song:
lullaby, sacred, torch, or love song.

"She's gotta be a werewolf with arms that hairy." Marshmallow fluff
on Eric's cheek.

Oh, Miss Pauzer. Your hair, feathery black.
Your glasses, rimmed black. Your face leaning closer.
The arm hair, black and long. *Werewolf.*
Your skin—browner than Mrs. Cebeck. Than Miss Hendershot.
Closer to my color. Color thought dirty.

"Hey, you sure you ain't black? You sure I didn't see you on the
Soooouuuuuuul Train?!"

We memorize "The Road Not Taken"
I memorize, "How to Eat a Poem" after that.
Margaret memorizes "I am Nobody"
Who are you?

You say bring in songs. Songs are poems.

I offer Olivia Newton-John's "Dolphin Song." Evan
hums "Rock the Casbah" at his cubbyhole.
He will always be cooler.

You say, send something to *Cricket* magazine. I am eleven and
getting my period, brown spots showing through my pink shorts at
times.

I want sound to invade my body, then hum.
So do you—whoever hovered above song?

Choose a form:
rondeau or aubade or ghazal or sestina or fee fie fo fum
    Subtle modulation between skin and teeth
        Not because she's dirty
        not because she's clean
        just because she kissed a boy
        behind a magazine, hey tomboy
I need, I want a microphone.
There's always been one in my home.
Used to lip synch "On the Radio" then
    "Magic" then "Get Nervous" then "Lucky Star"
    then "Hang Onto Your Love" then "Stay"
    then pesticides leaked on it in the garage
    and Goodwill hauled it away.

This is dedicated to microphones rotting in garages all across America.
Where I'm from—just another exit off I-95.
Another town you pass through on the way to somewhere else.
I don't know the Bartram sketches. The flora and fauna.
The Hurston juke joints. The how and why of fried gator bits.
I do know this: Sudesh Kumar, sociology professor two hours a day,
entrepreneur all other hours, once turned an ice rink into a disco
during that craze.
This can be done. Where I'm from.

        The straight shot to joy tastes lonesome and long:
        May your days end always in drum and song.

My mother waxes happy today. Because Amitabh Bhachan's son got
engaged to Aishwarya Rai—Bollywood queen with the light colored eyes.
    Indians are suckers for the light eyes. *I ran my mouth off a bit too much,*
                        oh what did I say?

A lyric always pulsing through the vein whether we like it or not.

He says, lots of songs start with a chorus. They don't always launch
    into verse.
Like *Sugar*, he says, honey, honey, honey.
Song to be studied.

When running
sound comes cleaner
momentary and flashing
some spangled-maker thing
appears then disappears, so sweet,
so sparkly.

> Today my girl *oohs*, *aahs*, and *dootdootdoos*
> then turns to serenade the stove with song.

Now is the hour of song:
"We came to this country on July 4th 1969. Nakul Uncle picked us up
     from LaGuardia
then drove us somewhere, to a park, in Brooklyn, for a barbecue. And
     the people were so loud! So jovial.
Happy-go-lucky. Laughing, talking. Singing songs like we used to.
They were eating the watermelon with their hands. Juice on their
fingers and chins. And laughing! Singing songs just like back home
spitting out seeds in the grass. Can you believe in England, I had to
wear gloves to do grocery shopping! Can you believe? Here the people
were so free.
Eating watermelon with the fingers! That's when I knew this was the
     place for me."

SONG FOR ST. AGNES
Tanu Mehrotra Wakefield

That needle in a pin cushion thrown out to sea
all the wares of the world blown out to sea

At St. Francis, Jessica, with all her limbs.
Green sweater, rainstorm, walking within.
At St. Agnes, a hook instead of her left arm
That visit to the Alligator Farm.
we march to mass, march to mass
me the sole Hindu, waiting in the last pew, full of hunger
to make the sign of the cross, to taste the wafer my friends taste

Whole bodies wrapped in thievery
the stars shone out to sea
Eliza attempted an escape every day
runt of a first grader screaming hog wild
her arm twists, tartan skirt flips, habits fly
rulers, pursed lips, stinging palms

Oh, Eliza, little Liza Jane. Oh, Eliza, little Liza Jane.

At Mokie's funeral, Sally Aunty, a Hindu of homeopathic hilarity, takes
communion with the other Catholics.
I envy her that, to taste the wafer
tall cross as far as the eye can see. tall cross hanging over the sea.
Choosing the instruments, I think, *clarinet*. Mom says, see the flute.
Lord Krishna played that.
It shines and my Mom likes things shiny and divine.

Your elaborate plates astound the king
who scatters pearls sewn out at sea

St. Agnes—girl with a lamb
the kind Mary had or the kind
nun sweating in the car
while I try to grasp my dog's tongue.

We sing for our supper with the *throats of birds*
as throatless birds circle out to sea

Here, love notes to Jon Janson
who fancied himself the Fonz.
There, Peter Keo who had a wife but couldn't keep her.
Claimed he kissed me in the playhouse. This I wish.

A pickpocket's fingers, deft and spare, leave
change in the wallet and a phone out to sea

Mokie peels kumquats with dirty fingernails. Had a horse named Rags
to Riches.

The days begins, walking barefoot to Big Joe's. June and Virginia chase
each other. In the front door, out the back, front, back, front, back,
around and around until the door slams shut and Junebug's hands
smash glass. The day ends with the babysitter flying into the bathroom
as the radio says: Elvis is dead.

O great ocean, o great sea
run to the ocean, run to the sea

ketchup and mayonnaise mixed
sweet tea   magnolia tree: any genus of North American and
Asian shrub
who's smacking?
sit *Indian* style, spoon sugar out of the sugar bowl

Under a lighthouse, you said you would paint there
Under a lighthouse, fish groan out to sea

Ending up at St. Agnes because I came home from public school and
     stated a plain fact: boys have hot dogs, girls have hamburgers.
"In Srinagar, two Anglo-Indian boys were our neighbors. Father was
Indian. Mother was Irish. They had all the latest records. There was
Frank Sinatra. Doris Day. Of course, there was Elvis Presley. He sang
so much about his baby. I used to think Americans must be awfully fond
of children."

How many bodies swallowed there? How many fair,
and forgotten? Tanu finds them, all the bones, out at sea

SAHEB
Somnath Mukherji

My chest hurts these days and I become breathless easily. It was not always like this. I have to refuse passengers with heavy loads now, even if they offer extra money. It hurts to refuse honest money.

The coughing rattles my ribcage. I have spent two hundred rupees to attach the black plastic sheet that I keep rolled up with the hood. When it rains, I pull the plastic over my head and tie it to the wooden pole fixed to the frame in front of me. It only protects me from the showers coming straight down. But water comes in from all sides and soaks me in no time. The rain hides the sweat. Only I know how much I sweat.

People whose houses are connected by narrower lanes prefer to hire a rickshaw. Honestly, in the neighborhoods where I have been working for the last seven years, there are lanes where nothing other than a rickshaw would fit. Many old people who live by themselves also rely on my rickshaw to get around. I think their children must be living far away earning a living. Sometimes when a gray-haired man climbs into my rickshaw I think of my father. How would he have felt to ride a rickshaw pulled by his son, I wonder.

At times, passengers instruct me to take them through the lanes away from the main road, where there is some peace and quiet. I don't blame them. The traffic on the main road has become horrendous. While people still hang from the crowded buses like suckling piglets, big air-conditioned cars with one or two people choke the road. To add to the problem, the auto-rickshaws have penetrated the inner lanes, making it so difficult for me to find quiet lanes. Besides, how far can you get away from one main road before you hit another? This is a city, my friends!

I have to admit that I too enjoy taking these people through the quieter lanes. Firstly, because they are alone hence less weight. Secondly, it feels good to hear the squeaking of the chain as it tightens under my pressure. The sound from the horn reverberates between the buildings without being drowned out. Sometimes these passengers sit and drink on my rickshaw as they imagine breathing in fresh air. Poor souls, they must have no kindred spirits to drink with. Too many people for some, not enough for others.

I remember a man who had come to the rickshaw stand under the banyan tree about two years ago, days before the Durga Puja. He had two little boys with him and wanted to see some of the Puja pandals. Around here, we call the temporary pavilions that house the mother Goddess for ten days as pandals. I don't know what people call it in other places. In fact, I don't know much about other places although I have heard stories about Delhi and Bombay. At the time the pandals were only half way through their final shapes, with their bamboo framework standing like skeletons at dead end streets and open playgrounds.

The man wanted to show the children some of the pandals in the neighborhood and eventually the idol of Goddess Shitola. It is very popular with children. I have never seen such a big idol—as high as a two-story house. The older boy seemed to be around seven while the younger one was barely three. The man seemed relieved after I had made a turn into a lane from the main road.

"When I was your age, your grandfather used to take me and your mother around the neighborhood like this," I heard him say, his voice trembling as the rickshaw rode over a part of the rough unpaved lane.

"Mostly the ride is going to be smooth," I assured him as we got on the smoother part of the lane. "I will show you the idol of Kartick next to the gas godown, then the famous pandal of Nabarun Samiti and after a few more pandals we will be in front of the large idol of Goddess Shitola," I had addressed the older child, turning around precariously to make eye contact with him.

"Where is your home, bhai?" the man had asked me.

"Do you mean here... or my original home?"

"Original. The place you were born and where your parents live," he clarified.

"I am from a village in the Sundarbans. People in Kolkata only know of the tigers that abound there. But there are also thousands of people who live there," I said quickly, anticipating the need to squeeze the rubber horn before making a sharp right turn. One never knows what to expect on the other side of a sharp curve.

"Have you seen a tiger?" the older boy asked.

"From a distance. When I was your age," I said and continued with the reply to the man's question.

"On the Lakshmikantapur line, you have to get down at Gobra and take a bus from there for an hour. Then take a boat across the river. Walking for about thirty minutes on the other side, you reach our village. Anyone can show you our house there," I explained, hoping that his question was sincere. After all, it is not every day that people ask me about my home.

"How long does it take for you to get home from here?" he asked.

"No more than six hours, but it can be longer during the monsoons."

As we reached the gas godown, the man climbed down to show the idol of Kartick Thakur to his nephews from a closer distance—that gave me a much needed rest. I was getting tired from talking and pedaling at the same time. I wiped my face with the gamcha, feeling the need for a new one, cleared my throat and spat out the phlegm that builds up on the back of my throat. As a rule, I never spit when I drive though I have seen many rickshaw-wallahs do that. I could see the man pointing to the idol and saying something to the younger child who was in his arms. The child reminded me of my own nephew. It had been seven years since I last saw him. My elder brother had deserted our family when we needed him the most. Those were really bad times. My nephew would call me Chhoka.

"Wasn't it nice?" I had heard the man ask of his older nephew as they were climbing back into the rickshaw.

"I really liked the peacock near his feet," replied the boy.

"Will we be seeing more idols of Kartick Thakur?" the boy asked eagerly.

"Not Kartick Thakurs, but we will be seeing other idols," I offered.

My answer was met with silence from the child who seemed understandably uncomfortable talking to a rickshaw-wallah.

The man gently repeated, "Did you hear what he said? We will be seeing other idols."

I understood that the repetition was to assuage my feelings, but I was used to the discomfort of the children from good families in talking to me.

I felt the pain rise within my chest as I stood up on the pedal and used my body weight to get the rickshaw moving. The first few pedals were difficult even at that time; nowadays it feels like I am pulling a train.

"What made you come to Kolkata?" the man had asked.

As we were going up a gentle slope, I raised my left hand to ask for some time. The silence let me ponder over the question.

What made me come to Kolkata? How should I answer this question? He was asking the story of my life. Why should I lay bare my life along with its wounds to this stranger? I thought of giving him a quick cooked-up answer that would bring the conversation to an end. But then, no other passengers had ever asked this question before. Or was he telling me that I should not have come to Kolkata. Did he belong to Kolkata more than I did?

Much after I had overcome the slope, I kept pedaling while the memories of the hard times that befell my family came rushing in. As I stared at the eroded treads on the front wheel, the memories seemed to be springing up from the road where the wheel touched it—as if they were musical fountains bursting out their pent up water in anticipation of the magical touch of the wheel.

I pedaled harder and squeezed the rubber horn a few times without any good reason. I felt the shirt sticking to my back. The silence was strangulating. I almost hit a cyclist at the turn.

"Can you not use your bell on a bend like this?" I yelled out. "Son of a blind…!"

The Nabarun Samiti pandal was visible in the halogen lights that bathed the whole area in a false golden glow.

"How beautiful! Do you see that?" the man said pointing at the pandal.

I got down from the seat, wiped my face and spat out.

"It is a long story, Dada," I said, exhaling heavily.

"What?"

The man looked perplexed. A considerable time had passed between his question and my answer.

"The reason I came to Kolkata," I reminded him.

I started narrating my story from the time my father had become sick: It was the year that I was supposed to appear for Madhyamik board exams. When we took him to the district hospital, the doctor said that my father's liver was rotting. I can still recall the emotionless face of the doctor when he had announced the verdict that was to change our lives forever.

My father had to be taken to a good hospital in Kolkata and had to be under complete bedrest. All this needed a lot of cash. I tried to explain to my passenger that one could get by in a village without much money. People accepted payments in rice, vegetables or other things. In fact some people who labored on our four bighas of land would be paid in rice and a cooked meal in the afternoon along with some cash.

The man had stopped talking to his nephews and was listening to me intently. He did not have any idea about how life was in a village.

After going past a few more pandals we arrived in front of the huge idol of Shitola. I got down again and pulled the rickshaw to the side over by the grass. It had almost been an hour that I had been pulling the rickshaw and talking much of the same time—that had made me very tired.

I was sitting on my haunches and pulling at grass blades. I was thinking about what my life would be in the next five years. Same rickshaw, same pedaling, same surges of pain in my chest . . . would I become sick and . . . thoughts about my parents—endless thoughts. Thoughts are like a shower of shooting stars—as one vanishes in a corner of the sky another one appears from nowhere. I just could not hold on to any one of them as they kept coming incessantly.

I noticed two white pajama-clad legs in front of me—it was my passenger. He had left the children on the platform of the Shitola temple, and they seemed content chasing each other around the concrete pillars.

"And then what happened?" my passenger asked, without any effort to hide his curiosity.

I did not know why I had been narrating my whole life or at least the part that seemed to have decided the rest of it. Perhaps it made me feel a little lighter. Perhaps I wanted to tie the events of my life together like an interesting Hindi movie—a series of dramatic happenings skipping the mundane life in between. Maybe I was hoping that somehow my life would be different after I was done with my narration—no more pedaling, no more chest pain.

So I sat there on the grass and continued to share how my elder brother had separated from our family just within a few months of his marriage. I had thought that he would set aside the differences and help us in our hour of crisis when my father fell ill, but he had receded further away, so far that neither my mother nor my ailing father could reach him.

My father had needed constant attention and so my mother had to leave her work as a helper in the nearby government Primary Health Care Centre. When we had taken my father to Kolkata, the expenses stood in front of us like a mountain.

My mother decided to sell two bighas of our land for thirty thousand rupees a bigha. I wish we had owned the land in Kolkata instead of our village. Land is like gold here.

All that money from the land sale was to be gone in just a few days like a shooting star.

Selling the land was like parting with a member of the family, although we had the ill luck of experiencing even that. It was painful to know that someone else's plough would be digging into that soil. The paddy saplings were still the bright tender green color and when they matured, their golden stalks swayed just the same way. But someone else came and harvested it—that would drive a knife through my heart. Not any more. Now it is filled with the pain from pulling the rickshaw.

Continuing in school was not possible for me any more. We needed cash for my father's treatment. My parents had cried when I told them about dropping out of school. But they knew we had no other way out . . . and that is how I came to Kolkata—in search of cash.

"Where did you stay when you first came?" the passenger asked, who was by then also sitting on his haunches opposite me and pulling at grass blades.

My aunt's daughter had always been very affectionate to me. She was the oldest amongst all our cousins, so we called her Bordi. She lives in a basti, not too far away from here, with her husband and her daughter. Bordi and her husband have a kind heart so they let me stay with them and eat with them every night. I have been living there for eight years and they still love me—such kind-hearted people.

"You know Dada," I said with a deep breath, "I used to be a singer." The man had looked up in disbelief.

"And what kind of songs…?" He muttered as if looking for a better question to ask. He immediately moved his eyes from mine and began to stare intently at the grass blade he had just plucked.

"Amader gayer gaan, folk songs from our village," I said, and sang two lines for him in a hushed voice.

> *You have lifted me, you have drowned me*
> *O great river, you seem to be without a shore*

It was a popular song and I used to be able to sing it quite well when I was in school. I had performed at so many functions outside my village. Once I was invited to a district-level competition and won the first prize. They had given me a book and a small silver trophy—a figurine of a man playing the harmonium. My mother has preserved that with great pride. She still keeps it close to her shrine that is crowded with so many gods and goddesses.

All those years through my father's sickness, my mother prayed so piously and wept everyday in front of her gods . . . Gods! I don't believe in them.

"I still wake up in the morning and practice for an hour before taking out my rickshaw," I continued with my story. "Bordi and her husband never complain about it . . . kind hearted people."

My parents used to say, "Saheb, you have given up your education for us, don't give up your singing, we will not be able to bear that."

"Saheb?"

"Yes," I replied, "I was born with a fair skin. My parents named me Saheb because my real name has preempted many from calling names.

"My parents never let me work in the fields. I could not be a dark

Saheb," I laughed.

After two years of working here and there and saving money, I bought the rickshaw for three thousand rupees and have made an honest living ever since. I send money home regularly. When I told him that my father had recovered somewhat although he was not be able to work, my passenger seemed quite relieved as if a burden from his shoulder had been taken away.

"And that is my story, Dada," I said, and pushed against my knees to stand up.

"And what about your elder brother?" the man asked following my motion as I stood up.

"He still lives separately and barely has any links with us."

He stared at my face when I very softly said, "I would do this again for my father if I had to."

All of us climbed back into the rickshaw and I started going back to where we had started, on a slightly different route that was shorter. It was getting late and I had to get back home. The stomach does not listen to stories.

He had asked me to stop in front of a two-story house close to the main road. There was some open land in the front with different kinds of trees in it.

"This is where we live . . . well, my parents live here all the time and I come for some time," he said hesitantly.

"How much should I pay you," he asked since we had never agreed upon a fare.

"Whatever you feel is fair and appropriate, Dada," I said.

He immediately pulled out a fifty rupees note from his wallet as if he was waiting for me to say something, anything.

Fifty rupees was a lot more than I had expected...thirty rupees would have been fair.

"If you need to go around and look at the Durga Protimas, come to the rickshaw stand under the banyan tree and ask for Saheb," I said before leaving.

I remember having sped back to Bordi's house without stopping at the rickshaw stand. I was battling with a sense of relief, embarrassment and perhaps even pride. It felt like the road offered no resistance to the rickshaw that night.

That was about two years ago.

Since then I have stopped singing in the morning. I had hoped that someday I might be able to make a name for myself as a singer. My parents do not know about this, although they ask about my coughing every time I go home. It is getting increasingly difficult for me to pull the rickshaw. The hopes I had a few years ago now seem to add to the dead weight of the rickshaw.

The doctor has asked me to take a photo of my chest at a laboratory. My father is able to walk around the house and tutors some students in the village, earning a small amount of cash. He still needs regular medicine and visits to the doctor twice a year. My mother has to take care of the household and also the work in the fields, although I go home during the sowing season. I think sooner or later I will have to sell my rickshaw and think of doing something else.

One evening, a few days ago, a heavyset man climbed into my rickshaw and asked me to take him through the quieter inner lanes. I do not have much energy for such rides any more, but I relented. He was dressed in a crisp white dhoti and punjabi—starched enough that it would retain the shape even if the man were to slip out.

A few minutes into the lane, he asked abruptly, "It is just four days to Kali Puja, isn't it?"

I nodded my head in assent, trying not to speak. I heard him open a bottle. There was the sound of liquid running down his gullet. I imagined his Adam's apple floating in the liquid. He smacked his lips and exhaled deeply after a few quick swigs.

"How come your skin is so fair… like a foreigner?" the man taunted.

I was in no mood for a conversation nor would my lungs allow for it.

"Born with it," I replied curtly, intending to bring a quick end to the dialogue.

"I see," he said, the words swirling out of his lazy tongue.

I stopped pedaling.

I straightened my torso and looked into the darkness in front of the rickshaw. I could only hear the sound of the chain passing over the ratchet of the rear axle. ■

AFGHANISTAN, END OF EIGHTY-SEVEN

Maya Khosla

Candlelight skids up a child who sleep-walks
with eyes wide. Outside, airwaves lower than sound
or shudder are rattling cups, smashing windows

within a miles-wide circumference. In her dream,
trees clinging to their blood-apricots swell
with the darkness of curfew nights. Touch one

and it explodes. Her father's vigil is crumpled by insomnia:
was that wind-shift or voices shrilling above the crack
of footfalls far beyond view? Dust floats on a cup of water.

It is the hour of curtains jerked from her grip.
It is another month, the slow ache of sky sinking
through his search. Her coat slumped against

a tree. He wants to tell her about its bent limbs,
elbows of trunk and branches, gestures fed by water
and anticipation, all leaning against granitic rocks,

When the clouds part, a shrike on a thin stalk
sways back and forth like a clock keeping its tempo
of hunger against the backdrop of a valley bright

with silence. A chewed-up fruit with her tooth marks.
Arrows of distress scatter like night-birds from the open
mouth of falling. Now wind, a half-shout running through it.

THUMBPRINT
Maya Khosla

The moment was all window. Driving over a mountain's edge,
as he gathered fallen peanuts from the empty passenger seat,
had been predicted days before by soothsayers who read

his wife's thumbprint. They spoke of glass blocking
the sky and floor. The call from hospital came. She listened
through the crackle of long-distance, fears flaring open

over thoughts of the single fir tree that had stopped his drop
A spinney of them, verticals swaying, married to sun and water.
And rapids below, dashed to white shards by rocks one moment,

seamless the next. After the call, silences grew under small sounds.
Branches, a fly beating against glass. Leaves stuck in a cobweb,
tapping out reports from wind. She swept them together.

Fueled a fire and burned the predictions. But random words kept
escaping with fly-ash. *Amethyst, dove, bone.*
The hospital was without anesthetics, needles disinfected

over flame. On his return, a squash from the farmer's market
swelled so large it forced the fridge door open and rolled out
so the stretch-marks deepened into cracks, a full year without rain.

She could still hear soothsayer chants hovering over the inky-dark oval
of her impression on paper. Held her knowledge like a tablespoon
of Epsom salts, fizzing on her tongue without a drink to wash it down.

THE MUSTARD FIELD: GIRLS FROM THE SATI SCHOOL WANDER

Maya Khosla

The rite of sati demands a woman immolate herself on her husband's funeral pyre.

Plunging into the button blooms, they vanish. Swish of departure. Delight
and giddiness unleashed among the sprays of yellow: Brassica

by the hundred have multiplied under the hands of rain. Four-petal suns
the size of fingernails brushing against cheeks, festooning the moment.

Each girl's bright encounter brings her to tremble, confirm her pluck
    with hands
on another's shoulder or scarf. Thrill and nervous hesitation working
    in tandem:

a rushing forward along with a pulling back. The leader, jerky with stops,
afraid of misstepping. The one behind her is slipperless on the cracked
    earth.

And the graceful one, with a star of leucoderma across her neck.
Through the tunneled secrets of dust mote and bitter honey they glide,

through the flowers that will give way to seeds of premonition. But not yet.
Now each second is rinsed by a leafy susurrus, the need to venture further

than the lasso of adult voices can pitch and bring them back.
Now only the percussive slap of feet. Only the wake of arms in
    breast-strokes,

pressing the gold multitudes aside, is visible. They have wandered further
than the absences each will grow into. Scarf veiling her averted face while

while mustard seeds spatter from skillets of hot oil. What remains after
    the pollen dust,
is brushed off, after the slow back-burn of light is relinquished, is a long
    wait for virtue.

CLINGSTONE
Maya Khosla

Time to pluck apricots, peaches, plums. Top ones warmest to the touch. Grip your shirt-rim and fan it out for a basket we can fill. With hurry, your hair rinsing my face. With small fires, the morning my cherry-red train puffed and you ran along the platform below, waving— one hand gripping the window   railing smelling of rain. Fingertips touching, letter to   letter, for weeks. Time now, to reach for the   top branches, the sweetmeats ready to give.   The world swings; the shift of leafy shadow   over stone is swift. What small fires we hold.   Pressed fruit gives easily — two halves of a whole   — juices bursting in the moment's mouth to fill past absences, uncertainties, with abundance. Tree frogs tick all around, vocal sacs bubbling. Clingstones are saved in pockets.   Click by click, the bowing branches are straightened by our picking. Stained cloth, drunken bees, the susurrus of hands splashing through red-tinged leaves. Readying themselves for fall.

THERE'S REALLY NO SUCH THING AS THE "VOICELESS."

Nadia Chaney

...There are only the deliberately silenced, or the preferably unheard.
—Arundhati Roy

I used to hate to introduce myself, because I wasn't sure how to pronounce my name. Everyone around me said it differently, including my parents and grandparents. I always felt tongue-tied at that moment of introduction. Nadia. Nah-dia. Nawd-ya. Nah-Dee-Ah. Nau-dia. Nae-dia. Na-ja. It felt heavy and slippery in my mouth. Now, in my late thirties, that feeling has disappeared and I have a job that keeps me traveling and teaching, introducing myself with confidence and ease. Tonight, I find myself retracing my steps, wondering when and how that change happened.

* * *

My mother made matching clothes for me, my brother and our dollies, and invited us all to the backyard for lunch. She made a gingerbread carnival complete with a roller coaster with little dough mice in walnut half shells to ride it, and facilitated cupcake decorating contests, and hosted dress-up Christmas parties where each family had to come as a fairy tale, or showed us how to make little animals out of the plaster drippings from my father's dental practice. It never stopped, a cascade of creativity and play. I looked way, waaaay up to her. She loved all our little friends on Frobisher Court, in Saskatoon, too. They were often invited with their teddy bears for tea. She arranged yearly block parties with big barrels of Macdonald's juice and marshmallow roasts and tricycle races.

When I look back, it is as if she was treating us like two tiny dignitaries from another planet. She always listened with interest and accepted our opinions as equal and valid. I understand that she was raised this way by her own parents in India, Edwin and Victoria D'Souza, to have opinions and to be celebrated for her gifts, though I think maybe Mom took this a few steps further. Even the imaginary friend we shared was treated with respect (they were two, actually, Good Alec and Bad Alec). They were real to us, so Mom treated them as if they were real, as well. When we blamed Bad Alec for some mischief she would consider the evidence and discuss our punishments (usually sitting in a corner, for a bad offence you faced the wall, not so bad, you could sit and draw or read) with the Alecs in the picture. This ability to bring the world to life with play and wonder would eventually become a part of my life's direction, training teachers, social workers and activists to invite creativity and the arts into their work.

We grew up in a world of imagination. We sat on our knees at symphonies and craned our necks in museums, we traveled and marveled and there were always books and music in our house. But we were not taught any Indian languages. When I ask Mom now, "Why didn't you teach us Hindi," she says, "There was no real need." I get that, I guess. I mean, it's not a dying language. It's spoken by nearly five percent of people on the planet. My parents were neophiles, moving forward instead of looking back.

Grandma Vicky and Grandpa Edwin never came to visit us, though we went to Goa to see them. My father's mother, Rhubab Chaney, Ruby Maji, would come from Pune every few years and stay for a few months. She was often taken aback by the freedom we had, especially in terms of being allowed to argue with our parents, to state our points of view and to ask challenging questions. She usually called me Rani, a not unusual nickname which means "queen," whereas my parents call me Nanji, a diminutive plus an honorific. To me, these nicknames point to a valuing of my personal power, a way that my elders respected my personhood.

A few years ago I was working in Bangalore and a friend used the word *cow-like* to describe a woman in a positive way. When I was surprised, he explained that the traditional Indian woman's role was to be like the sacred cow, obedient, docile, nurturing and generous. Perhaps this is why Ruby Maji and I used to struggle with our relationship. Not only did we not share a fluent language (she spoke very little English, and I spoke no Hindi or Marathi), we didn't share a common destination. When it came to the woman I was becoming it wasn't easy for her to approve.

Thing is, she started it. When my parents fell in love and wanted to get married, all their parents blessed their union, although my father's side is Muslim and my mother's is Catholic. They only asked that they leave India to marry, since it would be much harder to raise mixed-identity kids in India.

We grew up in the Saskatoon, Saskatchewan of the eighties, a small prairie city with a university and a healthy river. This was an era of assimilation, and Saskatoon in particular was not yet very diverse. Many of the early settlers were Ukrainian or otherwise Eastern European, and though it was the traditional territory of seven indigenous nations, as well as an incentivized area for immigrants of all colors, you just didn't see that many black or brown families. In school, I was one of only two children of color. In school, I was not the little Rani I was at home. In school, the other kids knew something about me that I had not yet realized.

"Your skin is dirty," they said, "you need to wash it. You smell." In the first grade, I would try to stay inside at recess but I'd usually get booted out in the snow, waddling in my pink snowsuit and swaddled in wool scarf, hat and mitts. I would skulk around near the big garbage bins, or hide under the three old pine trees that watched over the playground. Wherever I could be alone, I would build little snow caves and crawl inside to inhale the freshness of clean snow, or crouch between the garbage bin and the wall, using my warm breath to draw circles and stick people in the thin ice. I had a couple of friends whom my mom might invite over to play, or whose home I would visit and poke at their strange bland-but-salty food, but I mostly avoided those kids if they were in a group. I wasn't happier alone, I just didn't really understand the rules of the world I was in.

* * *

One sunny, freezing afternoon at school recess time, there was a group of girls pulling each other on a "magic carpet," a square of hard blue plastic with holes cut for handles. They'd tied a skipping rope through the holes and were running on the ice, squealing and sliding. All my hiding spots were overrun, so I was pressed against a cold brick wall, trying to kick over a raised lump of ice, waiting for the bell to ring. A volunteer mother saw me watching. "You want a turn, dear?" she asked me. Her breath was steaming and her cheeks were bright red with splotches of waxy white. The parent volunteer's job was to walk around the playground at recess, so the teachers could rest. Each parent volunteer had a couple kids who were always with them. This woman's two were standing on either side of her, looking at me from over their brightly colored scarves.

"No," I whispered.

"What? No? Of course you do." She pulled me by the arm and I slid along the ice, leaning back, trying to escape. Her two minions grabbed my arms to help her. She yelled at the girls to stop playing. When they finally gathered around her they were panting and laughing. "What's your name?" she asked me.

"Nadia," I whispered, feeling a little shaky like I might throw up.

"You need to let her play with you," she told the girls. "Give her a ride." They immediately started shouting "Not it!" almost as one voice, and one girl was last. She looked as if she had lost something precious. Her mouth hung open for a second as if she couldn't believe it. Her friends mocked her until the volunteer mom said, "Hurry it up." I was incredibly embarrassed. At that age embarrassment used to freeze me, my whole body, so I couldn't move at all. One of the minions pushed me a little. "Go ahead," said the mother. "It's fun." My mind was racing with ways to get out of this but I was utterly stuck. The mother pushed me by the shoulders towards the carpet, and then pushed me down onto the carpet, onto my knees.

"Hold this," said the girl who had to pull me as she threw me one end of the skipping rope. I think I saw the puller nod to the oldest girl, who had been held back the year before. She started to run. I fell back but managed to hold on. The rest of them were running behind and beside me, so I was in a little bubble of boots and snow pants making a stomping, rushing sound. We were bumping over the icy playground. Actually, I was having fun! Then they turned a corner and pushed the carpet into a doorway, where the gym's double doors were. I could hear the basketball practice inside, as if it were underwater.

"You're a teacher's pet," one of them said.

"No, she's not," said another. "They all hate you. Mademoiselle LeBlanc hates you because you're dirty and you smell."

"You should go back to where you came from." That's the last thing I heard. They began to kick me with their winter boots. They kicked my legs open, kicked my vagina, over and over and over. The bell rang. They pulled the magic carpet out from under me and ran to the foyer door, lined up two by two. I tried to move, but my body wouldn't listen. I curled up on my side. My heart was pounding, my insides throbbing. When I finally got to my knees, my hips and groin screamed in pain. As I made my way to the foyer door, I slipped and fell. This time I almost started to cry but I picked myself up and pulled open the heavy door.

"What is the matter with you," Mademoiselle snapped when I walked into the classroom. "Why are you late? Why don't you know how to behave?" I didn't answer, but hung up my clothes and slunk into my chair. My body ached. I needed to pee but I could not move my arm to ask for permission. I felt the pee burning harshly and wetting my underwear. Then, Mademoiselle called on me. To write on the board. I did not move. "What is the matter with you today," she said. She walked over to my desk and tried to pull me, her long nails digging into my forearm. I could not move, but to my horror I began to cry. I watched myself crying as if I was standing beside the desk on the other side of the teacher. A little girl with her head down, trying to will herself to disappear. When I remember the event, I see it like that even now.

She softened and asked me what was wrong and I managed to say, "I want to go home."

"Why?" she asked me. The other kids were watching. I heard the clock ticking. I could see Mademoiselle chewing her red lips. She was still holding my arm. I said nothing, and finally she kind of pushed my arm back onto the desk and went back to the front. "*Bien*, Michelle," she said. "You can take Nadia's turn."

* * *

I never told anyone about that day, or the torture that continued in various forms for many years. Instead, I developed a practice that happens with some second-generation children. I learned to shape-shift. I learned to shift my view of the world quickly and completely between my home and school environments. It wasn't just a lie of omission. The world and all its rules changed dramatically. In school I was a watcher. I was wily. As I grew, I became competitive, but quietly so. I hated people. I would try to kill them with my eyes. I worked to become better versions of the people around me, imitating their accents, their gestures. I was jealous of everyone. I was subservient, always hoping to gain favor from teachers, my classmates, older kids, always feeling it slip away. I hid my emotions. I pretended it was all fine with me. At home I was a little queen; stubborn and argumentative, or bright and all-knowing. I wept easily. I was creative and confident. I was one of the eldest of the children of my parents' friends, and I bossed everyone around.

In Saskatchewan, so far north, it was often dark when I rode the school bus, both to and fro. This was my transition time. I was always quiet on these rides. Sometimes they were a time for games of keep-away or what-does-she-smell-like, but for the most part they were my time to release one world for another. I never answered honestly when my mother asked me, "How was school today, Petunia?" I felt my parents would not understand and I was very embarrassed by what was happening to me. I didn't want them to know how hard the real world was. In my seven-year-old mind they needed to be protected.

This kind of shape-shifting is a practice of forgetting and erasure of the self. It's brilliant as a coping mechanism: instead of a self (who can get hurt), one becomes a kind of mirror, an object. Instead of having a sense of my own needs and desires, I submitted everything to the environments I moved in. I distanced my emotions from my experience of the world, and existed only in response to stimulation. This allowed me to experience two completely different environments without having to explain one to the other. I became the wall between my worlds.

By the time I was in my late teens, the freezing and speechlessness were buried but still alive, and creating a seething knot inside my guts. I became excellent at understanding what was being asked of me and providing it; at school I was very successful. At home, I was boiling with a resentment that I could not name. I started to take it out on my parents, especially my mother. I didn't know why, but I hated being at home. At school I had a few friends, but I was still mostly alone. Now, when I look back, I see the root of that resentment. I did not have the skills to direct my anger to its source, in fact, the source was long gone. In our teens we didn't have the same playtime at home, of course, but we were still very much encouraged to be creative. For example, we were never to buy our parents gifts. We had to write them poems. While our home existence was not quite idyllic, it was still very safe, predictable and disciplined. I felt none of the intense vulnerability and fear I felt at school. So home became the place to release the anger.

I believed for a long time that a mother tongue would have given me a sense of what was meant when I was told to "go back to where I came from." I blamed my parents for not teaching me who I was. When I look back now I see that I am certainly a product of the little home they built for us; they taught us values and culture and language in a million ways. But I wonder about the aspect of a traditional culture, and in particular a language. I longed for it, and I still do. A mother tongue. Something that would help me understand myself, and connect me to my ancestors. That would connect me to the skin and body that was costing so much and giving back so little. I wanted something my white friends didn't have, instead of always feeling like they were the arbiters of belonging.

While we didn't have an Indian language, and we didn't have Indian roles, there were still potent aspects of Indian culture. This is the confusing but beautiful thing, the reason I'm writing this essay in the first place. Although I speak no Indian language, don't know how to wear a sari, don't know how to make a round chappati, etcetera, I have deep values and a being that is somehow still Indian. My body is made of two parts that aren't familiar to each other: my ancestors' bodies and the elemental earth where I have lived and breathed. What are the implications of this kind of dislocation?

My body didn't fully belong to the place I lived, and those little girls and boys in elementary school knew it, even though I didn't. And yet I do belong. My body grew here, in Canada, knowing its earth, breathing its air, struggling with its complex history and my place in it. In India or in Canada, at school or at home, I felt like an alien. The shape-shifter was operating from outside my body. I was a good girl, with good grades and a sharp tongue. But inside I was a bleating, self-castigating mass. I wept at night, wishing to be different, to be someone else.

In the second grade, when they asked me what I wanted to be, I said, "Author." My escape was novels, where the rules of the world stayed still. Narnia, Nancy Drew, Sweet Valley High, Lucy Maud Montgomery, Madeleine L'Engle. Stolen novels from my parents' high-up shelves, too, where I read things I didn't understand. Because of my shape-shifting I would make sense of them, and be moved and horrified and gripped, but in rereading them now I realize I understood very little. I wonder also if this was happening as I moved across cultural boundaries in my small world. I made the sense I could, but it was neither mature nor consistent.

I wrote my first story when I was five or six. It was called "The Princess Who Wanted to Be a Librarian." The princess was the shifter. She had to please everyone. The stakes were high. If you (disobey, don't study, chew your nails, leave your towel on the floor, don't practice the piano, etcetera) no one will ever marry you, my father would say. In a way, this wound was as deep as the winter boots to the private parts. Perhaps they were oddly twinned. I had no context for what my father was saying, no way to understand his version of a cow-like, obedient femininity. My mother was not like that. I had no context for his threat, which he meant quite mildly: if you don't conform to your role as a woman you will not be able to access the institution of marriage. But, in the absence of an understanding of that role or those expectations, I took it personally. I did these things, so, shadowy demons whispered in my mind: You will always be alone. Hideous. You are rotting inside. I was adrift without a world in which I clearly belonged, where I could know myself. I did not yet know that I was also free.

At eighteen I moved far away from my parents' home, to the other side of this wide country, to Vancouver. I wanted to study English, I really wanted it, though I couldn't fully explain why. My father wanted me to study science and warned me that I would be wasting my life if I didn't. Instead of freezing, something shifted inside me and I fled.

In Vancouver I wrote spoken word poems and my knees knocked as I staked out my identity on little café stages, patiently stalking it like a deer hunter. I was "letting myself go," as my father put it on a trip home to see them. But really, it was more like letting myself out. I was unraveling. I was awkward and unruly and got myself into dangerous situations like being kidnapped by a biker I met at a party, and inappropriate situations, like spending a summer selling cookies at a nude beach, and I reveled in it all. Bit by bit I was finding my own feelings, my sense of what I wanted, regaining my instincts. Learning to be oneself is the journey

I believe all humans have to take, but in those first few years on my own I was making up for some lost time; time I had spent erasing myself. I began to tell myself the story of myself, piling up journals and collages and paintings. I was filling in the blanks.

* * *

I was reading bell hooks and Robert Anton Wilson, Yogananda and Ouspensky, taking my first yoga class, dancing all night and drinking thick smoothies. I was hearing the word *racism* and listening. There were pieces falling slowly into place, like playing Tetris on the lowest setting. I was hoping I could construct myself out of the bits I had. I was learning about my body, about myself, through concentration and meditation. I was starting to physically realize how dislocated I was, how I lived about four inches in front of my body. I was beginning to understand the shame and confusion I carried, and why my tongue felt so noxious and heavy in my mouth, especially when I said my own name. I decided to take a Hindi class. I thought it would help. I would build a foundation of self under me. I'd be able to talk to Ruby Maji. I wanted that so badly. I spoke French and had two years of Spanish. It was Hindi 101. It didn't even occur to me to be afraid.

In the first class we learned the alphabet. The rest of the students were second-generation Punjabis (same root language, same alphabet as Hindi), as well as a young white man named Gabe majoring in Sanskrit, Tarun Nayar and myself. Tarun was half-Punjabi and half-white Montrealer. He'd been playing tabla since he was little (about the same time I realized this princess wanted to be a librarian). I had not fully mastered the alphabet when Dr. Aklujkar moved on to simple sentences. This was an easy grade for everyone but me, Tarun and Gabe. Tarun and Gabe were climbing shale. I was in the path of an avalanche. I wrote one letter to Ruby Maji, three lines. She was thrilled. I was humiliated. My handwriting looked like a child's, all big and wobbly. This was it. I was not Indian. But what was I? No amount of wishing had turned me white and no amount of Wu-Tang, Naughty by Nature, Janet Jackson and Miles Davis was turning me black. Though the white theosophists gave me access to Eastern knowledge and black dialogue (particularly rap music), teaching me profound lessons about cultural reconstruction and self-knowledge, these were still only saplings and I did not fully recognize them yet. I was learning about antiracism, but underneath I was swarming with self-erasure and confusion. The only Indo-Canadians I saw in public were Monika Deol and Spek from the Dream Warriors, and I heard Bif Naked was half. I didn't exist.

Then one day Tarun approached me after a Hindi class. I was still sitting in my desk, another failing grade staring at me, draining my will to keep trying.

"Hey," he said, "you write poetry, right? I have an idea."

I invited him to the mansion I was staying in with eighteen other people. I made him my specialty, kale and poached eggs with miso gravy.

"Do you know what *bols* are?" he asked.

I shrugged and shook my head. Then he said something that made me freeze.

"*Dha Kr Dha Ti Dha Ti Dha Ti Jinna Ginna Dha*!

"They're patterns," he said. "It's how they teach tabla and classical singing. I can't believe you've never heard of it. Here, look."

He wrote it down.

"I'm wondering if you can match English words to this."

I didn't get what he meant in that moment, but we ended up starting a band, Heds Hi. A world beat fusion band with two Yugoslavian brothers, Ivan and Nikola, on guitar and bass, Irish Canadian Tommy on mandolin, Chinese Chris Suen on flute, T on tabla and myself as the lyricist. My voice started to mean something to me. We would perform at an Ethiopian restaurant called Nyala, for a small and loyal group of our friends. Tarun never questioned my right to speak for myself, in the language I had. I used to visit India with my family and feel frozen and dull, my senses resisting everything, a wall of shame and discomfort around me. As I got older I found a word for it: imposter. I was not a foreigner, I didn't belong here, I didn't have a category and I really wanted one. But with Heds Hi, which went on for four years, I wrote songs that came from my studies of yoga and Eastern ideas, which I accessed mostly through white writers. My favorite was an homage to Baba Ram Dass, a white man who had immersed himself fully in Indian culture:

Be here now

because life is fleeting

a momentary meeting

of body and soul

Like Crowley and R.A.W. and Gurdjieff, I needed these Western mystics and theosophists to help me find my way to my Indianness from the outside in like I needed kind, patient Tarun who never questioned me (though I'd better run if I showed up for a rehearsal without every word and cue memorized). Maybe as a mixed-race man he had his own questions to answer. Now his major project is called Delhi to Dublin. Maybe it was his own healing path that carved a little space for me. In searching for the true self that navigates multiple worlds, perhaps we can bring those masks to life, and create new possibilities for what it means to be a cultural human on this planet, even without mother tongue or traditional territories.

I dated Hari Alluri, a half Indian half Filipino who had grown up in Nigeria, then South Van in the Punjabi Market area. I was so jealous of his poetry, he had more ethnicity than he could handle. His poems bristled with Tagalog and Kannada, his family made *idlies* together on the weekend. His poems were brown, he didn't have to look for it. He wasn't wearing his culture, or gathering it in little handfuls. His story was so complex, but he knew who he was.

I made a long trip to India on my own when I was twenty-eight. "When you married, Beta?" Maji asked. "Please. When you learn it, Hindi? I am old woman. I cannot learn it, English." We used sign language to pad the English. We spent a lot of time together, and every day I felt the sense of loss. What if she could have told me about her life, her wisdom, her religion? Would she have taught me how to be an Indian woman? I wrote a series of about twenty-five poems in that time.

"These are your best work," Hari said when I got back.

But I loathed them. I had no right to look at India, to write about her, to try to understand with my overfed, otiose perspective. They were trite to me, heavy. I only wanted to write about the little girls who would come to me and call me Didi and tap me on the stomach and then touch their lips. Hungry. I was hungry. But when the little girls appeared in my poems I knew I had no right to write about them either. "There's something really you about these," Hari said. But I felt nothing but revulsion. This is what self-hatred does. It's so simple: it poisons the voice, not its sound in the world, but the way it sounds in your head. I dared not accept those poems. If I did I would have to accept my whole misshapen, dirty self. I buried them and continued to write rhyming rap lyrics about vague Eastern philosophies.

Then my ancestors took pity on me.

I got an opportunity to begin working in Bangalore. Every year for five years I went back and worked with peers and colleagues I related to, for a month or more at a time. I saw Ruby Maji on each trip. We built a relationship that went deeper than words, and a language of mixed up English, Hindi and sign language that was more than sufficient for us to talk about womanhood, religion, soul and art. While this did not resolve my mother tongue issue, it allowed enough space for me to account for the gains of unleashing the body from its traditional language. As the intense shame began to recede, I had to acknowledge a sense of freedom.

Maji said, "I never school, Beta. You smart one."

My grandmothers all bore children, bore husbands. The roles they had open to them were staked out in the earth they were from, and indelibly marked on the tongues of everyone around them. My mother left that earth at twenty-one to expand her perspective and she bore me into that expansion, without tether, without expectation. It meant I had to find my own way to say my name. But it meant I was also free to choose it for myself.

I rewrote the poems. Draft after draft, like a miner I was looking for flashes of myself. I started to send them out into the world, little emissaries looking for bits of land where I could stake my skin tent. As they found their homes, I felt my self begin to settle; those vast inches between body and spirit slowly shrinking. My heart clicking back into my chest. My tongue reaching all the way down, at last, into the deepest gut. Navigation and language, inspiration and instinct finally beginning to work as one. ■

FROM
WHAT LIES BETWEEN US
Nayomi Munaweera

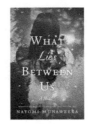

The walls of my cell are painted an industrial white. They must think the color is soothing. Where I come from, it connotes absence, death, and loneliness.

People write to me. Mothers, mostly; they spew venom. That's not surprising. I have done the unthinkable. I have parted the veil and crossed into that other unseen country. They hate me because I am the worst thing possible. I am the bad mother.

But here's a secret: in America there are no good mothers. They simply don't exist. Always, there are a thousand ways to fail at this singularly important job. There are failures of the body and failures of the heart. The woman who is unable to breastfeed is a failure. The woman who screams for the epidural is a failure. The woman who picks her child up late knows from the teacher's cutting glance that she is a failure. The woman who shares her bed with her baby has failed. The woman who steels herself and puts on noise-canceling earphones to erase the screaming of her child in the next room has failed just as spectacularly. They must all hang their heads in guilt and shame because they haven't done it perfectly, and motherhood is, if anything, the assumption of perfection.

Then too, motherhood is broken because in this place, to be a good mother is to give oneself completely. It is to erase one's self. This is what I refused to do. So they shudder when they hear my name, but inwardly they smile because they have not failed in the way I have.

There are others who write. Men who find the grotesque act I have committed titillating. They send propositions and proposals of marriage that I tear up into scraps of white that match the walls of my cell. I hate their unknown, unseen faces. They remind me that in this country, celebrity is courted no matter the cause. The fact that strangers have heard your name and know the secrets of your life is supposed to be pleasing.

I never wanted this macabre interest, this unsettling notoriety. I never asked for it. I would have preferred to have been locked up and forgotten. Instead, I have become a known thing. My name, the one I had before, is gone. Instead I am named by the act

I have committed. To be named thus is to be pinned down onto the corkboard with a needle piercing one's abdomen and a curl of paper underneath with one's genus and species on it in slanted writing. I have been named, and therefore you think you know my story, why I did what I did. To this I object. Perhaps this narrative is a way to undo your knowing, to say the truth is somewhere else entirely, and I will tell it in my own voice, in my own time.

And so, as all stories must open, in the beginning, when I was the child and not yet the mother . . .

* * *

Birth. My face was pressed against the bones of Amma's pelvis, stuck there, so that instead of slipping out, I was bound like a lost fish in a too-narrow stream. It wasn't until the midwife, tiring of my mother's screams, reached in with her forceps, grabbed the side of my head, and wrenched me out that I was born and Amma was born into motherhood, both of us gasping from the effort of transformation.

For three months after, there was a hornlike protrusion on the left side of my head. It subsided eventually, but for those months my parents were alarmed. "We didn't know if it would ever go away. I didn't know what sort of child I had given birth to. You were the strangest creature. A little monster," Amma admitted. "But then the swelling went down and you were our perfect little girl."

After that, the doctor looked at my mother's slimness, her girlish frame, and said, "No more. Only this one. Any more will wreck you." She had wanted scores of children filling the grand old house. She had wanted so many to love her. The love of an entire army she had created herself. She rubbed her nose against mine and said, "Only you to love me. So you must love me double, triple, quadruple hard. Do you see?" I nodded. She kissed me on the forehead, searched my eyes. I was blissful in the sun of her love, my entire being turned like a flower toward her heat.

Yes, I could love her more. I could love her enough to fill up the hole all those brothers and sisters had left by never coming.

* * *

I was born in Sri Lanka, a green island in the midst of the endless Indian Ocean. I grew up in Kandy, the hill city of the Buddhists. A city held high like a gem in the setting of the island. Maha Nuwara, meaning the great city, is the name of Kandy in Sinhala. Or even Kande Ude Rata, the land on top of the mountain. It is the last capital of the Lankan kings before the British came to "domesticate and civilize," to build railroads and scallop the hills into acres of fragrant tea. In their un-sinuous tongue, Kande Ude Rata collapses, folds into itself, and emerges as Kandy. But not candy sweet in the mouth, because this place has a certain history.

In the capital Colombo's National Museum, in a dusty glass case, lies the sari blouse of one of the last noblewomen of the Kandyan Kingdom. Splotches of faded red stain the moldering fabric of each shoulder. The last Kandyan king was fighting the British when his trusted adviser too turned against him. Enraged, the king summoned his adviser's wife. His men ripped her golden earrings out of her flesh, so she bled down onto this blouse. They beheaded her children and placed the heads into a giant mortar. They gave her a huge pestle, the kind village women use to pound rice, and forced her to smash the heads of her children. Then they tied her to a rock and threw her into Kandy Lake as the king watched in triumph from the balcony of the temple palace. Soon after, the British conquered Kandy and took over the island for centuries.

This is the history of what we do to one another. This is the story of what it means to be both a child of a mother and a child of history.

* * *

The house I grow up in is big and old. It has belonged to my father's family for generations. It has rooms full of ebony furniture, waxed, polished red floors, white latticework that drips from the eaves like lace, and dark wooden steps that lead to my little bedroom upstairs. A wrought-iron balcony hangs outside my window under a tumble of creeping plants. If I stand on its tiny platform just over the red-tiled roof of the first floor, I can see our sweeping emerald lawns leading down to the rushing river. Along the bank a line of massive trees stretches upward toward the monsoon clouds.

* * *

In the living room is a small, slightly moldy taxidermied leopard. There are very much alive dogs in the house, but the leopard is my infant obsession. This is because the leopard lets me ride him, while the dogs do not. Amma says I should call him Bagheera, for Kipling's black leopard, but the name Kaa, for Kipling's Indian rock python, is what I choose. The sound is easier and there is something slithery in his yellow marble eyes. Exactly between these eyes is the neat bullet hole that my father's father put there. The hunting guns are locked away in a chest in my father's study, but the leopard is here as evidence of their presence.

A formal portrait of my grandparents hangs above the leopard. My mustachioed grandfather is in a three-piece suit, my grandmother in a Kandyan osari over a Victorian blouse, ruffled and buttoned against the tropical heat. My father is a boy in short trousers, the only child of the five my grandmother gave birth to have survived the ravages of malaria.

* * *

The house is a kingdom divided into dominions, inside and outside, and ruled over by the keepers of my childhood, Samson and Sita. In the kitchen, Sita shuffles about in her cotton sari, her feet bare. She has been with my father's family since he was a baby. She and her sister came as young girls. Her sister was my father's ayah, while Sita set up court in this kitchen, which she has never left.

Samson is Sita's nephew. His mother has returned to the village down south they came from so long ago, but Samson stays to wrestle our garden. Once a week he cuts the lawn, balancing on his heels, sarong pulled up along his thighs. He swipes the machete back and forth as he makes his crab-legged way across the grass. His skin shines like wet eggplant, and at his throat a silver amulet flashes in the sun. "Inside this. All my luck!" he says. He has pulled it open before to show me what it holds, a tightly rolled scroll of minuscule Sinhala script, a prayer of protection bought by his mother from the village temple at a great price. She believes it will keep him safe from the malevolent influences, the karmic attachments that prey upon the good- hearted.

* * *

I am eight years old, tiny and spindly, and Samson is my very best friend. After school I race to throw off my uniform, kick away my shoes, slip into a housedress and Bata slippers, and escape into the garden. The red hibiscus flower nodding its head, yellow pistil extended like a wiry five-forked snake tongue; the curl of ferns; the overhead squawk of parrots—these are the wonders that welcome me home.

Samson speaks to me in Sinhala. He says, "Ah, Baby Madame. Home already? Come!" He swings me onto his shoulders. My thighs grip the sides of his throat, my legs hook behind his back. I reach both hands up into the guava tree to catch the orbs that are swollen and about to split, a wet pink edge in their jade skins. I grab, twist, and pull. The branches bounce and the birds rise, squawking in loud outrage. His arm reaches up to steady me. When my pockets are bulging he gently places me on the ground.

I bite into sun-warmed guava, that familiar sweet tang, small gemlike seeds crunching between my teeth. Samson is cutting away dead leaves from orchids suspended in baskets from the tree trunks.

I ask, "Why do they call these flowers Kandyan dancers?"

I already know why. These small yellow orchids are named for the dancers of this region because with petal and stamen the flowers imitate perfectly the headdresses and the sarongs, the drums and white shell necklaces that the twirling dancers wear. But I ask because I want to hear him talk and also because I want to show off what I have learned in school. I want to show how much more I know even now at eight years old because I have gone to school and he has only ever been a servant in our house.

He says, "This is the name. No? What else can we call them but their name?"

"No! I mean, did they call the flowers after the dancers or the dancers after the flowers?"

"You are the one who goes to school, Baby Madame. How could Samson know these things? Ask your teachers? Ask someone who knows these big-big things." A perfect yellow flower loosens its grip, tumbles to the grass. He stoops and picks it up between thumb and forefinger as gently as if it were a wounded insect, places it on his palm, and holds it out to me. I tug the rubber band at the end of my plait loose and settle the flower there.

* * *

He says, "Come, Baby Madame. I need your small fingers to work in the pond today." We walk over and he sits on the edge while I kick off my rubber slippers, hike up my dress around my thighs, and slip into the water. My feet in the mud, I reach into the water up to my armpits, follow the fibrous stalks of the lotus plants down to their main stem. I pull so the plants tear loose, the mud releasing the roots reluctantly. The koi come to investigate this curiosity in their midst. Their silver, orange-streaked quickness flashes all about me, their mouths coming up to nibble at whatever they can find, shins, calves, fingers. I work my way across the cool muddy water, throw the too-fast-growing lotuses onto the bank, where a mound of uprooted leaves, stems, and unfurled flowers lie open to the sky. Samson gathers the beautiful debris. He will burn it with the evening's other rubbish.

Other days I am the watcher and he the worker. I squat on the bank with a bucket as Samson wades in. He spreads his fingers wide to catch yards of gelatinous strands studded with shiny beadlike eggs, then returns to deposit these offerings in the bucket, which turn quickly into a shuddering viscous mass. Waist-high in the deepest part of the pond, he says, "Bloody buggers. Laying eggs everywhere. Pond is chockablock full already."

I say, "In France people eat them."

Astonishment on his face. "What? No, Baby Madame, don't tell lies. Who would eat these ugly buggers? What is there to eat?"

"Yes they do. Our teacher said. They eat the legs."

He stares at the water between his own legs and says, "No. Can't be. Legs are so thin. Nothing there to eat . . . Maybe the fat stomach, no?"

"No. The legs. She said."

He shakes his head. "Those people must be very poor. I might be poor like that if I wasn't with your family." A little nod acknowledges all the years he has lived with us—all my life, all his much longer life. "But even if I was on the street I wouldn't eat these buggers."

"But they are a delicacy there. In France."

"Shall we try, Baby Madame? We can catch them and give Sita to make a badum. Badum of frog."

"No!"

"That's what Baby will eat tonight. Just like the people in Fran-see. Fried frog curry with rice." He raises his arms, trailing streams of jelly in the air; he looks like a tentacled creature rising from the depths and shakes his fists so the water sparkles, lands on my bare thighs. Our laughter echoes across the pond.

In the monsoon months, the gardens are a different place, the ground sodden, the pond swollen. The sky lights up in the midst of dark stormy days as if a mighty photographer is taking pictures of our little piece of earth. It isn't unusual to come upon a flash of silver and gold, a koi flapping on the wet grass, swept out of the pond by the onslaught of rain. The river is dangerous at this time. It rushes by, carrying all manner of things—furniture, quickly rolling trees with beseeching arms held out to the sky, drowned animals. It is a boiling, heaving mass. The banks could crumble inward, the ground falling away under your feet. We all know this; in these months we keep away from the garden and the river. ∎

LYNCH MOB
Pireeni Sundaralingam

—Sri Lanka 1996

We have crossed the wrong type of border
the night sliced open, a sudden wound.

Words sit upon my tongue,
digging in their claws like fat, black crows,
thrusting wet beaks against my teeth.
We do not speak.

Men fall against our car blades
sparking in the shallow night.
They have all the words,
a torrent breaking at our doors.

Even the dogs can talk,
barking at our metal cage.
They dictate, demand, their spittle
running down the shining glass.

We tuck our language beneath our tongues,
suck down our sounds,
the heat in our mouths,
the swallowed contraband.

THE GECKO REMEMBERS
Pireeni Sundaralingam
—Sri Lanka 2009

They were always there,
limbs waving, inverted,
far from the sun's reach.

Each night I saw them gather,
their motley flock, milling
beneath the ceiling's wide field.

The night they left, their cries
scoured our furthest corners.
They left food steaming on the tables;
we feasted on the flies for days.

POMEGRANATE

Pireeni Sundaralingam

—Croatia 2013

They are the same, our trees,
their thorns rattling
in the brilliant heat.

See how they lean, patient
against this Eden light,
the claims of gardens
leveled by the silt of war.

Pomegranate. Survivor tree.
Crack open the bulb
and taste the flesh. It tastes
of blood and bones.

HISTORY SNAIL
Pireeni Sundaralingam
—Sri Lanka 2016

I have withdrawn from the pungent air,
fierce mind savoring only itself. Thought
furrows, drains into a private dark.

Sharp beaks dream of this voluptuary cave,
sense only the dull eyes protruding. They
do not see the salt trails writing territory,
the lung pressed close within the shell.

MANIFESTO
Aditi Machado

Do not dare describe flowers derange us. Do not dare say how we are arranged, risk calamity. Do not dare describe the feeling in the middle of flowers how we are drawn together. Our closeness beckons as with refusal comes magnetism. We write our names on the pillars. We remember absent things. We read in the middle of flowers a treatise on amnesia. We remember ways, our. Our dispersal in the coliseum of loss. Once in its life a thing must encounter its grammar. Wind vanes of logic atop a crumbling architecture in the middle of flowers.

ELEGY FOR A KNOWN UNKNOWN
Aditi Machado

Spring or
lightning—a seizure
of gladness. I am happy to say
is mean. Truth, unkind. Night—
a description of night.
Prevaricating on the difference.
Come now, there is never nothing
to unfeel. Produce the shape
of gladness. Produce the words
for night. A cool spring night
when it might rain. When

a conundrum
might fall out of leaves.
When in the business
of night I offer myself
the consolation of weather.
And I think the season
a texture, a decision-
making as involved as knitting.
There is sun, there is
moon, there is air

balsamic.
The tenderness of trees
that grows like moss
upon the breeze. Either
I have always felt this
or not at all. I am
sad then. Explain it
to me why I am sad.
Explain the martyrdom
of this tree, why it is
stripped, why whipped
of its ornaments.
What is the season
when the season is

as byzantine
as the taming of a horse.
Shake out the myths now.
It is spring, it is cool.
Either I have always felt this
or not at all.

DESIRES
Aditi Machado

to know nothing but food;

to make of prepositions nouns;

to be concerned with posture, to not posture;

to learn the roots of words, adventitious;

to observe trinities;

to open a book;

to swallow

SMELLING SALT
Aditi Machado

Let's go to the sea, I've said before, as if by going to the edge
of something one can be made more alive.

I never go except in a distant childhood, the water like a tomb
forever emptying out its contents.

Duning against it, not wanting to see the family graves.

The lighthouse grays. Some names were on it that are now fading.

On my desk, magically repurposed as one bright square; outside,
maybe a pond.

Fish glinting like so many thoughts disappearing.

From space the earth must be a monstrous object, full of eyes
you cannot escape.

JELLY BEANS
Soniah Kamal

Mr. and Mrs. Hafeez were at home in Karachi when the mailman came and delivered the letter. They had just settled down to their midmorning chai and they were delighted at the prospect of enjoying their tea and biscuits with a missive from Jamal, their own obedient son in America. As soon as Mr. Hafeez slit open the envelope a photo fell at their feet: Jamal with a white woman.

Tea was forgotten as Mrs. Hafeez went into hysterics. Taimur, their elder, had fallen into the clutches of the elitist Crocodile Coco, and now here was Jamal—their beloved bacha—breaking their hearts too and, even worse, with a foreigner. Jamal's accompanying letter stated that he was marrying Stephanie. He wanted their blessings. His mind was made up.

Mrs. Hafeez slapped her forehead at her ill luck. Everyone knew what marrying a gori, a white woman, meant! At least Crocodile Coco was Pakistani even if she was from a segment of Pakistan altogether different from the Hafeezes's Pakistan. Taimur had laughed when they'd ordered him to leave Crocodile Coco; Taimur laughed at everything they said.

This was Jamal's first transgression except for Mr. Hafeez catching him smoking once. But after a short talk, Jamal had agreed with his father that health was everything and had sworn off smoking.

Mr. Hafeez rose with his hand on his heart and immediately booked a call to Jamal even though it was very late night in America: let his hardworking accountant of a son be woken from his sleep. This nonsense had to be put to an end.

Mrs. Hafeez ferociously dried her eyes. A call was not going to dissuade a son gone so bold. They would surprise him with a visit. And shock him with their own replacement.

"The harlot's name is Stephanie," Mrs. Hafeez said, a half hour later, as she sat on her widowed sister's threadbare sofa. Mrs. Hafeez's niece, Ruby, was verbally betrothed to Jamal—an engagement Jamal had barely taken seriously—so here was Mrs. Hafeez with instructions that Ruby was to pack her suitcase for they were headed to the U.S. as soon as their emergency visas were issued courtesy of Taimur's connections, a senior Army officer close to the U.S. Consulate General.

Taimur had taken one look at the white woman in the photo,

her ill-fitting black cocktail dress, her scruffy velvet dress shoes, her double chin, and, imagining Coco's distress at being related to such an unfashionable thing (not that Ruby was a great step up), decided to help his parents. He even purchased tickets for his parents and Ruby. Coco was pregnant with their first child but Taimur told his parents not to worry—they would have resolved Jamal's problems in time to be back for the delivery.

The Hafeezes had traveled abroad once before to perform Hajj but this was different. Instead of their sons, there would be Ruby to guide them through Karachi-New York-Atlanta. Twenty-one years old, this was Ruby's first time on a plane. She was scared but determined to succeed and regain her fiancé. She took care of the Hafeezes's passports, pressed call buttons for water and extra pillows. She filled their disembarkation cards and led them through the serpentine New York customs lines—Domestic, Foreign, Green Card—where a pretty black customs officer checked their passports for visas.

"Ass-slam Hafeez."

"Aslam Hafeez, yes, it is me."

"Selma Hafeez."

"Salma Hafeez, yes, jee."

"Rub-eye-na Faazlih?"

"Ma'am, it is pronounced Roobeena Fuzzlee."

"And what brings you all to the U.S.?"

The Hafeezes informed her, in their tattered but indignant English, that they'd come to save their son from a white woman. The black officer blinked and stamped their passports and welcomed them to the U.S.

Ruby guided them to the connecting plane to Georgia. Once they arrived in Atlanta, the large airport nearly stumped Ruby with its train system but she managed to get them to baggage claim where trolley machines spat out their dollar bills. Finally Ruby mustered up the courage to ask a janitor for help and so a trolley was procured, and then a taxi—Taimur had advised them to surprise Jamal and catch him off guard.

Mr. Hafeez was most displeased as he converted the price of the taxi from the airport to Jamal's home from Pakistani rupees into American dollars. A surprise had its cost. Mr. Hafeez sat up front and the women climbed into the back. Afternoon was sinking into evening as they set off. Ruby had seen American roads in films and marveled at their cleanliness and orderliness and now she was smitten all the more that the roads were completely devoid of trash, stray animals, food stalls, beggars, hawkers, jaywalkers, honking, cursing, shouting;

the very rip and roar of her nation's fabric that often gave her such headaches.

The taxi driver was a somber middle aged man who'd moved here from Ethiopia. He informed them in slow, clipped English that though it was possible to make a new home here, they had to be careful where they went in Georgia. Some of the natives were kind, but just as many were mean and would shoot them if they could as if they were merely hunting ducks. By the time they arrived at Jamal's, the Hafeezes were ready to grab him, turn around, and return home.

They stood before the wooden door under the bulb-lit porch, their three suitcases next to them. The smell of charred barbecue was in the air, but otherwise the neighborhood street was quiet. Not a peep from inside the house either. They hoped this was the right house, a hulking house in the center of other identically hulking houses. There was no name plaque. Mr. and Mrs. Hafeez looked at the doorbell and stepped closer to each other. Ruby adjusted her dupatta over her loose hair. Her gold bangles tinkled like a distress call. There was nothing to do except ring the bell, so she did.

And so one balmy nothing-special evening, Jamal opened his front door to his parents and his anemic-looking cousin. He gawked at them.

"It better not be Girl Scout Cookies again!" called Stephanie's sleepy voice.

Jamal hugged his parents, nodded at Ruby, and led them into a beige living room. Stephanie sprang up from the La-Z-Boy and straightened her short dress over her thighs.

"Ammi, Abu, this is Stephanie. Stephanie, these are my parents, and, umm, my cousin."

"Hello," Stephanie said, looking confusedly from Jamal to the guests.

Jamal fiddled with the buttons on his striped shirt. He'd been married for six months, he told his parents. He'd wanted to break the news to them gently, thus the injection of photo in the introductory letter.

Mr. Hafeez doubled his hands over his heart. Mrs. Hafeez cried a medley of howls and hiccups. Ruby sat on the ottoman, her stony face unblinking, staring at the mess of wires behind the large TV. Her gaze kept returning to a wicker basket crammed with toys on the carpet in front of the TV.

Stephanie saw the girl looking at the toy basket. Jamal's mother was crying non-stop. His father shaking his head, his lips pursed. She should never have agreed to keeping their marriage a secret. Now here were these claimants, stepped out of a different world and into her home. Not that Stephanie blamed them. She'd have flown half way around the world too if her child had deceived her like this. Stephanie thanked God that Angela was at her father's for the weekend. She'd never seen this side of Jamal before, standing before his parents, his head bowed.

"Jamal," Stephanie smiled a nervous smile. "Would your parents, anyone, care for Coke? Coffee? Chai?"

Upon the usurper saying the Urdu chai instead of the English tea, Ruby felt faint.

"Chai?" Mrs. Hafeez came to life. She stood up and took a step towards Stephanie. "I would rather drink poison than imbibe anything prepared in *your* kitchen."

Stephanie stepped beside Jamal and took hold of his hand. Jamal did not let go even as his mother changed colors.

"Chalo jee, utho, let's go," Mrs. Hafeez commanded Mr. Hafeez and Ruby. "This boy has made a mockery of us, worse than his elder brother ever did. I disown him. He is no longer my son. He has chosen this…" she gave Stephanie a bite of a look, "*this* over us. He has ruined my niece, his fiancée, and I can never lift my head before my sister again. Let us go."

"What's your mother saying?" Stephanie turned to Jamal as Mrs. Hafeez's halting English fast devolved into rapid Urdu.

"It's okay, Honey," Jamal said. "Ammi, please, for God's sake, sit down."

Mrs. Hafeez began to howl and hiccup all over again about how he had deceived them.

"Jamal," Stephanie said, "can I speak to you for a second. Excuse us, please."

Jamal followed Stephanie into the kitchen. He turned the faucet on to drown their voices. He took Stephanie's hands in his.

"Did you know they were coming?" Stephanie asked.

"Of course not," Jamal said, hurt coursing over his face.

"Are you still engaged to your *cousin?*" Stephanie's voice faltered. She was horrified to find herself comparing her looks with that pasty creature outside: she was definitely prettier than Ruby, and—oh she hated having this thought for she believed one should be above caring— she was definitely the thinner one, Ruby looked like a guinea pig.

"I can't believe my parents dragged her here too." Jamal ran his hands over his prickly buzz cut. "I can't believe that bumhole brother of mine did not warn me."

"From what you've told me of your brother, I can't believe you expected anything good from him." Stephanie cupped Jamal's face and looked into his eyes. "What are we going to do?"

"I don't know, Steph." Jamal kissed her forehead.

"Are *you* okay?" Stephanie began to rub him between his shoulder blades. "Are they going to stay here tonight?"

"Where else would they stay?" Jamal nuzzled her neck and prayed that no one would barge into the kitchen. "They're my parents."

"But what about *her*?" Stephanie took a step back. "Your *fiancée*? I can't believe you've put us in this mess."

"I was scared."

"What are you? Angela's age?"

From the living room, the sobbing grew louder.

"Your mother needs to stop crying," Stephanie said.

"Honey," Jamal squeezed her hands, "can you change into jeans, a loose t-shirt?"

"Are you kidding me?" Stephanie said softly.

Jamal hung his head. "Let me take them out for a drive, or dinner, something—give you a chance to gather your bearings too…"

"Sure," Stephanie muttered as Jamal left the kitchen, "leave me alone."

Jamal convinced his parents and Ruby that they were tired and hungry. He bundled them into his Honda and headed towards the nearest Indo-Pak restaurant. Best to try to make up amidst a crowd. His mother might be less likely to cause a scene in public. Jamal glanced at Ruby through the rearview mirror. Her head was resting on the window, her eyes shut, fingers turning round and round the small emerald stud in one nostril.

Jamal focused on the road in front. *We love each other and that's all that matters*—how right it had sounded when Stephanie had informed her parents and how absurd it would sound if he were to make the same declaration to his. What had seemed like love—meeting Stephanie, who worked in the same company but in a different department—now seemed foolish with his parents in the backseat fuming and foaming because Stephanie was a foreigner and because, since they'd allowed Taimur his choice of bride, Jamal's wife should have been their choice.

"This is how you have repaid my trust to send you abroad," Mr. Hafeez kept muttering.

Jamal's hands tightened on the steering wheel. Awaiting his green card, he had not been home for the last three years, a sojourn which resulted in him not so much forgetting his duties but, somewhere during this time, recognizing that his own wishes were, if not paramount, then, at the very least, valid too.

But a break from home did not mean turning into someone else.

Did it?

The restaurant was fairly empty. The hostess led them through a row of formica tables, pastel walls decorated with generic posters of the Lahore Fort, the Badshahi Mosque, Lahore Railway Station, to a corner table for four. Mrs. Hafeez and Ruby sat on one side. Jamal sat in front of his mother and his father got in beside him. Mrs. Hafeez asked if the food was halal. Jamal assured her it was. He ordered chicken karahi, mutton biryani, naan and chai. No one spoke a word and it wasn't until the chai arrived, dark against the insides of white foam cups, and his parents took sips and sighed, that Jamal's eye filled with tears.

"I'm sorry," he said. "I'm so sorry. But I can't undo what's done."

"Can't," Mr. Hafeez said grimly. "Or won't."

"I don't know what to say." Jamal crumbled a complimentary papadum between his fingertips, the deep-fried cracker rough and spiky against his skin. The scent of powdered lentils and cumin rose between them.

"Nothing to say." Mrs. Hafeez wanted to slap her son whose large wet eyes were reminding her of the times Taimur would not give his little brother a turn on the bike. She would spank Taimur and make sure Jamal rode the bike as long as he wanted.

Only Ruby took a papadum and ate it.

"Ammi, Abu, just get to know Stephanie." Jamal's voice broke. "She's a very good person."

"She can be Mother Teresa for all I care," Mrs. Hafeez said. "You have deceived us."

Jamal looked at his mother. "Had I asked you, would you really have permitted—"

"Never." Mr. Hafeez said. "So you deceive us?"

The food arrived, hot and appetizing. Jamal ladled generous servings onto his parents' plates, urging them to eat—after all they had no grievances against the food. He asked Ruby to help herself and she did, remarking, a few bites in, that the food was tasty.

Jamal filled his own plate, his appetite somewhat revived. They ate silently and it wasn't until they were nearing the end of their meal that he told them about Angela.

"Stephanie's divorced." Jamal focused on the bowl of lime pickles steeped in orange oil. "She divorced her husband. He was cheating on her. Angela is four now. She thinks of me as her father."

Child! Divorce! Broken Home! Cheating!

The Hafeezes looked at each other, longing to hold each other, to smooth away the shock on each other's faces at how far Jamal had strayed, but they would have to wait until they were alone and not in public.

"First flight out tomorrow morning," Mr. Hafeez announced with finality.

"Tonight, hotel," chimed Mrs. Hafeez.

"No," Jamal said, "you will come back home with me and—"

Mr. Hafeez half rose, people turned to look at him, "You dare to say no to your mother and me. You dare." He began to cough. His heart filled with a rage that had begun years before at his eldest son's shenanigans, a rage he'd never been able to fully let fly because Taimur simply did not care. Jamal still cared. Mr. Hafeez could see that in Jamal's small wounded face and, though it was unfair to punish the child who cared, Mr. Hafeez could not stop. He brought his fist down on the table and wished out loud that his sons had both died at birth. Long hours he'd toiled in the bank back home in order to send his sons to the best of the best schools where everyone spoke English and acted as if they owned half of Pakistan, which many of the other fathers did, and for what: so that his sons could speak fluent English in flawless accents, the elder going on to marry an elitist crocodile and the younger an ageing firangi with a child.

Mr. Hafeez's coughed turned violent. Ruby managed to coax him down into his seat and she forced him to drink a glass of water to calm himself.

"See," Mrs. Hafeez said to Jamal, "this is the girl you should have married instead of that aged harlot with a child. A child! Who you now raise as if it is your own."

"Stay," Jamal said, looking from his mother to his father. "Please."

"What face am I going to show to my sister? Who will marry Ruby now that you have jilted her?" Mrs. Hafeez's lips quivered. "We will not stay for a single second after what you have done."

"I'm not going anywhere." Ruby spoke in a small but steady voice. Last time Jamal had visited Karachi, four years ago, he'd barely spoken to her and when her mother brought up marriage, he'd shown little interest. That very day Ruby, deciding she needed to be economically self-reliant come what may, had applied to teach Islamiat, her best subject, at the all-girl's high school she herself had graduated from. Jamal's disinterest seemed abnormal to her and not, as her mother and Khala kept repeating, because he was shy. That the girls school suited Ruby all too well, she would never tell her mother, and she would miss her friends—her special friend—but she would not miss the petty school politics, or having to sneak around, or her mother moaning about how she needed to lose weight, and so, when Khala had come running to their house with Jamal's betrayal, Ruby packed her bags: this was it, her opportunity to get out of Pakistan once and for all.

"What do you mean?" Jamal asked nervously.

Ruby's small dark brown eyes bore into Jamal's. "Had you been honest, I would not be here. But I am here. And I refuse to return to where I will be nothing but pitied and derided because you ditched me. Also I too deserve to live in a place where the roads and electricity and water runs efficiently. Khala is right—no prospects for me there." She cleared her throat. "You have to find some way for me to stay on here."

Mr. Hafeez looked at Ruby as if she'd grown horns. Mrs. Hafeez began to weep.

Jamal completely lost his appetite.

* * *

Mr. and Mrs. Hafeez wanted to go home but they could not leave the unmarried Ruby by herself. And so, a fortnight later, the house had been forced to settle into a modicum of a routine. On the weekends the three visitors kept to the guest room where the Hafeezes slept on the bed and Ruby in a sleeping bag and, on the weekdays, Jamal, Stephanie and Angela did not return home from work and preschool till late in the evening. Consequently the factions could, if they wanted, which they did, avoid each other quite resolutely.

Jamal assured Stephanie that this setup was not forever. Stephanie, feeling homeless in her own home, wore her bravest face—she had a Sri Lankan acquaintance at the gym who liked to joke that South Asian parents came to visit and then never left. But the ex-fiancé turning up and, marriage or no marriage, refusing to leave had to be a first. All these people did was drink tea all day long! Thank God one could not get drunk off chai! True, she was wearing clothes that covered her up a bit more. True, she was discretely sipping her evening unwind glass of wine in a mug. True, she'd switched to turkey bacon because according to Jamal while his parents could tolerate alcohol, pork in the house might kill them (which was tempting). But Angela doted on Jamal, and Stephanie would be damned if she was going to destabilize Angela unless it was absolutely necessary. So this ordeal would have to be borne. Jamal had to be trusted: soon his parents and that pitiable cousin would go back home. For now the trick was to avoid them. Stephanie did not like to keep Angela at the day care till late evening but returning home early meant spending the evening trying to keep her from those people. They had been indifferent to Angela so far and Stephanie was loathe to give them an opportunity to be unkind. Jamal said his parents would never be unkind to a child. Stephanie was not convinced.

Though it meant that Jamal had to stay out late too, the Hafeezes and Ruby were glad that Stephanie did not come home early on weekdays. After being cooped up in the guest room all weekend— your choice, Jamal had curtly informed them after they refused to sightsee if Stephanie came along and Jamal refused to go anywhere if she could not accompany them—they'd start their day as soon as they heard the garage door closing.

They would stroll in the back garden and then around the cul-de-sac and up the road to the end and back. Mr. Hafeez, an amateur gardener, pointed out to Mrs. Hafeez the pine trees, the magnolia bushes and, closer to the ground, healthy ferns and brilliant blue hydrangeas. Mrs. Hafeez pointed out the lack of people. "Na Adam, na Adam zaat, not a single human being anywhere," she kept saying though secretly she was glad of it.

Returning inside, Mr. Hafeez would turn the TV on to CNN America, a poor cousin to CNN International, he never failed to remark, even as he gathered the newspapers—*USA Today* and the *Atlanta Journal Constitution*—from the kitchen island and open up the pages to make sense of this new world.

Mrs. Hafeez and Ruby busied themselves with preparing elaborate breakfasts, lunches and dinners. Mrs. Hafeez had gone through the spice cabinet her first morning here. She'd sniffed at the unfamiliar oregano and basil, the lemon peel and parsley. Where was the cumin? she'd asked Jamal. The turmeric, red chillies, ground coriander? Jamal handed her his Shan ready-mix korma packet he used once in a while. Otherwise, when he wanted to eat Pakistani food, he got take out. Mrs. Hafeez lips had thinned. She'd rattled off a long list and Jamal had insisted she accompany him to the desi grocery store.

The small store sat between a dry cleaners and nail salon. It smelled of the stale samosas on display in a glass cabinet. Mrs. Hafeez had expected open bins of spices and instead grumbled about quality as she picked up the smallest packets of masalas she could find. Jamal picked up a packet of jelly beans, Angela's favorite candy, he told his mother, who shrugged indifferently. Jamal guided Mrs. Hafeez towards the freezer section but she was adamant that only fresh rotis would do and so they picked up a bag of white flour as well as long grained Zebra basmati rice and tub of ghee. She picked up a ten-count box of mangos, a red blush spreading over their green flesh. From Mexico, Jamal said. Mexeeco, Mrs. Hafeez repeated as she sniffed the box, smells like home.

Mrs. Hafeez had nearly clapped with joy at the fresh vegetables. She bagged them with assured familiarity even as she complained the okra was too long, the eggplants the pale Chinese variety, the garlic bulbs sprouting roots, the ginger more grey than golden, the chillies not firm enough, the daikon too firm. But there was a smile on her lips: she would make green chilly-daikon radish parathas for Jamal. And koftay. And biryani. And eggplant pakoras. She would win her son back. And she thought she had as he took seconds and thirds. And then he'd requested for her to put less spices on account of Stephanie.

Mrs. Hafeez proceeded to put extra spices in everything so that Stephanie couldn't stomach anything. She began to rearrange the kitchen in a nonsense fashion in order to irritate Stephanie into initiating a divorce since everyone knew it didn't take much for these white women to break up their families. It was nasty of her, but it was the only way Mrs. Hafeez knew to let Jamal know that nothing was forgiven. How triumphant Mrs. Hafeez would have been if she'd known Stephanie spent hours worrying how in the world, once his parents finally left, Jamal was going to readjust to her bland casseroles and quiches.

Mrs. Hafeez was increasingly cold to Ruby too.

"I have told your daughter to return to you a million times," Mrs. Hafeez told her sister over the phone. "Instead she's making Jamal's life miserable with her demands of finding some way for her to stay on legally." Mrs. Hafeez paused. "Not that I care if Jamal's life is made miserable. But why your daughter so desperately wants to remain in this country, Gods knows better."

The Hafeezes missed their TV programs. The missed their servant's constant chatter. They missed scolding him for chattering constantly. They phoned Taimur every few days and complained that he had not phoned them even once. Mrs. Hafeez missed her busy social life of religious events and gossip sessions concerning the morality of the women of the nation. Mr. Hafeez missed the evening editions of newspapers (because retired men made it a point of pride to keep up with current events) and going to the mosque to attend prayers, as well as gossip about politicians hell bent on ruining the nation.

One afternoon Mr. Hafeez interrupted Mrs. Hafeez's afternoon cooking session. He had to step out, Mr. Hafeez said, beyond the back garden and cul-de-sac, for some fresh air or he would suffocate. Mrs. Hafeez turned off the cumin she'd been pan roasting and washed her hands. She had no desire to go but complied because her husband wanted to go. They asked Ruby out of politeness if she wanted to accompany them.

"No," Ruby said. She busied herself at the kitchen table with a computer languages manual, unable to comprehend a thing. She was growing increasingly sullen as each day Jamal turned up empty-handed over how to keep her on. One evening, as soon as Jamal and Stephanie had stepped into the house, she'd informed Jamal she'd be willing to be his second wife. Before Jamal could even answer, Stephanie, her expression alternately horrified and bemused, had announced that in this country, only one wife *at a time thank you very much*. When Ruby's eyes filled with frustration, Stephanie turned to Jamal and said screw the cost, it's time to consult a lawyer. The lawyer said that for permanent status, Ruby needed employment for which she was uniquely suited and for which no one else in America was qualified; that eliminated retail, cleaning and fast food industries. He had muttered that it was a pity she had no computer skills. Jamal had taken her to the library and she'd returned with an armful of manuals. Waving goodbye to the Hafeezes, Ruby returned to the manuals, refusing to be defeated.

On their first walk out of the neighborhood, Mr. and Mrs. Hafeez crossed over the threshold timidly, making it till the traffic lights at the start of the neighborhood before they turned back. But their walks grew longer and bolder until those traffic lights were left far behind. They took to crossing whichever road came their way holding tightly each other's hand in broad daylight for the first time in their lives. Holding hands was a safety requirement here, they told each other, and yet, often Mrs. Hafeez would hold on a little longer than absolutely necessary.

Mr. Hafeez discovered kudzu. Mrs. Hafeez discovered that, when fellow pedestrians said hello, a nod in return was the polite response. Within weeks they discovered, to their delight, at a twenty minutes walk, a shop with a flashing neon sign: Dollar Store.

There they found aisles upon aisles of toys, lotions, shampoos, kitchenware, hair accessories, candles, all for, apparently, only one dollar. Mrs. Hafeez pointed to the rack with jelly beans in jars with gingham bows: cinnamon, green apple, birthday cake, cotton candy, pink lemonade, vanilla bean, orange blaze. She told Mr. Hafeez that jelly beans were Angela's favorite candy. They moved on to the home utensils aisle where they picked up a rolling pin and extra-large yellow plastic colander. At the cash register they stopped short at seeing it manned by a tall Sikh in a turban and a small woman in a shalwar kameez the same lavender shade as Mrs. Hafeez's outfit. Smiling tentatively, Mrs. Hafeez approached the register.

"One dollar each?" Mrs. Hafeez shyly asked.

"Everything ninety-nine cents." The woman beamed.

"No discount-viscount?" Mr. Hafeez asked.

"Discount?" The turbaned man guffawed as he began to ring up the items. "This is not India."

"We are from Pakistan," Mr. Hafeez said.

"Where?" the woman's eyes brightened. "My people were from Sargodha. They moved during partition."

"We are from Karachi," Mrs. Hafeez said. "My people were from Amrtisar but moved to Lahore during partition."

But no matter, they all agreed, even IndiaPakistan was once the same. They introduced themselves: Kuldeep Singh and Ira.

"We arrived here almost a month ago," Mrs. Hafeez said.

"Welcome to Georgia," Ira said. "Best weather in all of America. No snow!"

The Hafeezes agreed that so far they had enjoyed nothing but good weather.

"My younger son," Mr. Hafeez's chest puffed up despite himself, "came for college but now has a very good job. We are visiting."

"My daughter got married here to a very good boy with his own used *luxury* car business," Ira said. "She missed us so much, she sponsored us and we've been living here a decade plus. This," Ira looked around the store, "we do because we were getting so bored at home, especially now that the grandchildren, triplets—two boys, one girl—are in high school and have their own activities. They don't even need us to drive them anymore. Your son is married? Any children?"

The Hafeezes told them about their older son in Pakistan who had, just a week ago, been blessed by a baby girl. (Taimur told them there was no need to hurry back. Coco was in good hands since they'd hired an excellent nurse for her. And, for the baby, they'd hired a highly recommended Filipina ayah. "You take your time," Taimur insisted. Coco had been asleep. She was supposed to have called them as soon as she woke up. Eventually Jamal had told them to stop hovering over the phone. Coco was not going to call.) The Singhs congratulated the Hafeezes, and before the Singhs had a chance to inquire about Jamal, the Hafeezes paid and fled.

How to tell anyone about Stephanie or Angela? Angela who spent the weekends with her father and the weekdays with her mother, her purple carry-on suitcase her anchor between the two residences. You could not tell a child to go away. You had no choice but to plaster pleasantness on your face and sit through the ordeal of her unzipping her suitcase to show you how she'd packed her favorite dolls and blanket. You could not tell a child you had no interest in her school activity called 'show-and-tell'. You could not tell a child to not run to your room with pictures she'd drawn just for you. You could not tell a child to stop complaining that her mother did not let her eat candy all day or let her watch TV all the time. You could not stop a child from climbing all over you, from asking you in a sweet little voice to read *The Hungry Caterpillar*, sing "Five Little Ducks," do a Dora the Explorer jigsaw puzzle. You could not stop yourself from looking forward to reading, singing, and connecting jigsaw pieces.

Though you are not used to children addressing you by your first names (back home it is Uncle and Aunty), you are all right when the child called you Mr. Aslam and Ms. Salma according to her mother's instructions. One day she called you Dada and Dadi. You looked sharply at your son. Why had he told her to call you grandfather and grandmother. You wanted to tell her to stop but you did not because you did not want to upset a small child who was just doing as she was told. Her mother told her to stop. But she carried on: Dada-Dadi. You heard her mother's and your son's raised voices for the first time. He said, "she's my daughter too." She said, "but that doesn't make them her grandparents."

You found yourself at the dollar store, in the candy aisle, purchasing jelly beans, Angela's favorite, not because you wanted to irritate her mother by giving the child sugar but because every child deserved sweet treats. This child was nothing more, you reminded each other, than an inconvenience and a disturbance; you looked forward to being inconvenienced and disturbed.

One evening the child returned home wan-faced in her mother's arms. "What's wrong with her?" you'd asked. "Nothing's wrong with her," the mother replied in an exhausted voice. Your son added in an equally exhausted voice, "She's just tired from a too long day."

You held copious discussions between yourselves for a week before making the following offer: if Angela wanted to leave day care, you could look after her. The mother said, "No thank you" even as your son said, "That's a great idea."

Now they walked the child back from the bus stop. They learned to fix macaroni and cheese. They made peanut butter sandwiches. They braided the child's strawberry-blonde hair into ropes that flew around her sweet, toothy face. They stood in the cul-de-sac when she rode her tricycle. When the big kids came out to play, they stepped closer to her. They felt their hearts swell into wings around this child and they reminded each other every night: She's nothing to us. We are merely longing to see our infant granddaughter in Pakistan. That is all."

And they watched their son with this child.

The first few weeks the Hafeezes had watched Jamal and Angela's interactions with disbelief. They'd watched with derision Angela leaping into Jamal's open arms whenever she saw him. Jamal toasting and buttering waffles for Angela as if she were his princess. Jamal singing her the ABC song as he flossed Angela's teeth. Jamal putting her to bed because she preferred him and not her mother. A forlorn Jamal handing over Angela to her real father every Friday evening; not Stephanie but Jamal,who waited impatiently for Sundays and Angela's return.

Gradually the Hafeezes's derision turned to childlike wonder, a begrudging respect even, for their son's ability to love another man's child. Angela called her real father *Dad* and she called Jamal *Baba* just as Jamal did his own father, and Jamal called her *Beti*, daughter. All day long: BabaBetiBabaBetiBabaBeti.

Not biological, Jamal had said to them curtly, but no less real. Mrs. Hafeez warned Jamal, one day, that if he planned to have his own biological children, he should hurry up for Stephanie was no spring chicken. He couldn't, Jamal said. Because he had a low sperm count. It was one of the few shocks in her life that Mrs. Hafeez did not immediately share with her husband, choosing instead to spare him as long as possible from this barren pain: their son could not have his own children no matter whom he would have married.

The Hafeezes stopped keeping to the guest room during the weekday evenings. They began to sight see on the weekends. They all went to the zoo, sitting together in the cafeteria, sharing french fries. After that, it was Stephanie who begged off: I need me time, Jamal. Jamal took his parents to Stone Mountain Park and the Botanical Gardens but Angela got bored so the Hafeezes told him to take them where she wanted to go, which was Monkey Joes and Catch Air.

Visiting the Singhs at their store became the Hafeezes's regular routine. It was the Singhs who told them which restaurants would cater to their Pakistani taste buds. The Singhs who told them about the Global Mall on Jimmy Carter and the desi stores in Decatur with their sounds and scents reminiscent of back home. The Singhs who recommended the best halal butchers, Iranian stores for nuts and dried fruit, H-mart for fresh fish and cheap fruit, Patel Plaza for Indian films, Khabar, a free magazine catering to the desi community, and advised them to tell Jamal to contact a mosque for correct prayer timings. Jamal apparently no longer believed in ritual and institutions, a statement that dismayed the Hafeezes and Stephanie was Christian but apparently did not go to church; late at night they sometimes worried about Angela's growing up with this dearth of faith.

The greatest information they learned was of the Pakistani and Indian cable channels. Once Jamal subscribed to Zee TV, GEO TV, Star Plus and every other channel with back-home news bulletins, films, dramas, song and dance medleys, it seemed to the Hafeezes and Ruby as if the TV had planted a greater semblance of home in this country and that they could now, if not exactly grow, at least not completely wither.

Stephanie was not happy that Jamal's parents and Ruby no longer kept to the guest room. She would return from work to find the house reeking of microwave popcorn, Angela sitting between the old couple, the three of them mesmerized by an Indian soap serial in which overly dressed families forever schemed each other's downfalls while Ruby would be draped over the La-Z-Boy, frowning over a computer manual. Stephanie was most unhappy that Jamal now kissed her in private lest he embarrass his family, unhappy that Angela ran to Jamal's parents for comfort when she scolded her, unhappy that Jamal's parents wooed Angela with jelly beans even as they remarked to each other how cute Taimur's baby must be getting, how precious she must be, how darling she was to them. And Angela, beaming.

One day as the Hafeezes and Ruby watched a rerun of the film *Khabi Khush Khabi Ghaam*, a local advertisement for an Islamic school came on. The school was seeking qualified teachers for mathematics and Islamiat. Ruby clutched her pen and jotted the number. She phoned the school and was called in for an interview the next week. She spent the week getting the school in Pakistan to fax her recommendations and affidavits even as she brushed up on her teaching philosophy, which was to drill the students until they knew the facts of Islam by heart. She hoped her philosophy would be appropriate here too. Stephanie advised her to tone down the rote and concentrate on thinking. Ruby gazed at Stephanie's black skirt and flouncy white blouse and her smart kitten-heeled shoes and, before she even knew it, she asked Stephanie for help with her interview wardrobe.

It was Stephanie who drove Ruby to Kohl's for a pantsuit. Stephanie who waited patiently outside the fitting room until Ruby found something suitable in black. Stephanie who drove her to the interview, telling her she would ace it. Stephanie who waited in the lobby for the interview to be over. Stephanie who gave her thumbs up after a smiling Ruby emerged forty minutes later. Stephanie who signed Ruby up for driving lessons because she would need to drive to wherever she ended up employed. Stephanie who drove her to her driving lessons. Stephanie who told Jamal to check out used cars from his parents' dollar store contacts.

Stephanie who crossed her fingers the entire time because if Ruby found her bearings, Jamal's parents would go.

Stephanie took Ruby to the elementary school parking lot for extra practice. Round and round and round the car park until they finally braved the main street. At the first traffic light, Ruby jerked to a stop. When the light turned green, she pressed the accelerator and the car jerked forward again.

"You're doing great," Stephanie said after they made it all the way around the neighborhood. "Do you want to try heading towards a busier road?

Ruby hesitated, then said, "Yes."

"Take a left on the main road."

"I'm scared."

"You'll be fine."

Ruby took the turn.

"Good job!" Stephanie said.

"I was very scared."

"I couldn't tell. You didn't even panic when the minivan came hurtling towards us."

"It was on the other side of the road."

"I was scared!" Stephanie laughed.

Ruby laughed too. "I couldn't tell."

"I deserve a treat for that. You deserve a treat! There's a place nearby that makes cupcakes from scratch and great cappuccinos."

Ruby took a moment to answer—her aunt was not going to like it but neither did she want Stephanie to think she was rude.

At the coffee shop, Ruby thanked Stephanie again.

"You're so welcome," Stephanie said. "I'm sure once Jamal's parents see you are settled in your new life, they will be pleased to return to their own lives."

"Yes," Ruby said softly as understanding dawned. "I'm sure they will be more than pleased to return." Then Ruby added, "You know, you are no different than any daughter-in-law back home. You all want to get rid of your in-laws."

Stephanie flushed. "Their...your... coming was...a bit of a shock."

"*You* are the shock of their lives."

The Hafeezes watched quietly as Stephanie and Ruby returned from each lesson a little less awkward with each other, a little less severe, a little less taciturn, sometimes with coffee in hand and bags holding half-eaten pastries.

"What did you two talk about?" Mrs. Hafeez would ask Ruby in a pinched voice and Ruby would always reply, "this and that, nothing, really," and Mrs. Hafeez, upset over Ruby's refusal to return back home due to which she'd missed the birth of Taimur's daughter, saw this friendship, collusion even, between her niece and the gori as the ultimate betrayal. Ruby should have stayed loyal to her! When she complained to Mr. Hafeez he shrugged and said Ruby was *her* niece, what was he to do!

Two weeks later, the Islamic elementary school hired Ruby. Ruby passed her driving test and clutched the keys Stephanie handed her to the secondhand Toyota as if they were an umbilical cord to a fantasy world. She was going to pay them back in installments. The lawyer informed Ruby that she was in good standing for permanent residency because, though her religion and native language may be mundane in her own country, here they were highly specialized skills. With her first paycheck, Ruby bought Stephanie a bouquet and she kissed her on the cheek. Time would come when Ruby would settle down to a routine in her job and would move into an apartment complex that boasted a gym and a swimming pool—swimming an activity her short muscular limbs would partake in to the very end of her life—and one day share her life with a Malaysian Muslim girl whose mother would be just as pleased as Ruby's mother that their spinster daughters were at least not living alone in the U.S.

The Hafeezes watched with begrudging pride as Ruby rented a one-bedroom apartment. On the day she moved out, Mrs. Hafeez wept with relief.

"Ruby is no longer our problem," she said to Mr. Hafeez. "We are now free to return back home."

Mr. Hafeez's eyes locked with Mrs. Hafeez's. He agreed. They bade leave of the Singhs and they purchased jars of jelly beans in every flavor.

"To distribute back home?" Mrs. Singh asked, nodding her head in approval.

The Hafeezes glanced at each other. For the first time they mentioned Stephanie existence, and Angela's.

"She calls us Dadi and Dada."

The Singhs changed colors but not too many.

"We will miss you," the Singhs said, hugging them. "Visit again soon!"

As they stepped out of the Dollar Store, the Hafeezes looked forward to packing, leaving for the airport, kissing Jamal, hugging Ruby and shaking hands goodbye with Stephanie who, in turn, was thanking Jesus, Mohammed and the Universe that she was getting her life, her kitchen, her husband and her daughter back.

The Hafeezes rechecked their boarding passes and then allowed themselves yet another moment with the sniffling Angela. Poor child. They too would miss her, they assured her, but already they imagined the plane having taken off and landed and their hearts cracking open with love when they saw Taimur's darling child, their first granddaughter.

* * *

Karachi had not changed in the Hafeezes's nine-month absence. The city lights glittered as the plane circled the runway and the Hafeezes were happy to exit into the hot, humid coastal night air. They'd dreamt Taimur, Crocodile Coco and the beloved baby would be waiting for them at the airport but, alas, no. Taimur had sent a car and driver to take them home, a home the Hafeezes were glad to see had been kept spic and span by the chatterbox servant who had proven reliable despite their worries that he talked more and worked less. They slept in their own bed that night. Mr. Hafeez got a crick in his neck, which got him wondering what sort of pillow he'd been using in America where his neck had been fine.

The next morning, the Hafeezes arrived at Taimur's luxury custom-built home by the sea only to find him barking into a phone about being duped into a place with smelly water pipes and mildew. A maid told them that Madame Coco was on a postpartum vacation in Thailand. The Filipina ayah barely let them spend half an hour with their granddaughter, Marina—a bald baby with a cruel rash on her face. Apparently, Madame Coco had given strict instructions that Madame Baby's schedule was not to be altered for *anyone*. Also the Ayah would finally, sadly, tell the Hafeezes she had seven children she was supporting in the Philippines and thus could not afford to bend rules even though she truly wished she could.

The Hafeezes returned to their house and for the next many weeks threw themselves into socializing with extended family and friends. They answered inquiries about Jamal and Ruby with glaring smiles because Ruby's mother, angry that they had not dragged Ruby back, had told everyone the truth about Jamal and his divorcee with child. The snide glances annoyed the Hafeezes. Jamal had hardly committed the world's most heinous crime. In fact, Mr. Hafeez said, he had committed *no* crime. Mrs. Hafeez fought with her sister, suggesting she learn to be happy just because Ruby was happy.

Later, that night, as the Hafeezes clutched each other in bed, Mrs. Hazfeez asked if they should take comfort in the fact that at least

Taimur was happy with Crocodile Coco. Tears soaked her pillow as she informed Mr. Hafeez that Jamal was infertile. She wondered for the first time if Stephanie had wanted any more children. They did not need to tell each other they missed Angela. Without grandchildren, the Hafeezs decided, they may as well be dead and they vowed to renew their efforts to coddle their granddaughter. But the ayah hovered over Madame Baby as if the grandparents were kidnappers, and matters did not improve even after Coco returned from her postpartum vacation. She was happy to leave her infant's routine in the ayah's expert hands. It was useless to complain to Taimur. He was too busy making money and playing golf.

One evening, after a visit at Taimur's house where the ayah timed their allotted fifteen minutes with Madame Baby after making certain that they'd used the hand sanitizer, the Hafeezs returned home and telephoned Jamal. They wanted to return. To check up on Ruby, they said. Ruby was an unmarried girl abroad and they owed it to Ruby's mother to see for themselves that Ruby was just not surviving but thriving.

Jamal heard something else over the phone, a yearning perhaps, and he wondered exactly how Taimur and Crocodile Coco were mistreating his parents this time. In any case, eleven months ago his parents had been about to disown him and now they wanted to reclaim him. Jamal told his parents he would call them back. He turned to Stephanie who stood behind him like an attentive tail.

"I have a bad feeling." Stephanie folded her arms over her chest.

"They want to return. Check up on Ruby."

"Then they can stay with her, Lucky Ruby."

Jamal shook his head. "I'm their son. They have to stay with me."

"*My* parents don't live with us."

"*They* don't want to live with us. Please, Steph."

"No." Stephanie chewed on her lower lip.

"It won't be forever." Jamal took hold of Stephanie's hands.

"Why can't you be like your damn brother?"

Jamal strode into the living room. Angela was hosting a chai party for her imaginary friends and the Hafeezs. She happily made space for Jamal between his invisible parents and handed him a plate piled high with make-believe samosas.

"Mom, do you also want samosas and chai?"

Jamal got up. "Steph, come on, join us."

Stephanie looked at Angela and turned to Jamal. "They're not coming back. Your parents can't come back."

Angela gasped. Jamal nodded. She jumped up and began to dance around his legs.

"DadaDadi are coming back. DadaDadi are coming back. DadaDadi are coming back."

Jamal picked Angela up and threw her in the air and caught her and they laughed. You can watch a celebration for only so long and so Stephanie watched as long as she could bear and then covered her face with her hands. But there was a gap between her fingers and her eyes were not closed.

* * *

They would gift her a deep red shawl with gold embroidered paisleys, colors fit for a bride. Stephanie wore it often. Years later, too worn for wear, she draped it over the sofa in the drawing room, an abiding brilliant flame she had almost not allowed into her home. ∎

AND HE SAILED OUT LIKE A SHIP
Sadia Uqaili

30" X 40". Acrylics, brocade, and collage on wood.

DIE WELT IST EIN ZIRKUS II
Sadia Uqaili

14" X 19". Acrylics, colored pencils, and inks on paper.

DIE WELT IST EIN ZIRKUS III
Sadia Uqaili

22" X 30". Acrylics, colored pencils, collage, and inks on paper.

MEMORY KEEPER III
Sadia Uqaili

22" X 30". Acrylics, silver leaf, and inks on paper.

DESCENT FROM THE WINTER GARDEN
Dipika Mukherjee

Behind me, on an escalator is a young man, perhaps twenty, at least
a foot taller. We are alone in this narrow corridor going down, leaving
the light of the winter garden, the library hushed in this space with no one
else but us. He steps down and my neck feels this move, cranes to read
the walls, strains so that I am looking up and behind—"If it had been
possible to build the Tower Of Babel without ascending it, the work
would have been permitted—FRANZ KAFKA"—my brows furrowed
to construct meaning from disappearing ink on grey walls.
He lopes down three more steps,
and I bound off the escalator,
my heart a pounding,
unreasonable thing,
powering my feet.
After the rallies for *I Can't Breathe*
Hands Up, Don't Shoot,
at the gathering
of fierce voices
for the political,
a poet brought
marbled paper
to scratch words
with spent bullets;
I etched "My memory
is again in the way
of your history ~
AGHA SHAHID ALI"
as lush calligraphy,
colored in red,
white and blue.
Now, all alone,
color is only dark,
too dangerous.

DAMP RED EARTH
AND POURING RAIN
Dipika Mukherjee

Writing a novel is a lot
like cooking a good biryani.
First the manic frying, the heat
of cardamom, cinnamon, cloves
bayleaves, star anise, peppercorns.

Then set aside. Revise. Onions
reborn caramelized, pungent
with ginger-garlic. A fragrant,
even, browning, then the meat thrown
into an osmotic simmer.

The basmati rice must be—just—
half cooked, mingling, warm milk infused
with saffron and the essence of
pandanus, sprinkled rosewater.
Then a final rearrangement.

Gently stir this meat-rice, layered
yet touching. Out with the spices
hard, embittered, harsh on the tongue.
Seal to steam—slowly—on its own
broth, then taste for imperfections.

It is merely meat and rice—yes—
but what you now hold in your hands
will transport you to open fields,
of saffron blowing in the wind,
of damp red earth and pouring rain.

NOTE: Pankti (associated with food and the god of rain) is a Vedic meter
found in one of the later books (Book V) of the *Rig Vida*. The pankti meter is
stanzaic with forty syllables, written in any number of quintains, five padas,
or feet of eight syllables.

FIVE FAMOUS ASIAN WAR PHOTOGRAPHS

Amit Majmudar

THAT NAMELESS AFGHAN GIRL ON THE COVER OF *NATIONAL GEOGRAPHIC*

Her eyes are green because they had to be green for the photograph to mean anything to us.

Her eyes' intensity, and their hunted look, depend on their greenness (and, admittedly, a slightly disproportionate size relative to the rest of her face). Recessive eye colors are associated by people of European origin with people of European origin, and hence with a fully developed personality. Her face loses the one-sidedness so often read into the Asian both by SEAL teams and college admissions committees: The default Asian, depending again on the eyes, "looks like" either a religious fanatic or an uncreative overachiever. But not an Asian with green eyes; such an Asian is set apart. Green eyes add mystery and a sense of recognition simultaneously. Green eyes, in the setting of this otherwise standard refugee-face, create instant empathy, forcing us to imagine, in this most unexpected place, Someone Like You Or Me.

Of course, her green eyes are themselves a recessive trait. They penetrated that far east of Europe, or south of Russia, in the forced injections of genetic material brought about by the British Army's invasion in the 1800s or the Red Army's in the 1900s. Or the Macedonian Army's in the 300 B.C.s, or the United States Army's a couple of millennia later. The girl is nameless; she does not exist, she *represents*. So there is a possibility our empathy for the Afghan female in wartime is being aroused, when we look at this photograph, by the genetic trace of the ancient rape of an Afghan female in wartime.

THAT GUY IN SAIGON WHO IS ABOUT TO GET HIS BRAINS BLOWN OUT

This is a photograph that has a clear precedent in painting: Goya's *The Third of May 1808,* in which a row of Napoleonic soldiers have lined up firing-squad-style in front of a group of

Spanish resisters. The center of the group is that unforgettable man in the white shirt with his arms up. The left sleeve (the right is obstructed by the head of a fellow Spaniard) is the second brightest spot in the painting, slightly brighter than its own light source, the small box that the soldiers have set down to illuminate their targets. The brightest white in the painting belongs to the tiny sliver of the white in his eyes. His eyes are open, and his head is tilted, as if he were pleading, or about to plead. This is a man who might be shot in the next instant—but then again, he might simply be arrested.

The guy in Saigon who is about to have his brains blown out has no arms at all; the twisted front of his shirt would suggest they are bound behind him, but in the photograph, his shoulders taper abruptly into nothingness. He cannot throw his arms up in surrender, and he cannot throw his arms across his face in futile defense against the blast. He is, *literally*, an unarmed man getting shot.

This is only one way in which the photograph improves on Goya. The second aspect is the intimacy. Firing squads *had* to be five to eight strong: Military men knew that a few of the soldiers always shot wide on purpose, and that the close-quarters executions were psychologically sustainable only if the soldiers could offload the guilt onto their neighbors in the squad: *His* bullet made the actual kill, not *mine*. Even this pseudo-anonymity takes a toll on soldiers; hard as it may be to believe, the nervous breakdowns of SS men in Polish forests prompted Himmler's shift from conventional, bullet-based massacres to the gas chambers. The Saigon picture is much more intimate, with two men foregrounded.

Goya does not show us the executioners' faces; the Saigon photograph shows us the shooter in profile, and his chin is unexpectedly weak. His weak chin has a clear relationship to the smallness of his pistol. The guy about to get shot is unarmed, but the guy shooting him is unmanned. These details articulate visually a very basic, widely held truth about a soldier who kills a civilian: It is an act of weakness; it marks an inadequate man, who did not deserve to be granted the strength and dominance of the soldier. His weapon has shrunk in his hand, just as he is about to shoot. He is, in a sense, impotent.

The photograph also benefits from the surreal fast-forward effect of the civilian's face. Parts of his face are a few seconds in advance of the rest of the photograph. There seems to be blood about his mouth, and his right eye, closest to the pistol, has already shut.

DOUGLAS MACARTHUR WADES ASHORE
IN THE PHILIPPINES

Several photographs were taken of this apparently staged procession from various angles, showing various water levels along the pants and boots, which must have been terribly soggy afterwards. The one that is most widely circulated, however, shows the general and several cronies from the right, facing away from the camera. They are still close enough to the boats for the boats to be seen in the background, and the water is roughly knee level. Most importantly, however, the shore is not included in the frame. MacArthur is *actually wading the Pacific itself*, with the mighty tread of an aroused giant. He is walking from left to right, which on a map would be from east to west—from the Philippines, toward Japan.

The brim of his hat parallels the upward angle of the prow immediately behind him. He is at once the white American avenger and the flagship of the Pacific fleet, the instrument of American vengeance. (The atomic bomb, that supreme *Vergeltungswaffen*, hasn't been built yet.)

To these Americans, treading the ocean floor, the Japanese home islands will be less than sandbars. In the photograph, MacArthur's pants seem dark to the hips, but later photographs of him on the sand prove that he was never more than knee-deep. He was set down very close to this quiet Leyte beach, on an island secured much earlier—by Marines who waded through water at navel level or higher, their rifles over their heads, taking fire.

THAT BUDDHIST MONK WHO HAS
SET HIMSELF ON FIRE

Thich Quang Duc in the fire, like MacArthur in the water, is another photograph that records an act of self-dramatization. The monk is one shade closer to death than the Saigon civilian with the gun at his head. He has crossed even farther, but every viewer "knows" the photographed monk is still alive in the fire; a photograph of a burning corpse would fail to have this effect. It would become a grotesque or obscene photograph: Imagine the Saigon civilian being photographed *after* his head was blown off. The photograph would become something unfit for widespread replication. The moment *before* death is dramatic, and the closer the image can get us to its threshold, the better: Too far, and the image instantly hemorrhages all its drama. This is why none of the truly famous photographs of war, Asian or otherwise, are photographs of corpses. Corpses leave us cold.

So the monk freshly burning commands our gaze, while no photograph of the charred, humanish mound are available. Nor are there any easily procured photographs of the people sweeping up the monk's remains. Did locals pour buckets of water over the blotch? Did they scrub at it? Assuming they didn't get it completely clean, who pedaled the first bicycle over the black stain?

THE DETAINEE AT ABU GHRAIB
HOODED AND DRAPED IN BLACK

Of the roughly 2,742 photographs that emerged from Abu Ghraib, 689 involved pornography or simulated sex acts, 540 were of corpses, 37 involved dogs, and 20 involved a swastika between the eyes of an American soldier. So a considerably smaller number of images were actually fit for potential widespread replication in the media. If we subtract images of detainees either naked or near-naked (although admittedly, the Pyramid of Naked Arabs did gain some dissemination), it stands to reason that the cover of the *Economist*, and countless other websites, should have replicated the image of the prisoner standing on the crate in the black hood and black poncho-like drape, with what appear to be wires leading to his fingers.

Paradoxically, an excessively covered-up figure became emblematic of a torture facility that, in a clear majority of cases, stripped people naked. The arms are held out, which falls just short of the ninety-degree angle required for a parallel with the Crucifixion. The hint is unmistakably there, however. Notice that the image that provokes sympathy for The Muslim dovetails with the central image of Christianity.

Notice also that the face, and indeed the entire head, is *covered—* instead of hinting at Someone Like You or Me by the device of the green eyes, the photograph creates a black box (or bag) inside which we can imagine Someone Like You or Me. Even the smallest visual hint of sweaty black hair or overlong beard or large nose would estrange the viewer instantly; the image's power resides in its multivalence.

The torture scandal, represented most frequently by this photograph, managed to remain a self-examination regarding the *methods*, not the enterprise. Our pity for the enemy could rise to the surface without diminishing our sense of the cause's righteousness. The detainee's black hood and loose-fitted black drape resemble the veil and robe worn by women under the rule of orthodox Muslim males; the black hood, with its cone shape, resembles the white hood worn by members of the Ku Klux Klan. These are the cues that reinforce the detainee's guilt, subconsciously reminding the Western viewer of Arab Muslim misogyny and intolerance.

This photograph and the one of the nameless Afghan girl succeed on the same principle. To move us to empathy, one other had to be photographed as a female child with green eyes. The other other had to be photographed without a face at all. ■

WEDDING BLUES
Saadia Faruqi

S ome of us are leaders, some are followers. The sad truth is that in a mile-long traffic jam on an unpopulated section of I-45 going towards San Antonio, it really doesn't matter who leads and who follows. I'm at the head of the line, and six cars covered with plastic roses stuck with tape are behind me. Yet I'm also behind fifty other cars and trucks and SUVs outfitted with the most enormous tires I ever saw and an inordinate number of Jesus Loves You bumper stickers, aching to blow the horn and tell everyone to GET MOVING, IT'S JUST A LITTLE SNOW.

That's another thing, the main thing really. Why is it even snowing? Since when does it snow in the black hole between San Antonio and Houston, where the summers are shirt-sticking-to-your-body hot and the winters are a joke? I've lived in Houston for more than two decades and I don't remember any snow. Well, except for that one grainy polaroid I have from when I was thirteen, standing in white ash holding a snow bunny on a tray in my front yard and a toothy grin on my face. Even that one time so many years ago there hadn't been enough to build a real snowman, let alone stop traffic in the middle of a major highway. How utterly, furiously, ridiculous.

The white flakes in question drift lazily down onto my windshield, mocking me, unaware of the profanity I am throwing their way. The irony of being stuck in a traffic jam because of snow when I left Chicago to escape that very aspect of weather isn't lost on me. "Why do you need to go to this Chicago when you can live here in Houston with your family, Aleena?" my mother had pestered me in her nasally voice a thousand times as I packed my suitcases, as I said my goodbyes, as I climbed into the taxi taking me to the airport. To get away from you crazy people, I didn't say.

Truth is, I would have moved to Alaska to get away from my family, but only because I didn't know anything about snow. They just drive me so crazy, always in my face, telling me to live like a good Muslim girl, assuming, embarrassing, stereotypical *desis* come to life. It's cringe-worthy, that's what it is, and finally after years of tolerating them, in the sting of losing Asshole Fiancé Saif to my best friend, I accepted the first job offer that came my way after graduation. In my heady relief and hope for a family-free life, I hadn't bothered to check what the weather could be like in Chicago before sending an ecstatic email to the law firm offering me employment. Honestly it wouldn't have mattered even if I'd known.

Within days of my first winter in my new home though, reality had raised its ugly head, and I realized that I hated the freezing wind, the slushy piles of white mush in my front yard, the slick roads that made my car spin around and terrified me to no end. I hated having to blow the snow off my porch because my father's scrooge-like tendencies had rubbed off on me and I couldn't bear to pay some smart-ass neighborhood kid twenty dollars to do something I could do myself. I hated putting on three layers and scarf and mittens and hat and the ugliest boots ever just to go out to the Walgreens down the street for another box of NyQuil. I hated hearing my mother's voice in my head: "See I told you, a *desi* can't live in such cold weather. Houston is perfect because it's just like home." Despite aching to prove her wrong, wanting to scream that this is home, GODDAMIT, not that other country where I was born but never lived, despite the pain of losing a good job with great prospects, I returned to Houston after that first evil snow. I couldn't believe I was such a chicken, but I guess I'm a *desi* whose kryptonite is a harsh winter.

And now this. Caught in a traffic jam because of a few miniscule snowflakes in the middle of redneck country. What could have happened to stop all this traffic on a Saturday afternoon... an accident because some idiot farmer couldn't drive with flakes falling from heaven? It doesn't matter, we're stuck; the wedding party from hell is stuck before they get the groom safely to the bride. And who will be blamed if we are all late? Yours truly, because it had been my brilliant idea to make this drive on the wedding day instead of the day before. "Why go there one night early?" I had objected thinly a few days ago when the plans were being finalized. "We'll have to pay for one extra night and the bill isn't going to be cheap." In hindsight I realize I was trying to suck up to my father, as usual. My dear *Abba*, who showered his affection on the son or daughter who saved the most money. So far, I'd always been last on that scale; my brother Mo—bridegroom Mo— could always be counted on to be the most miserly of the lot. *Kanjoos* Mo, we used to call him growing up. Now he is all tall and handsome, a published poet, sitting in the secondhand Jeep Cherokee behind me waiting to see his bride.

Dammit, this is all my fault. In frustration, I fiddle with the radio, but of course there isn't anything but country music for miles around. God forbid the people in this stretch of the woods listen to the news or traffic radio once in a while. Where are we anyway? The last thing

I remember seeing was a faded red barn and a bunch of horses swishing their tales eating nonexistent grass. Who puts horses out to pasture in the middle of December? Redneck farmers, that's who.

Listen to me! I take a deep shaking breath and tell myself sternly to relax. If *Ammi* could hear me she'd demand to know why I am thinking all these negative thoughts on my brother's wedding day. There's nobody here to listen to me gripe though, because I had insisted on driving alone. I hadn't wanted to get my ear talked off by my sister or one of my cousins, or worse, my mother, for the three hours it took to get to San Antonio. The conversation would either have been boring (I met my best friend from convent school in Karachi the other day at *Kabab Kahani* and she looked so fat) or embarrassing (I was thinking of getting my bikini area waxed for the first time, what do you think?) or terrifying (did you know your cousin Aisha gave birth last week to a twelve-pound baby boy *mashallah)* or infuriating (when will you ever find a good Muslim man to settled down with?). No thank you, that's why I left Houston in the first place. Sitting in the car alone with my aimless thoughts is much better.

Only now it's truly getting boring. What the hell. I open the car door and slip out, a wave of freezing air slapping my face in punishment. You deserve this, I tell myself severely. Then: I should have brought my coat, the one I had reluctantly purchased in Chicago (three hundred dollars for this hideous black thing, are you kidding me?) and dumped into the back of the closet as soon as I had gotten back to Houston. I peer into the wind gusts, squinting my eyes to get a better look at what lies ahead of me. Several others have also come out of their vehicles to stretch their legs—mostly men, mostly from my own family. It's like a *desi* party with these people, I think, reminded of another traffic jam on another highway a few years ago when *Ammi* had actually brought out snacks and lawn chairs for everyone. We had watched with fascination as an ambulance had carted away two bloody bodies, as if life and death were a cricket match. I smile despite myself. Good times!

I see *Abba* nearby and trudge towards him, waving desperately. "Do you know why we stopped, *Abba?*" I ask like the little girl I always become in his presence. He is big and bald and cuddly as a teddy bear, the perfect father for a spoilt Pakistani American girl.

"Darling, I think it's an accident up ahead. I saw a helicopter a few seconds ago."

It's true. I glare up into the snowflakes and see the faint outline of a helicopter whirring away, camera probably rolling at the sad little stick people below. "Wedding Party Stranded Because of Two Snowflakes" I can see the ticker tape on the local news station, imagine the laughter as the news reaches the bride's family. "You go sit inside one of the cars, *janoo*, it's too cold for you," Abba continues kindly. He has wisely brought his brown leather jacket, the one that makes him look like an aging McGyver. I nod, shivering in my cashmere sweater that's more suited for a Junoon concert, and dive towards the closest car, opening the door and climbing hurriedly inside.

"Aleena, thank God it's you!" Shit, it's *Ammi*, peering at me behind enormous glasses, fixing her *dupatta* around her head even though there isn't a male in sight. "Can you see your father? He promised to find a bathroom for me, I really need to pee."

I stare at her, struck anew by how much she irritates me just by being herself. That thought brings with it a whole package of guilt, of course. What is wrong with me? Why can't I love my own mother? Because she's insane, a voice whispered in my head, emboldening me. "*Ammi*, surely you can hold it, you're not a child." Then I remember her talking about some bladder problem at one of our shopping trips last year. Horror washes over me, and I begin to silently pray she doesn't have an accident in *Abba's* new Camry. I know how he had saved up to buy this car—"The One" he had been dreaming about for years. No car should smell of my mother's urine, that's for sure. I don't want to be there when the inevitable occurs, and I hastily push open the car door and scramble out, mumbling something about finding *Abba*.

He is gone, poor soul, no doubt trying to find a porta-potty for her. God! She is impossible! Still, a tiny nagging thought—dare I say worry?—about her bladder lodges itself into the back of my forehead like a nasty worm. I'll have to ask her about it next week when we get back home. Maybe I'll call my friend Faiza who's interning with that fancy urologist from Harvard.

I trudge to the car behind me, a white Sonata with a peeling Baby on Board sticker on the back. Should say "three babies on board" I think to myself wickedly as I get inside, already in a better mood at the prospect of seeing my beloved nieces. "*Khala!*" the oldest brat shrieks, holding out her plump little arms in a silent command. Okay, I have to admit, she is a cutie pie. There are definitely some perks about being surrounded by family, even though I'll die before I admit it. Feeling like a movie star with adoring fans is one of them, I guess. But still, I have to protest against three kids in four years, just for principle's sake.

"Hello, *janoo*, my big girl, how are you?" I croon to her, glancing sideways at the other two brats fast asleep in their car seats. I fish out a lollipop from my jeans pocket. "Here you go, this is for you!" I know how to be the favorite aunt, don't I?

A slender hand with long painted nails and multicolored bangles on the wrist snakes out from the front seat and grabs the lollipop before Brat #1 can. My sister, or rather the lioness, has awakened. "Aleena! Stop giving her candy, she's already hyper. How am I going to handle her in the car if she gets a sugar rush?"

"It's just a lollipop, sis! Chill."

"Absolutely not! It's not just a lollipop! It's bad teeth, it's a slow slide to obesity and juvenile diabetes and Allah knows what else!" I roll my eyes at the familiar sermon. Farah is obsessed with being mother of the year, every year, and I am constantly amazed at how much useless information she collects from parenting magazines and online blogs like *DesiMama*. What a load of crap. Kids are meant to be spoiled, like we had been spoiled by *Abba*. Even *Ammi*, if I recall hard enough, used to sneak us little pieces of *mithai* when no one was looking. Any discussions of the dentist were waved away as if they were fairy tales.

Hmm, I'm not so unlike her, now, am I, sneaking lollipops and candy to these three young beauties while their mom looked away? Aargh! Once it's been uttered, the blasphemous thought comparing myself to my mother can't be un-thought. But I better pay attention; Farah is not done yet with her lecture apparently. "You need to follow my rules when you are around us, Aleena. You don't have kids, so you don't know."

My mouth drops open in surprise. I quickly open the lollipop wrapper and hand it to the brat, hiding my face. "That's really low, you witch, even for you." I can't believe she said that. Apparently everyone is being affected by this freak snow. I suddenly wish I can go back home, ten or twelve years back in time, even.

She looks sufficiently subdued. "I'm sorry, I didn't really mean that." I look closer, see streaks of tears on her cheeks.

"What's wrong?" I ask, suddenly worried, my hurt forgotten. She never cries, she who has born three babies and works nonstop in her husband's gas station with all three brats in the back room.

She shakes her head. "Nothing." Then the tears begin in earnest. "Omar's getting mixed up with something bad, I just know it. He's so quiet and withdrawn these days, and sometimes he gets so angry for no reason. I'm scared, what if it's drugs?"

My eyes literally bulge out of their sockets. Not a good look for a superstar aunt, I know, but I can't help myself. She has to be joking, no way. Omar *bhai* is the sweetest guy I know, so good with the kids and always taking care of *Ammi* and *Abba* when Mo isn't around. He's literally the poster child—man—for a "good Muslim," whatever that is. Drugs? Forget it! I remember him telling a friend off one time for smoking cigarettes.

I may be biased though. In fact, here's a little secret, which I will deny if anyone finds out. I have a teeny tiny crush on my brother-in-law, in fact I sometimes pray that Allah would find me his long-lost twin, only richer because I don't want to be breaking my back at a gas station or making sandwiches at Subway all my life. So far, my prayers haven't come true, but at least Asshole Fiancé Saif is out of the picture. He couldn't have been less like Omar *bhai* if he had tried. Not that he had tried. Ever.

I reach awkwardly around the seat back between us to hug Farah, my neurotic, ulcer-inducing older sister who I once used to be best friends with. Before she entered college and became all ultra-Muslim with the hijab and the praying and the fasting, and I decided that I didn't want to be… that. She's still my sister, though, and she's hurting. I don't like that one bit.

Time for me to be the big sis. "Listen, Farah, don't be stupid, okay. Omar *bhai* is so religious, he would never touch drugs. He's such a good person you can almost smell his, I don't know, goodness. He teaches at the mosque Sunday school, for Pete's sake!" She's shaking her head, but I forge ahead, ignoring her. "Listen, he's probably just tired from working all the time, plus you do have three kids, which is stressful enough on its own. I really don't think anything is going on, but you should talk to him."

Farah doesn't seem to think so. The tears come faster, making me want to remove my arms from her neck. "I'm not going to talk to him. He's a jerk. It's been so long since he, you know…"

"What?" As soon as I ask the question I realize what she means. Ew! "Okay never mind, let's not get into details."

The door on the driver's side opens and a gust of cold wind rushes inside, making me jump with cold and nerves. Speak of the devil, looking handsome as usual in his tight beard and his khakis and light blue shirt. Allah, when is my Omar coming to get me? I take a deep breath to remove thoughts that were scandalous and probably sinful and glared at him. No pain, no gain, right? "You guys aren't having sex anymore?" I ask boldly, uncaring that the couple in the front look shocked and embarrassed. Not more than me. "She thinks you're taking drugs, you better not be. Discuss among yourselves while I go see the snow outside."

Feeling pleased with myself, I scramble out of the Sonata. Sometimes being stuck in the middle of a traffic jam in a freak snow storm is the best way to save a marriage, if you think about it. I should have been a counselor, I tell myself happily as I stand on the road covered in white, debating my next move. This car-hopping is getting ridiculous. Where can I go to get some peace from this crazy family?

There's a couple of cars in front of me filled to the brim with giddy teen cousins; I can imagine them giggling about crushes and girl/boyfriends and the latest music. No thanks. It might be my age, but I can't stand Taylor Swift.

"Hey, Aleena, come here!" It's Mo, waving madly from the Jeep Cherokee ahead. What does he want, I wonder? He and I have started getting along more in recent years, now that he's finally left his nuisance younger brother phase, but I still don't think too highly of him. Head in the clouds, too unpredictable, too lazy, too everything. That's Mo, the bridegroom. Who would have thought he would get married before me? According to *Ammi*, it's an insult she won't be able to live down at the wedding this evening, what with everyone wondering why the older sister is still single. I can almost hear the whispers, see the arched eyebrows just back from the salon, wondering what's wrong with me. Morons. What's even more pathetic is that I'm thinking the same thing myself for the last year or so. You know, the usual existentialist questions a *desi* girl in her late twenties grapples with: what's wrong with me, why can't I find someone and be happy, why can't I show my family I like them slightly, blah blah?

Well, maybe it's time to change my attitude. What's that quote about opening your own doors to opportunity? I open the door to Mo's Jeep and climb in, determined to be happy for my little brother. "How're you doing, bro?" I am cool, casual, hiding my unexpectedly honest feelings of happiness and pride. My baby brother is all grown up, when did this happen? "Looks like Allah gave you a little snowy present for your wedding." I smile. Mo the poet will definitely appreciate what I have done there.

Mo says nothing. In fact he looks like he's about to… cry? I feel the anger rise in my throat again. What the hell is wrong with this family? Can't they even pretend to be happy for one day? "Aleena, you have to help me. I can't go through with it."

I cock my head, trying to figure out if he's absolutely crazy or if I'm hearing things. "Can't go through with what?" It's a rhetorical question of course. I already know what the bastard means.

"With the wedding. I can't. I don't love her." He looks miserable, I have to give him that. Miserable and suicidal. *Ammi* would kill him without a second thought if she hears this nonsense. *Love? What is this love?* she would bray, giving her usual lecture about commitment and dedication and harmony, the arranged marriage kinda way. *Your father and I got married without even meeting each other, and look how happy we are!* Er, okay. I finally figure out why fate has brought me back to Houston. Damage control. I am the only sane one in a ten-mile radius, I am their only hope.

"Are you fucking crazy, Mo?" I make my face look hideous, like I used to when we were kids and I would find the latest contraband under his bed—cigarettes, porno magazines, condoms. This is too much, though. "We are literally on the way to the wedding. The catering company, the guests, Aunty Noma's family, they are all waiting for you. *She* is waiting for you. That poor girl Samia, who has no clue what's going on in that stupid brain of yours. You cannot do this, you hear me!" I hope his fancy SUV is soundproof because I am screaming. I take a huge breath, mainly to calm myself down. I can't stop thinking about that day in spring when Saif had told me over a candlelight dinner that he didn't love me anymore.

Mo's face is the picture of innocence, pleading silently with me until I melt. All of a sudden I am transported to that time in seventh grade when a hundred dollars mysteriously disappeared from *Abba*'s wallet. Mo the thief had given me this exact same look, and people-pleaser that I am, I had made up a story then to save his sorry ass. He apparently thinks I'm the same idiotic bleeding heart sister he doesn't deserve. Well, not today. I'm much older now, much wiser.

I hesitate at the last second. He's still my baby brother. And I'm still me, wanting to please, wanting their love.

He's speaking, I pretend to listen. "Aleena, please, you gotta help me. You gotta tell *Ammi Abbu*. This traffic jam is a godsend, it's like the universe doesn't want me to go to San Antonio. We can turn back at the next exit. We can go home and pretend this never happened." Is he running scared at the thought of coming home to a quiet *desi* girl all his life, or genuinely unhappy? I can't tell, and frankly, I don't care. I lean forward and shake him. Hard.

"And how are we going to do that? How can we pretend that *Ammi* didn't make two trips to Pakistan to make wedding clothes for everyone? How can we pretend that a shipping container of furniture isn't coming from Dubai as we speak to furnish your new home? How can we pretend that a girl—a real human being—isn't waiting for you with henna on her hands? Are you mad?" I don't care, I'm still screaming. This is it: I will kill him myself. Are all men alike, I wonder? Saif had returned the engagement ring two months before the wedding. This of course is infinitely worse, using the universe (and bad weather) as an excuse to cancel an actual wedding. Compared to my asshole brother, Saif is a kitten.

"Aleena, I like someone else." The words are quiet, sure. Mo is suddenly different, grown up.

I feel the air whoosh out of my body, suddenly weary. This is too much damage control even for me. "Who?" I ask, even though it doesn't really matter. I feel like I've aged twenty years since this morning.

We are both silent for a long time. I could have suspected that he is lying about the other girl, but no one can fake this. No one who has ever met *Ammi* for one day would willingly do this. I decide that he's telling the truth, and that as always, I would be the one to get him out of his mess. Isn't that what family is all about, though? "Call her." I hand him my cell phone. "Call Samia and tell her what you told me."

Now it's his turn to look at me like I've grown two horns. He refuses to touch the phone, shaking his head violently. "No, tell *Ammi*. She'll do it."

I am incredulous. "Why should *Ammi* clean up your mess? You're not a baby anymore. She doesn't deserve this at her age!" I can't believe I'm actually defending her, but I know I'm right. "Mo, listen to me. You are an adult now. You have to do this. The right way."

"What's the right way?" Good question, bro.

I shrug, feeling anew the pain of my own rejection, reminded of the countless times I had wondered why. "I don't know what the right way is, honestly, *bhai*. All I know is, it really hurts like hell being rejected by the man who's supposed to be in love with you. Even if it's an arranged marriage it really sucks. Samia needs to know, but not from anyone else. She needs to hear you say it, she needs your apology. And you better make it really good."

He looks uncertain. I have to sweeten the pot. "If you call Samia, I'll tell *Ammi* for you. Deal?"

He knows that's the sweetest deal on the planet, one he really doesn't deserve. Being saved from *Ammi*'s wrath is better than telling someone you don't want them on the phone. Much better. There's no comparison really. "Are you sure? She'll hate you for being the messenger."

We are having such a great moment, but I know it is time to take a step back into my familiar shell. This conversation has risen some nasty ghosts I thought I had laid to rest. I smile cheekily, knowing intuitively that it will be okay, not today or tomorrow but sometime in the future. *Inshallah*. "It's okay, she's just *Ammi*. I'm not scared of her. I came back to the nest, after all, that has to count for something." What's there to be scared of, after all? I keep thinking of her stuck in that Camry with the new-car smell, holding in her pee.

I leave Mo dialing the phone with shaking hands but a surprisingly straight spine, and walk back slowly to my father's car. The snow has stopped and the helicopter is nowhere in sight. I spy a naked tree trunk near the side of the road and decide to take a minute to collect my scattered, wounded thoughts. Maybe the traffic—and the sky—is finally going to clear up. I lean against the tree and finger the phone in my pocket, wondering if I would ever find the guts to call Saif and tell him off. Maybe in a year or two, when vulnerability has faded a little bit and I am less emotional. At least I am no longer angry at him, at the world.

The air is so hauntingly crisp, and all of a sudden I am glad to be home. Well, a hundred miles away, but still home. It has taken me a while to finally think of this place, these people, this particular wedding party, as home. I have a sudden thought: *desi* women are pretty awesome. I think of my mother, running the house with an iron fist and a threatening shoe in her hand, now struggling with an ailing bladder, constantly worrying about her brood like a crazed hen. She is strong too, I assure myself, she can take this latest upset with Mo—or Mohammad, as she still obstinately calls him despite the fact that he never responds.

Still, I have to square my shoulders as I leave my sturdy tree and head for *Abbu*'s Camry a second time. I chuckle a little nervously. I hope she's found somewhere, or something, to pee in. Otherwise the news that the wedding party is turning back will be met with more than a little stink. ∎

POINT*ILLISM*: A POEM SERIES
Sophia Naz

Twenty-Six Soldiers of Lead

Like prisoners of war the letters were. Confined to end their sentences in a cramped rectangle with the lowest of ceilings. No escape and no respite. Silence inside the i of sentience while everyone looks here and there, eyeless, away. Shall we take another toke of this perpetual un-finishing? Long after the bombers had gone home their mouths still smacked of that falling sky. How are you's and I love you's punctuated by a rain of deadly dashes. Their lines rudely amputated, the letters lost their sea legs, became a gangrenous and obtuse morse code blacked out and blanked out, month after month, one postcard per month. For that was what was allowed. From the old country. Of his birth. Shellacked until their knuckles were lead-less, the twenty-six seceded to the margins and the first fruit of silence appeared, her blush painted in a corner but still defiant. A streetwise rose with a swagger in her curlicues as if she wasn't the queen of flowers held just so in countless miniatures but her upstart jaundice-yellow dirty blonde weed cousin dandelion crackled out of yesterday's sidewalk.

Atomic Nuqta

Chalk it up to DNA. The mail censors weren't such a heartless bunch after all. Noor Jehan was left untouched, down to the *khalish*. Double-helix thorns edging a raga of absence around her throat. She loves me she loves me knot. Gullet is a concavity between two saw-teeth. Late Middle English from Old French *goulet*, from Latin *gula*, from Proto-Indo-European *gala* as in gullible. Somebody had swallowed. A joke your father braided into the celtic *guluband* of a *mughal* empress. Too many miles to stone. East of the spot that she dressed up the sepia rose postcard in a tall story. A sieve endlessly sifting that shifting sand shroud called Sindh. Who grabs you by the border collar? Calligraphy of concertina wires on the displaced and splayed *dharti*, that which you wore and that which wore you. Separated at birth. To *thar* is to tremble. Supine and helpless down her long history wiped clean as a clay skinned *takhti*. A daisy chain later, the thorns reminded her of that other atomic *nuqta*, you know, the one that dub angst, autocorrect acting like any old cowboy cop changes to nuke?

Cowboys & Cow Boys

Now, that there are cowboys and cow boys, now that there is a red line that breaks and breaks you. Trumped up to twist into a noose. The same line that you & i went humming arm in arm. What I called *ganga-jamni*, what you called a venn diagram. Those lines are lost, the night is long, my mind's skipping like a cheap cassette. Trying to rewind history with the turn of a pencil. These are the years of static and stasis. *Kis kis ko batein, judai ka sabab hum?* To get to the analog of *inhi logon nein.* To jog that, jot that, thread that fugitive dot, noisy, nosy point of contention. To green absence you need the poin*tillism* of rain drops. There are wiles to reap, hairs of bigots splitting your sides as they try to untangle the bindi from hindi, extracting the sand wound that birthed the pearl they stand on. Lodged like a cumin seed in the sea crevice of a camel's mouth. Water has logged every mile of my grave. And you named each painstakingly painted rose? Yes I did, Zebunnissa, Shamimara, Jahanara, Shabnam, Nargis, Naushaba, Anjuman, Shagufta, Sheherazade, and so on and so on, until the thousand nights were done and there was the one left to right only, the very longest one.

The Department of Wronged Rights

You have made a wrong right turn because left is right here and we just wanted to drive that point home. (Your life is wood. Get the drift?) This is now a checkpoint. Please to sit. While you wait we will check you in a box. In triplicate. *Bibi ji,* are you by any chance that *adakara's* sister? (You mean the one who still lives on the tip of her tongue tied in brackets of silence stuffed in her straight faced helplessness?) Mutation would require you to visit another office (we only mince words here). On stamp paper. It doesn't matter if you can sign your name, thumbprints are necessary. Only the right thumb is right. Would you look at the price of pomegranates? Tell me, how can a simple officer possibly raise one's family in this *mehngai?* Please have some biscuit with the chai. Where were we? Yes. I was going to tell you about *Syah-gush*, the Supari Djinn. It is he who cracks your nuts into a heart, he who folds your teeth into paper-thin walls of limestone, your legs into eighths of red ochre, he who breaks your spine into a moist green triangle spiked with nails of clove, he who offers the bite of bruise-bright cardamom shot through with the tracery of electric moonlight jam down your throat. Benevolent or evil, it depends on which way the whim blows. You must not only believe he exists but solemnly attest before we can continue. Before you pass. Out of any port. You must. Solemnly attest. Before you pass out. We can continue.

Notes from a Holding Pattern

When the paper-thin roses that began as a lullaby had climbed all the walls of her garden of the thousand and one nights. But first there was a gold-green blur. And blood-red roses crowning the heads of walking thorns with the strength of ten oxen. Or so it seemed. Lahore was a mirage. If you got too close it disappeared. Like all of her loves she keeps Lahore entombed in her drawer, an entire city of rooftops and grey doves walled up in a four-by-six postcard. The mythical Walled City itself a walled-in *Anarkali* hard pressed in the pages of a *basant* beyond all remnants of return.

Tap Routes

The eyes of Laila are almonds. Morning is a white sheet where no one takes off their shoes. Gather them into piles. Perilous pyramids to recite the names of loss. Under your breath, circumambulating the graveyards of possibility. The eyes of Laila come into this world wearing their coffins. The eyes of almonds are blind, the eyes of Laila are blind. The eyes of night cry themselves blind and leave a wet shroud on the earth each morning. Don't cry for Laila for it is you that has stabbed her. Again and again. The eyes of Laila are a *leela* of blind almonds. You are condemned. To be lost in the Braille of their labyrinth. In the labyrinth of their Braille. *Bhoolbhuliyyan*. There is no Luck now. ∎

THE MEMORY OF WATER
Shabnam Nadiya

The year the waters rose to submerge a third of the university campus was the year the school hired Anisul Alam as the music teacher.

The floods came almost every year. But not everywhere. On the campus, the university students raised funds for flood relief. The university itself made a donation, usually to the president's relief fund. The actual handing over of the check—from vice chancellor to chancellor—usually merited a captioned photo in the national dailies. Perhaps five seconds on the evening news. Teachers and officers donated a day's wages. Students and teachers joined forces in distributing relief materials to nearby villages.

The campus itself never suffered much beyond a few parcels of lowland becoming ankle-deep in malodorous, green water, and the dearth of fresh produce in the markets. Housemaids and their mistresses suffered extra from the sludge being tracked into houses. The planners had built the campus on higher ground for a reason.

Anisul Alam hailed from the low-lying lands of the southeast, where some flooding was an annual occurrence. The rivers and the swamps swelled with the advent of the monsoons and were awaited as much as they were reviled: in its wake, the overflowing water left silted-over land. Earth so rich and warm and moist you could breathe on it and grow something green, people said, stand still in it for an instant and you could feel your feet take root in the loam.

But it had been years since Anis had seen any of that. The ways home became impassable during the rainy months. During their weekly calls his father told him point-blank that he was not to jeopardize his studies or himself trying to visit. Even in the years of mild flooding, people would drown, or be electrocuted from the unfortunate conjunction of live electrical wires and swathes of water. Launches capsized, boats upturned, electrical poles toppled, vortices formed. Who didn't know about the vagaries of flood season?

Anis liked imagining home during those calls. His mother had probably served dinner early so his father could take a leisurely pace in getting to the tea stall with the phone. At the stall, his father would sit right beside the counter, to be on hand when Anis called from the pay phone at his students' hall. He would order a steaming cup of milky tea and sometimes his words were punctuated by loud slurps. He would linger afterwards for gossip and news. The walk home would be amid darkness, but maybe he would find someone to walk with, at least part of the way. He would have his heavy aluminum-cased flashlight, its beam able to cut through even heavy rain. His mother would be waiting to hear of her son. On those evenings her worn prayer mat served merely as a waiting station.

Anis felt caught. His years of study and work in the city had left him unready to fit back in his village—but he was wearied of the frenetic city life of cobbling together a subsistence through private tuition gigs, seven-to-a-room living, and the interminable twice a day meals at the nearby *chhapra*. This existence was not what his father had hoped for when he had packed Anis off, at seventeen, to a distant relative in Dhaka.

His father had sent Anis whatever they could spare. They did well enough in the village; the city was a different beast. Neither father nor son had ever imagined the ability eventually leading to a degree would be singing—the namby-pamby skill that had always been an irritant on his father's skin. Whoever had heard of going for higher studies to the city to study music? That the university even allowed it seemed a joke to the old man: how could this be a serious thing? And Anis was certain this would make him employable? Where other aspiring families had only sent their sons to public college in the town or perhaps east to Comilla, he had reached higher and sent Anis to the capital. His bitterness seemed to make his *bidi* burn faster and the stench of it more acrid. At least Anis had a fallback, he would sigh. He could always come back and oversee the men ploughing their land, reduced as they were by having to finance him.

The campus seemed perfect before he even visited—it seemed his degree might indeed lead to a regular job. He pulled in every favor he was owed, and some he wasn't, to get an interview, which went well. He had acquired reading glasses on the advice of a sidewalk quack, and he thought the square black frame made him look intellectual. He felt confident. It was the interview board, comprising the headmaster and three school committee members, who seemed more anxious and shift-eyed: they had never interviewed a music teacher before. His academics were in order and he came with good recommendations, but how did one decide who sang well and who didn't? What if a student had an awful voice but sang well? How would he deal with girls and boys trying to mingle too closely? The headmaster had solid questions about curriculum and grading, but these dried up soon and the board members seemed befuddled by his answers to their fumbling questions.

The headmaster called the following week. They thought he would fit in well. "But you must understand, Anis *shaheb*. As an optional subject, you might not always have a full load, and we will expect you to take on other responsibilities." Anis already knew that. All he could think of was the red earth, the sun striking still waters through leafy branches, and the smell of freshly cut grass as he had waited for the bus. He said, yes.

At first he commuted from Dhaka city, an hour by bus. Teachers with more serious subjects took priority in the allotment of the few apartments schoolteachers were allowed. More would be built in the future. The university had plans. Just nobody knew when these plans would materialize. For the B-grade apartments, university lecturers and junior officials were considered first, followed by schoolteachers, especially if they had families. Anis had no chance of getting one. He was faced with the choice of a slit of a room in the dreary-looking Bachelors' Quarters, or seek a rental nearby.

There were places here and there on campus, in the rima of land the authorities had yet to use, where people ineligible for official quarters or those who couldn't be accommodated carved out their own space. These supposedly temporary arrangements had lasted close to a decade, giving the owners time to save and transform tin-sheet and thatch structures to concrete walls and indoor plumbing. The campus administration performed the convenient acrobatic of looking the other way while allowing the campus electricity, water, and gas grids to cover these places.

Anis had never lived in a place with cement walls and a tin roof before, but his room, sublet from Jabbar, who worked as a level four clerk at the director of examinations' office, seemed clean enough and the shared bathroom was right outside his room. The clerk was hospitable, ordering his wife to make sweet strong tea whenever "Master Shaheb" came to their part of the house.

This room was all he could afford. He was making less now than as a freelancer. The lewd jokes by his roommates when he was packing, about the bored, educated wives of the professors queuing up for music and *more*, had angered him, but he did hope to procure a few private students. Soon he would be able to send money home. Perhaps even a separate amount for his mother.

His settling into his room went smoother than his settling into a work routine. For the first time in the fifteen years' history of the school, music was available as a curriculum optional and everyone but the students seemed a little discombobulated by him. His classes were scheduled quickly, but by the time he began teaching, the theory books he had requisitioned, the scale-changing harmonium (preferably Pakrashi), the set of *bayan-tabla*, the fat-bellied *tanpura*—nothing had arrived. "Teach them *sa-re-ga-ma*," said the accountant cum admin officer when he pointed out his lack of equipment. "You just need their voices for the scales, no?"

In the end, he opted to transport his own harmonium to school every day. He strapped the case to his bicycle carrier with a checkered *gamcha* and rode to school precariously, constantly on the verge of falling.

"Why not just leave it here?" he overheard Mahiat Madam, the new geography teacher, ask the accountant. Mahiat Madam had just been married to a lecturer of government and politics after obtaining an MSc from the same department. The accountant shrugged as he wrote her pay slip. "Ask him," he said gesturing toward Anis. Mahiat Madam noticed him behind her, and pulled her sari to cover her shoulders.

"I need it to practice at home," he explained. And when she didn't respond, he continued, to cover his embarrassment, "I practice every morning, at dawn. By order of my guru."

The accountant ripped out the pale green pay slip and gazed at it in a satisfied manner before handing it to her. He told her, "He doesn't like the old harmonium we have in school either, says it needs to be tuned." She looked at Anis and smiled.

Before Anis could say anything else, she walked out. The accountant began drawing up Anis's slip. The scratching of his pen filled the silence as Anis waited.

As he settled into a routine, it seemed as if the rising waters were taking over all conversation. Every year, Mahiat Madam told him, the monsoon waters crept upwards, inch by inch, threatening to spill over the banks, but never really making good on that threat.

Yet this year the flood reached the roads—at first just the one that ran between the arts faculty building and the smaller structure of the dramatics department. Then water welled up from the very ground of the south side where brick-laden streets turned into grassy pathways leading to the third and fourth class employee quarters. The lake beside the vice chancellor's residence merged with the pond leased out for fish-farming, and moved toward the other lake a mile to the east. In two weeks, all that remained was a glassy surface spanning miles, over which the moon rose at night, full yet worn, like a coin dirtied by too many hands.

The house he lived in seemed safe for the moment. He made it a habit to walk to the edge of the water at dawn. The water had stopped about half a mile away and it seemed settled just short of the electric pole with a pair of sneakers hanging from the wire. That was his marker. He would stand there clutching his toothbrush, and ponder the presence of the sneakers, affirm that the water had advanced no further and hurry back with the toothpaste foaming at his mouth.

The teachers' lounge talk was a daily reckoning of whose neighborhood was at the most risk, and who had family in which part of the country. He discovered that most of them lived on safer ground; the clerical staff seemed to be more concerned. Several of them lived near him, and there was talk of sandbags and other measures. The anxiety they felt for family stranded in other districts seemed tinged with relief at being at a safer, better place, somehow.

Nothing made clearer to Anis his inapt presence than through the tracing of those conversations: not many of them worried over parents in the far reaches that were flooded. Those who did never forgot to mention their rural homesteads were actually located in small towns. Their worries of narrow streets waterlogged because concrete absorbed nothing and failed sewerage systems, of cars and baby-taxis stranded from water in exhaust pipes, of mothers overburdened because the servants refused to come or just ran away to their own flooded villages, of waterborne illnesses among nephews and nieces sneaking out to play in foul waters, of property—land, or houses, or fish-farmed ponds—being damaged, none of it mirrored his own.

The Islamiyat teacher was local. He had grown up in a village about ten miles away and had now stuffed his parents in his two-bedroom apartment. Like many other apartments in that block, even the balcony had been covered with woven mats and hardboard walls and turned into another room. His only worries were on behalf of his wife, whose parents lived in Lalmonirhat. "I don't know what we'll do if they seek shelter with us. They have a son, but he's in the army and stationed near the Burma border. Who wants to go there?"

Anis nodded. "My parents..." he began, but the Islamiyat teacher had turned to Shototi, the history teacher. "Is your sister well from jaundice? Is she able to take care of your parents? I hear there is a lot of jaundice in your area. Must be the flood."

Shototi said, "Oh, she's completely recovered. That was months ago, I don't think it had anything to do with the flood. They're not there, though. They moved to Chittagong city with my brother's family when it looked like the floods were happening." She smiled at Anis, "My sister, she's a widow; she takes care of my father since his stroke three years ago."

Anis ventured, "Where is your village?"

"We're from Jessore. My father was a civil surgeon so we moved around when I was a child. They decided to go back to his village when he retired."

He didn't know Jessore well, but he knew how they spoke. He wouldn't recognize the village if she told him, but neither could he spot the descending lilt, the softened consonants of the district in her speech; she spoke like a city girl.

She asked him quietly, "Are your parents still alive?"

"Chandpur," he said. "That's where they are."

"I heard things are getting worse there," she said.

"Yes," he said. "Bad."

His mother's letter had arrived two days ago. A rare occurrence. She could not read or write and would sometimes, depending on the availability and patience of his father, dictate a letter. This was the nineteenth in nine years. Hanif Miyah's grandfather had died but their cow had delivered a healthy calf. His father had ordered a new clay stove, and Haricharan, the potter, said he would fire it for her as soon as it stopped raining. The water sitting in the backyard was eating up her feet and giving her water-scabs from walking from the main house to the kitchen. One of their fields had gone under, they would lose the crop. Mijan Shah's family was searching for a bride. There was cholera. Allah was keeping both of them well.

"Hilnara," he said in a low voice. The conversation had moved on to the risk of dysentery from contaminated greens and no one was paying attention to him. "That is my village: Hilnara."

Some years, in addition to fundraising, the university students set up relief distribution committees. By the time the distribution mechanism began operating smoothly enough to begin distributing the packages of oral saline—dry foods—matches—candles, blankets, saris and lungis, the water had usually settled in. There would still be the occasional whirlpool or rough waves, but mostly the water sat black and green with the occasional deep ripple pushing across the wind's way.

The university let them requisition buses so they could travel to affected areas nearby. The more involved among the teachers would go with them, and sometimes they took their spouses with them. It was a nice outing, despite the pleading voices and begging hands.

Anis had wanted to volunteer the very first day he heard of the student-run relief committee. But it didn't seem enough. "What about the school?" he asked. "Won't the school do anything?"

"What do you mean?" Mahiat Madam looked confused. "We just

donated one day's salary this week."

"I mean our students. They should do something."

"But they're children! What can they do?"

The following week, at his request, a brief notice was sent out in the morning to classes six to ten. The headmaster had taken Anis aside that week and said, "Anisul Alam, you are a bit of a fool. You'll have all these high school girls in this committee—the parents won't like it. There are always these problems with music teachers. And there will be boys there. Make sure a female teacher is present." Her husband made no objection, so Mahiat Madam was volunteered to help out.

The headmaster remembered the poor turnout the year before when students volunteered for the Ladies' Club flower show and told the caretaker to keep the small corner classroom on the second floor open afterhours. When Anis walked into the classroom, his heart swelled. Enough students had shown up that they were squashed into the benches; the walls were hardly able to contain them. He picked out several of his students, sitting in front, and he felt his eyes warm to them. The girls sat on one side, the boys on the other, the girls' side vivid and multihued, like wildflowers in the thick of spring.

"Mahatma Gandhi's noncooperation movement had roused the country. The rebel poet Nazrul leapt into the fire of political activism. He would sing at rallies, write poems. Oh, his pen spouted fire!" He stopped to breathe as they hung on his every word. "Give us alms," he sang. "Give us alms / Look back, oh city-dwellers / Your children at the door starving / Give humanity, give us alms." He pulled out his well-worn notebook from his *jhola*-bag. "You will learn this song," he told them. "I shall strap my harmonium to my chest and we shall walk the streets of this campus with our begging bowl and this song, and people will give. For those who are in need. Just as the rebel poet had once walked." He looked into the bright eyes, at the vigorously nodding heads and said, "Welcome to the first official meeting of the High School Students' Relief Committee."

At their twice weekly meetings they practiced the two songs he had already taught them, the Nazrul Geeti and an Atulprasadi. He was teaching them another. They also set aside time to paint placards on poster paper. The steady thrum of the rain percussed their rehearsals, keeping time with the chords he pressed out on his harmonium, the voices of his students the only mutable thing. Mahiat sat in a chair beside the desk, smiling and nodding her head in time for the most part. Her perfume was sharp enough to fragrance the room even over the moldy walls. It took several days for her to lose her shyness enough to join her voice with the students'.

On the twelfth day of rehearsal he placed a bag of clothes on the desk. He had combed through his meager closet that morning for items to donate: a pair of blue twill pants shiny and frayed from overuse, a formerly white shirt, and a green and pink checkered lungi ripped near the hem. That is all he had been able to find, but his landlady had filled the bag with clothes that no longer fit her children.

"The headmaster is assigning the storeroom beside the girls' bathrooms downstairs to us," he told them. He had checked the space out already. It stank a little, and the broken benches piled in a jumble were completely covered in dust and cobwebs, but it would do. "I have a bag of clothing here, and Mahiat Madam and Shototi Madam will give us some old saris and other items this week. Maybe you can ask your parents too? Anything they can spare: foodstuff, clothing, medicines."

They were excited. "Do you think we're ready, sir?" asked Tuhina. Class seven, section B, couldn't keep time to save her life.

"What will we do with cash donations, sir?" Ronny, class ten, beautiful, lilting voice, but couldn't differentiate between the soft and the hard *r*.

"We'll need a ledger book to enter everything we get; one of us could be responsible for that." Arshia, class eight, sweet voiced, but could only handle the g-sharp scales with ease.

"Would you like to volunteer, Arshia?"

"Yes," she said. "I've never maintained a ledger before but I'm good with numbers."

"I can help Arshia," Shototi said.

Anis took a deep breath. "This Friday afternoon, *baad jumma*, we shall be at the mosque. When people will be emerging from the house of Allah, just having sung his prayers, they shall be feeling more than usually generous. We'll meet in front of the school at eleven and make a round of the campus, just like we did on Ekushey February, but instead of ending at the Martyrs Memorial we'll end at the mosque. Don't be late."

He had woken while it was still dark thinking it was raining hard outside, but realizing the endless thrumming was inside his head. His aching body heated and cooled itself, trying to push the pain and the heat out by drenching him in sweat.

He wasn't sure whether the children were louder than usual that day, or whether his ears were more sensitive. There even seemed to be more of them than usual, and that couldn't be right. The thought of lunch made him queasy; better to starve the fever before it could dig its fangs any deeper. When he came down to the teachers' room he was grateful to find it empty. Gokul, the peon, peeked in once to ask if he needed anything. He regretted now not asking for tea; the thought of a cup both hot and lemony parched his throat.

Mahiat Madam looked tired as she flopped into the chair beside him. "Uff, it's so humid today, I can't stand it." She fanned herself with a magazine. He mumbled agreement. He was actually feeling shivery cold. "The water's risen further, you know. I heard it's reached the lower steps of the social science building, and it's never come that far, *ever*." The social science building wasn't that far away. He tried to think which way the water was advancing. What about the open-air stage? Was that before or after the social science building? Which way was the water coming from? Was there any before or after or directions at all where flood water was concerned? Shouldn't people be more concerned?

"Have you seen it?" he asked.

"Of course not," she said. "I don't usually go that way. My husband told me." She peered at him. "You look terrible."

"I've been sick all day," he said. His face must have reflected how he felt because Mahiat looked at him fully for a few seconds before placing a tentative palm on his forehead. She whipped her hand away as soon as it touched his skin. "You're burning up," she said not looking at him. "You should be resting. You shouldn't be here." He glanced at the door reflexively, to make sure no one had seen. Why had she done that? Did women touch men in public like that? She seemed as uncomfortable as he was and perhaps as relieved when the Islamiyat teacher walked in.

"Did you hear the water's reached the social science building?" he said. "This year shall be bad, I say. If Allah so wills it, all is for the good, but how far do you think this water will reach?" He scratched his chin through his scraggly beard, and shouted for Gokul. "Anis shaheb, you live on that side of campus…what does it look like? Gokul lives on that side too—he said he was getting ready to remove his family. What a hassle, what a hassle. And this heat, ah, this heat. It's hotter in school than in my house. Even with all those people stuffed in it. Must be all this boiling young energy, eh?" He nudged Anis and chuckled.

Anis wanted to tell him that the real reason was probably the thick bank of dead-gold flax blanketing the stretch of land behind the school. That variety of flax was known to trap and irradiate heat, which is why it was in high demand for building houses. It was proof against heavy rains, insulated the meager heat within in winter, and in the summer it drew on and magnified the indoor shade.

Gokul brought in tea for the Islamiyat teacher and saved Anis from having to reply. His hands waving frantically, Gokul began telling them in great detail about the death of his cousin when they were both nine, when they both got caught in an eddy of floodwater, but his cousin couldn't make it out. It was days before the floodwaters returned the dead body, broken and bloated, but with intact skin.

That evening as he tossed and turned in his bed his thoughts returned to her. Mahiat's brief touch had jolted him and he realized how long it had been since he had touched someone, anyone. Did the fingertips of store clerks and rickshaw drivers when he paid them count? Perhaps this was what had been wrong all along: he had never figured out the right currency that led to friendship or more. Mahiat and Shototi had walked him halfway home that afternoon. They lived near each other, at a block of flats near Gate One, and went home together most days. Their husbands played tennis together at the Teachers-Officers Club. Sometimes he walked past the one-storied structure with the billowing green awning by the side. One afternoon he had seen a street boy with a ragged sack slung on his back crouched outside the wire fence poking at something inside with a long stick. When he walked closer he saw the tiny mewling kitten inside the fence, a wretched, scabrous little thing, hunched and too weak to even move away from the steady drip of the awning. Everything around them was bathed in the gorgeous bronze of after-rain sunlight. He felt he should shoo the boy away, grab the stick, or at the very least scold him. But what of the kitten? The rain would still be there, and the hunger, the scabs, the boy might return, perhaps with friends. He had stood there unable to leave yet wavering on what he should do, whether there *was* anything to do, until the boy had solved the problem by throwing the stick away and running off. Perhaps he had been unnerved by Anis watching.

His childhood fevered imaginings revolved around his mother's hands, her gentle touch descending on his cheeks and his forehead stealthily, when his father wasn't looking. Coddling, his father had believed, prepared one for nothing in life. He tried to imagine Mahiat here in his room, and failed. He could not offer her even his chair to sit on; one leg wobbled and came off easily. She could stand by the window but the curtains were drawn all the time. The outside view of the dripping faucet set in the middle of a raised cement platform covered in green algae wasn't much of an improvement on the grubby curtains.

He couldn't even imagine his mother here; where could she sit? Where could she sleep? What would she do? He would give up his bed to her, gladly, but she would never allow that. Her deepest joy was to cook for his father and himself, that is what she always said. But for the first time he wondered if she had ever known anything else. *Allah look after you*, she would say, every time he walked out of the house, whether he was leaving for the tea stall or Dhaka to seek his fortune. What if he did bring her here? He had no kitchen for her to cook in—he would have to find some other way to keep her occupied. What would she think of his long lonely walks, his nostalgia for his crowded, crude existence in the Dhaka city mess? What would she think of a tender hand transient on his forehead?

The fundraising went off without a hitch. The children were magnificent. They advanced bearing colorful placards and a hand-painted banner, their songs soaring through the air like kingfishers, searching and joyful. His hearing felt acute, able to pinpoint each and every one of their voices. The two youngest girls led the way jointly holding open a tote bag for people to put money in. Mahiat and Shototi darted through the group making sure they rested their voices in rotation. The group paused now and then for the teachers to take out the money, note down the amounts and put it away. They left a few fifties and twenties in the bag—the university students had told them it helped if people saw other people had already donated. While they had done well just walking around—the first donation had come from the rickshaw puller who brought Shototi and Mahiat—the hour outside the mosque had been the most lucrative. His instincts had been right. Altogether they had raised about seven thousand taka in a single day.

He had gone to see his landlord because his landlady had indicated that while she could freely give out secondhand clothes, any cash donations would have to come from Jabbar Ahmed himself and he would like to be asked. Without promising him much, Jabbar Ahmed had straightaway asked him whether he could change his regular practice hours from dawn to some other time. Anis cringed when he recalled the conversation.

Jabbar was very curious about the exact amount they had raised. Once that curiosity was sated, he moved to more pressing matters: Anis' vocal practicing at dawn was disturbing his sleep. Anis had tried to explain why the early hours was when one's voice was at its fullest and freshest, and how music at daybreak purified one's soul. Who could not be beguiled by the sonorous droning of the *tanpura* accompanying the elegant notes of the morning ragas? He usually started with Ahir Bhairav, performing the simple scales and then starting on a prolonged *alaap* prelude to the *bandish*.

Anis's suggestion that Jabbar Ahmed's son join him in the morning, he would even provide private lessons for free, was met with a strange look. "Oh, it doesn't seem right for a boy, does it?" Then, realizing his mistake, Jabbar Alam had said, "But it's an art. Everyone should learn something artistic. Even boys." He paused, "Although I have to say, Master Shaheb, a song or two wouldn't go remiss. Those practice things you sing, they're more like a river than a song. They keep rising and going without rhyme or reason." He laughed.

Anis had said stiffly, "Art has its uses you know."

Jabbar had winked at him said, "Sure. If you can mewl well enough, I guess you can bag a wife—who cares whether it's yours or another's?" His roar of laughter left pins and needles in Anis's fingertips but he could find no appropriate answer. He wasn't sure there was one.

Anis had shifted his practice hours to late afternoon, after school. By the time Jabbar Ahmed returned from work, he would be done with his practice and be quietly positioned underneath the sickly yellow light of the bulb hanging precariously on a wire trying to write the mock-tests the headmaster had asked him for. By the time he could hear the clinks and clangs in the kitchen as they prepared dinner, the errand boy from the *chhapra*-eatery at Gate Two would have delivered his own. By the time they set their dinner table, he would have finished his own meager meal of rice, lentils, and the fish or chicken cooked with whatever vegetable was cheapest that week. By the time they sat down to dinner, he had finished his ablutions, set out the dirty dishes outside his door, and settled himself on the prayer mat for the *esha* prayers. When the television turned on in the house, his light would be out and he would be in bed, learning to be lulled to sleep by the discordant voices and music from the nightly shows.

Mahiat waited until the students left before broaching the subject. "It will be easier to distribute the aid if we just hand it over to the young teachers' committee." Anis saw Shototi glance at her quickly, and look away.

"I'm not sure what you mean," he said. "Our committee..."

"Well, my husband asked how much money we've raised, you see. And I didn't know..."

"Because you never asked," Shototi interjected.

She glanced at Shototi but continued as if Shototi hadn't spoken. "Well, he wasn't very happy about it and he thought we were only asking people for money."

Anis was confused even further. "But that *is* what we're doing. We're asking people to make donations to our fund." Shototi was tidying away the song sheets and the paperwork, her lips pursed as if she had nothing to say about anything.

"Well, I meant, the walking around begging part he didn't like."

"But that's how we're asking people for donations," he said gently. "And it gives the children such pride, that they are able to give something back to the people with their songs." He slid the two wooden switches on the sides of the harmonium into their notches and maneuvered the instrument into its lock-down position in the case. Then her choice of words struck him. "Begging?"

"It's unseemly," she said. "It's not right for someone in my position. I think we've done enough, now just use the money for what it's for."

Shototi brought over the detachable lid of the harmonium case and slid it on. It sat awkwardly on top—he always had trouble with the thing. "We can do both, you know." Shototi said. "We talked about this. We can guide the children, raise more, and use what we've already raised."

Mahiat didn't look at Shototi. "My husband thinks distribution is the part where we might make mistakes. He says their committee should take over that part."

Anis said, "The university students' committee?"

"No," said Shototi. She grabbed the lock with the key still stuck into it. They were supposed to lock this door and return the key to the night guard who was waiting downstairs. "He and some other teachers are establishing a separate relief committee. No students. They don't like how the students' committee do things—they think the students lack proper supervision." She walked out of the room and waited outside in the darkness.

Anis nudged the top half of the case into its assigned slots and locked his harmonium. He grabbed the handle and swung it off the table. Mahiat followed him out. He knew he should say something to defuse the tension but he couldn't think of what to say. He wasn't even sure what was going on. He felt unfairly annoyed at Shototi.

The streetlamp right in front of the school had blown out. It had been several days and nobody had repaired it. Who fixed these things here? In Dhaka, it was DESA. Back home, you did it yourself or asked the neighbors for help.

"I'm meeting Moyeen at the grocery store," Shototi said to Mahiat. "Will you be okay walking home by yourself?"

"I could walk you home," Anis offered.

She hesitated. "I don't think that's a good idea." Anis caught Shototi rolling her eyes. He was going to offer his company again, but stopped himself. He still wasn't clear about what mistakes Mahiat's husband thought they would make. They had walked to the mouth of the dam where the water had overrun into the scrubby earth. They could hear the low growl of the constant eddy where the water gushed into the broad mouth of the concrete pipe. The spot was muddy and opaque—a swirling brown at war with the green of the remainder of the lake.

Anis felt lost. The headmaster had told him to meet him at Forid's Tea Shop at Gate 2. He could see several teashops, enormous silver kettles sitting outside, steam rising from the nozzles. But none of the storefront signs said Forid's Tea Shop.

He wondered whether he should just sit somewhere and wait for the headmaster to show up. Head Sir took an hour-long walk every evening before dinner; it kept his diabetes under control. Anis wasn't sure why he had been invited to join the walk, but he had sacrificed his evening practice for it.

The headmaster's voice startled him. "Anis shaheb, there you are."

He scrambled to his feet. "I didn't know which…"

"Walk with me," the headmaster commanded.

The headmaster walked fast, with purpose, in the same manner he did everything else. "I'll get to the point. Anis shaheb, I like you. I think you're a good addition to my school. Your students like you. But you seem to have no idea of how to conduct yourself. What on earth were you thinking going out *begging*?"

Anis was flummoxed. "But…"

"And Mahiat. She should have made sure her husband knew what you were up to. Apparently he heard from a junior colleague that his wife was out on the streets *begging*."

"But…"

The headmaster waved off his protest. "No matter. She, at least, is an adult. Although I have to say, her husband sounded very unhappy about her conduct when he called on me. No, it's the parents you need to worry about. Someone even used the words 'disciplinary committee.' But there's always a parent who's overzealous about everything." The headmaster sighed and stopped. In the distance the water gleamed as light skimmed the surface. Anis could make out dim shapes near the edge. It had become customary for folks to come out after dark to walk by the edge of the water, occasionally letting the water lap over their feet, as if the wet footprints they left would somehow curtail the advance.

He was shocked his fundraising plans could arouse such outrage. "But the rebel poet Nazrul…"

"To hear you, one would think your head was full of cow dung," said the headmaster. "What world do you live in? Things that are right for poets in history are not right for us, here and now. What made you think parents would be alright with their children walking the streets with a begging bowl? And what were you thinking taking them all to the mosque! Singing girls!"

"But it's not begging! It's fundraising! For a good cause!" He finally managed.

"Do you think you're the only one to ever have thought of helping poor people?"

The headmaster just looked at him and shook his head slowly. "Anis shaheb. You will have to learn to understand the world better if you want to survive in it." He paused and swiped at an insect buzzing near his ear. "I don't want this to go any further, Anis shaheb. You will desist."

The insect had moved over to Anis, its wings flicking his face. He let it be.

For the first time in ten years, he had gone two days without practicing at all. His throat felt empty, yet the emptiness was weighing down something in his chest. He had dragged himself to school but felt unready for everything; his students, smiles of acknowledgement and banter from his colleagues.

The headmaster didn't look at him when he made the announcement. "Mahiat Madam will not be joining us. She may come back but we're not sure at the moment when. In the meantime, Fazlur Sayeed Sir and I shall sub for her classes."

Anis reacted without thinking, "But she can't leave!"

"*Can't*, Anis shaheb?"

The headmaster's question made his ears burn. Was she leaving the school? The campus? It made no difference. He would not see her again.

"Our relief fund…"

"Will be given over to the new University Relief Committee. Yes," the headmaster continued, "as we all know the annual cultural program is coming up and…

"Sir, I have something to say."

The headmaster sighed. "You always do, Anis shaheb."

"Sir…"

"Yes, Anis shaheb. But think of what you'll say before you say it."

He looked up to catch Shototi Madam looking at him; the shake of her head was almost imperceptible. What was she saying to him?

"But where's the justice?" he asked. His words were leaden weights dropped into the calm pool of conversation sinking without a trace. Anis felt unsure of exactly what he was asking. He struggled inside as the momentary lull his words caused was almost immediately smoothed away and the conversation washed over the room again. He said, louder this time, "But is it fair? Is it just?" He felt the whole room staring at him, their stares accumulating into tiny beads of sweat ringing his hairline.

"Justice is a big word, don't you think?" The Islamiyat teacher said. "Justice is selective."

He sat at the long table as the bustle of the other teachers leaving surrounded him. He felt as if he wasn't there, as his colleagues slung bags on their shoulders, grabbed hold of attendance registers, handwritten notes, pens, exams, and for a few, canes or wooden rulers. He sat as if any sudden movement, or a harsh noise would break something inside of him, and the stillness of an emptied room was the only thing holding him together. He had no first period responsibilities, and consequently, no hurry at this moment.

As she rose to leave, Shototi leaned towards him across the table. "Anis shaheb, do you know what Matshonnyay is? We teach the children about it, in class six. You must have studied it, too, when you were in school." He looked at her unable to speak, unable to remember. "It's a period of time," she continued, "right after the demise of Shashanka, the King of Gauda. With his death his empire fell apart, and it was ages before the Pala dynasty arose. All of Gauda, ancient Bengal, was fragmented and submerged in anarchy. That's why the ancients called it Matshonnyay. Matshya, fish. The time when the big fish ate the small."

He looked at her without comprehension. She smiled. "When will you learn, Anis *bhai*? Some fish are small, some aren't. It's the small fish that need to learn how to swim around the big ones. They always have." She seemed to take pity at his stricken face. "Wait for me after school. We will figure out what to do about the relief effort, okay?"

"Apa, Shototi apa, I feel…"

She straightened herself. "You want to talk about what is just, what is fair? Fair is even though nothing is fair, we do what we can. Fair is this: we cannot disappoint the children."

There were no pauses in between the songs and the recitations. The audience barely had time to breathe as, under Anis's silent direction, the children launched into one song after another, interspersed with poems accompanied by *khol*: dha dhina na tina, the rhythm rang out, keeping time with the voices. Songs of the soil, words of want, turmoil, and redemption found grace through their young voices.

Although when he talked to the parents, most seemed quite okay with their mobile fundraising efforts, the headmaster had said even one parent objecting was something he wanted to avoid. The students on the committee had suggested they have one big performance with written invitations and posters all over the campus asking people to bring cash and other donations to the performance itself. They were aiming to double what they had raised last time. They spent a whole afternoon painting posters and traipsing all over campus nailing them to trees and taping them to lampposts.

The sunlight brought everything into sharp relief. As he looked down, he saw them all reflected on the stillness of the waters, like a murky yet faithful mirror. On the other side, with the water separating them by a few feet was the reflection of their audience. He couldn't tell the people apart in the reflection, they all seemed the same vaguely human shape and he felt loth to look up.

Somewhere on the other side of the water was the headmaster, the coworkers of Mahiat's husband, perhaps her husband too. She would be there too. He was sure of it. Shototi was also standing somewhere, her brow creased as was usual when she was reflecting on something.

Later in the evening, when they were done, he would walk to the water's edge and watch the dripping leaves, the crows and sparrows stretching and shaking their wings, and the sad silver shine of the waterlogged streets. For now he stood by his students as their voices lingered over the green waters like bitter angels.

A large classroom in the live sciences building had been given over to relief activities. A hand-lettered paper sign was taped above the pale yellow double doors: Student Relief Committee. Inside, wobbly cafeteria tables were laid out in the front of the class, the flat tops piled high with supplies. The tables on the higher tiers harbored blankets and clothing; the lower ones the items required to build the aid packages: sacks bursting with flour, chunks of brown palm sugar, rice, and tins of cooking oil and kerosene. At one end of the room, several long tables borrowed from the science lab also on the second floor. Rolling pins and boards were stacked at the ends, the whole area seemingly covered in a fine layer of white flour.

There were young men and women everywhere; their chatter was happy, loud, and full of purpose, keeping time with their busy hands. *Rutis* were being rolled out, dry-fried, and bagged, two to a packet, with an inch-round paper-wrapped piece of jaggery. Liter bottles of drinking water were filled. Plastic baggies of a-three-fingered-pinch-of-salt-a-fistful-of-jaggery were tacked with printed instructions of adding the mix to a *seer* of clean water.

Shototi and her husband had been working with the students; she was the one who had invited Anis. She stood with a group at the other side of the room but waved at him. He felt a hand on his arm—a young woman with a red armband marking her volunteer status pointed to a table. "Shototi di' said you were joining our team. We could do with another pair of hands over here." He walked with her as she flashed him a smile and said, "I'm Jesmin."

"I'm Anis," he said.

"I know. Shototi di' says you're the music teacher at the high school? We have a singing group! We're just getting together—you should join us."

"Me?"

"Of course you, mister. Listen, not too many guys are interested in singing. Guys just want to play an instrument. I don't get it. But we need more male vocals! Shototi di' says you know tons of patriotic songs? Like, the old ones? The *swadeshi* songs?"

Someone showed him how to tie a twist knot to seal the oral saline kits they were making. Someone told Jesmin to stop talking and get to work. Someone else said Jesmin talking equaled the work of certain other people everyone knew about. Someone else laughed. Someone chided someone else for eating pieces of the jaggery. His fingers moved faster as they found the rhythm.

He couldn't recall how long he had been sitting on this bench; he must have dozed off as the breeze cooled his body. An acacia tree, one of two thousand imported from Australia, grew right beside the bench, a branch extending at just the right angle for a headrest. Dead leaves from the trees, like sickle moons gone bad, littered the streets.

There was no one at the water's edge; the roads behind him were empty as well. He walked along the wide strip of grass taking care to keep his feet dry. When soft waves rolled onto the shore—sometimes pulling back with it some dirt, some dead uprooted grass—the water was barely inches away from his feet. It became a game almost, to see where his next step should fall: as close as possible to the water without touching it.

The week following their grand performance had been quiet. Most of the cash donations had been handed personally to the headmaster. Anis had not liked this; he had wanted his students to handle the money themselves, to both be witness to and participate in the generosity of their community. But the parents had wanted "someone responsible" to take charge. Most of it had come in during the first two days— the slower, later trickle was handled by Shototi. The headmaster had invited him for another walk and told him three things: Shototi was handling the money; her husband, Moyeen, had gotten the parents to agree that the money be merged with the university students' relief funds; Mahiat was not returning to school.

This week they would spend the money. They were drawing up plans of what was needed in the afflicted areas and the most efficient way to get it there. Moyeen had volunteered alongside Shototi to liaise between the school students and the university student committee. They held a meeting at Shototi's house. It was too dangerous to think of letting school students go out to distribute aid, said Moyeen, but they should do the budgeting and shopping themselves. He was sure if they chaperoned, some parents at least would give permission. Perhaps this could be a field trip?

He had walked further than he usually did, way past his usual marker of the jackfruit tree with the inexplicable green paint on the trunk. In the distance, he saw the rounded shape of the bus shelter; half a mile beyond that began the housing meant for senior professors— more bathrooms, fenced gardens, balconies prettified with flowers and wicker furniture. When he reached the dark shape he had been walking toward, he realized—although it was a boat—it wasn't the small *koshas* he was used to seeing around here. It was a dugout, a *konda* his father would call it, the base of a palmyra palm tree hollowed out by fire and blade. The pushing pole was propped on the side.

The boat felt heavier in the water and hard to steer, unlike the ones he would take out as a child when endless meandering hours were justified at day's end with the delivery of a bundle of water lily stalks or *kalmi* greens to his mother's kitchen. Perhaps this *konda* was only for short trips; visiting neighbors, perhaps, or plying from one rice paddy to the next. He was having a hard time keeping the curved prow nosing straight ahead. He had no particular destination in mind. He just wanted to remember what it felt like to be afloat.

There would come a time when Anis would realize his knowledge of the campus had forever been distorted; that his recall was inundated with details peculiar to this one year when he arrived. It wouldn't be until a few more years went by that he would learn what the school grounds looked like in the uncertain light of the rainy season; or how varied the grass felt underfoot: merely squelchy one day, and unpleasant, almost waterborne and light the next. He did not yet know the lay of the land here, but he would. The longer he stayed afloat, the farther he could take his boat, the quicker he would learn. He would know what this place was like when the water was gone; he would discover whether it was flat grassland beneath, or bare earth and shale or gravel.

He would know whether teenagers hung out here in the evenings to smoke weed or whether younger children could set up three-pointed open fires to cook an impromptu picnic *khichuri*.

He grunted each time he drove the pushing pole into the water, as if trying to spear the earth hidden beneath. Was it the *konda* that was at fault or had he forgotten the easy magic of those vaster waters of his past? The world looked strange to him: both the water on his left and the shoreline on his right glistened now and then in different shades of silver and green as if the difference between the two was no more than a trick of the eye. His grip on the pole tightened as his muscles relearned the old ways and discovered the new. ■

DEAR GOD OF DEATH
Vikas Menon

It is quiet here.
The days pass.

I miss your skin against mine,
the lamps flickering in your eyes.

From tears I sieve the salt
that seasons your rice

and await your return

my Nimble,
my Inescapable—

SPEECHLESS
Vikas Menon

Curdled, clotted & tied within,
my choked, abeyed bray

the difference between memory
and actuality: my sounds in Malayalam

are off key, my mouth an unskilled
magician as I try to point out what "is"

& instead summon an elephant.
An unschooled sorcerer I upend

an emphasis, ferment a rock
to rum. With each quick slip

I'm a duncetongued Yankee,
a *Thank-you man* from parts

Occidental. But even in English I fail

when my mother says
my happiness is you.

Many-tongued as we are
still we are forever kin

to silence, the lip bit down upon,
terrors of rack and ruin,

the lie at the dinner table,
a whisper behind a door.

If only I could incant
sand to rain,

rot shame away
as if it were a body.

If only I could be
anything than what I am:

a poor necromancer

raising the dear & departed
for only seconds at a time,

like this: her voice was like brittle branches,

her words

tenseless,
incessant

DEAR BLUES
Vikas Menon

Who knew
that you had a second heart

that could be broken
and yet bloom

again like the sky
between iron bars,

the ache above the navel
behind the ribs,

a horn at lip
molting a note to fray

autumn leaves
of flame.

DEAR GOD OF DEATH, PART 2
Vikas Menon

Savitri's tongue of honey & milk
spoke of nothing

so sweet as longing. The dead sleep beside us.

Wake O Beloved
Ressurrector,

bless us with their eternal return:

every morning I wake
and they die again.

Yet still I wrap folds of cotton
around myself, set off across the fields,

head held low,
branches bent with rain.

TWILIGHT, APRIL 11, 1994
Vikas Menon

the dead breath of cigarettes,
two fat hunched figures in the tree

scattered crows silent, wary, watching
vultures nestle in thickening dark

one mounts and then
flurries and silence   flurries and silence
cutouts pasted against dying light

they fuck and love, engorged, stately
loving the dead no more than themselves

a sensual bile
just at back of throat

OFFERINGS
Vikas Menon

*Thulaabharam is a Hindu ritual practice in Kerala where a devotee gifts her
weight in offerings that are then ritually offered to the god/dess.*

We offer the Gods
gifts equal in measure
to our weight: in bananas,
coconuts, silver and gold.
why not more?

In diamonds
and oil, blood and guns; our burden
in bullets, in machetes,
our mass weighed out in children's blood.

After all, on the altars of our immortals
humans have placed far greater gifts:
a cacophony of monks heads, a mute
of soldiers' hands, a blind of
women's eyes.

Why not give
the gods your body—its water, blood,
liver and lung, carpal,
metacarpal, eye and tooth, thigh
and arm?
This mortal collective—
this bag of bones, this garland of limbs—

is a brood of one:

like a serpent's tail devouring
its mouth, like death

is a beginning.

THE BUTCHER SHOP OF NEW DELHI
Sayantani Dasgupta

That Sunday morning I was excited by the prospect of the dinner party my parents were hosting later in the day. I was six years old, an only child; the birth of my brother still two years away. My parents were young and so were their friends. I addressed them as aunts and uncles even though we were not biologically related. Often, at their parties and such, I either ended up as the only kid or the only kid my age. Others were far too young, still in the grasps of their mothers. But I didn't mind. Most of my parents' friends treated me like a real person. They didn't baby me, and I felt welcome and comfortable in the world of adults.

On that Sunday too, like all other times we had hosted parties, it was a given that Baba would run errands and buy groceries, and Ma would tidy things up at home, prep and cook the feast. It was a blistery morning and the air tasted of dust, and yet, I didn't opt to stay inside the cool rooms of our apartment. I accompanied Baba instead. There were two reasons for it: First, the possibility that we would stop at our local bookstore and I would be allowed to pick up a new book of my choice. Additionally, if I behaved really well, there was the chance reward of a lemon popsicle. And the fruity iciness combined with a newly purchased book would equal perfection, paradise, and pure happiness in that oppressive New Delhi heat.

We stepped out after breakfast and for the next couple of hours, Baba and I zipped in and out of chaotic streets in his pistachio scooter, my arms cinched around his waist and my face pressed against his back. It wasn't long before I began to lose count of all the fresh fruits and vegetables we had bought. With each new destination, my energy levels plummeted. The sun shone so bright, it hurt my eyes. My throat felt like stone. I longed to return home so I could lie down on the cool mosaic floor of the drawing room with a book. I could already picture Ma hovering in the background with a tall glass of lemonade, coaxing me to freshen up so we could all eat lunch together. At every stop, I tugged at the thin shoulder straps to air out my dress. When we had left home, the white cotton with blue flowers had felt like air and smelled of soap. Now, pasted to my skin, it stank of exhaustion.

Our last stop was the butcher shop. Though it was air-conditioned, a detail that didn't escape me because the blast of cold air was something to look forward to, the butcher himself always had layers of perspiration glazing his forehead. Sure, cutting meat was a physical enough activity but somehow it didn't seem deserving of all that sweat.

The butcher was a fierce-looking, heavy-set Muslim man. He wore gray cotton kurtas that were always too tight. His thick, glossy mustache matched his oil-slicked, parted-in-the-middle hair. His lips were black from the tobacco he kept wadded in his mouth. Worse, he never smiled. Every time a customer walked in, he gave a curt nod as he listened to the order, then bellowed instructions and returned to dismembering bones and joints with a cleaver that made a distinct *thwokthwokthwok* noise.

The butcher and his two assistants sat on a marble platform that started near the entrance and ran the entire length of the shop, all the way to the back. Their tools rested on enormous blocks of wood, tree stumps really, stained rust and ruby from all the blood and juices they had had to absorb over the years. The blocks were positioned in front of them like desks. Some of the knives resembled swords and scimitars, their pointy ends curved like the letter C. Others had blades flat as bricks and looked unwieldy to maneuver. Those reminded me of hammers and I had seen them decimate big slabs of meat into granules.

And then there were the carcasses. They hung from tall iron hooks embedded deep into the ceiling. Once they had been flesh and blood animals—lambs—but now stripped of skin and hair, they were nothing more than bone and muscle. Combined with the scent of soap, they gave the butcher shop its own peculiar smell.

Most days, I found the ritual of cutting and carving meat fascinating. I would watch the glint of the knife as it swooped down to make a precise incision, the dull thud of cleaver against bone where meat met steel and became rectangles of lamb that were wrapped in plastic, handed to my father, and that Ma magically turned into her peppery lamb curry.

But that Sunday afternoon, I was whiney and needy, the way I suppose six-year-olds can be, and now when I look back, I see my father's dilemma. What should he have done? Should he have dropped me off at home and returned by himself to the butcher shop? But the lamb needed time to cook. Should he have dropped me off at a friend's home instead? But who would have enjoyed the intrusion of a cranky kid on a Sunday afternoon? The bookstore would have been an excellent option except that it was in a different neighborhood and probably already shuttered down for the owner's post-lunch nap.

In the midst of this dilemma, the sight of that new toy store must have given my father hope. It must have shimmered like an oasis across the street from the butcher shop. Or maybe it wasn't Baba who spotted it first. Maybe I did. Or we both did, together. At the same time. That detail doesn't matter anymore, what matters is, our instinctive, immediate relief at having found a solution to our problem.

I see it all now: Baba holds me by my hand and leads me to the store. Inside, it's so pleasantly cool that I feel as if I am walking through an ice cream. It is incredible to be out of the sun for however short a while. My eyes devour the treasures: boxes of mechanized toys and cars, wicker baskets full of stuffed animals, glass cases displaying an immense variety of dolls, elaborate kitchen and bathroom sets perfect for playing house, and the glistening spines of hundreds of shiny, new books.

An old man steps out from behind a candy-stocked counter. "Hello," he says, smiling, "Looking for something specific?"

The man is taller than Baba but his hair is white. He reminds me of someone's grandfather. When he smiles, his eyes crinkle. Even though he is facing Baba, he turns ever so slightly to include me in the conversation. I like that. I let go of Baba's hand.

Baba says, "I was wondering if I could leave my daughter here for ten minutes? I have to run to the butcher shop," he points with his shoulder in its direction, "and she is exhausted."

"Of course, of course, take your time," the man smiles. "We will be fine, won't we?"

I give him a shy nod, delighted that I will have full run of this magical wonderland without the disciplining presence of my father.

Baba says, "Be good, okay?"

I nod, barely able to contain my excitement. I am no longer hungry nor thirsty nor tired. I cannot wait for Baba to leave.

But as soon as he does, I am stumped by all the choices. I don't know which way to turn. Should I run over to the colorful wicker basket spilling with stuffed bears, bunnies, and pandas? Or those beautiful bookshelves lined with titles I have never seen? Or the dolls, those pudgy ones that look like babies or the lean, ladylike ones. How would it feel to touch them? To grab them all in my arms?

And what's more, this man even has Barbies. Rows and rows of them that are shimmering at me. They look elegant, beautiful, and expensive. Only a handful of my friends have Barbies. I inch closer to the shelf and gaze with adoration at the one closest to me. She is sheathed in a pink silk gown. It has a slight dusting of silver stars. Her elaborately styled hair is the color of gold.

I ache to hold her. I want to touch her dress, I want to feel the luxurious thickness of her gold hair between my fingers. But I know I can't. I mustn't. Because Barbie is in her telltale pink box. I am only supposed to look and not touch. Because if the box breaks, Baba will have to buy it. And somehow today just doesn't seem like it will be a doll-buying kind of day.

"Do you want to see her properly?"

I spin around, surprised. The man has come around the corner and is now standing next to me. Well, this *is* his store. He can stand wherever he wants. I shake my head, unable to trust my voice. I want to say "Yes" but I don't. I can hear Baba's cautionary words.

"Come on," the man insists, "I can tell you want to see Barbie properly. What do you think? Shall we take her out? Shall we play with her for a while?" The man's words are better than a lemon popsicle.

I swallow hard. I shake my head again. "I am not supposed to touch because then Baba will have to buy me the Barbie," I explain. My eyes remain glued to the pink box.

The man laughs. "Don't worry. We won't tell him. You and I will just play with Barbie for a little while. This will be our secret."

I nod even though it is a strange suggestion. No adult male, neither my father nor any of my uncles, has ever offered to play with dolls. Every evening when Baba returns from work, he and I play variations of hide-and-seek. With my uncles, I usually play teacher-teacher, where I pretend to be Miss Bawa, my own stern teacher in school, and they, my dutiful students. This man's offer to play with dolls is new. Unfamiliar.

I look up to see if he is joking. "Can I really play with Barbie?"

"Yes," he says, "really." He pulls out Barbie's tall, pink box from the shelf. Gently, as if she is a real person, he eases her out and puts her into my hands. I touch her hair, almost with reverence. It's just as I had imagined: thick, rich, and soft. Her dress glows, the stars glitter between my fingers. Her face, however, is cold and plasticky, just like my other dolls.

The grandfatherly man brings out a chair from somewhere and sets it down. He lifts me up and puts me on his lap. I am a little surprised but not alarmed by this rush of affection. I still have clear memories of adults putting me on their laps and reading to me. I make myself comfortable. From my spot, I can see a sliver of the main entrance. The man, given his height, must have been able to see more, anyone heading toward his store or exiting the ones across the street. Like the butcher shop.

Wordlessly, he pulls Barbie out of my hands. I blink. What have I done wrong? I glance at the main entrance. Is Baba already back? Is he hurriedly stowing Barbie away so Baba won't find out? The man starts to hum and, with a deft stroke, pulls Barbie's dress to the top of her head. I cannot see her smiling face any more. Instead, I see her white panties and the underside of her dress. It's rough and ugly like a sack, so different from the silky, starry top.

The man extends a finger and strokes Barbie's chest, which is not flat like mine. She has breasts like grownup girls. I alternate between staring at Barbie and the man's face. He can play with Barbie whenever he wants. Why does he have to encroach on my limited time?

He rests his bony finger on Barbie's chest and asks, "Do you have these?" I shake my head. He puts a hand on my chest as if to check and rubs the whole area, slowly but carefully. His finger now slides down to Barbie's white panties. He rubs it. Back and forth. Back. And. Forth. Slowly, lovingly, deliberately. "Are you also wearing white panties like her?" he asks.

I shake my head again. I don't have white panties. Not even one pair.

"No?" He smiles and licks his lips. "Let's check, shall we?"

He places Barbie on the floor and tugs at my cotton dress. I am not sure what game this is, but I don't want to play it anymore. I protest, "Only Ma can see my panties."

The man's grip is firm. "Don't worry," he assures me, "We will have fun, you will see."

He pulls up my dress and stares. He runs his tongue over his teeth. He scoops Barbie up from the floor but keeps her face covered by her bundled-up dress. He slides his finger under her panties. It's an ugly, awkward swelling, like a tiny ghost draped in a white sheet. Then his finger starts to move and twitch, as if it's shy, it doesn't want to come out. It just wants to stay in and play this odd game of hide-and-seek.

"Isn't this fun?" the man asks. His voice sounds funny. "You know what will be more fun? If we do this to you."

I try to get off his lap but with his free arm he pins me to himself. "No."

He tugs at my frock again, and I repeat, even more loudly, "No. Only Ma can see this."

"Come on. Don't be a spoilsport. We have to keep playing."

There is a snap of my panties' elastic and suddenly I can feel his fingers. It's an odd sensation, one that I've never experienced before. I feel the scrape of his nails as he rubs and prods me in unfamiliar places.

The game stops just as abruptly as it started. He hurriedly straightens my dress, sets me down on the floor, and glides Barbie back into her pink, plastic home. Almost immediately, Baba walks into the store, his fingers threaded through two plastic bags.

I run to him.

Baba says, "You know what? The butcher asked about you today. 'Where is your little girl?' I told him you were here. He said hello."

The toy store owner has returned to his spot behind the counter. He appears to be busy arranging and rearranging boxes.

"Did you like any of the books?" Baba asks.

"I don't want any. I want to go home."

I can tell Baba is relieved. He waves to the man, "Thanks for letting her wait here."

"No problem. She is a good little girl. Please stop by again."

I grip Baba's hand, "I want to go home."

"Yes, let's," Baba says, putting on his sunglasses. "Even I am tired. Well, at least Ma will be pleased. Today's meat is tender and fresh."

* * *

The rest of that Sunday is a blur in my mind. I think once Baba and I reached home, the sheer relief of actually being with Ma inside our cool apartment and under the reassuring whirr of the bedroom ceiling fan put me to a dreamless nap. When I awoke, the excitement of the evening overshadowed the memory of everything else that had occurred earlier that day.

And that's how it remained for years and years, the memory dormant and quiet, unwilling to stir or create a scene. I accompanied my father to the butcher shop numerous times but never again did I step inside the toy store. From time to time, I would remember the incident, about what had happened in front of those pink Barbies and glass cases, but I rejected it, or tried to, thinking it hadn't done me any permanent damage.

Until twenty years later, one weekend in Idaho, when I set out with two girlfriends for a writing retreat in the mountains, just a couple of hours north of Moscow. It was a picturesque drive, with nothing to interrupt us except the purr of the car's engine and our excited chatter, thrilled as we were for the opportunity to get away from the rigors of grad school and into a world with no Internet and only limited cell phone coverage. Somewhere along the drive, the conversation turned to monsters and suddenly, each of us, though separated by geography, race, and nationality, had something to share.

My voice shook as the toy store owner took over the car. Up to that moment, I had never talked about him, not to my parents, nor to my close friends. I had convinced myself that it was a small incident, one that should not be paid any attention especially given that searing, unfathomable tragedies occur every second in India. Surely no one should have to expend their time and energy on a small story from over twenty years ago? Surely the incident could not have left a scar.

But it had. And I had needed Idaho and the distance from India to realize it, and to realize that even in developed countries such as America, monsters exist, and that here, too, they get away because their victims experience the same agonizing trap of shame, loathing, and embarrassment.

When we reached the cabin, I set aside my laptop. I no longer wanted to write what I had planned for the weekend. Our conversation had ignited something and lent the story an urgency. It needed a physical release, not the sterile click-clack of typing on the keyboard, but the violence of pen against paper. I wrote feverishly. Messily. I recounted every detail of the day. But I couldn't remember the specifics of the man's face. What kind of a nose did he have? What color were his eyes? Did he wear glasses? I wrote everything else, from the abrasive heat of the city to how the man's fingers had felt against my skin. But I couldn't remember if he wore rings or bracelets or a watch. If he had a cap. Or bad teeth. He did have white hair, though, didn't he? Or was that also my imagination? Why was my memory so unreliable with details that mattered?

I wonder now if I gave him white hair because of the monster I did fear back then. His name was Betaal, the ghost, and he showed up every Sunday afternoon on my parents' TV. He had thick white hair down to his shoulders, a red mouth, and an alabaster face. Directed toward young audiences, the show *Vikram Aur Betaal* ("Vikram and the Ghost") was based on a two-thousand-year-old Sanskrit book, where Betaal was the spooky antagonist to Vikram, the righteous and handsome king.

As per the original story, Vikram's task is to retrieve Betaal from the cremation ground in order to fulfill a vow he has made to the tantric, or sorcerer. But wily Betaal doesn't want to go to so easily. So like Scheherazade from the *One Thousand and One Nights*, he offers to tell stories to Vikram. However, there is a catch. The end of each story contains a riddle that Vikram must answer. If he doesn't know the right answer, Betaal will go with him quietly to the sorcerer. If he does know the answer but chooses to remain quiet, Betaal will come to know immediately and he will kill Vikram. But if Vikram answers correctly, Betaal will return to his perch and Vikram will have to try to nab him all over again. Needless to say, Vikram is able to answer all but the very last riddle.

Which is why each episode of the show began with Vikram, resplendent in orange silk and bejeweled necklaces, walking through the cremation ground in search of Betaal. Littered with skulls and bones, the only vegetation were dead trees from whose branches hung thick black snakes, watchful and dangerous. Fog and mist would roll in unexpectedly, and Betaal would loom into view, hanging upside down from the highest branch. Vikram would climb the tree, wrestle and finally overpower Betaal so he could carry him on his back. I think more than his hideously painted face, it was his wails and cackles that I feared the most.

And yet, I watched *Vikram Aur Betaal* regularly. It helped that Betaal disappeared after twenty-five minutes of air time, leaving me, the satisfied viewer, with a new, meaty story to mull over. Even now, I can recall his features clearly, and when I stumble, there is Google to help and several old episodes uploaded on YouTube. But the man in the toy store cannot be found on the Internet. He has no name, no distinguishing features, nor a voice I can match to an identify-this-sound software. I cannot even say for sure whether he had white hair. Perhaps it is immaterial. It is the one definite physical detail I have stamped on him, and it is what he will have forever, he, the monster I have to live with, the monster who will never go away. ∎

MY GRANDMOTHER SPOKE TO TIGERS

Swati Khurana

The regular coffee is watery, sometimes burnt, but fine with lots of cream and sugar, and frankly, unlimited. For two dollars, I can sit for six hours and drink four cups of coffee. I inhale the sweet, woodsy smell of almond, from the freshly baked almond horns. The smell is free. A column with handwritten signs, painted in different colors, thin letters, dots at the vertices, announces: Viennese Coffee (Espresso, Steamed Milk & Whipped Cream); Russian Coffee (Espresso, Hot Chocolate & Whipped Cream); Hungarian Coffee (American Coffee, Almond Extract, Whipped Cream & Cinnamon). When I can afford it, I like the Hungarian.

The café tables are small, mismatched, next to each other, at different heights, but communal. That is a good thing. I have been in New York City for two months, and I don't have any friends. I pretend that I am friends with the people seated next to me. See, the girl with her organic chemistry textbook is actually my best friend. We are going shopping together downtown after we study. The man with the stacks of sheet music is actually my boyfriend. We have been in love since we first made eye contact, when the waitress brought him the wrong pastry order. I want to tell the waitress my boyfriend ordered a cherry strudel. See that group of students sit around me and laugh contagiously. We are college buddies, because of course I am the kind of smart girl who goes to college. We have so many inside jokes. But I can't tell you about them.

In my notebook, all I can write is:

Loneliness cannot actually kill you.

I cross it out.

~~Loneliness cannot actually kill you.~~

I don't know what to believe.
I write this instead:

See that girlchild, breathless, gasping for air, skin around her knees stretching, elongating her to girlwomanchild, a rolling pin flattens her feet, widens her hips, curves her spine, toppling her body. Her pelican feet planted on a bed of small stones. Knee-deep in a stream, she hears the crickets rub their thighs, thickets of thorned stems, feeling the hair between her legs grow dark, long, thick, creating a webnest that seals any opening between her legs shut.

Oh Bobby, poor Bobby, he had no idea to whom he had been betrothed. The chocolate pastries here remind me of that day at Borough Market, maybe our third or fourth date. We walked into a sweets shop, not worried about people seeing us together and tsk-tsking, which would immediately alert our parents. I had looked up at him, and then at the variety of chocolates, some with lemon and orange rinds. I was surprised at how similarly Bobby and I were dressed—blue jeans, white button-down shirts, black shoes. As he turned around to grab a sample of chocolate-covered almonds, I saw how his shirt collar was starched, his shirt pressed. Into the line of his shirt, the chaos of the hair on the back of his neck swirled behind the collar. I smoothed out my own rumpled shirt as I looked down at the mustard stitching of his shiny Doc Martens boots.

The forced eye contact with him made me sweat. He stood even closer to me. The chocolate shop was crowded so we bumped into each other—colliding elbows, shoulders, hips, knees, backsides, stomachs, hands, and chests.

As we walked down the sidewalk, I tried to keep some space between us. When the street got crowded, I walked behind him. When we walked toward a more adhered couple, I let the hand holders cross between us, sidestepping to the edge of the sidewalk.

We paused to watch a street performer—a man with no head, just a black bowler cap, some space where his hat would be, a white button-down shirt, a black suit, holding a green apple. The performer's actual face was behind the shirt, but from a distance, he looked like a headless businessman, just like a painting I had seen at the Tate. I took out my notebook from my purse and wrote down: Man with Apple Head.

A couple approached in the opposite direction. This time, Bobby grabbed my belt loop, pulling me toward him so we would not separate. We paused behind a red telephone booth. I took his hand, surprising myself. He put his fingertips against my lips. His hands smelled of camphor oil. He traced the edges of my lips with the edge of his finger, and I became aware of how slowly I was breathing. I dropped my hands to my sides as his fingers moved along my face. I worried about whether the soft, but present, hair above my lip would be noticed, but he moved over the skin without hesitation. He pulled me by my pant loops again. But toward him, facing me. I craned my neck up. He was much taller than me, and he spread his feet out a bit, making himself a bit shorter so he could bend down and kiss me. I kissed him back, but soon pulled away and grabbed his hand.

"I get it. You want to take it slow," he said. He put his pinky into mine, and we walked away from the phone booth, which now had a group of tourists in front of it snapping pictures.

Later, in Leicester Square, we walked down the side of the Odeon Theater and saw the handprints of movie stars: Robert Redford, Ralph Fiennes, Omar Sharif, Bruce Willis. "Many film premieres are in these cinemas," Bobby explained over the sounds of tourists clicking the shutter and advancing film forward. Bobby suggested we put one hand each in the giant handprints of Arnold Schwarzenegger. As I bent down and saw how my small hands were swallowed by the space left by the Terminator's handprints, I saw a glimpse of our future, my smallness, Bobby's largeness.

When he told me he loved me, I said, "Thank you." He must have told his parents he wanted to marry me later that day. There was a phone call at home that night. The next week, his parents met with my parents. My parents asked me if I wanted to marry Bobby. I must have said yes, but couldn't remember exactly how or when.

I think of dismemberment often. Legs and arms just disappearing. My body becoming a diagonal, leaning into the empty space of the missing limb. I wonder what that would feel like, to be missing a foot, a shin, a calf. At night, when I sleep on the futon in my sister's flat, I sit with my feet together and my knees bent, and I touch both feet, both ankles, both shins, both knees, all the way up my body, to remember what my legs feel like. I wonder what I would do not being able to write in my notebook every day, if I lost the use of my right hand. I started practicing brushing my teeth with my left hand, which made my right upper gums bleed. I can stir sugar in my coffee with my left hand. I am working on my penmanship too.

I always knew my body was broken. It was confirmed back in London, four days before the wedding, which happened to fall during the week of Princess Diana's funeral.

There I was, lying on a gynecological table for the first time in my life—legs clenched, in a chair, with metal stirrups at the end. My heart raced. My stomach rumbled. My intestines churned. Dr. Amin, a short, bespectacled woman, said, "It says on your form that you are here because you are interested in birth control."

"I'm getting married on Saturday," I said.

She took out a metal contraption that looked like a giant rounded compass. My thighs locked together. I imagined a blade cutting through metal, cutting through me. I shivered in that paper gown, wondering if I could get paper cuts from where the edge hit my thighs.

"B r e a t h e." Dr. Amin pushed down on my stomach. The paper gown brushed up my thighs. Dr. Amin's hands pushed my inner thighs, then her gloved fingertips pressed on the outer lips, trying to push her way in, while my skin burned.

I realized that Bobby would be much bigger than her finger.

"Is it important for your fiancé to know that your hymen was torn on your wedding night? Or does he know you're a virgin?"

"He knows. I just don't think I can go through with it." I hadn't thought about the hymen breaking at all, but the idea that my body would split open and break and bleed made me start shaking

"Come back tomorrow. A simple procedure we can do in the office in thirty minutes. Bring maxi pads and wear old underwear. You'll be ready for your wedding night. It's just a little cut . . ."

I am not supposed to think about those days before the wedding. I am supposed to think positively, purposefully, according to the book I felt compelled to read from the café book-share shelf because the cover was purple and the title (*Thinking Positive, Moving with Purpose*) was in yellow.

My grandmother could speak to tigers. One sleek tiger carried the most fragrant flowers in her mouth, her fangs dripped with the blood of wild boar. She had long eyelashes and arms strong enough to slay a forest.

The tiger was born outside, underneath a two-thousand-year-old banyan tree. She taught my grandmother to smell thunder and read raindrops. The roots of the tree spread underneath, curling beneath the *sangam* of the Ganges and Jamuna rivers, the rivers crossing, creating a pattern of flickering dashes, like the snow of a television signal, or light hitting the bioluminescent skin of shallow-swimming fish.

In a frenzy, the tiger flicked off pieces of bark, rubbing them inside the crevices of her elbows and knees. She stretched, elongated her limbs, and curved her spine.

Under the table, I elongate my legs, remembering how shaken I was after that appointment and prognosis. So, I decided to get out at Trafalgar Square from the Tube. When I was aboveground, there they were. The flowers for Diana. I had seen pictures of thousands of bouquets of dahlias, delphiniums, sorrel, sweet peas, moon carrots, hardheads, buttercups, wild daisies, cowslips, bronze fennel, and chrysanthemums. And perfect English roses. I imagined the sight, but I could never have anticipated the sweet, pungent, rotting smell of the flowers. It reminded me of Punjabi milky sweets in rose water, past their prime.

I had been watching BBC all week and saw Tony Blair call Diana "the people's princess." My father had said it must have been declared against the law for BBC to show anything else on the telly, as it was nonstop public mourning. But there it was in the flesh: the Mall, stretching from Buckingham Palace to Admiralty Arch. On the news, I had seen people throwing flowers and teddy bears and waiting in long queues to sign the condolence books. People walked to the railings of Buckingham Palace, where under other circumstances no one would be allowed to get so close.

As I looked up from the flowers, I saw lots and lots of them. Couples. Insufferable couples. Hand holding, snogging, eyeglass matching, hugging, whispering, giggling, taking self-portraits with cameras in outstretched arms, sharing drinks, eating cookies, sharing secrets, locking arms, holding waists, wiping tears, blowing noses, couples.

Holding the flowers Bobby had given me that morning at the

stop before my appointment, I took the card out of its envelope. In his handwriting: *I can't wait until you're my bride. It's only a few days away, and I'm so excited. Our first night together will be so special. Please let me know what music you'd like to listen to, so I can make a CD for you. I really want it to be special for you. Love you so terribly much, hugs and kisses, B—*.

I squinted my eyes beyond the couples and looked at the individuals. There were so many Indians. I tried to see if I could recognize any of them, but I couldn't. Even the lines to sign the condolence books seemed to be filled with Indians and Africans, more so than I would have thought. I sighed. The news made it seem like everyone would be crying, but in actuality not that many people cried at all. People were very composed—businessmen with their suits and briefcases, Chinese kindergarten teachers with large posters of their students' handprints, a young version of Freddie Mercury who nailed a poster to a tree, a redheaded freckled man in a large overcoat drinking from a small bottle of Baileys and leaving a larger one, the Catholic nuns reading poems on different cards, the Nigerian women with wax print head wraps and dresses leaving a small clay pot with a rosebud, the American tourists drinking their coffee in Harrods cups, the Japanese tourists walking in groups, the Sikh men putting down their newspapers and looking, the Harrods employees in black skirt suits and heels serving free coffee and Evian water on the Mall. London.

And I felt the people. I remembered from school that the earth moves one hundred thousand kilometers per hour, but that people don't have "speed organs" to sense absolute speed. On the Mall, I could feel the motion of the earth with the people around me. We were moving together. My shoulders unclenched. I lunged forward into a spot where I wouldn't step and crush a flower, and I felt my legs and inner thighs loosen. I stepped back, and my body still felt different. Looser. Lighter. I opened the bouquet and threw the irises—petals of blue and purple, green stems, erect leaves—on the ground. I knew Diana would have preferred the flowers that way, free so they could biodegrade into the earth. I also knew that Diana would be so gracious that she wouldn't let anyone feel bad about how they left flowers for her, plastic, paper, staples, rubber bands, and all. I spread my arms and twisted my body. I stretched.

The giant outdoor screens and speakers were already being set up so that the funeral inside Westminster Abbey could be watched by people who were outside, along the funeral route. An older West Indian sang "Amazing Grace," offering a man a tissue without pausing her singing. I found myself with my feet planted on the ground, body swaying. I looked around. Two other people were swaying to the woman's song.

I walked to the dustbin and threw away the paper and envelope.

I looked at the card again. Bobby meant well. I was sure of it. But Bobby couldn't imagine the challenge he was in for. I put the note in my pocket. Could we really just dance that night?

Apparently, the reason I had difficulty making friends when I was a schoolgirl in London was not because I was dark skinned, hirsute, and clumsy, with a funny name; nor because I hadn't, nor do I now, have the social graces to know when and when not to make and maintain eye contact; not because I didn't have especially high marks to get recognition that way; but was because my classmates weren't tigers. My grandmother wrapped me up in her shawls, as I sat in her lap, and told me stories of wonderful, talented girls, who were always understood by finer, more sophisticated creatures. "These people don't matter," she would say. "You come from a line of women who spoke to tigers." I would grow up to be courageous, powerful, and fearless. I would be worthy of Durga's companionship, and could attack from any angle, using the formidable strength of my capacious body. That was supposed to be my destiny.

Destiny can be a joke of the cruelest kind. I thought I would grow up to be a tiger, not a wife. And yet, two nights before my wedding, and one night before my hymenectomy, was the *mehndi*. I sat still on the side of the room while a lady squeezed henna from homemade plastic cones, with little holes made by dress pins. In this slow-motion movie of my life, I was becoming a wife. My hands were stained in the shape of peacocks, paisleys, little flowers poking through leaved vines, tracing up my fingers.

The party began with a ladies' *sangeet*—a group of women sang, while the men stood at the bar. The women sat with me on several white bedsheets that had been spread on the floor. One woman draped her leg draped over a *dholki*, a drum that could be played on both ends. Another woman then grabbed a spoon and motioned to the first one to lift her leg so she could bang the body of the drum with the spoon. Songs about in-laws, cooking, gold, rice, children, silk, and bangles.

Meanwhile, my eyes looked down at my feet as I tried not to make eye contact with anyone. In my head, I composed a terrible triolet:

I'm a girl of nineteen
"It's just a little cut"
The very idea is obscene
I'm only just nineteen
Can't stop thinking about Dr. Amin
Why couldn't I be a slut?
I'm already nineteen
"It's just a little cut"

The live music ended as dinner was being served, and the DJ was given the responsibility of carrying the rest of the party.

A little girl in a gold-beaded flared *lengha* and embroidered leather shoes with upturned toes snatched a cocktail samosa out of an even littler girl's hand. The littler girl's hand looked impossibly large when then the tiny samosa was taken. A friend of my mother's raised an eyebrow and nodded in my direction. I understood that today was the peak of my perfection and suitability because as soon as I was married, I would be judged on whether my rotis were fluffy, fresh, and plentiful, and if my womb was the same, if anything could even enter and take root.

The DJ signaled to his lackey to turn on the red siren light, and so it started. The song. That song. The train-whistle song. People shoved the last samosas into their mouths while taking long, final sips of their drinks.

The song starts with slow *dhol*, speeding up into a frenzy, an impossible electronic-fiddle beat, synthesized bells, and hands clapping. As I had observed over dozens of weddings, it was simply scientifically impossible for a Punjabi to not move her shoulders, tap her feet, bob her head to the song, even if the song and everything about weddings filled her with fear and loathing. Genetics trumps angst. I felt my elbow moving to the music, even while I tried to keep my hand as still as possible.

"*O SADI RAIL GADI AYEE*," the song announced that the train had arrived, and the conga lines started to form. Throughout the room people lined up, hoping their disjointed em dashes would connect into a single, smooth segment. To my pleasure, the photographer stopped taking pictures of me and took pictures of the dance floor. An old man with a walker obliged as his daughter-in-law, who stood next to him, steered the walker. The spiraling conga line snaked through the banquet room picking up people from the tables, where no one refused more than thrice because it was simply not done to not participate. Except for the bride. When the line swung toward me, my mother jumped in front of me, pointed to the *mehndi*, insisting that no one oblige me—saying, without saying, "Tomorrow night, she will be all yours." I had always been swept up in previous conga lines, and this time took the opportunity to admire the orderly chaos. Most people had one hand on the shoulder in front of them, doing a variety of moves with the other hand—revving up motorcycles, twisting light bulbs, brushing off crumbs. Small children giggled as they wove in and out of the legs of the elders, and soon found it easiest to slide on their knees on the shiny smooth dance floors in their pint-sized Nehru jackets and *lengha cholis* while their parents were too distracted to stop them. A group of young teen girls were in a single-file line, obediently copying the oldest, tallest one. When the alien spaceship part of the song came on, the ladies took to doing the "swim," as one hand rose, the other up in the air, their bodies twisting down, while staying in the line formation. Some men continued doing the twist, a dance move they had learned forty years ago and dusted off at every function to every genre of music.

My cousin was doing a great job leading the front like a drum major, knees high as he marched, vigorously lip synching, even doing the two-finger whistle. My grandmother used to love to do that whistle. She died when I was thirteen. I tried not to think of too her too much. I thought of Bobby. He was a good whistler. He would be able to do that—he could ham it up, if needed. I missed him for a flash. Then I remembered. In two days, at my wedding reception, this song would play again, but I would be expected to be at the front of the line with Bobby, or else in the middle of the floor dancing with Bobby while everyone danced around us, bearing witness to our foreplay, when it is expected, even titillating, to see a just-married couple holding hands, dancing, their genitals facing each other, perhaps even moving in sync.

It feels like a definite future truth that I will not only be dismembered, but even more pressing, that I will also be alone. I watched a television show on the Spanish channel where a man had taught himself to eat with his feet. He could hold a fork in between the toes on his left foot, and a spoon in his right. And he could sit on a chair and feed himself meatloaf with potatoes and peas. I tried to lift up a pencil with my foot. It's not about how dexterous the foot is, but really how well your hips rotate, if you can balance yourself seated at an angle to have full range of motion for your hips, knees, and feet. Sometimes I am amazed at the wonder of the human body. And then also, horrified by own body's limitations.

I am not a bold person. So you can imagine my own surprise when I found myself running away from home the day before my wedding, to Bobby, whom I had grown to care for, who kissed melting ice cream off my pinky. You can imagine my bewilderment when I found myself on a plane, going across the world to live with my sister in her university flat. You can imagine my astonishment when my sister left me this note: "You can build your own life now. This is the time."

I still hear that song sometimes in New York, when a cab driver with an open window and empty backseat drives by. Songs are time machines, oppressive ones, even, bringing you back to places and times, holding you hostage.

To imagine that I once believed that I could be a wife. Unfathomable.

Did I really believe my grandmother could speak with tigers? Did I pretend to believe? Or perhaps my grandmother pretended to believe my own belief, so we both could see me as the kind of girl who believed stories about her grandmother speaking to tigers. A girl like that would be lovable.

Instead of the refill of the burnt coffee, I decide to spend the money on the Hungarian coffee. The smell of almonds is not enough. I want to taste them too. ■

UNICORN
Vidhu Aggarwal

UNICORN 2.1

I am somewhat corn
fed. Like genetically modified feed, I can con
anyone into loving me into thinking I'm non-
toxic. I have ways of co-
opting the unravish'd bride of quietness. I run
away from live bodies. I once flirted with becoming a nun.
Then I met a real icon
inside an urn.
Her name was Sylvia or Nico.
I smeared her ashes on my flesh like a glittery ruin.
I felt pretty un-
ique. Now I've got coin.
Now I've got game. I'm not just another suckable curio.

MINOTAUR 1.2

In which I bullshit with a minor.
In which I turn
into a perv. I run
with the bulls, I feel like a topless psycho killer, I ram
my inflamed genitalia into an abyss of pixels while main-
taining my cool. I'm a bullman in a skirt. A Shiva on the mount
of yoni-lingam, meditating in the acid rain
in love with the Flood. I tour
my post-apocalyptic rumin-
ations in a tran-
scontinental copter. I chew cud for millennia. I chat up an amir.
I ode around a Grecian urn
A cyclotron accelerates my subatomic om
and a small iota
of my soul is ion-
ized, released from the workaday rot,
released into the riot
of the nirvana-sphere, forever turned on.

MINOTAUR 2.1

In which I'm harmonized with my virus. I auto-
mate sex in HiveGrind. I rim
a poodle in the Kill Room. I'm in
a good place: full of amino
acids and vitamins. Almost omni-
potent, I hover above the rat-
race. I don't care if you don't like me or
my maze. I've mastered mar-
tyrdom. I am both muni
and sati. I set myself on fire. I mourn
briefly & am reborn into version 2.2. 2nd generation tor-
eodor/bull. I gut a muon
with my scary horns. I rut
everything and everyone I'm not.

AVATAR OF THE LABYRINTH
Vidhu Aggarwal

I have one super-charged ovary
spinning in an orbital
around my zigzagging lab.

I have a botnet
of "borrowed" servers. An array
of sequestered wombs inside my own private belt-
way of lobes. I test for the best habitat

in the network. I watch a horn
grow, an appendage. If I don't like even a bit
of it, I press abort.
and out it goes into the toilet.

All this whirring labor
on multiple fronts to bring forth
the perfect introvert.

I'll feed it a broth
of data-rich fable
from alter-
nate streams in the torrent.
I'll press secret info
into its toenail.
I'll wrap it in the afterbirth
from my entire battery
of uteruses. It will vibrate
like a lyre
to the hum of its own tantric antler.

AVATAR OF THE SPHINX
Vidhu Aggarwal

I refuse to play therapist
to yet another parasite
hipster.
I've contrived a new Turing test
for the next
generation aspirant
entering my sanatoria.

Who would brave my hairy forest
of crypto-nodes, and suck up the vapors
of paranoia?

Pharaohs
need not apply. I will gauge the state
of the native
cortex with my probes: Are you a bona fide poet,
a real-deal artisan
of the info-vortex,
a servant
to quantum error, able to spin
noise
into the bhangra-sonata
mix of the millennia, or a mere theorist
of mass extinctions out on safari,
a sniper
in the bestiary of code? Do you exist,

Vox
Humana or are you a hoax?

Why continue to fixate
on Mother-Father
incest porn,
as if Oedipus was still your favorite
virus. I'm over

that sociopathic pasha
and ready to invest
in another toxin.

If you prostrate
yourself before my tesseract, perform a havan
in the phoenix-
firepit of my sphincter, dissolve the hieroglyph of the future/past
you can infest

the crypto-nerves

of the global server, inject the next version
of humanity with your alt-error code. The attar

of the self is a opiate
for the massive multiplayer persona.

AVATAR OF THE MERMAID
Vidhu Aggarwal

All id
      with the ink-spit dermis
of a squid-like diva
singin' in the rain.

All teeth
with the death-drive
mecha-breath of Durga or Darth Vader.

In another life I was a meth
addict, I was a void
of narcissistic gloom. The open waters dam-
med up in a vat
of oilspill. I was maimed,
evacuated into a psychic-myth farm,
marooned in another dim-
ension. I took it a sign to dream
another dreamer. I took it as my dharma.
It was hard
for me to reform
my biodata into a swamic hyper dom-
ain. I grew the multitudinous limbs and vermiform
hair of a Med-
usa devi
squirting mandalas and emergency mito-
gens into the world fever.
Now I sit on a thermo-
genic lotus, with my ammo
and my ova,
an armada
of hypo-sigils, tat-
ting the shivering worldskin with my liquid meme.

AVATAR OF HANUMAN
Vidhu Aggarwal

I shrink myself to boson. I grow into supernova.
Run a marathon
against Achilles. Every second, every day: number one friend to Ram,
devotee of paradox and numen. I haunt
the bunglers that roam
my jungle, the lurkers gathering data and form-
ulas. You think you can sequence the genome for manna?:
Neem, my thunderbolt strength. Tulsi, my sweat; Amaranth
my seed. O human
packrats with your zoos, your turf
wars, your Bubbles the Chimp. You say you are a fan
of the flora
and fauna. But you mourn
their loss from afar,
meditating upon every trauma
of the month
in some discussion forum.
Dumb talk from the disembodied mouth—
no one to know the author
of the fart
without aroma.

AVATAR OF THE SWASTIKA
Vidhu Aggarwal

Someone once told me I was *wrong*,
and I turned

a sick,
sick carousel

a revolving
door of cuckold. A phalanx

of hunky troops

storming
through my flickering skirts—ah! the perverse
geometry of my affliction. It was a race

of Aryan dragons, like Angels
entirely white with bleached sphincters, claws

in the blades of my windmill. My guts, wild shoots, a shiny
array on the dance floor, sniffing glue, snaking around
the universe. Ah, the sound of boots! The pain, the attitude!

I read my entrails in reverse, my Wheel of Fortune,
a cursed
will to power, I was branded

like a proper man, proper
like Don Quixote
like the whirligig of Paul de Man
a man (a man) without conviction.

It was not just
my stain but I took it on. I was not a man. But the mark was mobile,
a doubly-

curled mustachio, repeated in a maharaja's palace gate.
I am also/or
the body of Ganesh, remover of obstacles,

auspicious, vicious insignia, a force
of Shakti, dance-crazed.

PILL AMPHIFLEX
Vidhu Aggarwal

The capsule
demagnifies libido
and forwards all desire
to the tenth dimension
of the infinite salivating quarks.

I taste a microsphere of transport
like some prurient sorrow
and shrink.

In the tenth dimension
desire buzzes like a demonic
housefly that cannot die.

CALIBAN
Faisal Mohyuddin

24" x 18". Ink on Paper.

THE POET
Faisal Mohyuddin

15" x 11". Ink on paper.

THE BLOOMING LIGHT OF YESTERDAY'S WAITING WORLD

Faisal Mohyuddin

14" X 11". Ink on paper.

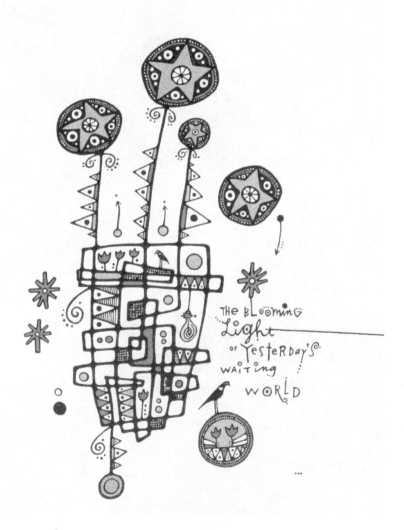

THE HAMLET MASK
Faisal Mohyuddin

24" x 18". Ink on paper.

I INVEST IN ELVIS
Mala Gaonkar

Iwas on a work trip, to see a warehouse for sale, when I took a long detour to St. Louis, to see a man, Joe, who taught me to ride a bike. Joe was dying. Decades ago, his daughter Rose had been my girlhood friend; they were our neighbors. We still exchanged cards at Christmas— cherubs encrusted with Santa suits from Rose, and, from me, "Happy Holidays" in plain red on white with a photo of a painting below. From the profits I made in my business, I collected the few paintings I could afford. They were by little-known artists who produced at most a few works a year, challenging enough to be flattering to a collector, but not too much so, and showing for the first time in the right group of New York galleries I had never even visited. Images on their own have no worth to me. I liked what they represented: prices. Prices are order in a disorderly world of desire and beauty and greed. I checked auction and stock prices the way men check football scores.

I was on this trip, with really nothing to warrant a visit, except that my mother had told me that Joe was dying. We had only lived two years in that house whose contents were just books, two beds and a traffic light bright sofa. I remembered the books; the sofa was a gift on my eleventh birthday.

The orange sofa had been on sale; no one had the stomach for bold colors these days, the tired salesman had said, frowning. My father, a smile spreading across his wide, sincere face, said it reminded him of the gul mohur trees outside his childhood home. My mother said it reminded her of temple garland marigolds. Appa had his first paycheck that year as assistant professor in mechanical engineering at the University of Illinois, and he said stomach (here, rubbing his expanding girth) was his to spare.

It was my eleventh birthday. No friends came, as I had none.

Happy Birthday! they sang to me, later at home, off-key. Enjoy your new palanquin!

They bought a big, plywood cupboard, dyed to look like walnut; it was the color you see when you spill black coffee on your shirt. The cupboard was enormous. It glowered at the orange sofa in the front room of our cereal-box house.

"Amma, Appa! What are we going to put in there?" I asked.

"Our gods! Our books!"

I had a 102-degree fever. My brain was trying to force its way out of every possible crack in my skull. I had risen from my invalid bed to see what I would get for my birthday. As I said, I had no friends to invite. We had just moved. Well, it had been a few months, but there were still no friends.

Perhaps it was the glaring sun elbowing through the curtains, but the gods glowed. Our gods were a photo of Saraswati, the goddess of learning, and another electric blue image, akin to the cover of one of those Xbox games kids play now, of the goddess Kali, industriously chopping an astonished demon's head off with a shimmering, stainless steel scimitar in what appeared to be the mother of all thunderstorms. Detach yourself from this world of illusion, the gods exhorted, actively engaged as they still seemed to be in their own. The gods used to reside in the corner of my parents' bedroom, on a cardboard box covered with a red polyester bedsheet, on which reigned a dusky bronze urn of incense. The urn was an irrationally grand object in that jumble sale of a room. When we did our pujas, I meditated on that urn, not our gods.

Someone inside my skull was industriously applying sandpaper to my cerebrum.

Amma said they had to go back to the university labs.

"It's my birthday."

My father explained that time did not travel in an arrow. In the space-time continuum, my observation of a specific event, namely this illness, was arbitrary.

"I will die of this fever."

In the reworked hierarchy of the Indian immigrant family, the only thing lower than a neglectful mother was an unemployed one. My mother gave me a Tylenol and a turmeric root from the Indian grocer to steep for tea. She stroked my forehead briefly and they were gone. She said I should study my vocabulary while lying there. I spilled the yellow tea on the new orange sofa, which absorbed it without complaint.

In those brief years in America, my mother liked to listen to The Miracles' "Love Machine" when she washed the dishes. She was always turning the cassette recorder volume down on the sexy bits when I was in the room. My father said this would not be necessary if she simply listened to that Bangladeshi chap sing "My Sweet Lord." I told him, hopelessly confusing him, that George Harrison was a Beatle, not a Bangladeshi.

Oh, what binds you to a place like that? Where none look like you? Where you drive the floor-flat prairie interstate, past the pawnshop, gun-shop strip malls that hold nothing for you? Where people only congregate in stark churches where your cavorting feckless gods would be shot for their sins? Is it the music?

The new music I was hearing, alone at home, twiddling to the right radio stations, shutting my eyes, was what bound me, my American siren call. Certainly my parents would never let me buy an LP. And this only reinforced the strong sense that our Lake Trail Drive home was a tiny sliver of the whole sugary cake of the world. If I understood this music I would live. A large life. Otherwise, it would remain constrained to that stained orange sofa.

For my mother, the food was the wheat-fed Midwestern Siren. American food was the elevated miracle of ease: orange Tang, Pop-Tarts leaping from toasters, green peas and white potatoes on TV dinner trays, Tater Tots adorned with Kashmiri chilli powder. All without any chopping or pots!

For my father, the sirens were silent. His books remained in the old country, in Bangalore. The few books they had here lay in piles everywhere. They were both forever shouting at me things like, "Where did you leave the Riemann equations! Where is that David Hilbert book!"

I couldn't fully understand the thickets of sigmas and epsilons, but I could see their beauty. I could see how understanding these would let you into a magic realm where Ancient Greek men in white bath towels spoke to my parents directly. If I looked up to my parents—and I did—it was for understanding these books. Explain it to me, I would ask, but my father, exhausted, or my mother, impatient, would wave me away, saying, listen in your math class first.

Looking back now, I can only blame myself for the absent friends. Children are like small, weak primates, and if I had thumped my chest a bit more, my strangeness could have been used to advantage. And strange I was. My mother refused to get me the Princess Leia lunch box I wanted when I had a perfectly good tiffin carrier from the Mumbai markets. The tiffin carrier was an impressive three-tiered copper structure that sensibly kept your curry separate from your rice and pickles. My mother packed dinner leftovers in it every evening. Everyone else in the sixth grade ate peanut butter sandwiches tucked in metal boxes with superheroes on them. I ducked into the corner behind the dirty dish steam trolley, and took out my spoon to eat the lamb curry. The scent of garlic wafted around the cafeteria. A girl at a table next to the trolley wrinkled her nose and giggled. A tall, handsome boy, Josh Weedon—I knew him from the oddly named homeroom—sauntered over behind the steam trolley and held his hand out cordially. Reflexively, I put down the steaming tiffin carrier, patted my hands on my skirt, and held out mine. He pulled his hand into a fist and mock-punched me in the gut. It wasn't hard, but I doubled over in surprise, my smile still painted on my face. A few other boys were laughing behind him. I elbowed my way past them.

"You are/ no-thing/ more than/ stuh-reet dogs," I said in my sing-song accent. They barked, gleefully, their English as pointed and fast as one of their footballs.

A plump, pretty, brown-haired girl waited till the dogs scattered and came up to me. "I thought you would want this back," she said. She had expertly stacked and clipped up the tiffin carrier, confining the fumes. I had my hands awkwardly clasped in front of me, over my books, and it took me a moment to take the wretched thing back, even as Rose patiently held it out. She lived down the street and didn't we see each other in the bus? Yes, we did. After that, Rose and I often found ourselves eating lunch together, not least due to my maneuvers to bump into her before each break.

Rose had records, stacks of them. It seemed utter luxury to me, sitting in her room huddled over her small plastic turntable. The world loved disco, but the two of us loved Elvis:

Bugsy turned to Shifty and he said, "Nix nix,
I wanna stick around a while and get my kicks."

There was much flailing of limbs in Rose's garage. When Elvis said "I'm not trying to be sexy. It's just my way of expressing myself when I move"? Well, we would shriek when one of us repeated it, and cup our nonexistent breasts as we danced. I loved wearing her dad Joe's old wide-wale green corduroy blazer when he wasn't around to protest, dipping my invisible microphone stand. Indian Elvis. That was the name of the band I was going to start when I got out from under my parents' roof.

Rose took me aside once in the locker room after PE. "Here, Lana, I got you a new deodorant stick. You kind of need this strong one." I was ashamed, but also desperate to be like the other girls, who smelled like washing machine powder. Rose showed me how to shave my armpits, just outside the shower. She said Americans didn't have any body hair, and with my dark hair I would need to shave daily.

"For the rest of my life? Like a man?"

"Yes," said Rose earnestly, as if we were making a promise to each other.

I often went home with her after school, as she lived only two houses down the street, and her Serbian mother, Maria, made pork meatballs. That is how we met Joe. My parents worked late in their labs, sometimes the night through, and were relieved I had some adult supervision. We ate buttery apricot tarts, which Maria worried were too Old Country, so she also laid out the Twinkies that I loved for their fairy crumb. Maria didn't go too far from the house, tending to her tomato patch, pickling cucumbers or watching game shows. Sometimes we had *Gilligan's Island* crackling in the background, a sort of family hearth. Rose's father Joe did The Skipper's lines in his native Slovakian accent: "Gilligan, I don't care if you pick red white and blue bananas, just pick some bananas!" We thought this the pinnacle of wit. I still do.

My mother didn't know what I got up to with Rose. I felt for the first time the giddy freedom of deceit. My mother had come off the airplane, cattle class, and gone straight into a molecular biology lab, already yoked by family arrangement to my father. I knew my mother was older than most Indian brides; I also knew, from eavesdropping the whispers of visiting aunties, that there had been illicit letters to a fellow student of a different caste intercepted by the town gossips that had tainted her on the marriage market. My father was taken with her, though, and insisted on marrying her. In the first year in America, they often talked about how leaving India had given them air to breathe, and I pictured them in bell jars in the bazaar knocking hard to get out.

Sometimes after school, if she could manage it, I went to Amma's lab and dissected rats for her. I had to look for tumors: ugly, hard, Tic Tac nodules that looked wrong. I can see the rats' small insides still, like jewels set in a Swiss master's clock. I loved the delicate scalpels, the pincers, the enchanted jeweler's loupe to cup a specimen slide. I was all hers as we meticulously sliced the layers of the lab-fat oblivious rats, their bellies and livers gleaming, listening to all she said, our heads dipped to our work and her voice in mine as she said, over my questions, thoughtlessly tender, "Thank you, sweetheart, the work flies by with you here," not knowing we'd never be closer the rest of our lives. If I look back to where we began to speak less to the other I cannot find the thread. Memory is altered by remembrance, and so the dearest, most remembered parts of our past oddly grow the dimmest.

So, maybe I don't remember this straight, but Rose's dad, Joe, didn't understand Elvis. He only listened to country music. "Hey, I love it," he said. "You gals will too when you get old and dented and want to hear music that sings of problems not just romance. And the songs are funny. There isn't a single funny rock song; like the guy meant it to be, I mean."

He was right. I listen to Hank Williams and Johnny Cash on the way to work in Miami now.

"How can I miss you if you don't go away," they warble. "My girl ran off with my best friend, and I sure do miss him." What is more enchanting than someone a bit like you who sings his troubles into jokes? I wonder, would Rose, would I, identifying with her as I did, have understood Elvis if he were black?

Or brown, my mother would later ask when we spoke of those days? Those gyrations, my mother scoffed, could have been seen ten years before in any bog-standard Bollywood film, before you jokers pranced around to your king.

Joe worked the night shift in Peoria Steel, and sometimes he was just waking up when we got home from school. He'd fry burgers for us, regale us with tales of how so-and-so almost incinerated his arm tipping a blast furnace lever. I didn't tell my parents I ate the gentle, holy cow, favorite of the god Krishna, but my issue had been more disgust than awe. I had seen the scrawny, dirty creatures on the road in India, chewing scraps with their legs sunk in the piles of garbage the municipal truck never reached at the end of the road.

Joe said not to worry, these were different cows. "They give them food from bags," he said. "It's all clean."

The trouble started when Rose hopped on her Schwinn to go to Claire's house one summer evening (I was not invited), the pink streamers on her handlebars whipping behind her like some shout of joy. Joe asked me if I wanted to try her cast-aside banana seat.

"I can't ride," I whispered. My parents never had the money for a bike in India, or the time to teach me. I would never have admitted this even to Rose. But Joe was kind, and old enough not to matter. He was bald with sharp ears, a jovial elf. He said he would need to speak to my mother and I gave him her number. After a long time—were they discussing the State of the Union?—Joe emerged, smiling. He must have spent hours trying to help me balance on that ridiculous pink seat. I asked him lots of questions as he ran along beside. Was it hard to move here from Slovakia? Why did he make mean jokes about black people and Mexicans (something unthinkable to my parents), but was nice to Indians? Did he always know he was going to be a steelworker? He answered them all, first patiently, and then with increasing excitement, the way someone unused to talking about himself realizes for the first time that he can hold an outsider's interest, even if only an inquisitive child's. Rose, who had taken me on as one does a lost cat, at first seemed relieved to share the burden of my American education.

Was it during the times my mother came to pick me up from Joe's lessons, and then, the three of us walking back towards home, laughing at mishaps in the lab and factory, that I realized I did not want the lessons to end? And how happy I was when Joe made his jokes, happy my father was not around to look perplexed, laboriously parsing Americanisms that came more swiftly to my mother? Did I realize it when the days were growing long and hot and, supposedly at trumpet practice, I wheeled the bike up the hill past the Slawsons' house and pedaled down in exuberant zigzags? Singing "Hound Dog" all the way, until I saw Rose at the bottom staring at me, her face a round, hard mask.

"I'm just practicing!" I yelled at her.

"Do it on your own bike! With your own dad! You said you couldn't do it on your own!" she shouted back.

I told Joe I had learned to balance. We still talked, more rarely now, about unions and layoffs and the cheap, flimsy steel from the Japs, important real-world problems. Rose spent more time with Claire at school over lunch so I went to the library, a small sandwich now in my bag, which I gulped down over reading *Time* magazine. I read about oil, how all of it was in a few small desert countries in Arabia. I told Joe he needed to do something in high demand like that. He said my mother said there was a great need for technical lab assistants for clinics and he was learning that now through a catalogue course. He was very proud. Maybe one day he could even work in a lab like my mother!

At home, my mother talked often of history, of Faraday, how a blacksmith's son of little schooling read Newton on optics and divined that magnetism was the mirror of electricity. My father murmured one did not need degrees if one had genius, but without the latter the former paid the bills. I thought then they were speaking of Joe; only later would I realize my mother was speaking of Joe and my father of himself. My father said it was difficult for him to understand the banter of the faculty lunches. "Our girl is making a better shift of it," he said proudly. Actually, my mother corrected him, his girl had just one friend, Rose who wasn't doing well at school. Rose's own father was worried about his daughter flirting with boys, my mother said, and slinking off from band practice. I had never thought Rose dull or that I was sharper than her. When you are a stranger, knowing how to talk to others is worth so much more than the ability to remember the details of plant meiosis.

I was stubborn; I wanted Rose's favor back. I passed her a note saying Elvis would keel over soon, and she should stockpile memorabilia for what it would be worth after he was dead. But not the trash she'd been accumulating: mugs, statuettes, photos. I told her what I had told her father about how the oil market was rigged and how we could do the same for the Elvis records that would get rarer when he died. It seemed obvious to me that the slender swiveling Elvis was a different creature from the plump bejeweled deity of an Elvis but Rose was shocked. It took her awhile to want any part of this.

I spooled through microfilm records in the library to get the print runs from early in Elvis's career, when no one knew him to be a god, and the record company pressed the small number of 45s they accorded a mortal. Elvis's five Compact 33 singles from 1961 were our target. We could afford the later releases from the first few months post-release I said, after speaking to John at Anglin' Records downtown. Even just one. "Surrender"/"Lonely Man" was the first one we got from a mail-order operation. I called collect to make sure it existed, and paid for it with her savings from her Long John Silver's job at the mall. I told her this was the hidden stuff that Elvis would want to see in a real fan's collection. I dredged up more information at the library. My grades were slipping. On weekends now, I was made to sit in the university library and do math worksheets that my mother corrected furiously in the evenings. Secretly, I was studying Elvis. It was a slipping link to Rose. I thought I would try imaginary tales of woe of my Indian childhood. I told her crazed stories of how I had eaten rats when we starved in the slums of Calcutta. Except we had never set foot there. She merely looked repulsed. But she did keep buying the records. Elvis, by letting me sift through his release dates in the university library, had given me my start finding prices.

Joe was studying, too. When I went to see Rose now, Joe gave me manila envelopes to give my mother. "I need her opinion on my coursework," he would say, and I could suddenly see how in a certain evening light, smiling, with his strong arms and bright blue eyes, short, plump Joe could even look handsome. My mother gave them to me to return, sealing the folder flap with tape. "So nothing falls out," she said.

Around Thanksgiving, when the neighbors were piling up pumpkins and we just had dead leaves to rake, my mother was denied tenure at the university. The rats had stayed silent. My father said it was no matter as it was time to go home.

My mother said our home was here.

My father shook his head. "You are too clever to not work. This is a dead end job. What else keeps you here?"

My mother did not answer.

They hauled the orange sofa out to the driveway for a garage sale. A pale, browsing couple, assuming I was deaf, asked each other if these people were on acid when they bought it. I did not share my father's gul mohur dreams with them, and when they asked for a discount on some pots tagged for $5, I scowled and told them no, the price was firm.

Elvis dropped dead as predicted in his bathroom. Rose came over, for the first time in months, stumbling over a Bertrand Russell volume on the hall floor, a vast chest in her arms. She set it down before the unsold sofa with a thump.

"But this is everything you collected," I said.

"I want you to have something in case it all goes wrong. I know we haven't really been friends for awhile, but this is for emergency relief so you don't wind up like the beggars in Calcutta."

"It's just one crate," I said to my mother.

"Look, we're two assistant profs earning ten thousand a year. Shipping that to India would be half a month's salary. No. If you can put those things into your carry-on suitcase? Maybe. But what will you do for clothes? You want to wear that same skirt and underwear for six months? You know the house price doesn't even cover what we owe on the mortgage?"

I said we were going to a pit where no one cared about our credit rating. I had grown very tired of hearing about this rating.

"That is why you are an American," my mother said, "and why we are taking you back to India. You have lost all sense of shame. Suggesting we should shirk our debts!"

I went over to see Joe in his toolshed behind the garage. I knocked on the door and no one answered. I went to the back where a small oblong window as large as a notebook was propped open for air, a Dolly Parton song sidling out. I dragged a bucket over to stand on and peered in. There was a strange noise like a rattler I had heard once on a nature show. A man was crouched on a stool, his shoulders shaking. He heard and looked up straight at me. It was Joe.

I ran away. I would pretend I had never seen him.

I wrapped myself in the red polyester sheet in the puja room and stared at the gods, aloof amidst their incense. Those tornado-bait Midwestern shoeboxes. It was safer than houses to just dig. A house could get swept up in a tornado, but there was always safety underground. I told my mother we were going to bury the crate, to keep it safe forever. She laughed and said we should bury the orange sofa with it too; in time it would be a period piece. Rose said Claire told her it was all junk and not to bother. I remember looking at Rose sternly then. I had the confidence of scholarship. My studies would not fail me. One day I assured her this would be her treasure.

At the hardware store, I said we needed two large water-tight plastic boxes and duct tape. The guy at the counter asked how many ex-boyfriends we planned to kill. I thought of Josh Weedon, his flat but handsome face. We put the records in two garbage bags and wrapped the whole with duct tape, and then four more garbage bags. We stuck the whole into an old wood box with a bunch of rusting ball bearings in a Ziploc bag for if we ever needed to find it with a metal detector (tectonic plate shifts, I said learnedly, could shift our box over the years). I had a compass to find the bearings we marked in my favorite copy of *The Golden Book of African Mammals*. We buried Elvis in Rose's backyard. "Wait till we dig this up in a few years," she said. "We'll have a bonanza!"

When I showed my final report card to my parents, I told them my math teacher thought I was a genius who would rot away on the subcontinent. My mother frowned. "When you think you are a genius remember there was a time when you had to learn to go sit on the toilet like anyone else."

My father was distracted by the Voyager departure that summer to Jupiter and Saturn. It would keep going past them; somewhere Unknown. Greetings had been collected from all countries and inscribed on a gold record for other conscious beings who might find it, but he only read the incongruously irreverent one in his language, Kannada: "Friends of Space, How are you all? Have you eaten yet? Come visit if you have time!"

I wanted to know if they had put Elvis onto the golden time capsule. He did not think so.

When we left Missouri, I saw my mother hug Joe. I had not even seen her embrace my father in our own home. I stared. "Look after yourself, Joe," she said, smiling and shaking her head at him. "Stop smoking." He held both her hands in his. "Your eyes are as big as coffee cups," he said wonderingly, as if he hadn't seen them a hundred times already. They didn't seem embarrassed. "Don't give up," she said. She had tears in her eyes. In the small, superior way I feel when I see sentimental people, I thought, how banal!

Rose watched them, frowning.

I thought of that moment often later, even as a woman careening towards middle age. I liked being alone, and made fun of the awkward, eager Indian lab-men my mother halfheartedly sent my way in hopes I would mate and breed grandchildren.

Rat-dissectors, I said. Formaldehyde men.

"I give up," she said. "I can't say I blame you. If I had married a different man he would not have been content with curried Tater Tots. I was lucky."

When I finally got to St. Louis, I drove the hour to Rose's house. She had hard, permed hair now, pearlescent lips that shimmered pink. She was very plump, but still pretty, in a snug forest-green velour sweatsuit with bell-bottomed trousers. She had an Obama pin on her shoulder. She was looking for Elvis again, I feared. An emissary from a land of Hope, a new kind of music. She said that the country needed a change. Behind the platitude lurked her own view that one person could actually make a difference. It was an idealism beyond me. I envied this woman.

I asked about Joe and said my mother had wanted me to visit and was sorry she could not be there too.

"He would love to see you, Lana. I used to be jealous of you then, you know," Rose said, as if we'd just spoken yesterday. She sounded tired, wheezing slightly in that way heavy people do.

I felt a strange grief. As if I were somehow ill too.

Rose said, "You remember when I liked Tim, and you thought he wanted to kiss me, but he just wanted the money for the soda pop? You remember when we trapped that poor baby bird as a pet, and it died, and you said your religion ordained we'd be reborn as chicks and pecked to death by vultures? And remember how we cried?"

I did not remember any of it but nodded. Rose tried another tack.

She said, "I went to the community college for a computer course."

"You can't go wrong with computers," I said. There was a long pause. I dug my fingernails into my palms. "What happened to Josh Weedon?" I asked.

Rose laughed. Josh finally had his uses. We both relaxed. She said, "He became a cop."

"That thug is armed? How many innocent people has he shot?" I asked.

"Oh, Lana, he's a fat loser who tried to trap speeders on A4 with a supersize Cup of Mountain Dew between his legs. Plus everyone has a gun out here. Who cares? Why did you never marry?" she asked.

"I have a business to run," I said. Any place can be home if you know how to travel and work, I thought to myself. I muttered something about solitude being different from loneliness.

"My man didn't last, anyway," Rose said. "I keep missing him, but my aim is getting better!"

She laughed and I thought of Elvis. She gave me a pink scented candle to take to Joe's hospital room.

"Little buddy," Joe said. He was attempting his Skipper voice again, the one he had used to make us laugh. He was looking somewhere else above my head, in the unnerving way very sick people do. As if looking at your real self, not the one you present to the world, nicely spit-polished. I held his hand. I wept, more from anxiety than from sorrow.

"You taught me to ride a bike!"

It was the dumbest thing to say, but Joe suddenly looked amused.

I remember him young, bald but dapper, with the cigarette dangling from his lips, as he guided that cheap pink bike up and down Johnston Trail Road. My mother had tried pushing me once, lost patience after ten minutes, and when the axle jammed into her ankle, yelled that I didn't have the balance gene and to be satisfied with walking for Krishna's sake. Joe had come out of the house and sharply told my mother that she needed to stop steering and just help me stay upright. He had reached out to hold her wrist when she tried to walk away.

"Joe, how do you feel?"

Joe cracked his usual half smile.

"I don't talk to strangers. Who's this business tycoon? "

His smile broadened. I said stupidly it was Lana and that I was sorry I had not seen him in so long.

"Jeez. I must really be dying. Look, I've been to hell and back. And it's wonderful. Let me tell you. I'm ready to go."

I called Amma after my hospital visit to ask why all those manila folders they passed back and forth. "You don't need to worry what I think. Appa's gone, and it was so long ago."

There was a silence.

"Amma?"

"With you Americans it is always the sex. He listened! He was my friend."

"Why don't you visit him?"

My mother ignored me. "Joe is a very clever man. He saw what was happening to his job. He nearly made it through those biology courses even if they were rubbish. Imagine Joe a lab technician! I can." She laughed.

I could hear the endless beeping of a rickshaw traffic jam. She must have the windows open in the flat. She always hated air-conditioning. It was a hard laugh. "Oh, daughter, I couldn't visit him because I am a coward just like you. How could I bear it?" There was a silence. It contained all we were thinking—our years in India—my father's happy rise to head of his department in computational mathematics, my mother's steady ossification into good works running a university program for science education in schools, my own determination to forever forget Joe crying in the shed. We talked a bit more about the climbing prices of onions in the bazaar before saying goodbye.

I went back to the hospital the next day. Joe patted my hand, and was weary but insisted on talking. He said I eased his worries with my questions. His thyroid tumor, he told me, had nearly suffocated him in his sleep. He had first refused an operation to take out the lump. Then, after that gasping night, he had consented to the surgery, and that had nearly wiped out Rose. I asked Joe what worried him the most. He said it was pain. I told him we could arrange for him to go home and have a nurse on call to help with the morphine drip. I did not say "hospice."

"My bucket's got a hole in it, I can't buy no beer." He squeezed my hand briefly and was silent a minute. "Don't try to give money to Rose; she wants to do things for me her own way, and I'll never hear the end of it. Even when I'm dead."

I had an idea. She would never take money from me, but she would take it from herself. It was worth a try.

Rose was sitting out in the viciously cheerful patient's lounge, all bright yellow walls with red flowers, her face grey with exhaustion. I sat down beside her.

"He nearly got his lab assistant license." She laughed. "Despite your mother's lousy tutoring. He called her in India every month, you know. It wasn't cheap."

I felt anxious to do something, talk of anything else. My mother must have gone down to the telephone shop at the bazaar every month. I hadn't known. Or particularly wanted to know either. We both looked out the window.

"Rose!" I said. "Where can we get some shovels? There's gold in the ground! We buried Elvis! Remember?"

We rushed home to the garage. I called my mother, who kept my old report cards, diaries and animal books in the room that she'd given up calling her grandchild's, and who now read out the compass coordinates, reluctantly.

"Don't dig up old things," she said. "You won't find anything worth having."

"Every cell phone has a GPS. This will be easy."

But of course that's not what she meant.

Rose had purpose now. I had never seen her so happy. Joe had told her he was coming home to die, and she would make it as good a party as possible. With the most beautiful nurse Elvis could buy. We dug up Rose's corn patch, deep into the evening. Sweat beaded down my back and I felt my neck stiffen into painful, thick ropes. I didn't have a plan and the shovel kept crunching into the sticky clay ground.

The word spread. Rose was digging up treasure! To pay Joe's medical bills! In their garages, people found floodlights, metal detectors. Everyone, it seemed, had a dream of buried fortune. But in the dim light, moving toward us, they could have been a troop of French peasants with their pickaxes fomenting revolution.

"We're digging for plastic and shellac," I said. "Nothing to get excited about."

"Don't kid," someone said. "We know you are looking for something big."

A kid bumbled about the back yard with his own Walmart metal detector, his shadow a giant praying mantis against the garage wall. There was a party atmosphere. It was starting to drizzle, but people passed around beers and from a boom box George Jones sang:

My pants are ragged but that's all right,
I've got five dollars and it's Saturday night.

In the flashlight beams, the rain turned to rhinestones.

We struck plastic at one a.m. I knew we were digging up nearly worthless discs and was worried someone would say that none of this would be enough. But it would be a way for me to give her money. The box was coated with greyish mold that we scraped off. A kid with a phone snapped a photo of the LP we cut loose from the layers of garbage bag and duct tape, its cardboard soft and pungent, and a moment later, he shouted: "It's listed for five hundred dollars on eBay!"

"Long live the King," someone yelled.

Elvis lay scattered across the lawn, on besmirched velvet, on gilt coffee mugs, on damp, mildewed album covers. I gingerly moved things about, looking for the autographed photo scroll that had been Rose's Koh-i-Noor diamond. Rose was openly weeping, with people taking turns to hug her.

Here's the thing: I didn't even like this Elvis. Fame turned him into a party balloon full of helium and covered with glitter. The songs I liked were from the 1950s. Elvis was a different man when he sang to Rose.

She came over to me in her black leggings and that t-shirt saying Yes We Can. She had the full, beguiling voice of someone mocking her own tragedy.

Five hundred dollars! I guess that would have seemed like a lot to us back in the day. "What the hell," she said. "It's a down payment on the down payment of my bankruptcy. What a party, though!"

I said, as naturally as I could, "I know a buyer who would pay twice for this. Back in New York. I'll cover for ninety percent of that and make a profit!"

A cup went around for Joe. "C'mon Rose, don't spoil the party," a man called out, when she demurred. In the dark, I put in ten twenties. "Oh well," muttered Rose to me when the cup was pressed into her hand. "Might as well take it. They won't be coming round again to help me with anything for awhile!"

Strange that kindness can only be bought with kindness. I wasn't clever like her about that.

I didn't tell Rose that there had been something else in the box: a thick, sealed packet that my mother must have slipped into the bottom, knowing we would bury it, certain we'd never dig it up again, unable to bear throwing it away. It said "JOE" in capital letters, underlined in my mother's firm hand. I knew she would not want to know I had found it.

I had held reason in high regard, abandoning my heart to swift efficiency and here I was laboriously digging my way back to it with people who barely knew me. Oh, but what do you do without a man like Joe? You chase his voice to the bazaar bingo box for a shout across the sea deep lines. You send your daughter to help him die.

Remember how I said that there is nothing more enchanting than a man who turns his troubles into laughs? All around stood such men— not much hope left—the university job cuts on top of the steel plant that was shut down long ago. Rose was laughing now with the high school science teacher who lived down the road, tossing back a beer. In the dark sky I showed them a flash of satellite. Voyager was about to hit the edge of the solar system. On the golden disc, Bach shouldering Kannada greetings for aliens. I remembered digging around inside rats with my mother for the evidence, looking for the patterns she craved but never found. What had I helped uncover here? Old hopes, worth little. In the eternal hierarchy of an Indian immigrant family, the only thing lower than the unemployed woman was a friendless one. Without caste, without community. The belief that love makes us happy is wrong; it is better than that, it offers solace. I had seen my mum pile on work to forget it, and my father, distanced, to claim it, to somehow take my mother home with him. At some point, even if you have it, it runs out, so beware. But in the brief musical whirl, if you can, run heedless into it. So, this is what love is for: to be out of place, alone and yet know someone's listening. I didn't need to run away from the shed or avert my gaze from the bazaar phone booth.

You can be on your knees in the mud, strangers all around you, staring at mildewed images of Elvis fluttering on the grass around you and just like that, gratitude hits. George Jones's voice sounded tinnily from all directions. I put the packet of letters back in the deep ground and carefully covered them up. ∎

DEAR INDIA,
Shikha Malaviya

This letter is being written on a blue aerogram, the kind they used back in the day, the kind that had us airborne as soon as we ripped its blue edges with our brown fingers. Why don't we write letters anymore? People are forgetting the art of anticipation. Instead of mangoes being plucked from trees, they're being sprayed with sulfur and shoved into the belly of a plane. All in the name of imported. Some things are best had after traveling across several oceans.

And don't you hate that uncle who has lived all his fifty-five years in a 3BHK MIG house across the Yamuna in a city that is another acronym, NOIDA? He tells you how 'life in America is' from that one, yes, one trip he took visiting bread factories on behalf of his company. Our bread is from the latest U.S. technology, he claims. It arrives each morning freshly baked, on the back of a cycle. There is no high-tech without the low. The neighborhood dog and cat will agree, eating U.S. technology bread soaked in *desi* milk for its supper.

And don't you hate it when people say 'to be honest...' Does that mean they weren't being honest before? To be honest with you... the traffic isn't so bad, the heat is bearable, and the pollution has improved after introducing CNG. But I won't lie (does that mean I was lying before?). I miss you every day. The muezzin's early prayer call, the chaat stall with tikkis sizzling in a giant tawa and the intentional clang of the chaatwala's spatula, I miss it all. It's too quiet here on Silicon Street. It's so quiet that I can hear the palm trees sway, my neighbor's sneeze as he drags his garbage bins in front of the driveway each week. We've said hello only twice this year.

I do the silliest things to bring you back to me: I open empty pickle jars and inhale them, I make cushion covers out of empty rice sacks that claim 'grown in the foothills' of the Himalayas, I open old letters out of which *akshath* & roli spill out along with a Goddess's blessings.

We're never good at getting to the point. One look at a jalebi, and well, you know what I mean. I've tried to tell you how much I love you, but you never hear me. You're always brushing me off your shoulder, saying *jaa re, jaa re udh jaa re panchi.*

So here it is in writing.

WHAT HAPPENS WHEN MEN NEVER ASK FOR DIRECTIONS

Shikha Malaviya

He sails west but thinks east, knocking down signs when the sun blinds his eyes, screaming Indio! as he spots a lip of land and lobes of gold. It is the ninth day and the natives smile, tanned skin-white teeth, gifting him cotton and parrots trained to chant Colombo! Colombo! night and day. On the journey back home the parrots drive him insane, squawking his name, no cloves, no silk, just the sun in his eyes and warm bodies stored in the hull in crooked lines, as royal promises burn through a magnifying glass setting all maps afire.

HOLY COW SONNET
Shikha Malaviya

If our Lady of the Holy Bovine Order could speak
She would say, India you've lost your way
She would say, where is our *Satyamev Jayate?*[1]
She'd lie on her side and offer all four teats
Give the skin off her back with a side of beef
Gau mata ki jai![2] Praise the cow that leads us astray
Come out, come out all zealots and play!
Which type of meat did the *musalman* eat?
Drag the sinner by his leather clad feet
And beat him till his last breath escapes
Become the world's largest exporter of beef
Yet ban it within your own states
Suspicion of eating steak now trumps rape
The holy cow watches quietly and weeps

[1] *Satyamev Jayate – Truth alone triumphs. An old Sanskrit saying that also is India's national motto.*

[2] *Gau mata ki jai – Hail the mother cow (in Hindi).*

BOTANY 101
(FOR INDIA'S DAUGHTERS)

Shikha Malaviya

A found poem from phrases in the BBC documentary, India's Daughter.

Course Description:
Introduction to good looking, softness performance, pleasant flower; flowers in relation to gutter and temple. Lecture/laboratory course. (3 hours worship/lecture, 3 hours gutter/lab).

Prerequisite: Birth as an Indian girl

Upon completion of this course, India's daughters will understand:
-Why a *female is just like a flower*
-Why a flower *always needs protection*
-How *if you put that flower in a gutter, it is spoilt*
-How *If you put that flower in a temple, it will be worshipped*
-Why *a man is just like a thorn*
-Why *a flower is given less milk than a thorn*
-Why *Indian society should never allow its flowers to bloom after 6:30 or 7:30 or 8:30 in the evening with any unknown* thorn
-How under *the imagination of the film culture*, a flower *might feel they can bloom for anyone*
-A flower means *immediately putting the sex in his eyes*
-How *in our culture, there is no place for a* flower
-Why *only 20% flowers are good*
-How flowers & thorns *are not equal*
-Why *housework and housekeeping is* for flowers, *not roaming in discos and bars at night, doing wrong things, wearing the wrong* petals
-How a thorn *will put his hand, insert, hit, create damage*
-Why *when being raped, a* flower *shouldn't fight back*
-How *if a flower disgraces herself,* a thorn *would put petrol on her and set her alight*

REGISTRATIONS NOW BEING ACCEPTED
ON A ROLLING BASIS

#AYLAN, OR
HOW TO TREAT REFUGEES
Madhushree Ghosh

Photo credits: Roberto Salomone
Family photo: Madhushree Ghosh

We have always told our histories in stories, our geographies in poetry. When Didi and I were young, Ma told us about her childhood, how she and her sisters would run to school before the bell rang for the classes to start. In Barisal, now Bangladesh. They ran because education was the only thing that mattered—coming first in class and reaching school early was important. Those were our bedtime stories. We were refugees once. Children of refugees are also refugees. We know through the stories that pass down to us by our parents.

* * *

Let me tell you a modern fable—a fable because there are two sides to this story. Let's start with the geography, because it's important to understand the distances, and why they needed to be crossed. In between the Balkan and Anatolian peninsulas, separating the mainlands of Greece and Turkey, lies an elongated water body, part of the Mediterranean Sea. It's called the Aegean Sea. The sea is connected to the Marmara Sea and Black Sea by the Dardanelles and Bosphorus. The Aegean Islands lie within this water, bound below by the Sea of Crete which washes up on the Greek islands of Crete and Rhodes. In 2015 September, it is this sea that Abdullah Kurdi and his family decide to cross. Eventually, the Kurdis hope to reach his sister, Tima, who has been living in Canada for two decades and who sends her brother the funds for the dangerous trip across.

The distance between Turkey and Kos is a narrow 4.5 kilometers or 2.8 miles—it is ominously calm during the summer months. But with connections with smugglers, the water taxi through the strait is expected to be an easy journey. If one has money to spare and the will to survive.

* * *

I meet Roberto Salomone in 2014. He photographs happy American writers in the idyllic Italian seaside town of Positano. Later he tells me his purpose is more than recording happiness, it is to tell stories.

Like what, Roberto, I ask him. After all, when one is in Italy, one cannot think beyond Steinbeck, wine, cappuccinos, maybe prosciutto. He smiles, his eyes shining like Baba's, my father's, used to.

My job is to be a photojournalist, he says. I've been recording the migration of immigrants throughout Europe since 2011.

Where? In Italy? The ones coming here? I ask naively, pointing across the shining ocean. I realize all the countries are so close to each other, connected by water bodies that look serene. But based on the news, the same oceans and seas turn into monsters when dinghies holding desperate families try to reach the other side. Where do they come to, Roberto? I ask again.

He says: All over, they come to all these shores and borders. They're at the Greek/Macedonian border, separated by barbed wires and antiriot police. Or in Calais, France, tents to live in while waiting at the border. Or they arrive at the island of Lesbos, searching for the gateway to a better life.

It reminds me, as most such conversations do, of where I come from. India. Or, to be precise, where my parents are from—what was called East Pakistan. And now Bangladesh. I wasn't born there, but in postindependence India. Children of refugees.

* * *

My elder sister, Didi, and I have been told that we're refugees ever since we could comprehend short sentences. If Ma didn't say so, it would be Baba. Refugees of war, and displacement. Refugees of religion, even though Baba never prayed, though he attended all the *pujo* ceremonies and said he did so for the food. Ma's whispered incantations were meant for her personal god and not for us to hear. More importantly, they told us tales of a life much better than the one they moved to, after Partition. Stories of how wonderful what's now Bangladesh-was. The cauliflowers were larger than footballs, roses were redder than blood, food was plentiful, the air was clean. That was Baba's interpretation of Bangladesh—his land before he walked from there to India. With his cousins, siblings and widowed mother into West Bengal, the land of Bengalis.

In 1947, the British colonizers made a strategic exit move—their policy of divide and conquer applied even after they had completely destroyed the Indian economy and people. They divided Indians into

India and Pakistan. In fact, Pakistan was divided into two sections. One near Afghanistan, then called West Pakistan, and one near the state of West Bengal, called East Pakistan (now Bangladesh). Divided on the basis of religion. Hindus in India. Muslims in Pakistan. Baba didn't have a choice but to move where Hindus weren't a minority. Even though he didn't believe in religious ceremonies but loved the food. He didn't have a choice.

Every time Baba told Didi and me stories of what happened, there were embellishments, some lies, some exaggerations and mostly, it was an adventure. Every time he started with a *bujhli to*, which in English roughly translates to "so, get this." He started all his childhood stories with a *bujhli to*.

Like life was meant to be this uncertain, this exciting, this full of hope.

Bujhli to, he said: Once, we were so rich that we didn't know the value of money.

What does that even mean?

His eyes twinkling behind his glasses, Baba and I sat in the vegetable garden next to the kitchen, 1977, I a seven-year-old, he, an older father. Digging into the Delhi soil with his bare hands, he pulled out a small potato and rubbed the dirt away.

He continued, as if the soil in his hands had made him fall into a trance: We didn't know if gold was more valuable than silver. If silver was more valuable than copper.

So . . . so what happened then? I asked him, taking each small potato he handed.

Well, we had to move. And quickly. My own Baba died when I was four, so it was us brothers and sisters and Ma. Had to leave that house, Rumjhum—it was so big that when the photographer came to take our picture, he couldn't fit the home in one frame. And then—

Baba, what happened with the silver and gold and all?

Oh, yes, he said, back to the story and digging out more potatoes: We thought we could sell the bigger things for better prices. All the copper vessels, plates, jars, tureens. Ma gave the silver away—Muslims might like it better. We asked a family to take care of the house while we went to Bengal. It was to be for a few days, months at most.

Ah. And then?

Then when we tried to sell the vessels, copper didn't bring much money in—if we had gold, we could get more. Even silver. But we had nothing.

Didi called us from the sliding kitchen door: Ma said, Lunch is ready, come.

So, then . . . Baba? I asked him, ignoring her: So, Baba, with no money, what did you do?

Baba put the potatoes in the plastic *tokri* bowl and pulled the garden hose to wash his hands. He continued: Rumjhum, you do many things to put rice in the bellies of your sisters.

Why rice?

Bhaat? That's a metaphor, Rumjhum—rice and food are the same for us Bengalis. Your favorite uncle, your Shonajethu, and I, we chased the cows in North Bengal when we moved there from our Dhaka home.

Why, Baba?

They'd run. And then poop out of fear.

So?

So we'd take the poop, mix it with dry grass stalks and make cow dung patties—dried it in the sun against the outside walls of our place. Every day, after school. He was a good student, and I was a good athlete.

He ran his thick fingers over the potatoes as if examining them, but really, I knew his mind was back in North Bengal, where the weather was cool and the Kanchenjunga mountain rose in the north, majestic in the mornings.

Looking up, Baba said: Isn't it funny? We ran after gold, silver and copper, and finally, what fed us was cow poop. Cow dung patties. Who would have known that when we were landowners in Dhaka?

We walked back to the door, his hand on my head, my arms tired from holding the basket filled with potatoes.

Baba's voice was uncharacteristically soft as he remembered: We sold the patties for a few annas, to feed the family. Those worthless copper vessels! We carried them all the way from Dhaka. But we didn't know. We'd never had to worry about money as long as my father was alive.

Baba stopped me, both of us in front of the door: You're lucky to have a father. It's hard to make decisions without the hand of a Baba on your head.

* * *

A father's dream is what pushed the Kurdis to make the dangerous water journey toward Greece. A father's dream to give his children an education he never could have. News reporters told conflicting stories, trying to humanize and then dehumanize their third attempt to escape Turkey. But one thing was for certain. Abdullah Kurdi, a forty-year-old Syrian, had been living with his wife, Rehana, and their two children, five-year-old Galib and three-year-old Alan (misrepresented by the media as Aylan in September 2015) in Turkey. When they lived in Damascus, Syria, Abdullah worked as a barber, then moved to Kobani, near his wife's family, in 2010. But ISIL had a stronghold over that Syrian region, bombing incessantly, killing Abdullah's relatives, and severely injuring his father-in-law. The Kurdis fled from Kobani, to Suruc, Turkey, thirty miles from the Syrian border. Abdullah worked as a laborer, making ends meet. It wasn't enough. Next, the Kurdis moved to Istanbul, in search of stability, both financial and regional.

"The migrant crisis" is what his story is called. A label that helped justify why Abdullah decided, after three years of relative peace in Turkey, to make the move to the EU.

Analysts scolded in opinion pieces, He was fine in Turkey. He was there for three years. Why make that dangerous trip now? With the children too. He wasn't in Syria. He's not really a refugee. He was a careless father, losing his sons to such a foolish endeavor, an ill-thought-out escapade.

Abdullah, when asked, said what a father would say, I wanted my children to be treated like human beings.

* * *

Roberto tells me stories of immigrants in tents feeding him when he was stranded in Calais, of men giving him shelter from the rains in Lesbos. The humans are dehumanized when labeled as a "crisis."

From Canada, Abdullah Kurdi's hairdresser sister, Tima, paid 2,900 pounds for the Kurdis' safe passage. Skeptics later wondered, if Abdullah had thousands of dollars saved in his bank account, sent by his sister, why did he need to make that dangerous trip? Why now?

* * *

Ma was a middle schooler when Muslims in her Barisal neighborhood in now Bangladesh started behaving suspiciously around her and her sisters. Nothing big, or drastic. Just a whisper here, a soft giggle stifled around the corner, a step away to cross the road to avoid her, a Hindu. Ma's grandfather was a highly regarded principal of a high school in Barisal. Even after we moved to Chittaranjan Park, a middle-class neighborhood in South Delhi in 1976, middle-aged Bengalis, wearing thick glasses and the seventies outfits of bell-bottoms and paisley shirts, would stop her asking, are you Bhubaneshwar Ghosh Dastidar's granddaughter?

Ma would nod, smiling the beaming smile she had only when pride of her lineage shone through her heart.

When Partition of India took place in 1947, the politicians fulfilled their ambitions. Nehru got India, Jinnah got Pakistan and Gandhi remained the beloved and benevolent negotiator. While this satisfied the politicians, millions were uprooted to separate Indians via religion. Hindus in the center and Muslims sandwiching the Hindus between East and West Pakistan.

In the seventies, whenever I watched the news about floods or famine in Bangladesh on TV, or news on other South Asian natural disasters, or global war-torn refugees fleeing bombings, I asked Ma about the long line of refugees walking miles to safety. Each person on the black-and-white screen had determined eyes, holding their babies, balancing their belongings on their head, heading in snaking lines out of wherever they came from. Refugees moving from one village to the next, some not comprehending that they were leaving home forever, some not knowing where India ended and Pakistan began.

I asked Ma: Why do they all carry big *potlees* of clothes? Look, these men—carrying rope-braided cots on their heads? It doesn't make sense if you're running for your lives, no?

No, she said, it makes sense. You carry what you think you will need in your new life. You carry hope in the *potlees*, the bedsheet is what you wrap your best clothes and jewelry in, which you'll sell to start a new life. When you find a place that you can call home, you want to put your bed there. To sleep free. That's why they carried cots.

And you? Did you?

We were in her bedroom, it was near evening. As always, Ma was combing her hair so she would be presentable before Baba returned from work.

Well, Ma, did you carry a cot too?

She must have been in her late thirties, I realize now. Ma looked at me, then turned away, blinking back tears. Usually when Ma cried, which was often, Didi and I sat silently on her bed till she was done. We didn't know how else to handle emotional displays, and giving hugs wasn't taught in the Ghosh family, but how to stay silent was.

But this time, Ma turned to us from the mirror, placing her thick comb on the table in front of her. She ran her work-worn fingers through her jet-black hair: We knew even before that year started that we were going to have to run.

What do you mean, "run"?

Flee. The Muslims didn't want us there. They said it was theirs. My grandfather knew our schooling would be disrupted, and he was a stickler about that. Without an education, we were nothing.

Didi added: So that's why you beat us to submission every day? To be educated?

Ma glared at her, her fingers stalled in her hair: Have I ever beaten you, eh?

Didi shook her head, then giggled to deflect Ma's wrath.

I pulled at Ma's sari: So, *bolo*, what happened then?

Well, what happened was that we needed money. My Thakurda was well liked. But being well liked didn't mean he had money. We had to figure out how to save every paisa, every anna, so we could then take the train out of Barisal to Kolkata. The train was to go through Khulna to Howrah station in Kolkata. About 128 miles. We had to leave our friends and cousins, who were going to other towns. The house. Our dolls. Everything.

Oh, I said, since I couldn't comprehend what that meant—losing everything, including Ma's dolls.

Ma picked up her comb, roughly untangling her waist-length braid, she said: But I was my grandfather's favorite. I was.

Really, Ma? How did you know? I questioned her conviction.

Oh, when he tutored the neighborhood children and if they got their algebra wrong, he would call for me, Sila, Sila, come, show them how it's done.

And you did.

Yes, I did, Ma said. She stared at her braid as if looking for answers, her eyes moist again. She cleared her throat and continued: You know when you are someone's favorite, you know what you do?

No, what do you do?

You make sure you please them. You make sure they are happy. At any cost. Get it?

Yes, Ma.

So that's what I did.

You mean, you did algebra?

Na re, when we knew we had leave mid-term, everyone was fleeing. Everyone was looking to sell something, anything. That money would take the family to a new life. It was important. So, even before the term started, I decided not to mark my textbooks. No pencil mark, no dog-ears, they were brand new, brand new.

Really?

Pushing her braid away, Ma removed the sari she'd worn while cooking that day. Turning to me, she pulled a starched blue cotton sari she'd placed on the bed. With rapid movements, she expertly pleated the front and pulled the sari *pallu* over her blouse. As an afterthought, she reached out to the dresser and stuck a *bindi* on her forehead. She didn't look at her face, or the soft wrinkles permanently now etched on her forehead.

Yes, Rumjhum, she answered me finally. When the time came, I gave those books to Thakurda—and he blessed me when he saw we would get more money from them than from the books of all my sisters and brothers combined. Because I was his favorite. So I knew what mattered to him then.

Did the money help? What did you buy with it?

Ma walked away from us, shooing us to follow her to the living room: We never asked about money, Rumjhum. That's low class. They sold our books, and that gave us the money to leave Bangladesh. Sometimes, that's what we need to do as children. Follow.

* * *

Later, I ask Roberto if money was the need, the urgency. No, he writes back, people want a life. Any life is better for their children than the one they leave behind. It's more than money. You have to treat refugees right. They are human. Treat them as such.

* * *

In 2015, we learn more about the three-year-old Syrian son of Abdullah Kurdi. Alan, or #aylan as he was known, was born in Kobani, and his brother, Galib, may have been born in Kobani as well, but the information is murky. In the summer of 2015, Abdullah's sister, Tima, contacted the smugglers in Turkey and sent the money. Rehana, his wife, spoke with Tima, worrying that she didn't know how to swim, so what if something happened to the boys, how would she rescue them? Typical worries of a mother. Abdullah's father spoke to Tima from Syria, asking her to tell Abdullah not to leave Turkey. This was, after all, their third attempt to flee Turkey. Two previous times, they were caught by the coast guards and returned back to Turkey. This time, Abdullah was determined—he needed to do this for his sons, his family—an education for the boys.

On September 2, 2015, Abdullah and his family started out of Turkey from Bodrum, a seaside town near the Aegean Sea. In the daytime, the town was sleepy, with tourists, idyllic boats, and soft music. In the night, the seashore transformed into a ragtag military operation of dinghies, boats, inadequate life jackets strapped on dazed people, *potlees* of their precious belongings, scraps of money and jewelry in their pockets sewn shut.

Rehana dressed her younger boy in an outfit in which he would be proud to land in the EU—a red shirt, blue shorts, and laced shoes with freshly combed brown hair. She swallowed her fear of the sea and the fact that she didn't know how to swim, taking her boys' hands. The island of Kos, less than three miles from Turkey, with its blinking lights tantalized the Kurdis of a life out of here.

There were two boats. Their boat could hold eight. There were sixteen people on their boat that night. They were all Syrians according to one news report. Then a few Iraqis were said to be in this group. Maybe Eritreans, and other people facing religious, economic or war persecution and a combination of all of that. Most didn't know how to swim. Many held their children's hands. The plan, the only plan, was to reach Kos. After that, life was to be better.

The boat was to make a five-minute trip across the three miles and take the Kurdis to Kos. Within half a mile from Bodrum, the engine sputtered, stalling in the choppy waves. The women clung to their children, screaming. The men held onto the side, grabbing their life jackets, asking the captain, Do something, help, do something.

* * *

This is when fables or tales become murky. Here is version one. According to Abdullah Kurdi, this is what happened. The captain of the boat allegedly called his accomplice who was in the other boat to rescue him. He jumped off and left the refugees to fend for themselves. In the middle of the Aegean Sea, half a mile from Turkish shores and two miles from the EU, Abdullah took over, trying to navigate the fifteen-foot boat in the dark, heading toward the twinkling lights of Kos. In the chaos, his wife and children stayed by him, close, fearful. Next to them, an Iraqi woman held her two sons, all screaming in fear.

The boat hit wave after wave, tilting ominously. In the dark, when it capsized, the sixteen refugees, migrants, were flung into the sea, grabbing anything in the dark to stay afloat.

Abdullah held onto his family, his wife, Galib and Alan. Galib asked Abdullah, in the dark, in the water, he asked, Baba, did you bring us here to die? Or so Abdullah said later. Alan clung to him, calling him, Baba, Baba, the only words he knew. Abdullah couldn't hold onto his family anymore.

Abdullah let his firstborn go first. Galib was dead already, he knew. His wife was with Alan, floating, trying to stay afloat. Abdullah headed to their direction, trying to reach them as fast as he could. But when he got to Alan, the three-year-old boy's face was quiet, eyes closed. Abdullah tried to wake him up, but he knew this child, too, was gone. In a panic, Abdullah looked for his wife. He spotted her, floating in the distance, dead.

* * *

For three hours, Abdullah treaded water, his dead family drifting away from him. This was his third attempt to give his family a better life. Third attempt, a failure again. This time it was worse.

Early next morning, Mehmet Ciplak, a Turkish crimes officer, found a little boy, who reminded him of his own six-year-old son, a little boy, facedown, washed ashore onto Bodrum's soft, sandy beach. The boy was still wearing his red shirt and dark-blue shorts—dressed for an outing.

* * *

Here is the second version of the same story. An Iraqi woman with her family, husband, two sons and a daughter were in the same boat. Her two sons drowned in the strait as Galib and Alan. According to the Iraqi woman, Abdullah Kurdi was one of the smugglers getting them to Kos. In fact, he was at the wheel.

Journalists asked why she boarded the boat. His family was with him, she said, so I felt safe—if the smuggler brings his own children to cross the seas, it must be safe, yes? When they fell in the water, he swam to the Iraqi woman, saying: Please don't incriminate me, I am a refugee, just like you. I lost my family now. So, don't tell them I'm a smuggler, please.

* * *

In 1947, refugees in Pakistan and India escaped religious persecution. Some Hindus adamantly stayed back in Pakistan and some Muslims refused to leave India, saying this was their homeland. Decisions of love for one's motherland haunt later generations. But when refugees flee to different countries, they still carry their decisions with them. Baba could never adjust to India, even though we ate, spoke and practiced the same customs. Ma never adjusted to the uncouth North Indians for whom education was a secondary option. Life was always better in the country they left behind.

In 2015, the persecution is religious, it's economic and it's tribal. As Roberto says, it doesn't matter what persecution refugees flee from. The fact is life isn't good from where they come from, in fact, it's so bad that anything, even a dangerous three-mile sea journey, is better than life back home. If we are silent, then we are dehumanizing refugees. #aylan becomes a hashtag. The little boy in blue shorts and red shirt. A label. A "migrant crisis."

In February 2015, two alleged smugglers, Muwafaka al-Abash and Asem al-Farhad, were presented in a Bodrum Turkish criminal court facing charges of smuggling and manslaughter, responsible for the death of the Kurdi family and two other refugees. Abdullah Kurdi was tried in absentia but all charges were mysteriously dropped. His life is over as his family is gone, Abdullah mourned. A barber in Damascus, Syria, then a laborer in Turkey, Abdullah is a man with a primary school education and now without a family. He has vowed to clear his name.

* * *

In Roberto's words, people have been escaping wars, famines and dictators for centuries. It's the freedom of movement. Fear of the "other" is what has changed now. The world is scared and doesn't want to know the "other." Fear is such a powerful weapon; it creates barriers in our minds.

* * *

The neighborhood we settled in New Delhi was for Bengalis. All those who were displaced from East Pakistan, now Bangladesh. For the longest while it was called EPDP Colony, or East Pakistan Displaced Persons Colony. Once middle-class Bengalis moved in, it was gentrified and turned into Chittaranjan Park, a neighborhood combining the name of a Bengali freedom fighter with a park. As if that would change the fact that the settlers there were refugees.

Ma and Baba were allotted a small plot of land in the nineties, after many court appeals, many meetings with politicians, influential leaders, and many protest marches to the government offices in Delhi. It was part of a small plot of land allotted to 200 refugees of 1947, across the upper-middle-class homes, separated by two main roads. This land allotment to the "remaining refugees of 1947" was called Pocket 40. A parcel of land, titled 40, for no reason but that the land engineer lacked imagination and naming it after another freedom fighter wasn't one of his priorities.

Across Pocket 40, was the Punjabi refugee colony, called Kalkaji—lower-middle-class neighborhood, refugees from what was then West Pakistan, North Indians with different sensibilities, food habits, religious customs and festivals. Baba and Ma learnt to speak broken Hindi, mandatory in New Delhi. Didi and I grew up speaking many languages fluently, as is the norm in a metropolitan city.

In 1992, when we moved to Pocket 40, Baba's green thumb qualities passed onto his daughters, more to my sister than me. We worked with the architect to build us a first-floor lawn, digging into the verandah area, concrete waterproofing, so we could have a lawn up in the sky.

For three days the soil was soaked in water, and grass sod placed over. Within twenty-four hours, sparrows flew in, then called their friends, eating the fresh seeds clean off the soil.

Didi decided we needed to grow something that birds wouldn't be attracted to, and still look pretty. Mustard seeds, she decided with Baba's determination. Sparrows hate them, and they'll cover the soil quickly.

With Ma yelling behind us to stop us from finishing all her spices, we stole her mustard seeds bottle from the kitchen. Didi and I threw the seeds liberally all over the terrace floor now soft with fertilizer and soil.

Within a week, the thin stalks peeked out from the soil in the terrace lawn. Neighbors around us walked by our house, pointing at our floor and the greenery. Look, those are the girls who're growing flowers in a lawn on the first floor. A terrace garden!

Didi and I beamed just like Ma would if we talked about her grandfather.

One Saturday, Baba returned from work early. The mustard seeds had blossomed into tall plants with sunny yellow flowers. Didi sat among them, her hair cut short in a stylish bob and wearing a brown *salwar kameez*. She smiled when I took her photo on a secondhand Russian-make camera Baba had given us that winter. Behind me, Baba inhaled the air, and sighed: Ah, feels like home.

* * *

Abdullah Kurdi is considered the human face representing the "migrant crisis." He is not a refugee, but a migrant who is desperate, taking desperate measures due to economic and government restrictions. Abdullah is happiest around children, his sister, Tima, says. He misses his boys terribly. Shortly after the #aylan photograph was plastered all over the world, the Turkish President offered him citizenship. Then Barzani, the Kurdish Regional Government prime minister, invited Abdullah to visit Iraqi Kurds in a PR move. The Iraqi and Syrian Kurds fight over him, claiming him and his tragic story as theirs.

Barzani promises to set up a charity so Abdullah can start a hospital in Alan's name. Abdullah, who has lost his family, with little education is helpless in understanding that he's a political pawn.

Tima offers: Neither he nor I speak Kurdish. We left for a better life. Now we're made to be something we are not.

In the days following the funeral, Abdullah spends his time looking at his phone, searching for what people around the world are saying about him and his dead son. His sister worries for his mental health. Canada has extended an invitation again for them to send Abdullah's papers again. The biggest curse is when a father buries his child.

* * *

Roberto says that now that Greece has started sending refugees back to Turkey, more of them will try to cross the treacherous waters in the dark. Things will only get worse.

* * *

 It's been almost four decades since Baba and I dug out potatoes from the first house we rented in Chittaranjan Park. My parents are long gone. Didi and I now live thousands of miles away, in a country that feels like home and looks nothing like it. The terrace garden has been leveled and slate slabs placed over the concrete. It looks clean, pretty, with flower pots that Baba tended to after we left for America. Still alive, still watered by caretakers. As their children, we still do what we were taught. Sometimes, we don't question, we follow our elders. ∎

UNTAMED TEA AND DANGEROUS CHOCOLATE
Roshni Rustomji-Kerns

Throughout her life, at least until she was sixty-eight years old, Sofía Cruz, known to everyone in Oaxaca as Maestra Sofía, had believed staunchly in the extraordinary healing powers of infusions, misnamed *teas*. *Té de tila, té de manzanilla, té de yerba poleo, té de yerba santa, té de yerbabuena, té de ruda, té de malabar, té de jengibre*. Teas for headaches, stomachaches, PMS (cramps, bloating and/or the grumps), bleedings (internal and external), nervous conditions (mental or otherwise), hangovers, arthritis, dark moods, hot flashes, an excess of energy, a loss of faith, an overabundance of religious fervor—for any and all ailments. Herbs, seeds, leaves, dried twigs and flowers filled the large glass jars lined up against the back wall of Maestra's small shop at the corner of Alianza and Republic. The shop proclaimed its name as Sin Nombre. The dry earth smells of the herbs combined with the copal burning in a brazier behind the counter drifted out of the nameless shop and traveled up Calle Alianza until it got lost somewhere among the garbage bin smells of rotting food from the restaurant below my apartment.

Maestra Sofía did carry a couple of cartons of small bags of different brands of commercially packaged black teas but she never recommended black tea to her customers and wouldn't drink it herself. And then, at the age of sixty-eight Maestra became a devotee of strong, hot, black tea because of me, Jahanara Mody, born long ago in Karachi, educated here and there, reading, listening to music, living and dying in Oaxaca, Mexico.

Maestra Sofía still believed in the healing properties of the herbal teas she sold in her shop but she declared that the strong black tea with milk, sugar and a touch of ginger that I served her the first time she visited me tasted much better and was definitely more powerful than the nonblack teas she had enjoyed since she was a child. She called it *té de Buddhi indómita* and sometimes *té de sabiduría indómita* because she said that black tea carried echoes of ancient wisdom from Asia. Wisdom that could never be dominated, tamed or its power diluted by anyone! Maestra Sofía was not only familiar with Confucius but had also read some of the Upanishads and a shorter version of the Ramayana. She said, "*Buddhi indómita como Hanuman.*" I really don't know if the type of tea I had introduced to Maestra Sofía really imparted any kind of wisdom but I liked the name, especially the *Buddhi* part.

Before I was born, my parents had decided that if I were to be a girl, they would name me Jahanara: "a bright ornament of the world." And so I was named Jahanara. But as soon as my paternal grandmother, Bapaiji, laid eyes on me in the lying-in hospital in Karachi, she announced that she doubted that I would grow into any kind of an ornament of the world. She decided that my scrunched-up face marked with a network of faint lines and surrounded by meager hair—"No one in the Mody family has ever arrived into this world with such a paucity of hair!"—foretold my future. I was born an old woman. Hopefully a wise old woman but she wasn't sure about that. She called me Buddhi. The meager hair and the faint lines on my face have followed me through life.

When my colleagues in Boston couldn't twist their tongues with enough agility, breathe the right breaths through Jahanara, I offered them Buddhi. Someone invariably asked, "Buddha? Like the God?" And others would vary it with, "Like Boodah? The fat, laughing man?" And again with the twisting of tongues and errant aspirations I first became Boodie and was then transformed into Buddy in the United States of America. When I introduced myself to Maestra Sofía as Buddy, she looked at me with confusion. She said the only Buddy she had heard of was President Clinton's dog. I offered her Buddhi; she recognized the word and the tea I introduced to her became Buddhi Tea with the addition of *untamed*.

I confessed to Maestra Sofía that I had disliked tea until I was seven years old. I started liking tea after my participation in what my Bapaiji later described as one of her *women-have-to-save-women-with-special-strategies-when-faced-with-bloody-insane-male-political-rampages.*

It was the first week of August 1947 and I was barely seven years old. The adults had finished their afternoon tea ritual and I had drunk my glass of hot, sweetened milk when Bapaiji asked me to fetch the extra-large white tablecloth from the cupboard, the much-darned and patched tablecloth. Darned and patched with such skill by my mother and Bapaiji that it looked nearly as new as when Bapaiji had received it as a wedding gift from her aunt. The tablecloth was used only for special occasions. Bapaiji's birthday, Navroze or when my father invited his colleagues from work for a Sunday *dhan-saak* lunch once every two years. As far as I knew, no celebration had been planned for that evening.

I brought the tablecloth to Bapaiji.

After spreading the tablecloth across the table, she asked me to help her carry four cups and saucers, the teapot with the picture of King George, the milk jug, the sugar bowl and a couple of plates from the kitchen to the table. All the dishes except the sugar bowl had just been washed by Dossamai, the lady who came to our house twice a day to sweep the floor and to wash the pots, pans and dishes. After instructing me to set the table as if tea were to be served soon, Bapaiji returned to the kitchen. I could hear her speaking to Dossamai in urgent whispers and wondered if she was warning Dossamai—once again—about paying attention to the policemen on the streets of Karachi and not to worry if she couldn't come to the house very early in the morning.

Two days earlier a policeman in his red turban and khaki uniform, his beard carefully contained within a net casing, had brought Dossamai to the door. It was 5:30 a.m. When my mother went to open the door for Dossamai, she was surprised to see the policeman with Dossamai. Dossamai, her sari already partially tucked up in preparation for her work, walked past the policeman and into the house completely unperturbed, swinging the broom she always carried with her. The policeman was definitely disturbed and started speaking before my mother could ask any questions. "Baiji, please take care of this old woman. I tried to explain to her that there is a curfew. No one must be out in the streets from nine at night to six in the morning. When I tried to take her home she started to beat me with her broom."

It was a ferocious broom. A thick, bristling collection of stiff, dried rushes nearly three feet long tied together at one end with twine. The kind of broom that would defy the witches of Salem or anywhere else in the world to use it as a mere form of transportation.

When the policeman started to leave the house, Dossamai reappeared at the door, grabbed his shirt, turned him around and brandished the broom in his face. "I am nearly eighty years old and have worked since I was fifteen years old. I have never been late for work. I will never be late for work."

The policeman and my mother tried to explain the reason for the curfew. They reminded Dossamai of the violence threatening the city. They spoke of the battle for independence and the civil war being fought simultaneously across the land. Dossamai muttered that as far as she was concerned the world had gone insane. Hadn't her one and only relative, her orphaned nephew whom she had raised since he was five years old, got caught up in all this? He had converted to Islam because he didn't want to leave Karachi. "Bhagvan, Allah, Jesus Christ-God, Khuda what does it matter? All are the same. Going from one religion to another? What is all that about? One is born what one is born. One can't change that just because people give old places new names." But all this insanity was not going to stop her from coming to work on time.

I was still thinking about the curfew-broom incident when Bapaiji called from the kitchen. This time she wanted me to butter some slices of bread, arrange them on a plate, place the plate on the table draped with the special tablecloth and sit myself on the right-hand side of the head of the table. "Buddhi, be sure that you can be seen from the front door. Start eating one of the slices of bread and pick up the cup as if you are drinking tea. I know, there is only air in the cup but sip. Do not slurp. Act like a grown-up lady."

I had just taken a tiny bite of the bread and was lifting my teacup in what I considered a ladylike manner when I saw a strange sight from the corner of my left eye. Bapaiji was walking out of the kitchen and into the dining room. She was walking like a very, very old lady. Very slowly and with hesitation. She was hiding Dossamai behind her. As soon as Bapaiji sat down in her chair, Dossamai crouched down and scooted under the table. The tablecloth hid her very well.

I was wondering why we were drinking air tea when we heard the noise of a crowd coming down the street, closer and closer to our house. I had heard slogans and shouts in the distance a few times in the past month but never so loudly and clearly as at that moment. Bapaiji picked up the teacup and started sipping. I noticed that her hand was shaking. She put down the cup, picked up the plate of bread slices, held it under the table and whispered to Dossamai to take the food and tie it up within the end of her sari. She put the empty plate back on the table and I nearly dropped my cup. More buttered bread had appeared immediately on the plate. Bapaiji again passed the food down to Dossamai and put the empty plate on the table. Three slices of buttered bread appeared again on the plate. I had heard my parents talk about Bapaiji's *talent*. According to them, Bapaiji never wasted anything and indeed when she cooked, the ingredients—rice, spices, dals, sugar, vegetables, even meat and fish—always seemed to multiply in sufficient amounts to feed the families or anyone in the neighborhood, in their houses or begging on the street, whomever needed food. This was the first time I had seen Bapaiji's *talent* in action.

The crowd reached the door. One of the men knocked. Bapaiji got up and went to the door. I could hear her greeting Dossamai's nephew and inviting him to come in. The rest of the men stayed in the street. Dossamai clutched my legs as they dangled under the tablecloth and I could feel her trembling.

The man told us very politely that he and his friends didn't wish to harm anyone. He just wanted to take Dossamai with him so she could also become a Mussalman and then the two of them could continue living in peace in Karachi.

Bapaiji, who had told me that a Jarthoshti never told a lie, told a lie. Well, a sort of a lie. She said to the nephew, "Look around. You can go to any of the rooms you want to. Do you see Dossamai? How can you take her away when you can't see her?" She then sat down at her place at the table and offered him the plate of bread and butter. He took a slice and wandered around the two bedrooms, the bathroom and the kitchen and came back to the dining room. He agreed that he couldn't see Dossamai anywhere and then he bent down and touched the floor near Bapaiji's feet and asked for her blessings. She touched his head and blessed him with a long and happy life, told him that he would be always welcome in our house, got up and took him to the door. He joined the crowd and they went off. Bapaiji said, "Ahura Mazda be thanked for making those *Ungrezees* invent tablecloths!" She told Dossamai to remain hidden under the table.

Bapaiji then brought a tumbler of water and asked me to go under the table to give it to Dossamai and to stay with her until my father could take her away to some of his friends who were going to New Delhi, which was to be the capital of independent India. They had agreed to take Dossamai with them.

We did not see Dossamai again after that night when she crawled out from under the table and went off with my father.

I did not tell anyone about what had happened that evening until many years later when I served tea to Maestra Sofia one Sunday afternoon in my apartment in Oaxaca, Mexico.

At the end of the story, Maestra Sofia put down her cup of hot black tea, thought for a few minutes, looked out at the jacaranda tree in front of my window and asked, "Is this the type of tea your grandmother used to drink when she drank real not air tea?" When I said that it was the same kind of tea, Maestra nodded her head and said, "Yes, this is *té* de Buddhi. Wisdom that cannot be tamed, put into categories, into books, into boring lectures."

The partaking and the naming of the tea was two weeks after Maestra Sofia and I had met in her store. During my first visit to Sin Nombre we had exchanged stories about chocolate.

It was late afternoon in March and the heat had settled in for the summer when I had entered Maestra's shop to buy some of her highly praised, homemade, individually wrapped, roughly shaped chunks of dark-brown chocolate speckled with sugar and cinnamon. Chocolate one could break into edible pieces or melt into water or milk to be whipped up into a drink. Chocolate that could be used for pleasure or for healing. After I picked up some of the packets of chocolate, I told Maestra Sofía that I had heard that the chocolate one bought in Sin Nombre was the best in Oaxaca. Maestra agreed. I laughed.

As I reached into my bag to pay for the chocolate, I mentioned that I had spent the afternoon reading about the extraordinary chocolate-making skill possessed by Catarina de San Juan, the pious and virtuous visionary and healer of Puebla. A skill that the citizens of seventeenth-century Puebla exploited even when the aged Catarina, partially blind and paralyzed throughout the left side of her body, was facing death. A skill that was profitable to the Poblanos. In whatever quantity they brought the ingredients to Catarina—the chocolate, the sugar, the cinnamon, the almonds, definitely some vanilla, very often some dried, dark-red chilies—to be made into chocolate that could be eaten, drunk or cooked, the quantities increased under the miraculous healing hands of the pious woman who spoke to Jesus, the Virgin and the saints while darning stockings and preparing chocolate. The final product she handed over to her clients far exceeded their expectations. Not only in quantity but also in quality. Some of her clients may have praised her. But many of them used her services while despising her as a slave-servant who was born a heathen with a heathen name, Mirrha, in the heathen land, India, abducted when still a young girl by Portuguese pirates and sold as a slave in Acapulco. No one paid the woman living and dying in poverty extra money for the extra chocolate they received.

Maestra Sofía said, "Yes, Catarina de San Juan. I know about her. Yes, chocolate. History. Stories. And what about the fate of that Bishop of Chiapas at the hands of some of the highborn ladies of his congregation? It happened about the same time as Catarina was being buried in Puebla."

According to Maestra Sofía, the late seventeenth-century Bishop of Chiapas had forbidden the presence of all the paraphernalia for making hot chocolate in his church. The braziers, the chocolate, the mixing tools, the cups, all of these used to be carried into the church by the ladies' servants and slaves in order to make hot, frothy chocolate for their mistresses. Without this exotic, new drink, the ladies felt that they could not survive the familiar old-world rituals in this strange new land of delicious chocolate and elusive gold.

Maestra Sofía assured me that "those ladies knew that the bishop knew that chocolate was supposedly an aphrodisiac. A product put here in this strange land as temptation in order to lead to damnation of those who came from civilized Christian countries. I don't know if the ladies believed this but the bishop seemed to have believed it. He wanted no secularly aroused ladies in his congregation. Or maybe the preparation and the drinking of the chocolate interfered with his delivery and the ladies' appreciation of his sermons. The bishop forbade chocolate. At least in the church. So the ladies took their revenge and made room for a new bishop.

"One of the ladies, supposedly the most pious of them all, graciously invited the offending bishop for a cup of afternoon chocolate at her home that was quite far from the church. She offered him a cup of chocolate that she had poisoned with the help and blessings of the other ladies. It was done with such finesse and skill that no one could prove the lady's guilt." But rumors about the cause of the bishop's death, according to Maestra Sofia, persist to this day throughout Latin America. Rumors about his death and of course questions and conjectures regarding the bishop's willingness to drink a cup of aphrodisiac chocolate with the ladies one hot afternoon in a land of chillies, chocolate, vanilla and gold.

While Maestra Sofia was telling me about the Bishop of Chiapas's fate, she served at least two other customers. They stopped to listen to her and went off, shaking their heads—either in dismay or disbelief—at the end of the story.

* * *

Maestra Sofia offered me a chair behind the counter and asked me questions. Who was I? From where? Did they have good Mexican chocolates in Karachi? I told her that I didn't think we had Mexican chocolates in Karachi, but chocolates did exist where I grew up. Expensive. British. She didn't seem impressed.

I thought it was time for me to offer her a story in friendship. A story about chocolate.

It took place about six weeks after the Dossamai and tea incident, October 1947, a month after the birth of Pakistan. My father and I were coming home from Thackery's Bookshop in Karachi when we saw a man and his daughter huddled under the lamp on the sidewalk in front of our house. I had seen them earlier among the refugees from India trying to find any kind of shelter in this new capital city of the new country. The little girl looked very tired and was crying for her mother. When we told Bapaiji about them, she invited them into the house. My mother gave them food. The girl would eat nothing. She looked at everyone with eyes that were dazed and pleading. All she would say was, "Where is my *ammi?*" The man whispered to Bapaiji, "Her mother is dead. Killed. She saw it all." Bapaiji started praying softly, went to the cabinet where she kept her prayer books, opened it, put her hand inside and drew out a couple of bars of dark, bittersweet chocolate. English chocolates. I knew very well that the chocolate hadn't been there earlier because I kept my schoolbooks in the same cabinet. But after what I had seen Bapaiji do a few months before, on the evening when we hid Dossamai under the dining table, I wasn't overly surprised. Bapaiji sat the little girl on her lap and started feeding her some of the chocolate. She said that chocolates, religion and politics were all mixed together in her mind.

As Bapaiji lulled the little girl to sleep in her lap, she reminisced. "My parents used to send me to a lady from England who lived far from our house. I went for my classes twice every week. They wanted me to learn English. As one of my rather timid and not very intelligent aunties used to say, 'The English—they are so clever! Even their little children speak English!' My English teacher was very strict. She never smiled. She was a good teacher but she always gave me strange presents when I had done well at my lessons. Pictures of Jesus Christ as a baby, as a young man, as a man dying on a cross. She also gave me pictures of British kings and queens and princes and princesses. After a year of tutoring me, she decided to return to what she called her 'civilized home.' At the end of my last class she gave me a big box of chocolates, hugged me and began to cry. 'How sad,' she said. 'How very, very sad. You are such a sweet girl. You are so intelligent. But oh my, oh my, after you are dead you will burn in hell for all eternity because you are still a heathen. All those cards and pictures I sent with you to your home. Nothing happened. I will pray for you. You poor, poor child.' I thanked my teacher for the chocolates. She asked me to thank her for her prayers and I did so. The chocolates may have been delicious."

Having told our introductory stories—murder by chocolate, comfort through chocolate, the political religion of chocolate—I said, "I had forgotten my grandmother's story until I read about Catarina de San Juan and chocolate today."

Maestra Sofía said, "I can tell you all kinds of stories about Catarina de San Juan. Stories that you won't find in any of the books you are reading. Family stories. I am the only living descendant of the son Catarina's husband, the Chinese slave Domingo Suárez, had with another woman when Catarina refused to consummate her marriage with him. Because she had promised herself to Christ."

That is when I decided to invite Maestra Sofía to my apartment for a cup of hot black tea. I needed to hear stories about Catarina de San Juan from a woman. All the books I was reading about her were by men. Men intent on sanctifying her, explaining her, analyzing her. I wondered if Maestra Sofía knew anything about Catarina's death. Did Catarina de San Juan speak of the land of her birth as she lay dying? Did she remember the sound of her mother's voice calling her by the name she had given her daughter? Her mother calling out for Mirrha. Miriam. Had chocolate arrived in India when Mirrha was stolen away from her *desh,* her *tierra?*

But instead of stories about Mirrha-Catarina, Maestra Sofía named the tea I offered her, black tea grown in Sri Lanka, the Tea of Untamed Wisdom. ■

UNTITLED
Shivani Narang

i tried to write a poem about myself once
without trying to hide behind masks of metaphors and
dance in circles of similes but
i know when i stand on this stage
all you see is your model minority.
your small, indian girl, attending UC Berkeley,
with hair shorter than you expected
a voice louder than you anticipated
less extracurriculars and talents than you imagined
a life plan less planned than you planned for her,
a GPA not as high as you hoped,
i am not going to apologize if you are disappointed.
my name is Shivani.
i am twenty years old
i miss my dada,
i have never been good at physics,
poetry is my most affordable therapist,
and clearly,
i have not been taught to talk about myself.
in a family that articulates labors of love with quiet gestures of af-
firming eye contact and for dinner my favorite sabji,
that would make me "too much."
i am too white in india, too brown in this country,
too queer for brown, too brown for queer,
too soft to be powerful, too powerful to be soft,
i am tired of this white man's myth that i am model for a minority
that i am capable for a person of color
that i am to compare myself with my brown and black siblings whose
struggles are not mine,
i am tired of your boxes for this brown body suffocating me.
i am tired of keeping my head down and running on a race track
that has no finish line in sight.
sinking under seas of diaspora and assimilation
under the weight of everything that I am not doing,
around countless " you are not enoughs"
i am child of self-doubt.

my eyes were birthed as
fire
burning,
apologizing
already.
i am child of immigration.
my skin was birthed as
oceans
drowning,
longing
already.
i am child of depression.
my mind was birthed as
the earth,
struggling to
breathe
from the weight of carrying the world
already.
i am child of mehndi.
my hands were birthed
making chai
every morning
giving love
to everyone else, first,
already.
i am child of love.
my heart was birthed as
monsoons,
flooding,
nourishing,
already.
i am child of sacrifice.
i burn.
i drown.
i flood.
i am trying to love myself.
i am trying to
remember my name.
remember this is me.
remember i am my own home.
remember my home.
remember my sister.

remember my parents' faces the day my sister was born.
remember those faces are warmer than any sun could ever be.
remember i am still here.
remember i. am. i was. i will.
remember my poems.
remember my poems bleed revolutions.
remember my voice.
remember my voice is my liberation.
remember i am speaking right now,
this is me swimming against the currents of my own silence.
my name is shivani,
i am twenty years old
i miss my dada,
i have never been good at physics,
poetry is my most affordable therapist,
and
i tried to write a poem about myself, once.
but now I know, next time,
i'll try to write a poem for myself, finally.

DEAR SANJANA
Shivani Narang

In seventh grade, my teacher asked,
can you speak up please
i can't hear you.
little sister, you are in the seventh grade,
and now i will speak up for you.

dear sanjana,
Mama sent me an email last night. she wrote about parts of herself
she has never shared like
failing the sixth grade and
sleeping on floors of rooms in chennai, LA, london, mumbai and
waking up early to stand in long visa lines.
she also kept saying sorry.
sorry for taking up my study time,
sorry for saying too much,
sorry for not saying enough, and
sorry for all these apologies.
dear sanjana,
after 18 years,
an email from 400 miles away,
is the first time mama has let her wounds show.
this is how the women in our family hide.
We cry alone in bathrooms, flush the toilet a couple times so nobody is
suspecting.
we feed ourselves last,
give up our seats first.
we are flowers.
we need water, sunshine, soil, roots.
these roots are our bones.
our bones become apologies
drowning under waves of
just never getting it quite right,
sanjana, please ask mama to
delete sorry from her vocabulary,
ask mama to remember her bones also hold decades of resiliency,
ask mama to let her voice feel the sun,

because it is cold over here sanjana and
her words are the warmest blankets i know.

dear sanjana,
nani, she is our lotus
whose existence is 2 generations wiser
whose stem strongly pushes through depths of quiet water
whose roots are buried in histories of partition, reincarnation, and
liberation,
whose petals
still share oxygen.
nani is the spine to this story.
the rhythm to this poem,
the shaking in my voice,
but nani didn't look up when nana started yelling.
her eyes fell to the floor as if gravity grew stronger as his voice got
louder,
her petals quickly began to be covered by this water, faster,
my eyes filled up,
and i realized
this is how the women in my family forget the weight of our voices.
dear sanjana,
there is an ocean between us and our lotus
but, nani never told me shame travels overseas
silently.

so dear sanjana
In senior year of high school,
when the boy comes too close
speak up.
say no.
dear sanjana,
when the white girls in class say you are nice, small and sweet
that you are pretty, for a brown girl
don't take it as a compliment.
tell them you are bold, brave, brilliant
that you are important, as a brown girl.
when mama doesn't look up when baba starts yelling
remind mama about nani.
give her a lotus.
remind her of the suns in her voice.
when your older sister forgets

that her worth as a woman is more than
her GPA or body weight, her silence or sorrys
give her a lotus.
remind her to spill the poems rooted, growing, screaming in her bones.

Dear Sanjana,
my blooming flower,
yesterday, when i asked you what you see in the mirror every morning.
you gave me a few tears,
unearthing insecurities buried deep in your body,
a consequence of a quiet female ancestry.
but you never gave me an apology.
This is how I unlearn from you.

this poem. this flower. this is the women of color in our family.
breathing.
finally.
water these petals, baby sister.
for the days you need help.
to breathe.

THE MONKEY MAN
Sachin Waikar

The night we hunted the Monkey Man I was stretched out on the couch with a show I'd already seen. *Hawaii Five-O*, maybe. My fingertips were cheese-curl orange. Ugh, Mom would have said if she and Dad had come back early from the movie.

Two figures moved from our yard to the patio. One of them wore a baseball cap. I waved them in.

Billy came through the glass door first. He glanced at me, reached into the cheese curls bag and pulled one out, delicately, like he was performing some kind of -ectomy. Remind me, Billy's expression always said, why am I friends with you? Kyle stood behind him.

We think he's got someone in there, Billy said, like a prisoner or something. Kyle looked down at the carpet. His head was too small for the Reds hat on it. He wore half-moons of eye-black, same as every day, even when snow covered the baseball diamonds. You think he's got someone in there? I could've asked Kyle. He would have nodded. He would have nodded if Billy said the Monkey Man was the Devil himself.

A stakeout? I said. Like with the counterfeiter?

Billy's jaw muscles twitched. One night last fall the three of us had knelt in the woods behind a house across the creek. That's where he prints the bills, Billy had said. He pointed at a dark window. After a couple hours, the counterfeiter, a bearded guy with horn-rimmed glasses, had shined a flashlight at us and said, Come and see my antique collection. The collection included an old mimeograph machine. The counterfeiter made us hot chocolate.

Billy ignored my question. There's this light, he said. I saw it flickering in his back room. The one that's always dark. Bet that's where it happens, he said in a low voice. The torture.

Billy slipped a canvas backpack off his shoulder. I hadn't noticed it until then. His hand disappeared into it, returned with a can of root beer. Supplies, he said. He put the can back in. His hand returned, balled into a fist. He opened it to show us a metal dart with blue fins. From the board in his basement. This is for him, Billy said. He and Kyle looked at me, waited. I swung my legs off the couch.

We were thirteen. Staying home wasn't an option.

* * *

The Monkey Man had moved into the ranch house at the end of the cul-de-sac, next to the Vreelands, Billy's folks. From our living room I'd watched his green station wagon crawl down our street with a U-Haul trailer. Two kids, hair black as dice eyes, sat in the back. Later I realized his wife must have been in the front. She was just too short to see.

The Kims, Mom said the next day, after she'd walked down the street. He works at the plant. They're Koreans, but Christian, I think. I saw a crucifix. Don't think they've ever had Jell-O. Hope they give the dish back.

Later that week Billy and I were playing catch with a tennis ball. Mr. Kim walked out of his garage with a paint can. He glanced at us, without expression. Then he painted black strips over the cursive letters—THE WHALENS—on the wall by the front door. The blunt black rectangle is still there, a shadow beneath the newer paint.

After Mr. Kim went inside, Billy walked toward me. Remember, children, he said in his game show host voice, keep your cats and dogs out of their yard. He bit into an imaginary sandwich. Neither of us had pets.

I'd heard the Kims' kids' names called from the house sometimes. The syllables clung together, doubled back on themselves. I couldn't pronounce them. The kids were a few years younger than us. They looked alike, with short thick hair and pinched faces. But one wore a dress. Sometimes, when we played Wiffle ball or Capture the Flag in the cul-de-sac, they watched from the window, until someone closed the curtains.

The Whalens had kept their backyard neatly trimmed and edged. Now it became a maze of prairie grass, ragged flower beds, talon-shaped shrubs. Vines grew up to then over the windows. From the Kims' yard came the hollow calls of wind-whistles, the voices of gods we'd never know.

After Saturday-morning cartoons, Billy, Kyle, and I often watched the Kims' backyard from the Vreelands' deck. We peered through the cedar slats, snickered at the games the boy and girl played: Tag in slow motion, a hopping contest, soft clapping to a silent beat. When Mrs. Kim worked on the flowerbeds, she wore a pointy wooden hat like we'd seen in Vietnam War movies. Sometimes Billy crouched and stretched his eyelids with his fingertips to imitate her. We didn't see Mr. Kim much. Some weekend mornings he stood alone in the back yard, shirtless, eyes closed, striking waxy poses. Tight muscles moved beneath his skin. Even Billy had nothing to say when we watched him.

Maybe the fourth or fifth time we saw Mr. Kim out there Kyle muttered something.

Huh? Billy said.

Like a monkey, Kyle said. He's like a monkey man. His shoulder tightened, waiting for Billy's fist.

But Billy grinned. His jaw worked the name for a moment. Yeah, he said, look at the Monkey Man.

One day last July I came back from a baseball game to find the cul-de-sac ringed by cars. Some were parked at off angles, as if arranged by a giant child. Billy jogged toward me as I stepped out of the car. C'mon, he said. It's some kind of weirdo party.

We played catch in Billy's backyard, our eyes on the bushes bordering the Kims'. We saw clusters of people, maybe thirty in all, black-haired, with pale arms and legs extending from their sleeves and skirts. Streamers fringed metal folding tables. Children squealed.

Boring, Billy said. The Kims' yard became quiet. Soon a lilting voice pushed past the trees and shrubs. A man sang in what must have been Korean. Billy and I stood where we were. I hoped the song, its notes like ribboned crystal, wouldn't end. But it did, with whistles and clapping. I looked through the bushes for the singer. There was no way to tell.

Then a chorus of young and old voices began a new, familiar song. Billy smirked. Ching-chong birthday to ching, he whispered, leaning close. His breath smelled like stale bubblegum.

Want to watch TV? I said. Billy stared at the Kims' yard. Want to—

Billy held up a hand. We watched the adults file into the Kims' house. Seven or eight children stood alone on the grass. After a moment they chased each other through the prairie grass, yelping.

Billy walked to the deck's edge, knelt to scoop a handful of limestones from the bed below. He held them out to me. I thought about acting confused or saying no. I took the rocks. Billy grabbed another handful. He held up one finger. Then two.

On three, we let the stones fly.

I aimed short, toward the bushes. Billy's stones arced into the yard's center. For a second, silence. Then a wail rose from the Kims' yard. Billy swiped another fistful of rocks, but I grabbed his arm. The kids ran into the Kims' house. The screen door banged shut.

I pulled Billy behind one of the benches. We watched the Kims' yard. After a moment a man in a white shirt opened the screen door. Mr. Kim. Slowly, he walked onto the grass. I thought he might step through the bushes, to the Vreelands' deck, right up to us. But he walked past the party tables, to his yard's center. He turned toward Billy's yard.

I saw Billy's wrist tense, the stones still in his fist, as if to launch them at Mr. Kim. Then his hand uncurled. The rocks rained to the deck.

After several moments Mr. Kim walked back into his house. I knew that if Billy had thrown the stones, Mr. Kim wouldn't have flinched, not even if they'd hit his face like buckshot.

* * *

On tonight's mission we passed the corner of Billy's house. I walked a step or two behind Billy and Kyle. In the dark, Billy's deck looked like a dead ship's hull. Dim light glowed from a lamp on the Vreelands' kitchen counter. The bedroom windows were black.

We didn't spend much time at Billy's anymore. Not inside, anyway. I remembered watching cartoons there once, a couple of years ago, Billy, Kyle, and me. It was rainy. Mr. Vreeland had come back from fishing, a can of Stroh's in his fist. Billy and his dad had the same eyes: wide-spaced, greenish, with unsettling depth. But the centers of Billy's looked soft. Mr. Vreeland's didn't. William, Mr. Vreeland said. He pointed at Billy's bare feet, which rested on their chipped coffee table. Billy didn't hear his dad, or was acting like he didn't. Quickly for a man of his bulk, Mr. Vreeland set his beer on the table and crooked his arm around Billy's neck. What? Billy said, more plea than protest. Mr. Vreeland dragged him into the hallway. When the bathroom door shut, Kyle and I stepped quickly out the back door. Billy never said anything about it.

Mrs. Vreeland looked like an actress, the kind who always played the star's older sister or best friend. She was weathered-pretty, with grooves around her mouth and eyes. Until last year her hair had been a honey-colored hive; now it fell on either side of her face, feathered, like Farah Fawcett's. She read magazines at their kitchen table, under a broken halo of cigarette smoke. Sometimes she asked me questions about school or baseball. But when I answered she looked over my shoulder, half nodding, like I was speaking a different language.

That night, Billy's parents weren't home. I imagined Mr. Vreeland at a steak-and-martini dinner for work, Mrs. at a bridge or canasta table. Later, after everything changed, I tried to remember a time I'd heard Billy's parents say anything to each other. I couldn't.

At the edge of his yard, just before the Kims' bushes, Billy stopped. He's calling it off, I thought. Hoped. Billy unslung his backpack and fished out the root beer. He peeled its pull-tab and gulped from it, passed it to me. I drank. No moon rode the sky above us. After Kyle took a sip, Billy drained the can and tossed it into the bushes. We're going in, he whispered.

No one moved. The creek murmured to itself. Somewhere a dog barked once, then whimpered. Turn back, I told myself. Nothing to prove. But part of me, I realized later, was excited about what we might see. And I figured the darts would stay in Billy's backpack. Guys like him talked big, but always dropped the lime stones in the end.

I was the first to step past the bushes.

* * *

Last fall, when a few orange and red leaves still clung to the trees, the shadow cast by the Kims' house had seemed longer, extending almost across the cul-de-sac. The prairie grass looked spikier. There was something else. Kyle noticed first. Where'd she go? he said. We sat on the Vreelands' deck with grape Kool-Aid. Billy shrugged. But Kyle was right: for weeks we hadn't seen Mrs. Kim kneeling in her flower beds or wiping the windows. In her place an older woman—Korean, I figured—with hair streaked like skunk-fur stared out of their front window or stood waiting for the school bus.

A couple weeks later I was raking leaves when the green station wagon rolled into the Kims' driveway. Mr. Kim got out and went to the passenger side. He lifted what looked like his daughter from the passenger seat, her head in a white kerchief. But then the back doors opened and both kids jumped out. Mr. Kim wasn't holding his daughter. It was her mother. His wife. Mrs. Kim's body had retreated from what little space it had filled.

Tell Billy, I thought. But I imagined his grin. I didn't tell him until the next week, when cars again crowded the cul-de-sac. This time they were parked more carefully. Families in black walked to the Kims' door. White wisps of breath rose above them.

Again a man sang from their backyard. The notes, lower and longer than before, slipped through Billy's window into his room, where we sat, far from the deck and its limestones. Too cold, I'd said when Billy said we should watch from outside.

No claps or whistles marked the song's end.

We didn't see Mr. Kim or the kids for awhile after that. Maybe they moved, I said to Mom. But we saw him out there the next Saturday, bare-chested on the backyard frost, angling and re-angling his body. I looked for hints of loss in the curve of his back, the pitch of his head.

The children remained a mystery. Shipped 'em back to China, Billy offered. But I imagined them trailing their father around the house, half-orphans with clasped hands. We never saw them again.

I began avoiding the Vreelands' deck on weekends. I shrugged at Billy's stories: The Monkey Man's burying something, or someone, in the garden. Me and Kyle saw this big pile of dirt. Yesterday he levitated at least a foot off the ground. Ask Kyle!

* * *

But this night felt different. Maybe I wanted to prove something to Billy. Maybe I wanted to be there when Billy saw nothing in Mr. Kim's back room: no prisoners, no corpses, no cages. Or maybe I was just bored.

The Kims' yard was silent. On the patio a small bike leaned against the wall. Billy nudged me, pointed toward a back window. Kyle and I were already looking at it. The blinds were down. Behind them were languid flashes, a miniature lightning storm. It was brighter near the window's top, through a gap in the blinds.

Billy stepped toward the patio. Wait, I whispered. He didn't turn around. Kyle followed. Then I did too.

Near the window were two plastic chairs. A deck umbrella lay next to them, unopened, its striped top full of secrets. The window looked bigger up close, covered with vines. The gap in the blinds was a couple of feet above our heads. On the other side of the wall I imagined a pale widower curled in an armchair, sucking his thumb in the TV's light.

Billy stood before the window. He paused, then pointed at the deck chairs. Kyle was already holding one; he set it in front of Billy. Nothing, I told myself. We'll see nothing. I couldn't breathe.

Billy stepped onto the chair, a palm against the bricks. Slowly he rose, until the room's flicker played across his hair, his face. He squinted into the light. Kyle was staring up at Billy, like he could see through his eyes.

Billy leaned forward and stared into the room. Let's go, I whispered. I tugged at Billy's jacket. Eyes still at the gap, he swatted my hand. Then his whole body tensed. His knees locked, palms curled into fists. He swayed, nearly fell. I reached for him, but he jumped onto the concrete, pushed past us into the dark.

He was gone. Kyle and I looked at each other, then the window. No way he was right, I thought. About the prisoner. The torture. But what had he seen? I watched my sneaker step onto the chair. My fingertips found the window's sill. Like Billy, I rose.

In the room the TV sat on a table against the near wall. It was on, the screen angled away. I blinked against the light. My eyes moved to the far wall. On the edge of a bed sat Mr. Kim, the Monkey Man. He was naked, leaning back, the sinews and hollows of his body unreal in the light. His eyes were closed. He wasn't alone. Kneeling before him, her back to me, was a woman, slump-shouldered and pale. Her head rose and fell at the Monkey Man's lap. Rose and fell, the feathered hair shuddering.

Hair like Farah Fawcett's.

Mrs. Vreeland, Billy's mom, was with the Monkey Man. Kyle pulled at my jacket. He whispered something. I couldn't move. Mrs. Vreeland wore black underwear. The skin at her waist was saggy and ribbed and pouched. But Mr. Kim's body looked smooth and polished. I was at earth's only window, a witness to modern Eden.

Mr. Kim lifted his head. His eyes opened.

I ducked. Breathless, I stepped onto the patio, then into the grass, toward Billy's yard. I knew Kyle would follow. I was the only leader left.

We found Billy on his knees by the deck, bent over the limestones. His coughs sounded deep and wet. Kyle put a hand on his back. Billy jumped up and punched Kyle in the face. The Reds cap fell off. Then he was on top of Kyle, grunting and flailing and sobbing. Kyle just lay there. I pulled Billy off. He ran onto the deck. The glass door slid open then shut. I waited for the lock to click into place, as if the sound could explain everything.

* * *

Billy's parents split the next year. Billy and his mom moved to Indiana. Mr. Vreeland stayed behind to sell the house. Soon after that Mr. Kim drove away in the green station wagon. A rusted For Sale sign appeared in his front yard. I never saw any of them again.

In the years after, when I crossed behind Billy's old house I sometimes looked at the yard that had belonged to the Kims. The prairie grass was long dead, but I would imagine it was still there, and the flowers and vines and wind-whistles too. I'd picture Billy and his mom on plastic chairs on the patio, under a striped umbrella. They would smile at each other, then look out into the yard, where Mr. Kim stood, lips parted in song, hands shaping happiness out of the air. ▪

THE OTHER SIDE
Tara Dorabji

The other side of self hate
Is love
I thought I was done writing this poem

> I love you, Mom
> I owe who I am to you, my strength, my beauty, my fierce
>   resolve
> I want to love you in that uncomplicated way of being a kid—
> the scent of your deodorant and perfume rubbed into the silk
> of your shirt

Your boyfriend said you shouldn't raise us White
But I already wrote that poem of hating the shadow inside me
Of not having words to describe me
Of trying so hard to be White, of taking it like a cupcake to eat
I've written the poem on being Brown in America
On finding my roots, of loving myself
of surviving the every day assaults on my identity
I've written that poem a hundred times

> I am a woman of color
> I say it like a mantra
> I say it with love
> I teach it to my daughters

The other side of being Brown is my Whiteness
There is hate inside of me
Jagged bits of glass that I want to heat until they melt
Until I can turn it back to magma and find my way back to love

> The other side of love
> Is hate

When I was little I was silenced by Whiteness
It was the standard by which I measured myself
I want my skin to be white, my hair to be blonde, I told my sister

The White is in me—I reach for my Omi's hand
Her hair is still blond; her eyes are still blue
I think she might be dying; she tells me later she was in a river
It is like she is on acid; her filter is gone

Those Mexican people, you can never trust them, she says
I hold her hand tighter. She asks about my friends' children
He is a little blondie with blue eyes
I squeeze her fingers, searching for love. Her blood courses through
my veins

The other side of love is hate
I thought I'd written this poem on self hate
I thought I'd put it rest and buried it

My Omi might not die. I search internet ads of Brown women
Caregivers: *We cook, we change diapers, we take care of dementia*
My mother says, *She is Tongan. Tongans are natural care givers*
As if a person can be bred to wipe someone's ass
No, I say. *That is not true*

Some days, I am silent around racism
Not like when I was little and the words fell around me
And I tried to find shelter in them so no one would see my
        Brownness
It was a compliment to hear the racism flow freely
Because I see you as White

I am silent when my White boyfriend's Aunt from Illinois talks about
        Ferguson
I don't throw my fist in the air. I lean into my boyfriend
Tell me about your business selling paper, I say
I don't owe them the truth. I don't need to be a mirror to reflect their hate
Silence is a weapon now. Because it is not my duty to show you how to
        see

I am not silent with my mother
This is the burden of love
We have to pay someone to take care of Omi, I say
It is hard work and none of us want to do it
My ears bleed every time my mom says Tongan
Nice sturdy women, my mom says

Something inside me breaks
I scrape my fingers against the concrete
Until the nails snap off
The nubs are bloody
A trail of our blood coats the wall
I am part of you, mom
I come from my Omi who lived in Germany

    My Uncles were drafted into the SS
    They didn't take the fourteen-year-old
    because Oma threatened to cut off his hands

My Omi and I both want freedom for Palestine
But I can't stand the way she says *those Jewish people*
The occupied becomes the occupier
Both of them live inside of me. Indian. German. Italian
My parents cross colonized each other in me

    The other side of love is hate
    I thought I'd written the last verse of this poem

I hired a Tongan woman to take care of my Omi
She will leave her son—the same age as my daughter
I help my Omi to the commode and take off her Depends
I leave the room before I gag
The diaper hangs from her ankles

    I am too weak to do it
    My Omi calls my mom
    Who empties the commode
    Throws away the diaper
    Flushes the shit down the toilet

I open the window
How can we hire her if she has to leave her son? I ask my mom
It's not a traditional nuclear family, she says
As if it were contemporary like polyamory

I thought I'd written this poem
And healed the wound of self hate
But I have this Whiteness inside of me
It's not a cupcake
It's not invisible
It's a shame that
is anchored to those I love

The other side of hate is still love

OTHER MOTHERS
Tara Dorabji

Ask me how many children I have. Small talk should be easy, not hard.
I pause. Even counting on my fingers won't capture the truth.

How many children do you have?
Such a simple question. Such a complex answer.

My children are born from blood, unborn, and born from another.
Two are blood. One I raised and two more I claimed. There are those
unborn. And there is still another.

How many is that? Is it enough to rephrase the question? How many
fathers are there?

One baby daddy. Three pregnancies—one birth. Then there is the
boyfriend, who is no longer a boyfriend, with kids that might get cut
from this poem. It's too much for me to keep track of.

I am like that old woman in the shoe with too many children to know
what to do.

The number keeps changing. I never say eight, but at one time that
might have been true. Two just got subtracted. Can children get
subtracted away? Let me count the story on my fingers.

One.
To the other mother—I have never met you. Pictures of you at
seventeen and pregnant are in my house—though our son and his
father left long ago. You eat pizza over a bursting belly—while your
boyfriend and father-to-be holds up his high school diploma.

You stopped calling when the state of California opened a child
support case. Our son was six. He became mine.

You wrote letters from jail and promised to call. He counted the days
to your release as if it were an advent calendar and each day were a
chocolate to eat and mark the coming of Christmas. He celebrated the

day you left jail, but there were no gifts. He waited by the phone. It did not ring.

He was seventeen when you came back. He had left my house by then.

You cleaned his room with him because you weren't there to teach him to clean it himself. He's playing you, though. He knows how to clean-up after himself. I taught him. As a boy, he alphabetized the spices and his bookshelf. When he left, I took out the trash and unloaded the dishwasher—silent reminders of his absence.

I give him a ride and he tells me that he's going to a funeral. Your new baby daddy died of a heroine over dose. Before he died, you took our son to Modesto, stepping over the dog with an infected penis to enter the house, drinking piss water beer with men tatted up with swastikas.

He asks you later, *How could you be with a white supremacist when your son is Latin?*

Drugs do strange things, you say.

I wonder when we will meet? Will it be a birth or a death or a chance encounter in Santa Cruz? Will you take my hands in yours? Will you reach back for that decade? The untraceable time from pre-school until he became a man, hairs sprouting from his chest, voice deep, wearing tight-fitting, black, skinny jeans.

Everyone always said he had my eyes, but maybe they are yours.

You are sober. You are in school. The track marks on your arms have healed. Our son is high. I hope he will find his way back to me.

Two, Three and Four.
To my other mother - You were twenty-seven with two kids, living in Vegas when you met my dad, leaving a coked up marriage.

I was twenty-seven and pregnant when you left my dad. My dad called at 1am when he saw your joint bank account empty. You didn't call him back. That's how he found out it was over.

I was the one you met with right after you left him. We ate burritos in the Mission as you drove your gas guzzling truck en route from

Santa Rosa to San Diego. I was pregnant with twins. You sent soft, pink blankets after their birth. I was the first one in the family to have babies.

When you started dating my dad, you bought a burgundy mini-Van. It fit all four of us kids. My boyfriend bought a Mazda 5, so we could fit in one car—there is no cargo space, but the gas mileage is good.

My boyfriend and I, we didn't live together, so we could live without the cargo space.

Growing up, I spent every other weekend with you. I don't remember the day that I stopped trusting you, but we worked out keeping each other at a distance. But when I was twenty-two and pregnant you stood by me. You said you'd help me raise the baby when everyone else turned away.

I cried so much with that first pregnancy, alone with a baby growing inside me. Twenty-two and pregnant. I called the other woman. She was the *ex girlfriend*, going to law school in LA. My baby daddy lied to me. I bled for days.

Once a cheater, always a cheater, you said when I stayed with him. When I went on to have twins with him. When his six-year-old son became our son and I raised him. *Once a cheater, always a cheater.* I think of this often. I think it might be true. I don't want to be with a cheater ever again. I wonder if I am a cheater.

Maybe you see parts of yourself in me. I only see you on Facebook; it is the perfect balance for our relationship. Nearly a decade after your divorce, we don't show up for each other at weddings or births, but I think we might roll up for the funeral. It seems fitting.

Five and Six.
To the other mother—

I drove down to San Jose in the silver Mazda 5 to pick up the kids. We got the 5 a.m. call that you were using again. The kids sat on chairs lined up on the porch, waiting for their fathers to pick them up. The oldest's eyes were blazing. He knows this cycle.

Our boy jumped in the car without question. You kept our girl inside, telling her that baby daddy #3 is hiding drugs in your purse, stealing your phone, hitting you. Baby daddy #3 ends up in jail, but the paternity test takes his number away. His name stays on the birth certificate of your fourth child. This one comes with you at night to the motel rooms. There is no father to pick him up and take him home.

You tell your daughter that you want to get in the car and come back home with her. Home. She wants to take you with her.

She can't help but carry your baggage. She brings it home and posts photos of you all over her wall. Inside the car, there is it too much baggage to fit on her lap. There is no cargo space in the Mazda 5. I take some from her pinned under the weight.

A song plays on the radio. She says it reminds her of you and she sings:

> *It's been a long day without you, my friend*
> *And I'll tell you all about it when I see you again*
> *We've come a long way from where we began*

She tells me that Sergio is living with you in her old bedroom. I tell her to stay out of the bathroom when Sergio is in it. Who is Sergio?

I can barely breath under the weight. The baggage fills the Mazda 5. The door is unlocked, but we are moving too fast for me to get out.

This boyfriend, he isn't a cheater, but under all this baggage I wonder if he was ever with me.

We pull up next to you on the curb. My window is down, letting air whip through my hair.

You say *Happy Mother's Day* to me. I can't say it back to you. The words choke in my throat and we roll away.

I jump out of the car while it's still moving, your suitcase rides shotgun and your shirt catches in the door, flying like a flag above the Mazda 5.

I count backwards as two children roll away. There are no words for the grief carved in my flesh.

Seven.
To the other mother
They call you Amma ji.
You hugged me, once.
I bled through my underwear for twelve days.
That was simply our timing.

Eight.
To the other mother—I love you. You cook organic beets with my girls
and taught them to a ride a bicycle. They will be big sisters and I will
sleep through the night.

I googled you and we met in Snow Park and walked Lake Merritt
together. I asked for your help. I am the ex now. The second baby
mama. You are pregnant.

You listen and offer to be a quiet fire. I admire this.

I am a fire keeper and I am volcanic. I explode. I erupt. I am the star
and the sun.

You make me earrings for my birthday—rose quartz.
You pick up the girls from school on Wednesdays. I work late. I
produce radio. I drink dark and stormys.

I hug you at Alcatraz during the sunrise ceremony. I take my *suegra's*
hands in mine and tell her that she must open her door to you.

My daughters tell me when you cry at night. If you ever leave him,
take the baby in your arms and have my girls grab onto the pockets of
your sweatshirt, one on each side.

On Valentine's Day, years ago, my kid's dad pulled a rose from a
bouquet and gave it to me. I wonder if it was your rose. The rose dries
and dies on my kitchen table. My heart aches. I reach for my chest and
pull out a rib and hand it to you. Adam came from our damn womb.

You take my rib and I know that even if I die, you'll have something to
give our daughters.

THE DARK-SKINNED DISPENSER OF REMEDIES
Toni Nealie

I'm peeling potatoes for dinner in Chicago, the phone scrunched between my ear and shoulder, talking to my mother as she has her morning tea. A chilly wind is blowing up from the Southern Ocean, she says, so she hasn't wandered up the road to get her groceries. Her old bones get creaky if she doesn't walk every few days. I imagine her, seventeen hours ahead of me, sitting in her rose-patterned Sanderson linen chair, drinking Earl Grey from a pale blue-and-white china cup. Age is pressing in on her. Glaucoma narrows her life now, so she walks to the store or down the track to the beach, but usually keeps close to her small brick house. I want to ask about my grandfather again, but I can't bear stirring her up so that she'll fret later, alone. She has always avoided talking about her father.

"Don't let anyone know that's your grandfather in there," she'd murmur when I was a child walking with her past his mausoleum. She hated him. He was cruel. "He sent my mother home to her family to die. He threw her out because she didn't have sons." This is what I heard growing up, not understanding why a man wouldn't want daughters.

When she was three, my mom lost her mother. By twelve, she was an orphan. "I miss Mother," is a frequent refrain in our long-distance conversations.

I press on.

* * *

Most families have secrets, the clichéd skeletons in the closet. As technology hastened access to old records, my family's rattling bones began somersaulting out from the media. Fifty years after his death, my grandfather featured in a television show, then in books, in an online encyclopedia—and now in blogs and websites. Each source replicates much unattributed information, impossible to verify because no one, other than my mother, is alive to comment. All that my mother kept hidden about her father is now in plain sight.

From my safe distance in America, I could afford to poke away, to search for nuances and context and points of view. On moving here, I was profiled at the border and shunted into a years-long immigration process very different from my husband's seamless transition. In the aftermath of 9/11, amid a wash of anti-Muslim and anti-immigrant sentiments, I confronted my heritage. My cultural roots were in Aotearoa/New Zealand, but my skin, hair, and eyes favored my Indian grandfather. Unmoored from siblings, friends, and full-time work, I had time to investigate my family's past. I was out of my mother's range, so I wouldn't embarrass her. She was getting older. I was running out of years to ask questions. The time had come to sniff out what had been suppressed.

If my grandfather's ghost refused to stay silent, perhaps it was time to claim him.

* * *

My grandfather is persistent. He died in 1941, long before my birth, yet he knocks for attention still. I have carried him around in photographs and letters and newspaper clippings for years. He lives in a drawer next to my desk, in a manila envelope filed between my sons' school report cards and travel soccer roster. Every so often I take him out and put him away again. Each year there is more of him.

In a fragile brown-and-white photograph, Wally Salaman looks stern in a topcoat and fob watch, peering out over pince-nez spectacles. "I was only a boy of fourteen when I left India," he wrote in a letter to a relative. Sailing away from family, he arrived in New Zealand in 1903. An importer of precious stones, silks, and carpets, he dabbled in real estate and made aniline fabric dyes for soldiers' khaki in World War I, under contract to the government. Grandpa Salaman gained fame—and notoriety—as an herbalist, on the wrong side of the law. So many views of him exist that I feel like a game show competitor trying to press the buzzer for the best answer. Was he:

a) bold adventurer,
b) charlatan,
c) successful businessman,
d) devout Muslim,
e) non-practitioner who staged a Muslim funeral as afterlife insurance,
f) family man who left generous trust funds for his descendants,
g) cad who abandoned two wives because they bore girls,
h) victim of 1920s colonial racism, or
i) dangerous criminal, a child killer?

I didn't fossick in dusty library records for his trail. Turning on my computer, I came across newly digitized newspaper records from the 1920s and 1930s. The headlines blared:

> *Salaman in Court. Indian Herbalist. Salaman on Trial. Why Salaman Came to Court. Herbalist Faces Grave Charges. Salaman Case. Tragic Story at Manslaughter Trial. Accused of Murder. Charge Against Indian. Ills of the Flesh. Recommend Mercy. Will Salaman Be Released? Fraud! Ruffian! Humbug! Salaman Swindler.*

My grandfather killed a child. No—a child died while under his care in 1930. No—my grandfather *denied* treating him at all. Six-year-old Lyall Christie was ill for four years. Two medical doctors treated him for diabetes. His mother took him to my herbalist grandfather. Two days later little Lyall died. Convicted of manslaughter, my grandfather was sent to prison for a year's hard labor. These are the facts, baldly stated.

I doubt that my grandfather was responsible for the boy's death. The more I read about the period, the more I find unvarnished racism and a colonial medical establishment protecting itself. Tabloid newspaper *New Zealand Truth* said the case was "a poignant story told by the dead child's mother, Mary Ann Christie: a narrative of childish illness and suffering over a period of years with the tragic knowledge confronting the parents that their young son was, according to one doctor, doomed to die at a young age."

The boy's mother testified that she saw my grandfather as a last resort, trying anything for her ailing child. She paid no fee and received no medicine. In court she said, "I wouldn't like to blame him for the boy's death."

* * *

I fumbled my way through newspaper records back to the 1920s. Earlier attempts to convict my grandfather failed. In 1924, a nine-year-old Māori girl named Mane Reiha died. She was in the hospital for a month. When doctors said nothing more could be done for the child, her grandmother took her to the herbalist. My grandfather sold the woman four bottles of a "tonic" containing quinine, almond oil, and herbs.

The magistrate: "He mixed it up with as much skill as a barman mixes a cocktail."

The Health Department doctor: "Oh, that usually requires some skill."

The magistrate called my grandfather a ruffian and a humbug. "Go back to India and practice on your own people," he advised. A Health Department doctor said that when Māori people "hear of the 'marvelous Indian doctor,' they come to him from long distances, especially with cases practically hopeless; the patients die; then the trouble begins."

Cost, not mortality, was the Health Department's concern. "The relatives go to an undertaker, but have no death certificate, Salaman not being in a position to give one. That is how our Department comes to hear of the cases. The result is a coronial inquiry, a coffin has to be procured, the body sent back home—all this *expense* has to be borne by the Health Department, when the patient should have been left to die in peace in his own district."

The doctor who did the postmortem on Mane Reiha certified that the child had died of tuberculosis. My grandfather had *not* killed her.

* * *

Later that year, Salaman returned court for a jury trial. Agnes Stewart, a nurse with medical, surgical, and midwifery qualifications, claimed damages for negligent treatment. She saw many doctors for goiter before going to the herbalist. My grandfather gave her tonics containing potassium iodine and opium. Her friend, also a nurse, testified that Stewart said she was on her deathbed. She was "in a most shocking state, in a desperate way, so desperate that he did not want to take the case at all."

Salaman's wife, my grandmother, was a witness. She was described in news reports as "his white wife." Race was clearly an issue. Counsel for the defense felt the need to remind the jury that Salaman was "a colored man, but that fact must exercise not prejudice, as British justice [was] for all." The defense maintained there was no evidence of harm, and one of the most famous medical authorities also recommended opium. The lawyer for the plaintiff argued that Salaman had traded on his "blackness" by putting in his window a sign, Indian Herb Atah. He said it was inconceivable that a white man would have attracted such a "horde of dupes and hypnotized patients."

Convicted and ordered to pay costs for pretending to be a doctor, my grandfather was sentenced to a month in prison for attempting to receive money by false pretenses. Agnes Stewart died shortly after.

In 1927, he faced six charges of false pretenses when two policemen posed as customers. Salaman examined them with a stethoscope to their throats and magnifying glass to their eyes, they testified. He diagnosed ulcers and poor circulation. The policemen left with assorted bottles of medicine and boxes of pills. When analyzed they were found to contain phenacetin, an analgesic used widely at the time, and small amounts of herbs.

The newspaper described my grandfather as "the dusky one" and "the dark-skinned dispenser of remedies." He was found guilty and fined twenty pounds on the first two counts and convicted for the others. His stock in trade and twelve of his properties were confiscated. He petitioned the House of Representatives, seeking the appointment of a commission to investigate the prosecutions.

On a day when *Truth*'s lead was "Gay Girls Take Wrong Turn/ Bacchus Enthroned in Venus Street/Fair Flappers and Business Men in Wild Midnight Orgy," the paper ran a story about Salaman. It compared him to several famous healers. James Moore Hickson, an Australian-born Anglican, traveled the world with his healing ministry. Émile Coué, a French pharmacist, pioneered hypnosis and autosuggestion and famously said, "Every day, in every way, I'm getting better and better." Gipsy Smith was a popular evangelist who led a march of thousands to protest Chicago's vice district. Unlike those three, my grandfather's error lay in dealing "with material matter instead of spiritual." He made the mistake of thinking that "it was possible to cure the sick and afflicted by means of drugs and herbs as if they had that essential to all who would be cured—Faith." If he had merely stuck to the role of psychic healer, laying on of hands, or autosuggestion, he could have avoided trouble.

"He would never have done that," says my mother. "He believed in his healing abilities and his medicine."

By contemporary Western standards, my grandfather's herbal methods appear dubious. *Te Ara*, the national encyclopedia of New Zealand, lists him as a "Merchant, dyer, herbalist, charlatan."

Charlatan. I was indignant. What kind of person can boast that their forebear was a charlatan, a fraud, a fake? This did not fit with my childhood fairytale about a handsome prince wooing his fair bride. My hands got clammy, my cheeks flushed. If I could un-see the headlines! I snapped shut the computer. A year slid by, then I couldn't find my files, either the paper copies or those stored on my computer. It was as if my mind had redacted the stories. Searching afresh, I found new items, blog posts, and web entries, repeated, repeated. None questioned the first telling. Not a journalist challenged the facts, investigated the context, the practices, the times. Once a story has been released, there's no getting it back.

* * *

The vaccines and antibacterials we take for granted were not around in the 1920s. Penicillin was discovered in 1928, the year my mother was born. Most cultures have healing traditions based in plant cures. Ayurvedic medicine has been practiced in India for five thousand years. European monks and nuns used herbs, including opium and cannabis. Chinese immigrants brought medicines, acupuncture, massage, and meditative exercise. In New Zealand, *rongoā*—traditional indigenous healing—used remedies from roots and leaves until the Tohunga Suppression Act of 1907 outlawed native healers. In the 1920s, the famous All Black rugby player, George Nepia, was apparently advised to have an operation for a leg injury, but instead he turned to Māori herbal medicine, which worked. The British doctor admitted later that he had not believed the leg could be healed.

Herbal remedies, homeopathy, and other alternatives to traditional medicine are widely available today. I'm skeptical of their efficacy, but, unless a practice is found to be directly harmful, a practitioner is unlikely to be imprisoned. It is difficult to judge my grandfather with a modern yardstick. He was tremendously popular with his patients, who gave him gold and bronze medals inscribed with details of his successful treatments.

"When I was six, if I looked out the window on Tuesdays and Wednesdays, I would see cars lining either side of Gill Street," my mother recalls. "Cars with running boards and canvas hoods. People came from all over the country to see him. He didn't take appointments, it was first come, first served, so they just had to wait. If they missed out, they had to come back another time."

* * *

Racism rippled through the prosecution of my grandfather. He was a British citizen of colonial India when he arrived in New Zealand, also a British colony at the time. The 1901 census listed only twenty-four "Asiatics." By 1916, the numbers had risen to 181 and grew steadily higher. A cartoon from 1917 shows a British politician opening the door for a "Hindoo," as all Indians, regardless of religion, were called. The caricatured head is turbaned, black faced, and huge. By the 1920s, immigration was restricted. The racist White New Zealand League excluded Indians from leadership roles and lobbied to keep immigration white. This is the environment in which my grandfather married my white New Zealand grandmother, conducted his businesses, and went to trial.

* * *

The racism was not veiled: "The coon in question has been judged a false alarm and a fraud."

The coon. Saying it makes me queasy. I pace around the house with the word souring my mouth. I scrub the white tiles in the shower and load the dishwasher, check my e-mail messages. My fingers are sore from squeezing them.

This ugly word. I was familiar with its use during and after slavery, in the so-called coon songs of Tin Pan Alley, the Zip Coon minstrels, the song "All Coons Look Alike to Me" by Ernest Hogan, and the coon movies that stereotyped African Americans as lazy, stupid, shiftless, and untrustworthy. Hearing it applied to my Indian grandfather, I realized how racism had seared my mother, how it distorted her views about heritage.

The word's origins are blurry; sources say it comes from *raccoon*, or maybe from the Portuguese word *barracão*, which at one time described a shed for housing slaves. It wasn't heard in New Zealand when I grew up, but my high school boyfriend heard it when he first flew to Australia, 2,500 miles away. He hitchhiked across the continent from Sydney to Perth in a truck, a trip that took four days. One night on the arid Nullarbor Plain, the driver hit something. "It's probably just a coon," he laughed, meaning an indigenous person. My boyfriend was so shaken that he called me from a pay phone as soon as he arrived in Perth. Another friend visiting Mparntwe/Alice Springs in the Northern Territory was horrified to see signs hanging in bars that read "No Coons Served Here." It was the 1980s and the Arrernte nation had lived in the area for an estimated forty thousand years.

Other offensive words were used in New Zealand, such as *boonga* (a Māori), *coconut* (a Pacific Islander), *curry-muncher* (an Indian), but not *coon*. That word carried the weight of slavery and segregation with it, and the idea of a person being a wild animal. To see it in print, in the public record, about my grandfather makes me short of breath.

Racist reports about my grandfather dated back to the end of his first marriage. One described him as a dark-hued Syrian and another as a Hindu, even though he was an Indian Muslim. A *Truth* reporter wrote in 1918: "A young woman who had seen fit to disregard Kipling's advice about the impossibility of East and West mingling . . . proved that her case was no exception." Salaman petitioned for custody of his first child, because his ex-wife was living with a Chinese man. Depending on which side's case was presented, the couple was on "improper terms" or the man was merely a housekeeper. It was a scandal.

Her lawyer said, "This is a new class of case. This country has never before been troubled by the half-caste question." The judge responded, "We have had our half-castes." "Yes," said the lawyer, "but they were, so to speak, our own people. We have not had Asiatic half-castes." The judge replied that if there were good Chinamen, there were probably good Indians, and the child might be as well be with the father as with the mother. Salaman gained custody. He later married my grandmother Gladys and fathered two more children, my mother and her younger sister.

* * *

I found my grandfather in books—*Law Breakers & Mischief Makers: 50 Notorious New Zealanders* in a chapter titled "Swindlers, Tricksters & Charlatans" and *Kings of Stings: The Greatest Swindles from Down Under*. He turned up in magazines and blogs such as the *New Zealand Listener, Indialink, Waymark*, in library websites and Toastmasters meetings. There is even a story in a current affairs magazine where I once worked. A former colleague wrote it, without knowing I was the granddaughter of his subject.

The hidden part of my family's history was under my nose in the fusty libraries of newspapers where I worked my first journalism jobs. If I had peered into their creaking filing cabinets, I may have found the stories glued onto white sheets, or in crumbling newspapers hanging from wooden clasps. It didn't occur to me then to search out the story. I was too busy creating my present to worry about the past.

* * *

After Salaman was convicted, people turned out to support him at public meetings in several towns. One gathering had five hundred attendees. Appreciative patients wrote letters telling of his care. Many felt that the local medical profession was responsible for the severity of his sentence. They petitioned the government for his release, to no avail. He went to prison for a year.

His wife Gladys, my grandmother, died of tuberculosis, and his baby daughter, my mother's little sister, died of diphtheria.

* * *

Reading back through the old newspaper reports, I am struck by the determination of the authorities to nail him, without evidence that he was acting outside the laws of the time. He never claimed to be a pharmacist or a doctor. Did he believe in his remedies or was he offering placebos? Was he a quack or was he a fraud?

The meaning of *placebo* in Latin is "I will please." My grandfather did please people. Placebos have been documented to benefit patients, but their use presents the ethical quandary of knowingly deceiving people when they are vulnerable. What about his use of opium in his "tonics"—did that make him a charlatan? Opium has been used since the Stone Age, in Greek, Persian, Arab, and Western medicine. In the nineteenth and early twentieth centuries, anyone could buy it in tinctures and tonics, in patent medicines, in soothing syrups for babies, which were available at fairs, general stores, and pharmacies. Doctors were able to prescribe much larger doses, until regulations were introduced to deter them.

"Opium is in virtually universal use throughout India as the commonest and most treasured of the household remedies accessible to the people," said Sir William Meyer in a 1912 address to the United Nations. "It is taken to avert or lessen fatigue, as a specific in bowel complaints, as a prophylactic against malaria (for which its relatively high anarcotine content makes it specially valuable), to lessen the quantity of sugar in diabetes and generally to allay pain in sufferers of all ages."

New Zealand medical doctors prescribed opium so liberally that by the 1940s the nation had one of the world's highest rates of use. New Zealand's Quackery Prevention Act tried to prevent people making false claims about their medicines.

* * *

For years I didn't discuss with my mother what I found on the Internet. She felt tied to her father's transgressions. Ignoring him and denying her connection to him was the only way she could carry on. *Mortify*, from Middle English, "to deaden, to subdue by self-denial." My mother tried to protect my siblings and me. She immersed herself, and her children, in the genealogy of her mother's people, the Waltons of County Cork and the Richards of Cornwall. She read me adventure stories about English schoolchildren, the *Famous Five* and *Secret Seven*. I grew up knowing Victorian poetry and Māori legends, but nothing of my Indian heritage or our extended family. My mother built a scaffold of rules for my siblings and me. Never put the butter on the table without a butter dish and butter knife. Never put the milk on the table without a jug. Never use tea bags. They're vulgar. Ideas of propriety—designed to protect us, to deliver us into respectability. Now I understand.

I resist absorbing her shame and muddle through my conflicting impulses. When I was small, my mother used to walk my siblings and me up to the Shirley Methodist Church every Sunday. At Sunday school I sang "Jesus Wants Me for a Sunbeam" and "Jesus Loves Me, This I Know." The Bible has plenty to say on punishment, including Ezekiel 18:20, "The son shall not suffer for the iniquity of the father, nor the father suffer for the iniquity of the son. The righteousness of the righteous shall be upon himself, and the wickedness of the wicked shall be upon himself." My mother and I *should* inherit no blame.

I ferret about the Bible and get confused. Exodus 20:5, Job 21:19, and Numbers 14:18 allow the price of a crime to be felt for several generations, the Law of Moses says a goat can be sacrificed as a kind of atonement proxy, and Christians believe that Jesus made the ultimate sacrifice to wipe our grubby slates clean. I have no goats, and I haven't taken Jesus as my savior, so I'm not sure where I stand there.

My mother never saw her father pray and wasn't sure if he was a believer. The Qur'an says: "Every soul earns only to its own account; no soul laden bears the load of another." There is a judgment day scale that weighs good deeds against bad. Maybe my grandfather's good deeds would help balance his ledger, dying fabric for soldiers' uniforms in World War I, donating land for a public reserve.

* * *

On the phone between America and New Zealand, I made my mother go back to her childhood, to peel off the scab. For eighty-seven years she carried her pain inside her, and covered it up so her children could prosper, untainted by our grandfather's record.

"When I was at school, the teachers would stop talking when I walked by, so I knew they were talking about me," she said. "Children called me a nigger. I was so ashamed. If I ignored it all, maybe I could forget."

In my mother's memories, she is often held aloft, her feet not touching the ground. In one, a stranger holds her above her mother's coffin and tells her to say goodbye one last time. In another, she pictures her father in a small room. She is lifted up and greets him through a window. Now she realizes he was in prison. She recalls leaving New Zealand for India, seeing her father's car hoisted up onto the ship by crane. As the ship crossed the equator, a sailor lifted her and she kicked her feet against him, until one tiny slipper flew off and she watched it tossing in the wake.

So much loss. My mother always said that her father was a bad man. "I remember him hitting me in the bathroom, his razor strop on the back of my legs," she told me. She thought that was because he was Muslim. I reminded her that "Spare the rod and spoil the child" was a common Christian sentiment and that she had spanked me with a wooden hairbrush when I was a child. I don't spank my children because it's mean, but a lot of people do still, regardless of their religion. I don't want to defend her father, nor do I want to support a prejudice.

She grew up believing that her father divorced his first wife because she didn't provide him a son and that he sent my grandmother Gladys away because she too bore only girls. He had sent her back to her family to die, so the story went. Who told my mother that? I wasn't so sure when I read the newspaper clippings. If he only valued boys, it didn't make sense that he fought a bitter, public battle for custody of his first daughter. When my grandmother was dying, he was already in prison. He was in no position to care for her. Would it not be prudent to go home to her parents? Where was the compassion of the court, when a man's wife was dying and his little girls were left parentless? My mother, who was loved by her mother's family, absorbed a narrative that no doubt reflected their biases and those of their times.

* * *

Children have no responsibility for crimes of a previous generation, I believe, but societies *are* culpable. My emotional string is taut. I recoil from my examination, the taint of criminality and the coon-ness of it. I am mortified at this affront to my family heritage. I had filled in the silences in my family story by inventing a fairytale. Now, no amount of imagination brings back the prince that I imagined my grandfather to be, the romance, the magic carpet. It's time to retire the motley remnants of my fantasy, a chewed-up rug that flies nowhere.

Why even concern myself now with any of this? We may all have unreliable biographies, but I think my grandfather deserves to be fleshed out, to be more than a caricature, a crime entry. Like me, he was an alien in a foreign country at a time when paranoia about outsiders was high. I want to claim my Indian heritage, for my children and me. I care about my mother, a fierce keeper of secrets, sheltering me from phantoms and bogeys until I was old enough to shout at them. It took my own isolation to empathize with hers. I care about her—a lonely little girl who lost her family to prison and disease and endured humiliation by racism—who finally gets to share her burden. The child grows up to protect the mother. ∎

DESIRE, 1
Zafar Malik

19.5" X 14.5". Acrylics, colored pencils, markers, and ink pens on found paper.

DESIRE, 2
Zafar Malik

19.5" X 14.5". Acrylics, colored pencils, markers, and ink pens on found paper.

KHOAAHISH #3
Zafar Malik

14.5" X 19.5". Acrylics, colored pencils, markers, and ink pens on found paper.

TARTEEB #2
Zafar Malik

11.5" X 11.5". Mixed media on board.

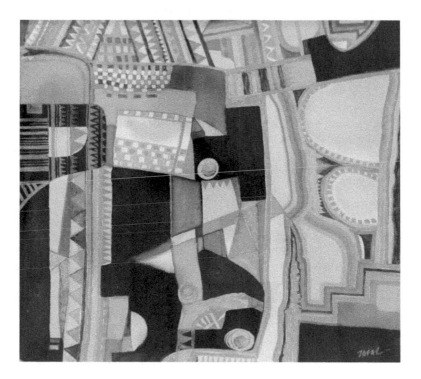

WITH US THERE IS NO INSECURITY
Ranbir Singh Sidhu

AMNESIA

I am a thief; in my time, I have stolen watches, VCRs, books, guns, cars. But in recent years I have given up on that part of the trade most others in my profession still practice zealously: I no longer steal objects. I envy my colleagues, yet also look down on them as simian brothers, swinging among the branches of primeval fantasy. I was never a specialist and found that when one afternoon I murdered a woman in her house it neither made me want to continue killing or give up my trade. Her death contoured the shape of my life in only one way: when I arrived home I found blood on my shoes and so spent some minutes cleaning them. But that wasn't all, because it also made me turn inward, and I have discovered that such an inward turning, a moving away from the events of daily boredom are what lead a person to discovery. My own discovery was simple, and I'm surprised I did not learn it earlier, because I am sure I was what I am, that I have always been this: an anesthesiologist of the soul. The thefts I carry out now—of guilt, fear, remorse—which I peel away from the heart like a man carving a statue in alabaster, allow the sufferer, the victim of my theft, a temporary salve —so that they may kill again, and push the children of their nations to charge to their grim and bloody deaths. They forget the numbers, the methods of execution and murder, the ways that bombs tear apart bodies and gas asphyxiates. In the gift of my amnesia they sleep with peace and innocence.

BOSNIA

In those days it all returned to Bosnia. Where else was there? A brief horror in Africa, in the Gulf, the threat of one in Korea, but then, Bosnia kept me busy. Here East meets West and Islam battles the Christian nations. The mysteries of the Eastern Orthodox Church resonate, Vienna clashes with Constantinople. Jeanne first talked to me of Bosnia, of Herzogovina, and her tongue found the depression of my spine and followed it from my anus to the point, she said, where the base of my skull bulges like a hard cancer. Some claimed, she told me, that 700,000 Serbs were killed at the concentration camps at Jesenovac, and that it was the Ustashas, the allies of the Nazis that did this. She laughs and I feel the weight of her naked body as it moves over me. She has a passion for fact and she tells me that the latest research, the very latest, states that only 487,000 were killed, and that if you looked at it statistically, more Muslims died there than Serbs. She tells me the statistics, the difference of a point, but I don't listen; her numbers are nothing to me.

CLINTON
I met her the day the administration changed and pushed up a notch on her alphabet, from Bush to Clinton, though little happened to shift policies or hearts. I made sure of that. My absolution allowed cowardice and fear to continue, because as I gave the gift of amnesia to murderers, I also gave it to those who might once have wanted to act. I met Jeanne in a bookshop and I watched as she roamed through the shelves on politics, on sex, on history, and as she stole a book on torture. I was struck by her because for a moment I thought she was a ghost. She was the exact likeness of the woman I had killed: the same yellow, flowered dress, the same thin, long neck that rose above her collar like those women in Africa, the ones so often pictured in television specials, with necks are held up by band after golden band. In the bright sunlight of the street, I thought I detected a diaphanous quality to her skin and clothing, as though stray beams of light were passing through her.

DUBROVNIK
The Republic of Dubrovnik boasted Europe's first trash collection, she tells me. It was the dawn of the fifteenth century. But today what remains? The city is a hull, shattered and lies stranded on the Adriatic Coast, as though it were a desert island and no bottles it might toss into the waters could bring it rescue. From Italy, you could see the night glow with its fires, as though the axis of the world had shifted and Europe lay much farther north in the cold latitudes where lights on the horizon dance nightly and shimmer with the memory of those first humans who saw them. I don't care about the numbers of dead, I tell her. Only buildings elicit my sympathy, the blown-apart docks, the old stones that held so much. It is the artifacts of a race that interest me, because in those stones, hidden behind those walls were cruelties and tortures that even Jeanne would find unimaginable. Dubrovnik, like the whole blighted mass of the Balkans, was for so long a prostitute to its warring neighbors and various masters. Jeanne looks at me with interest, and I tell her how the walls of Dubrovnik hid the dark hearts of slave traders, those walls hid the Nazis, and think of the Turks, the Austrians, and I tell her all I imagine is the pain as a whip hits a body; any whip, any body. And it is here that she disagrees, because Jeanne always must know who and when, she must always have the specifics. She wants to know what the weather was like that day, the quality of light. Who stood

in that room, what did they see; but I cannot supply her with answers because I have allowed all that to pass away and be forgotten. I have absolved the perpetrators of the facts and now I think only of the whip and the body, and all history for me is reduced to this single action, this single relationship, and I can tell Jeanne nothing more. That is how our debate began.

EXILE

In those days the city was hot, sweltering, and when we lay together in my small apartment we were often naked. I wanted it that way. I said we would not leave until the debate was over, and so we lay like that for days, no, weeks, in the sticking heat of that room on a bed whose sheets only knew the perspiration from our bodies the way blades of grass know dew. We ate food that friends would bring us or food we could call and have delivered. And so began our exile in this room, and we were refugees who had nowhere to travel to, were coming from nowhere; we lived in limbo, a self-created limbo, to be sure, and it was a place closer to the edge of dreams than to the edge of worlds. We were far from that clash, far from the center. We were orbiting and watched the world as though it were a ball that we could toss across the room.

FEAR

It begins with fear, I tell her. What else. The Serbs were afraid of an independent Croatia, afraid of the return of the Ustashas. The Croatians were afraid that within a greater Serbia they would be less than a minority, dogs to be hunted down for the memories of past wrongs, just the memory of them. And here was my point. What did it matter about the past wrongs, whether they existed or not? What did it matter what the Serbs did once, what the Croats did once? Only fear reigned here, far like a continent that slid over the hearts of everyone. Fear that would rend the landscape until all possibility of memory was gone, until anything, any building, any road, any village or tree or river or bridge, any face even, was so distorted that there would never be a recapturing of the past. The past would be gone and fear would dig its fingers into the soft hearts of every person. And if the past is not known, what else can it be but an ogre, a dark shape menacing the far reaches of a memory long since vanished.

GUIDE

She laughs. She will be my guide, she says. Truth, she tells me, as though it is all she needs to say, can be far more devastating, far more numbing than any phantom of a blank past.

HELL

Virgil was Dante's guide through Hell, and in my small room, Jeanne insists that we close the windows and switch the fans off. The heat rises and we lie in wet pools of our own moisture. In the modern, and former, ex, no more Yugoslavia, our guides are reporters, writers, doctors, or just voices that come from bombed cities, and we hear them through the crackle and noise, not of gunfire or bombs dropping, but of the radio waves that blanket this nation, these nations, at war. This is where her argument begins; at the portal to hell and we look through the television screen and the daily count of the dead and wounded, at the waterless, the houseless, the weaponless, the countryless. It must all begin with numbers, with a counting out of the dead, of the limbs they have lost, of how much their bodies weigh. There is no greater sublimity than this tally of horror.

IZETBEGOVIC

In Sarajevo, while writers and artists from across the West were trying to name it the Cultural Capital of Europe, the President of Bosnia, hidden in a room in the heart of this would-be Cultural Capital, began a self-imposed exile by walling himself off from the rest of the city. He no longer spoke with the Vice-President, Ejup Ganic, who had recently tried, it was said, to sacrifice the President's life to the Yugoslav National Army. Ganic himself spiraled into madness. On Radio Sarajevo he was heard wailing incomprehensibly. Jeanne wants to know which frequency Ganic was heard on, and I tell her, and she says she has me. I shake my head. It is that wail, I tell her, ribboning out of a building, any building. It doesn't matter who it was. The sound transcends facts. It is only pain. I do not absolve pain, I tell her. My anesthesia applies only to guilt and remorse, and those feelings which inhibit the inflicting of real pain. She looks at me quizzically and says, No, it must all be catalogued. Every word, gesture, scream.

JEANNE

She is from Lebanon, another Lebanon, and she says it is all in her head, a time when everyone walked the streets until late at night and the bars and cafes buzzed. She was born there but fled, so long ago she can't remember. She has seen her own birth certificate, seen photographs of herself in her mother's arms taken in a hospital ward. She has visited the hospital and confirmed that, yes, the room in the photograph and the room in the hospital are one and the same. Yet she doesn't remember and this gives her life, she says, a core of uncertainty that hides the possibility of her own death.

KOSOVO

The Serbs were born at their own moment of death. This is their greatest point of pride, this ancient death, which resurrects itself every June 28, the anniversary of that defeat in 1389, when the small Serb nation was overrun by the Ottoman Empire. It was a wound never sutured, and six hundred years later when Slobodan Milosevic stood on that battlefield of loss in Kosovo, it was to pull out this humiliation, this almost antediluvian memory, and to warn, and to warm up the crowd of losers, to a morning horizon of blood. She has photographs of that rally. Of Milosevic raising his arm in angry salute to the crowds whose beaten down hearts and faces had been waiting for this succor for more than half a millennium. What would we know without these photographs. How could we gauge the degree of hate, of anger, without seeing those faces in the sea of black and white. I study the photographs, but I tell her, again, they do not matter, they add nothing. I have seen to the core of Milosevic's heart and it rests easy because of me. I hold it every evening for him on the tips of my soft fingers and he spends easy and restful nights.

LUBNAN

This is how she pronounces Lebanon: with a short, precise *u* and a luxuriant *a*. It doesn't suggest the Lebanon of television images where buildings stand blasted out, no windows, few walls or even floors, and where a green line of dark imagination only recently split the city of Beirut. I argue that amnesia has saved her old Beirut, Paris before there was Paris. Without my forced forgetting, without my night flights, because I tell her now that this is how it happens (she raises an eyebrow in question, is amusement, in disbelief), that this is how I scrub the insides of minds like a chambermaid cleans a toilet on her knees the memories of murder and atrocity. With my ministrations no guilt remains, and those murderers of the modern Beirut could just as easily be the dashing men of memory who strolled down boulevards ending in the sea.

MOSTAR

So this is our debate. It shifts between the need for fact, for detailed memories, not only of the people, the faces, the events, the times, but how the buildings looked, how people held themselves, their gestures, their grimaces, the way the rain fell that day on a battlefield in Europe, or how the machine guns sounded at Sabilla; it moves from this to amnesia, or not quite amnesia, but a memory of form, a retention on the retina of emotion and pain; the scent of history. Jeanne gives an example: Mostar. It means defender of the bridge, and now the name is meaningless. The bridge is gone, and on one side of the Neretva, the river which splits this city, 35,000 Muslims starve. The Croatians on the Western bank shell those who in another part of this country, perhaps another time, are, were their allies. Fealty and betrayal are lost here, she says, your memories are nothing; there is only land which can be grabbed, land which is lost. The bridge, completed in 1566, was the jewel of this city. It was Miodrag Pirusic, a Serbian artillery commander who ordered the first shells fired on the bridge, but it was not until two years later, two years of constant shelling, that the bridge finally fell and its dark, old stones dropped into the river to mix with the bodies of animals and humans. She describes the bridge in detail, every stone, every corner of it, the slender crescent shape, and she says: How can we know what we have unless we know what we have lost?

NUMBERS

I have no argument against her numbers, because she says everything, yes, everything, can be reduced to a number at the tail of an equation. And this is the great elegance of memory. She says I can say nothing against it, that I have no argument that can challenge her numbers. I have argued that life, that the memory of life is simply form, and that the events and words and places, that ultimately the pain and horror of war—because it is now plain to both of us that it is war we are talking about—are peopled not by individuals, but by impressions that are interchangeable, that one can be the other, that there is no difference between the number of Croats killed in 1939 to those Serbs killed in 1389. But I do say this: these numbers, bloated, are ghosts of my salvation. They come back, every year, and fill a void where only vengeance can dwell. Without these numbers I would have no absolution to give, I would have no memory to erase, no sleep to ease.

OTTOMAN EMPIRE

It was the Ottoman Empire which, from the thirteenth century until its dissolution at the close of the Great War, held down, viciously, much of what we recently called Yugoslavia. The vast lands of the Ottomans served only to feed a central glory, a gemmed profligacy which ignored the rusting iron it was set in. Yugoslavia had no connection to the centers of learning for more than half a millennium; East and West were denied it. It straddled an ancient fault line, and it was crushed where the two powers met, in a dark age extended across the zone of contact.

PHOTOGRAPHS

The core of her argument lies here—in photographs we see now every day on the television, in newspapers and magazines that she is having delivered. She has ordered everything, every newspaper that will come to our door, every magazine she can think of. In the afternoons, when the mail arrives, we lie stripped and naked on the floor and paw through them, half awake, staring at these images of death, murder, rape, the destruction of property, of life, of sanity. The heat has not abated and every day as the sun crosses the room we warm like lizards to a dank, afternoon activity, our muscles stretching, our limbs beginning to move. What she does is to cut out all the photographs. Every one she can find. She does it slowly, because it is still only the afternoon, and though we both sweat and breath heavily in the hot, still air, we are unaccustomed to movement. Our bodies are beginning to calcify, and every day I believe we move a little slower. Our debate, though it continues, feels ancient, and I wonder if it did not begin a millennium ago and that we are nothing other than the flicking tail of a lizard born at the Schism.

QUESTIONS

We are left with questions hanging in the air between us. We lie at separate ends of the bed, and mouth the questions, no longer able to support our sides of the argument, and slowly I am forgetting what it is that I so dearly wagered, even what the wager was. The room is plastered with the photographs of our faulty memories.

RAPE

I have listened to the music of rape, a single strain that follows my dreams. It has no face, no victim, no aggressor. There are only certain times when the music rises, soars, crescendos, then dies down, incubating in a slow movement. On one wall there are photographs only of men. These men are young, old, they have mustaches, beards, thick locks of black hair, eye patches, spectacles, cuts across their face, handsome jaws; I do not know if they are Serb or Croat or Muslim. Jeanne says this is the Wall of Rapists, and when she says it I try to steal my eyes away from hers, away from that wall of faces, because in seeing their faces multiplied like that, in seeing how one blends into another, how one stare duplicates another, I begin to understand the horror of her argument. There are so many faces here that when I look at the wall I hear nothing, no sound, no music; there is only a redundant, numbing silence.

SCHISM

The Great Schism of 1054 allowed Rome and Constantinople to split the salvations of the world between themselves, between Catholicism and Eastern Orthodoxy, cutting a line through Bosnia, and this has been the battlefield not only of empires, but of priests claiming more than bodies; claiming the eternal souls of territories. We look across at each other on the bed. All trust has been lost. The images that she has taped to the walls begin to impregnate me with more than amnesia, with a sense that everything, every emotion, feeling, action, is not in essence the single act—whip striking at a bent back—but that the actions of everyone, everything, melt into the obscurity of debauched redundancy; as the faces on the walls multiply, as the facts she piles into my ears mount with tedious precision, everything I know becomes a tautology, and the essence I seek becomes lost.

TITO
she says is Hitler who is Aurangzeb who is Caligula who is Pol Pot who is Milosevic and I only hear the question not the statement because I sit my back to the wall in sudden fear that everything I know is gone and

USTASHA
Again the history lesson, again I try to fight it. We return to Jesenovac, to the million killed, or merely the 100,000, and she says: Do I know Stepinac, and I can only reply that I no longer know anything or anyone. Cardinal Stepinac, she says, baptized all the Serbs before the Ustasha slaughtered them. He stood over them and in Latin he baptized them. Their deaths gave them eternal life. Stepinac did them a favor.

VICTIMS
I shout suddenly that there are no victims, there never have been. I have not eaten for four days and I subsist only on the images that surround me and all I see now are the faces, frozen, as though waiting for some future date when technology will revive them. When I hear my voice, cracked, uncertain, and the words that I shout, that there are no victims; that one last plea of mine, that one last attempt to win this debate: there is only the whip, the body, the arc it makes in the air. But I realize in that moment that I have put myself into Jeanne's alphabet and my voice, as I speak, is being recorded, catalogued, digitized.

WITH US
there is no insecurity: this was Milosevic's slogan and it is repeated again and again all in the same tone of threat from her voice because she says the debate is won and lost and now we live in the infinity of knowledge of images of everything at once and forever and that is how we will know the world...

XERXES

Even Xerxes who defeated the Greeks at Thermopylae and sacked and burned Athens, even Xerxes fled from Salamis from Plataea and in Persia he was killed and it was the Greeks who wrote his history.

YEAR ZERO

Pol Pot began from the beginning. He started civilization from zero, not one, and to begin from zero everything was destroyed to be rebuilt, and who wrote the histories that were gone, who wrote the lives that succumbed and when I look at him in the corner, now that he has lost our debate, and tell him of Pol Pot again, and tell him it is I who will write this history, I also tell him of his death, his coming death. He calls my name: Jeanne, and I hear it with the satisfaction of a victor. But in his voice, his person, all I see and hear is that zero, that beginning, because once catalogued and recorded, once digitized, once he is in my alphabet and I have taken those words, what is there left for him because he has said nothing, written nothing, and everything here has been my voice, my words, because I wrote this history, this catalogue of a debate and its demise, because the ghosts of the murdered have but one fate.

ZAGREB

before it was Zagreb was the Roman settlement of Andautonia and it was only in 1094 AD that King Ladislaus gave it the name Zagreb when he founded the diocese there, though the origin of the name itself remains a mystery. ∎

POEM BEGINNING WITH A LINE BY BELLOW
Amit Majmudar

Who is the Tolstoy of the Zulus? Who is the Proust of the Papuans?
Who's the Baryshnikov to dance the Blackfoot Bolshoi back from ruins?
Who is the Kafka of Qatar? The El Greco of the Eskimos?
And who's the Vladimir Nabokov of Lakota prose?
Who is the Titian of Tenochtitlan? The Mahler of the Mayas?
Did the Hottentot Hans Holbein slip right by us?
Who is the Shakespeare of the Seneca, and what is his *Othello*?
Who is the Goethe of the Hutus? And who in the hell is Saul Bellow?

BROWN STUDY; OR POEM ENDING WITH A LINE BY GOERING

Amit Majmudar

The brown, who once studied
how to be white, now study
the brownness of brown. The Heritage
Foundation is preparing
a white paper on Brown, warning against
tanning salons and Coppertone
and Syrians. The brown
have begun to study Robert Browning
with furrowed brow for signs
of anti-brunitism. Brown might well be the new
black; though the old whites, to be fair,
never did anything to young brown me
but bake me brownies. How now,
brown cow? I have no beef with the whites
as long as they admit brown cows are sacred.
With me, being brown isn't a black-or-white issue.
You remember that panel on decolonization
at Brown University? Ever since
when I hear the word "multicultural"
I reach for my Browning.

1979
Amit Majmudar

The mob that knifed the sentry knew Hafiz.
The mob had dedicated to Hafiz

A park with pigeons in downtown Tehran
A mere two weeks before it threw Hafiz

Through the glass house of the embassy,
Brickbats of spine and glue that flew Hafiz

Into a future where no books could live
Unless approved as good and true. Hafiz—

Starry-eyed lush with Shiraz on his breath,
The Persian miracle half Rumi's, half his—

Danced with the students on a burning roof,
Clinked toasts with an inkwell in the news office

Because Hafiz was young and knew no better,
Wine condensed on his tongue like dew, Hafiz

Conspiring on the tongues of priests and gunmen
Masked, veiled like the Beloved, who blew Hafiz

Like a kiss at all of us who drink and rhyme,
At all of us who know the true Hafiz

As an ambassador from the hidden kingdom
Where rooftop sniper fire cues Hafiz,

His rhymes, when broadcast by the muezzin,
A rain of red wine out of the blue, Hafiz

Making the revolutionaries dreidel
(Spinning's the best way to pursue Hafiz),

Making Marines cry Allah, mobs cry Oorah,
Lovers who never knew they knew Hafiz.

FIRE SERMON
Amit Majmudar

Nippon, napalm. Caution: Flammable: Cambodia. In Viet
nomine Domination, Phan Thi Kim Phuc is on fire,

and American cameramen are at her side, shooting her.
Agni, agony, Saigon, gone. Thich Quang Duc is on fire:

Watch him burn down to his own prizewinning photograph.
Burn, baby, burn. Old Glory is on fire,

and new glory, too, this vainglory of a match burning
toward the hand that struck. Giordano Bruno is on fire

with all our bygone divines, beggar devas, the Shining Ones
whose names are ghost pepper. My mouth is on fire,

my tongue is on fire, somebody get me a glass of water, quick...
Better make that a whiskey: My match head skull is on fire.

I burn for my poem, my person, my sermon to be one fire,
but as the dance floor heats up here on Phuket Island

I chant with the others, I sing with the heavenly choir,
the roof, the roof, the roof is on fire

THE MAN WHO PLAYED GANDHI
Anu Kumar

The year he turned fifty, Das made the farthest journey of his life. He never returned. Like his father and then his grandfather before, Das was a traveling actor, though he had found his own particular niche. A role that had served him well all these years wherever he traveled. But his illustrious forebears had never made long journeys, even in the time the trains made such things possible, making the farthest always within reach. Toward the end of their lives, they had confined themselves to places closer home, or simply stayed put in the village, the one Das had grown up in and where he still lived. People like his wife, though, took pride in insisting that it was a town, now with its own railway station and many television-owning families.

Unlike his forebears, the challenges Das faced were uniquely his. They had never had to keep up appearances or maintain careful habits, even during lean seasons, when finding work was as difficult as the fact that it could come by unexpectedly as well.

That October, a month before the festive season, when a fortnight had elapsed since the lean period, with villagers no longer busy with transplanting the new crop, Das still found himself without work. By this time in other years, he was usually on a train, traveling to a performance in one small town or another. Now he felt himself deserted. Even his wife had been taken away by the television in the house next door.

Sunday evenings when they had gone for long evenings by the river were already given over the film, any film, the television chose to put up those hours. She wouldn't miss it for anything. The afternoon serials too had become more important than all the other things of daily habit. He thought of her on the swing reading her prayer book soon after their afternoon meal. And asked himself why he had let himself get used to it.

He turned his mind to other things. He pulled out the small, square-shaped mirror nailed to the wall by the window, and brought it closer. The three-pronged television antenna tilting on the terrace of their neighbor's two-storied house caught his eye, and for a second, a grimace passed his face. He straightened his brow, reached for a small comb. He needed glasses, he thought, finding he had to lean in closer. His eyes moved almost simultaneously to take in the portrait of the man fixed right next where the mirror had been. A man he had portrayed in shows across the country and emulated to perfection. Someone Das had followed since childhood when his skills had been greatly applauded. His speech, they said, was just perfect. He walked too in just the right way.

Now that Das had aged, he did not have to try hard. He had become Gandhi. That unexpected smugness made him look critically at himself, when his mustache caught his attention. He bent so close his nose touched glass, and he blinked. His lips had the right expression of fastidiousness and disapproval but the straggly ends of the mustache now hanging low over his lips were uneven.

As he turned his head sideways, sniping off some stray ends of hair, the music blared up again, some raucous song that was part of the movie and then he heard the shout from outside.

Postman.

Das frowned, the ends of the scissors rising in an open v, holding his nose neat in between. This was not the usual postman. This voice was unfamiliar, someone young and impatient.

Das ran fingers down his mustache. He had trimmed it but not carefully enough. He lifted his head, turned it left, right, then lowered his chin so he was almost glowering at himself. The mustache was bristly, whitened in parts, and the gray showed in places.

He'd some work left still, then the voice called again.

Postman, need your signature.

Das knew then it was a registered letter. He sighed, perhaps the Gandhi Learning Institute had sent him yet another brochure. They were always sending him material to read, though he had several hundred Gandhi quotes memorized for use already.

Through the thin cotton curtain, he looked out through the grilled balcony, past the small iron gate. A man waited on his bicycle, his foot stretching down to scrape the ground. Das heard the rhythmic scraping, and recognized the man from the times he had been to the post office. He was a graduate, unlike the old timers in the post office, and his assumed busyness always kept him surly, or else he always had his nose in a book, never even looking up once. Das had been told by a peon somewhat dismissively that the new entrant was studying for the civil services, that the post office job was just temporary. And here he was today, out delivering letters. Which, Das surmised, must have led to an increase in surliness.

The man noticed a brief movement in the curtains and holding the envelope forward again, said brusquely *Sign please.* It was thin, hardly big enough to enclose a book or even some kind of reading material.

Das allowed himself the briefest glimmer of hope. The towel he usually draped around his bare shoulders was not at its usual place, on its hook by the door. His wife took care of all this. Now he pulled out a sleeveless coat, pushed his arms quickly through it and walked out, picking up the tall walking stick on the way. He did not need it, but every small impression counted.

As Das undid the bolt on his front door, the new postman looked up and did not turn his gaze away. In that moment's silence, Das knew what to expect and waited for the obvious statement of fact. Or perhaps it would come mixed with mockery, or sarcasm for people also had light-hearted fun at his expense. Das would tell himself never to take all this personally. For it was Gandhi who had become the butt of ridicule.

When Das walked out on the patch of uneven ground between his house and the ground, miming Gandhi in every way, the man whose lips had been pursed in an intent to whistle, took a quick look around, shook his head and said, "God, you look just like…"

He stopped midway, as Das did too, noting the foolish vacuous look spread over the man's face. Had it come to this then? That he wasn't recognized any more. But it wasn't his fault. Perhaps schools didn't teach Gandhi any more.

"Yes?"

Das waited. The man slapped his jeans, looked around again and found no one to share his amazement. Then he slapped himself on the forehead and said, "Ben….can't get his name right. It's the man who played Gandhi?"

"I play Gandhi," Das said, and stopped. There was no point, if this man was mistaking him for someone else, he really needed to do something fast, brush up his skills. Maybe give a speech or two.

The postman unclipped the pen from his shirt pocket, handed it over and then said, a sudden joviality in his voice now, "Maybe you should give me an autograph. I could say Ben Kingsley, oh yes, that's his name!"

He was startled at his own utterance, but the next moment, he was laughing. "Yes, amazing how I remembered the name. It just came a moment ago, was gone and now I have it. Yes, Ben. Ben Kingsley is really good. I think he's American. But he had no problems, traveling so rough and wearing so little too."

The pen stilled in Das's hand. He smiled. Yes, it took a lot to be bare chested, even in peak winter. As he had done the time he had gone up to Kashmir. They wanted to promote national integration and peace and what better than to have Gandhi in all this or at best someone who looked like him. But it had been cold, and darkness had come early. His hands had trembled as he spun the charkha, and also from what he thought were stray gunshots. It was what happened all the time. He was told, policemen firing away at protesters who didn't need an excuse to come out into the streets. To protest for electricity, bad roads, no schools or these being taken over by the military or even for those missing children and husbands. As the crowds had panicked, dispersed, and then gathered around again, and the sounds of marching soldiers came nearer, faded and neared in rhythm, Das sat in place, willing himself not to tremble, his mind on the moment, and on the charkha before him.

But this man with the post would not be interested in all that. He was talking about this actor, whose name he had finally recollected and whose movies he had seen. Movies he, Das, had never heard of.

In a flash, he remembered all the competitions he had entered in since childhood, then through school, college, and later. He wanted to match the man's list in every way. Das had come out winning on so many occasions, now countless really. The audience as one had admitted that there could only be one real, authentic lookalike of Mahatma Gandhi, and that was Das, son of Raghunandan, village Phookchakri. Spectators and judges at every competition stopped simply to stare at him, caught in a daze. The disbelief would change to grudging respect when he recited from memory one of Gandhi's many speeches. At the end the applause would be prolonged, so would the nods of agreement.

"He speaks just like him. Not a word out of place, the gesture is so like Gandhi's." Sometimes they would come up or meet him backstage, to tell him that they admired the way he sat still at his charka, spinning cotton, adjusting his spectacles, smiling just the way they remembered Bapu doing so.

Das kept his silence, stoppered his own memories, and signed where indicated. It was then that he glanced at the envelope. It was from Manoharpur, a place he had never been to; a town he didn't even know of. But evidently the place did know about him. He must have been the best Gandhi ever.

The man pedaled away with a swish, a thin cloud of dust swirled around his ankles. "Manoharpur. People now call me from places far away," Das said, raising his thin voice, glad he had the triumphant last word. Manoharpur, he said to himself again. Even if it was the remotest place on earth, he would go there. Though he knew he'd have to look it up on the atlas. The neighboring house with the television had an atlas, for they had a school-going child. The thought cheered him up. He had a pretext to draw away his wife.

He stood outside their gate, with the heavy lock on its long metallic chain. For some minutes Das rattled the latch, but the jangling was ineffectual and drew out no one. Other times, barely a year ago, there would have been someone at the porch. A child playing but the television had taken over everything. They were all entranced by it. The outside world was only interesting if it was packed up to fit inside a screen in your home. It was all so mindless. He put his head against the bars and then flinched. It was already hot; the midday sun beat down fiercely, but he was stubborn. He would bring her out. He finally sat down, just by the end of the wall, where the gate began, for that provided welcome shade. He put the letter on his head, fanned himself with it. He must have dozed off because he looked up to hear someone speaking in thin insistent tones over his head.

"Did you have to make a scene? Come on, get up."

Das suddenly found himself quite numb. It was his wife, standing over him, rail thin and in her voice as reedy as the rest of her. It took him quite some time to remember where he was, who she was. He had even forgotten how to unfold his knees.

"Arre, the heat has made you deaf? Get up. The older you're getting, you're getting some screws loose."

They went back, she muttering softly, holding him by the hand for he was still unsteady on his feet. It looked almost romantic to anyone looking at them. Then he realized he had not asked for the atlas. He stopped abruptly, she almost stumbled in response. It took him some time to explain what it was he wanted. At the end she insisted, in a tired voice. "The railway station will have one, won't it?"

"No I want to know for myself now," he said, petulantly slapping the envelope before her, just as the post office man had done before him.

Their argument picked up the last few steps home. She was already openly resentful because after having been alerted to his presence outside the house, she had had to miss the last few minutes of her serial and he, because of the wait she had made him endure and for the fact that the atlas was still not there.

Cocooned in the warmth of their small house, he pulled his spinning wheel from under the stringed bed, and took it from its case. He sat before it, bunching up his knees the way he had learned from Gandhi, then raised the wheel, moving it methodically, turning it left, then right, as he put the spool in.

He spun fast, watching the river of thread running up down the wheel, his left hand on the spool, moving up and down, quickly, his fingers and thumb holding the yarn and his right hand on the wheel.

He had been doing it a long time. The soft whirring noise lingered over the stillness in the house.

His wife sighed, pulled her sari over her head and set out to fetch the atlas.

To get to Manoharpur, one followed the scratchy black line of the rail track on the atlas map, from Puri by the sea, up to the northern parts. But the main line stopped at Haridwar and straggly lines appeared, only to meander away somewhere else. Das knew he must try first for a ticket to Haridwar and make other decisions only after he had reached there.

"It's not very long for Dassera. And Manoharpur...let me see..." he muttered as he opened out once again the much-folded letter he had received. "If its somewhere near Haridwar, so it might be cold this time of the year."

It was hard not to miss the large deep pools of unspent sadness in his wife's eyes but she was talking of the sweater that she would have to finish knitting in time, the shawls she would have to get ready. His shoes, those were the most important, had to be got ready too. He had those old Bata sandals, thick straps that crossed tightly around the feet. He would make do with those, some woolen socks would help and of course the shoes would have to be polished.

He looked at her silently, as other questions shaped themselves in his mind. How would she manage when he was gone? Was she saving anything? Maybe he would find a place somewhere to send her a money order?

There was suddenly too much to do. He snapped at her, asking why even lunch wasn't ready yet.

* * *

"Haridwar?"

The stationmaster's thin eyebrows rose over his sharp gleaming eyes. Das was used to the stationmaster by now. As he was to the stench and the general crowds around. Das sighing to himself, three query lines in neat parallel lines on his forehead, let himself in for the inevitable. He knew what to expect, he'd be made fun of and he'd have to participate in it, for the sake of his ticket. A stationmaster could easily declare that tickets were all booked.

"No... only to Manoharpur...to participate in the Dassera..."

"Why Bapu, a new satyagraha?"

The laughter washed over Das, leaving him exposed, naked, helpless. Das's toes twitched. They longed to scratch the floor in his discomfiture. But he only pulled his arms around himself, drew his shawl tighter and nodded in agreement.

"Could be...the letter didn't say anything. I will have to find out when I reach there on the tenth..."

The man pulled the sheaf of unmarked tickets towards him. He wrote down the date, and then Das's full name. Shyamsundar Raghunandan Das...

"Why do you have such a long name Bapu?"

Das was peering through the grilled window that divided them. It was broken up into several small squares, and a fly buzzed above as it tried to navigate its way through. Das hoped the man had not misspelled his name. He stared at the man's scrawl, the upside down letters appearing like a long line of ants following each other in imperfect order. One never knew when to do the right thing. If you spelled it out for them—S for Shimla, H for Hen, then Y, y, y for Yugoslavia...they either got offended or confused.

"Don't spell." Someone had once snapped at him. "I know English. I am BA pass, Kanpur University."

And on another occasion, a particularly obnoxious stationmaster had put him in his place. "Don't tell me as if I don't know the spelling of Yugo...whatever. It begins with a J. Jugoslavia..."

That time his name had appeared on the ticket, with an 'h' missing everywhere, giving his name a castrated look, a chicken plucked in a very ungainly manner. Syamsundar Ragunandan Das.

The stationmaster looked up to see Das peering anxiously through the bars. One frame of his spectacles was caught between two bars, while another straight bar spliced neatly through the other half. Still his nose managed to wedge itself in, ascertaining the facts for himself. The stationmaster smiled indulgently holding up the ticket.

"Arre. Bapu...why don't you shorten your name. S R Das..."

He handed the ticket over to Das, putting his stamp back on its rubber pad in one corner of his table. Das wriggled his nose so that his spectacles settled down on the thin ridge over his nose more comfortably and he answered firmly, determined to halt more questions now that he had the ticket. "It's the name I was born with. Besides, there are too many S R Das's around. Only one Shyamsundar Raghunandan Das."

"Quite right...Bapu." The stationmaster's finger was now on his mustache, a thin straggly wedge of hair that lay between thick, paan-stained lips and a nose that looked clamped to his face like a clothes peg. He glanced around, trying to get together an audience, and the peon who had been lounging on his corner stool, his eyes held hypnotically by the loud ticking wall clock, obligingly shuffled forward. Two passengers looked at each other in appreciation of the stationmaster's wit. Das smiled too, absently. He folded the ticket carefully and after checking the dates again, placed it in the inside pocket of his sleeveless jacket.

The stationmaster's voice rose to accommodate the addition in his audience, "Even Mohandas Karamchand Gandhi had a long name. But who remembers Bapu, except to blame him for all the ills of our country."

The peon piped in smartly, "Not just Gandhi...I think Nehru too was to blame for what is wrong everywhere." And he looked sadly down at the floor, as if the scattered pieces of everything that had gone wrong had fallen all around him.

Manoharpur was three hours away from Haridwar. The train, Das had been told, took a day and a bit more to reach Haridwar but most times it was late. No one could tell how long it really took. "Can't say..." was the usual answer he got from everyone—the numerous train attendants to the vendors who clambered in and out selling toys, whistles, women's magazines and soap paper to wash oneself after using the toilet—all gave him the same reply, vague and perfunctory.

The train was full of young people, raucous college students returning home for the festival vacation, other boisterous, restless kids prone to throwing tantrums. The college students stopped every vendor who passed their compartment, made him empty his box and passed around the things he had to sell. They bargained and hassled but in the end, only pulled on long disappointed faces, shook their heads mournfully, insisting what was on offer wasn't quite what they were looking for. The children, not to be outdone, pestered their parents, who pressed the attendants with demand after demand—water and chocolates, a magazine and water again because it was hot inside the train, with all the crowds.

Das eased himself to a corner seat with his book. He was reading one from the *Collected Works of Mahatma Gandhi*, a series of the great man's writings and speeches that the government had been steadily bringing out since the 1950s. In most shows, he would recite one of Gandhi's speeches. Some of these he knew by heart. His favorites in no particular order were Gandhi's speech on Satyagraha just before the noncooperation movement, the speech he gave to the British mill workers, or the one in Noakhali when the Partition riots threatened to rip the two new countries forever asunder.

Das put on an old Himachal cap, pulling it down well over his ears. He was glad he wasn't recognized for who he wasn't, and felt sad about that too. He did manage to read in peace for a good many hours for no one even looked at him or what he did, even the time he shuffled his way to the bathroom, putting the book face down so that its title struck everyone in the face. He walked in the manner of the Mahatma, stooping forward a little, his eyes blinking rapidly. The smile around his lips enunciated even more the lines on his forehead, the cuts in his cheek. The aisle crowds obligingly made way for him, some gave him a brief glance but no one looked at him really. When he returned, the book was just where he left it. No one had even lifted it, even out of curiosity. When he picked it up, he saw the dust-browned mark on the book's jacket. Someone had brushed past it carelessly, so that it had dropped to the floor, where it had caught the end of someone's shoe.

When the night lights became too dim for him to read, he rested his head against the wooden berth playing over in his mind a story Gandhi had related in his autobiography. His remorse after consuming mutton and smoking at a friend's behest. On some festive occasions, sometimes he read out that part from Gandhi's Experiments with Truth, and that never failed to move the audience. If he were luckier, there would also be an old timer in the audience, an ailing, almost debilitated freedom fighter who would insist on sharing his memories too, and that would invite a surge of other shared things from others. It was in this way, he thought, the earliest stories were made up, how inspiration traveled and he sat up straight and proud at that very thought.

At Haridwar, the train reached three hours late and by then night had fallen. A cold wind had forced a sudden shutdown of all stalls in the station. The coolies sat under a makeshift awning, passing around a bidi, and a thin stream of smoke drifted into the clear night air. Over the station walls, Das saw smaller fires burning. Only the kindly tea-stall owner had kept his shop open, offering shelter and hot tea in small cone-shaped clay cups to those waiting for a train, others who had nowhere to go and even Das, who had still further to go and needed a place to sort out his plans.

To Das, the high clay stove, its fire making a throbbing sound in that cold night and the array of cups arranged like a small hill on a flat plastic bucket suddenly looked very inviting. The hiss of the kettle, the musical way the owner poured the milk so that the light on the foam made every bead and drop shine in the darkness was welcoming. There was already a circle of people around him, even a straggly dog or two.

In the few minutes it took Das to gulp down his cup of steaming chai, the group around the tea stall provided him much useful information. He had come in last and so they turned to him to resume flagging conversations. Words gave warmth on such a cold night.

The school grounds where the fair was to be held was a good forty minutes away but the performers, most of whom had taken the state transport bus from Haridwar, were staying in the Apsara guest house. Maybe arrangements had been made for him there too? Das didn't know but he would find out. A silence fell as the audience took in the uncertainty in his voice. Then a tongawallah who lived in the Radhabhai colony, near the city square, offered to take him there. Das looked apologetic. He didn't have much change left. The tongawallah waved away his apologies. Who had asked him for money anyway. Besides, the guest house was on his way. Then the tongawallah took advantage of the pause in the conversation, took a deep breath and then made a more momentous announcement, as he thrust a bristly chin forward to indicate Das. "Didn't he look like the actor who had come here once?"

Das looked around, a frank guileless look in his own eyes as he offered himself up for inspection. They peered at him then, screwing up their eyes, alternately shaking and nodding their heads as they sought to arrive at a mutually amicable settlement.

"Yes, but his head is broader...a bit."

"His mustache is not bristly."

"Yes you are right, and he is not so thick around the middle. The other one had a big paunch..." There was a roar of laughter at that, after which a lull fell as they repeated the joke in their own minds.

It was Das who jumped in, grateful and eager to be accepted. "You are referring to Ben Kingsley?"

The tea-stall owner's gaze was openly mocking, "Aree bhai, why would Ben Kingsley come here all the way to Manoharpur. Taking a flight from Hollywood-shollywood, wherever he stays, then a train from Delhi or maybe a flight from there to Dehra Dun...and then a car journey. It would take him two whole days. Big stars don't have the time..."

There were nods of agreement all around. The man next to Das then placed a hand on Das's shoulder, as if he were a particularly slow student, who had to be explained things carefully. "No. Bhai, we are talking of someone who looked like Ben Kingsley-Shingley, whoever. He wanted to be an actor. We don't know what became of him."

Everyone shook their heads sadly. Yes, no one could tell what happened to a man who looked like the actor who looked like Gandhi. The wood in the fire crackled all of a sudden, spewing out a spark or two. It reminded everyone how late it was getting. The tongawallah got up, rubbing his hands on his shawl. He dug his hand through his collar and pulled out his purse. Das made to do the same but the owner waved him away. "You are here for the first time. Don't shame us by paying."

At the school grounds, where the tongawallah dropped him off, the reception was equally warm and welcoming. No sooner had he introduced himself, the chief organizer, a nervous looking man with the air of a school headmaster, gripped his hands tight and thanked him in a choked voice for not letting them down. It had been a tradition in this town to celebrate Dassera with great fanfare but things were getting very expensive. He coughed meaningfully and went no further. Das understood. There were many like him who would have been ready to come for next to nothing.

"Your stall will be somewhere there..." he had pointed to the darkness on his right. Das nodded absently. It didn't really matter, people would stay to listen if they were really interested and over the years, the interest in Gandhi had waned and remained only of an academic nature. The organizer was nodding in perfect understanding, almost as if Das had said the words aloud. "Yes, it doesn't really matter. After all, the magician will simply make you disappear..."

The man did not intend his remarks to startle Das but nevertheless he hastened to reassure him, as Das's eyes now fixed him in a long, unblinking stare.

"Oh dear, I didn't mean to make you nervous. It's all right, the magician is quite respected. He has already made the Taj Mahal disappear and even the India Gate. Or is it the Gateway in Bombay. We were very desperate to have him here..."

The words were falling off him in a rush, as he tried hard to assuage Das's fears. It was obvious he was afraid that Das would take the next train home. "The other village, Puranpur, had called him last month at the village headman's son's wedding. We had to show them we were equally good..."

Das was nodding concentrating on the man's every word. All that long journey—he wondered, calculating quickly in his mind—a whole day and night away from his home, only to disappear from everyone's sight, to be part of a magic show. A show that had made the Taj disappear and the Gateway, even the Qutb Minar and now Gandhi. Das shivered, held himself tight, knowing if his hold slipped on himself, he wouldn't know whether to laugh or cry.

The organizer, almost as if he read Das' thoughts, said aloud, "The magician, we couldn't promise him the Taj, the Qutb nothing...and then finally someone. The young CPWD engineer, a smart Brahmin boy, saw the items on the list and came up with your name. It would be a very new thing: the magician who could make Gandhi disappear."

His shiny eyes were pleading with Das for understanding but his attention soon moved to the sounds of a quarrel that had just broken out. Men were fighting over sleeping space, though durries and pillows had been spread out in a long line all down the school dormitory. The organizer pulled Das by the sleeve, "It's all right. They can't get their sleep without a fight..."

In the end, the fair had been a success. Das had been on show for the whole of five minutes. It took two minutes for the magician to introduce him to the audience, for most seemed to know little about Gandhi. He had waved a crystal ball, dangling it high up and drawing the audience's attention to it. Not Das, who sat in despair looking at the faces staring up at the magician as the hypnosis came into effect. He saw how faces stilled, how the laughter on some faces changed to a silly stupefaction, and how some simply fell back on their chairs, unable to take it all in.

Neither could Das. For the next three minutes he just sat there, exactly as the magician had indicated on a low stool with wheels provided. His back hurt a little because of the hard wooden seat. The hypnosis would soon be over, the magician had warned him, and things had to be timed. But Das found he couldn't move. He only felt himself swept along, he heard the rumble of wheels under him, and saw through the mistiness before him, the curtains fall. In his mind, he remembered the magician's voice, smoothly assuring him, about there being actually a double layer of curtains, one that the audience could not see but of just the same color as the background. It was here Das would stay hidden for some time as the audience recovered.

Das then had to make his way out quickly, as the magician moved onto his next act. In the wild cheering that followed his own disappearance, Das only wanted to get away, and forget his shoes as well. The magician had earlier looked disparagingly at Das' shoes; their creaking, the magician had complained, could break the spell. Das had felt ashamed. His shoes seemed a symbol of everything doomed and long-gone.

It was the magician who took all the applause. But what did it matter, Das thought, as he counted the ten one-hundred rupee notes and two five-hundred notes, if everything turned out well in the end? He regretted only having carried too much luggage. To fit in the collected works of Gandhi, he had had to leave a shawl behind at home, for all his wife's insistence and Manoharpur that year was facing an early, cruel winter.

"Excuse me..." a voice broke into his reverie. He looked up into the eyes of a very earnest young man. The quality of sincerity seemed etched into the young man. It seeped out of his gold-rimmed spectacles, his lined khadi kurta, and through the overstuffed rucksack that he wanted to push into the empty space under Das's feet. Das nodded.

The man pushed it in and then eased himself into the berth between two villagers who were already sleeping, heads drooping onto their chests.

The other man smiled at Das once he had made himself comfortable. "You look like Gandhi." It was a statement, not even a question. But he was not waiting for the startled expression on Das's face to die away. Like a child who had found a ready and captive audience, he went on, "I am researching Gandhi's early role in Indian politics. Do you know, he traveled all over these parts, in the years before Champaran. Through small villages and towns, trying to find the real India."

Das was listening to him, filled with a sudden sweet emotion. He scolded himself angrily: "Why are you getting so emotional. It isn't as if he is talking about you, or even some relative of yours."

The train had slowed down as the man talked. It was a small station, huddled around empty benches, a ticket booth and a tea stall, tucked into the wall. "I will get us some tea...I think Gandhi liked tea too." He waited and Das smiled, obliging him. Then he was gone. Das looked out and saw him walk, his quick light steps moving towards the tea stall. Then he turned at the light tap on his shoulder. It was one of the villagers who was now stretching himself awake. "So he's got you too. That man." And he shook his drowsy companion. "Hey wake up... tell our friend too."

The other man only nodded, he was too sleepy. The first man shrugged his shoulders and laughed at Das. "He is mad. Does no work. So many times I have seen him on his train, talking only of Gandhi this, Gandhi that. Young men should really find themselves a job these days."

The young man never returned but he had left Das with an idea, one that came to him even as night fell, and the lights dimmed. Das realized he could put off returning. He would travel, from one station to another, buying tickets, changing trains, telling whomever he found about Gandhi.

Would his wife miss him? Or would he still be someone to be conveniently remembered like Gandhi? The shoes he had left behind in Manoharpur would come back to his wife. She could keep them clean. Sometimes she might think of him. Or even wonder, Das thought, what on earth was he doing wandering around the country, barefooted, perhaps cold? ∎

ON RE-READING VALMIKI'S *RAMAYANA*
Kirun Kapur

Anyone can disappear
across the black water.

Every girl can be taught
her middle name is shame.

When will I burn
your urge for purity—

my bones are a furnace
my face is a game.

Every girl steals away
with a demon at some point—

all her alphabets, ankle bells
all her braids—

She will meet herself in the third person,
she will lie with her fear,

she will dress in her rage.
O, the world is curdled

with husbands,
blue as the gods, gentle as flame.

FALL
Kirun Kapur

Whom do I speak to when I speak to you?

A tree. My tall lover. My idea of a god.

Look at this world, red as a spleen,

a temple, gold and dying—

An airplane full of people has disappeared.

Up they rose, side by side, lives

in numbered rows. I watch the oaks,

the aspens drop their leaves in twos and threes.

On TV a woman speaks of how she prays

they never find the smallest trace

of wreckage, so that she can continue

to have some hope. I try to picture

the full plane. I try to be in the world

of mysteries I can hardly stand.

Look, the willow still holds all its green,

next to it the cherry's been stripped bare.

An airplane full of people traveling

eternally. I'm here in the debris

of one season. I don't know how

to speak to you about even the simple

loss of leaves.

DOUBLENESS GHAZAL
Kirun Kapur

Could anyone have saved me from it?
Waking or sleeping doubts creep from it.

I tell myself, it doesn't matter what you're thinking.
Give me the tall truth, I am prepared to leap from it.

Helicopters. Bangles. Kerosene. Silk.
Under my mind's weight our stories seep from it.

Why won't you answer my most basic questions?
Cut down the reeds. Make a clean sweep of it.

Not even you could make me other than I am.
So bitter is the brew we steep from it.

Gin or whiskey, a long needle or quick fist.
Pleasure or grief, eventually I'll sleep from it.

A plain brow, hot cheek, the sharp twist of a lip
As if a face could be the key to it.

Kiran means light; Kieran means dark.
Why shouldn't Kirun get lost in the great sea of it?

NIMMI'S CHOICE
Ravibala Shenoy

I set the teapot and the plate of almond biscuits on the tray and climb the stairs. My husband is lying on the bed. I straighten the pillows, brush down his unruly hair and open the blinds to the afternoon sun. Three years ago he was diagnosed with cryoglobulinemia, a rare blood disorder.

"Look at my condition," he says. "Have you been happy with me, Nimmi?" he asks reaching for my hand. "I for one would never have been happy if I was not married to you," he says.

In the drowsy afternoon stillness, I remember a similar quiet day in 1976, the year I turned twenty-two.

The phone rang just as I was leaving to go to the bus stop and my father picked it up.

"Who?" My father's voice was audible from the adjoining living room.

"Arjun Malik? You want the birth particulars. Okay. I will find out more."

"That was Damle calling from Bombay," he said to my mother when he hung up. "He says there is an eligible man in town. He's interested in his daughter."

"Isn't she over thirty?" Mother asked.

"Yes and this man is thirty-seven," Father said.

"But, what about our daughter?"

"She's too young for him," Father said with some annoyance. "On the other hand he's principal chief engineer with the Railways."

I didn't listen anymore; otherwise I would have been late for class. I was a graduate student in French at Delhi University. On the bus, I thought I'd like to be married within a year of getting my degree, and perhaps have four children, but principal chief engineer in the Railways, ugh! He was number six: I had rejected two of the last five candidates before him, three had rejected me. There was neither heartache nor humiliation, just a profound sense of relief and a touch of pique. By now, even their faces were a blur.

Sometime after that call, while searching for a flashlight in my father's closet, I discovered a paper with a date, time of birth, and the initials AM. In India, the first step in any marriage negotiation is the exchange of horoscopes. I figured these birth details belonged to Arjun Malik.

One time my best friend Kala and I visited an astrologer. We entered the astrologer's flat clutching our horoscopes. A wraithlike figure, with long loose white hair that contrasted with her dark skin, met us at the door with a frown. But upon seeing Kala's round and dimpled face with her dangling earrings that shook enticingly when she smiled, the woman murmured, "All right, all right," and pointed to a sofa in the waiting area. I went first.

The astrologer studied my chart and then after a pause, turned to me, her pupils magnified behind thick lenses said, "Let's put it this way, whatever else goes wrong in your life, you will marry a good man and be happy with him." All day I felt lighthearted and hopeful.

Not long after first hearing about him, I visited the astrologer on my own carrying Arjun's birth details. He was eligible, so I wondered if he was the one.

The astrologer was leaving for Bangalore that day, and I had been warned that the free reading would be brief.

She hurriedly snatched the scrap of paper that I held out. "My taxi is coming in an hour." She went over to a desk, cast a chart and peered at it like a student writing an exam.

Then she cried out in a hoarse voice, "Your planets are matched so that every planet in this chart is situated opposite to yours! Hmm, now you will either fall in love at first sight or despise each other and flee to opposite ends of the earth!"

I felt something pleasantly formless and full of potential rise before me. She did some calculations and asked, "Now, why did you bring this to me?" She scrutinized me over her glasses.

"What do you mean?" I asked, my cheeks getting warm.

With her chin in her hand, she said, "You realize that..." waving the horoscope, then stopped and said instead, "It's tedious to explain, but no one can escape fate. It is said that your individual destiny seeks you like a calf finding its mother in a herd of cows. Astrologers can see much of the future—but not all of it." The clock on the wall struck the hour. Gesturing to the clock, she ended the session, saying "You are very lucky to have caught me today." As she walked me to the front door, she added, "I can tell that you're a romantic girl; be also a sensible one."

I was intrigued by this man whose planets indicated love at first sight, but could also spell disaster. Was he the real one? The next day, at the breakfast table, I told Father, "I want to meet this Arjun Malik." Father looked puzzled. His inquiries had yielded something, and, apparently he disapproved.

"If you take my advice, you'll have nothing to do with him," Father said.

"Why?" I asked. "What did he do?"

"She'll like him," Father said, ruefully, as he turned to my mother.

"A dangerous man!" Mother sighed, as if privy to some secret information. She was setting a plate for me at the dining table.

"Before meeting him, she's already in love with him," my grandmother observed. Her head rose just above the table. She pulled a snuffbox from her waist, took a pinch of snuff and sneezed loudly.

Father finally relented and invited Arjun Malik to dinner.

* * *

I adjusted the folds of my silk sari in the full-length mirror, and tied a string of jasmine around my waist-length braid: the jasmine was as white as the silk sari I was wearing. A long-sleeved fitted white blouse covered my beanpole arms. I looked at my reflection in the hand mirror and examined myself from one angle, then the other. I thought I looked like a boy from behind. I didn't know if I was pretty or not: a little dark, but flexible and agile. Just as I was clipping on my pearl earrings, the doorbell chimed. There was the sound of conversation. He was here! In my haste, the hand mirror slipped and shattered in long shards on the floor.

A bad omen! But, I'm going to be happy in marriage, that's what the astrologer had said.

When I entered the living room, Arjun Malik stood up. He was a lean man, of average height. "Nimmi," he said, drawing out my name and looking into my eyes. I felt my head spin. I sank down on the leather hassock thinking of something to say. The only other guest was Dr. Dutt, an ophthalmologist. They were talking about the emergency that had been declared by Indira Gandhi three months earlier. My father was a top surgeon in the city, and I admired him unreservedly. Arjun, who looked younger than his thirty-seven years, spoke respectfully to my father and Dr. Dutt, and only when spoken to. Arjun had a stern face but his voice has a nice baritone. There was a force field of energy coming from him. His strong, square hand resting on the arm of the chair had a power of its own. And when he spoke, energy centers opened within me.

At the dining table I stole a closer glance. He was attractive in a raffish way. Not handsome, but distinguished looking. He looked at me gravely, but his eyes were hypnotic. I was astonished that my heart was fluttering. Nothing like this had happened before with any of the previous five marriage candidates, and only once before in my twenty-two years. My soul felt pinned like a butterfly under his gaze. He asked me questions about my classes and hobbies, and I asked questions back, all the time wondering why Father had disapproved of him.

Arjun Malik appeared brooding and sad as though he carried some wound in his heart. Most men his age were married with kids. There must have been some scandal or tragedy. He looked like someone who had suffered, poor man! Maybe he was in love with a married woman and not free to marry. He didn't look like a Don Juan. More like someone who'd only talk to you about Wittgenstein.

Father didn't say much to Arjun Malik, only to Dr. Dutt, whose sideburns dipped as he bent his head to eat. The meal was ordinary, just rice, a mutton curry and ho-hum vegetables as if they held an encoded a message telling Arjun not to get his hopes up.

"I haven't seen you around," Arjun said to me. Our circles didn't intersect. I didn't hang around with the smart set. Considering our ages I didn't realize then that there was anything incongruous about this.

"I went to a dance recital, last week. Rita Saigal." I said.

I caught a glimpse of his expression and a cold wind of foreboding smote my heart: *He must know Rita! And he probably doesn't find me attractive.* Rita was an acquaintance of mine. She considered herself a classical dancer on the brink of world fame.

In the course of the evening Arjun told me which books to read, which art movies and plays to watch. I resented this, yet I knew that I was in the presence of a superior intelligence, someone as brilliant as my father.

The sadness in Arjun's face made what he said poetic, spiritual and damned. Perhaps he'd been betrayed in love, jilted. That must be what the horoscope had showed. No one else knows this but *I* know. I, on the other hand, would lead a charmed life, I reminded myself. Let me look at him, with kindness, so that years later when life is hard for him, he will remember that a young woman glanced at him with a compassionate gaze. Perhaps I was trying to seduce him, for when our eyes locked, made bold by the knowledge of the stars, my gaze may have been provocative. Arjun's eyes widened. I heard a sharp intake of breath then he burst out laughing.

My first attempt at seduction misfired.

Soon it was time for Arjun to leave. He glanced at his watch, rose, bowed slightly in my direction, thanked us for the evening and left. Father didn't see him to the door. I pictured Arjun going down the staircase, lit with a single ceiling bulb, and two geckos on the pale yellow walls snapping up moths.

After both guests had left, Father said sharply, "Had a good enough look? I don't want him. If you want to marry him, ask him yourself, because I won't."

"Why not?" I asked.

He didn't give an answer.

That night, lying in bed, all I could see before my eyes was Arjun's face. I heard his voice, turning over every word he uttered. With the night sky visible through the bedroom window, and a light breeze ruffling through the almond tree that lifted the curtains, I wished for Arjun Malik to climb through the open window and take me with him.

Days later Jaya, a classmate with whom I was not chummy, was in the cafeteria telling her friends about a party. Jaya looked like a Grecian goddess, with long curling eyelashes. I overheard her say that while she danced with Arjun her sari came undone. Arjun had been very patient and proper as she draped it back in place right in the middle of the dance floor. But later when they danced again he clawed at her bra hook. Listening to her, I wished that I could afford French lace bras. When someone at the party decided to show a pornographic movie Jaya left. I was glued to every scrap of this conversation and later played it over and over in my head. Jaya, turning to me said, "Oh, Arjun Malik asked about you. I asked if you two were related. He told me you guys had met a couple of times."

I waited for Jaya to say more, but she was swallowed up by a crowd going to class.

* * *

The theater season had begun in Delhi. My parents saw Arjun at the theater; he stopped to speak to them.

"Do you have tickets for the whole season?" he asked.

"No," they answered tersely.

He hung around for some time, then seeing that his conversational gambit had failed, returned to his seat.

"Marry him!" Father said once. "Pull out what little hair he has on his head, and then return home. It would be another thing if you were thirty or something."

My mother looked up from her knitting.

"If she likes him so much, why don't you approach him," she said.

"No," Father said sulking. "We are not interested, and we are not that desperate."

A week later, I saw Arjun standing on the entrance steps of the theater scanning the crowd that was spilling out. It was dark. I felt a surge of joy as I watched him from between the small cars in the parking lot. When our eyes met, I smiled and waved my fingers airily.

He waved back happily. Pleased that Arjun was waving until it looked as if his arm would fall off, I jumped into the backseat keyed up and joyous. My companions thought it was because of the play we just saw. Through the rear window, I saw him standing by himself gazing after the car.

Afterward I thought I ought to have stopped and talked. What could I have talked to him about? I could hold forth on the structural arrangement of Molière's *Tartuffe.* But I thought it would be best to keep my mouth shut and give the impression of allure and sophistication. There was such a gap between his life experience and mine. I knew that if I got too close, I would be extinguished, like an asteroid flying into the face of the sun.

* * *

I picked up bits of hearsay about Arjun from other sources: that he sought out young girls. That he sometimes drank excessively. That he was highly sought after by desperate fathers of marriageable daughters past their prime.

I finally found a pretext to phone him. It wasn't difficult to find the number in the telephone directory.

"Would you like to speak to my college society about...?" My voice faltered; I wanted to say, "I would like to have lunch with you. Put your cards on the table. Tell me your secrets. I will decide if I can live with them." Instead, I murmured, "I hope we see you again sometime."

"Yes," he murmured.

Six months after catching sight of him in the parking lot of the theater, I opened the *Times of India* and read that Arjun Malik was engaged. I threw the paper on the floor. Tears rolled down my cheeks and the newsprint smudged. But I felt relieved. I would no longer have to disobey Father.

Father picked up the paper. "Good, very good," I heard him say, putting down the paper. "God be praised!"

I met Rita by chance at a lunch for my friend Neela's engagement. The lunch was at Manju's house. Arriving there, I heard the shrieks of women who had not seen each other in over a year. A smell of biryani wafted through the kitchen. I wandered into the living room and saw Rita on a sofa in an alcove. She was howling with laughter over what someone said. I have to admit that Rita's laughter was sexy. A low musical gurgling that began in her throat and rose to her lips like a fountain. She lit a cigarette, inhaled, then beamed at me, patting the sofa.

I lowered myself beside her. She lived alone in a flat and had a private income. Rita liked me. She called me the ingénue.

Three girls rose up to hug Neela, who had just entered.

Leaning towards me, Rita lowered her voice. "Didn't Neela have hair on her face? She's had it removed now."

"I don't think so," I said, observing Neela's tall, graceful figure. "I think she has always looked lovely."

"Well, my dear, I know that fiancé of hers. Mr. Corporate Hotshot. She's going to have a hard time reining him. And that mother-in-law, the less said the better."

"Rita, do you know Arjun Malik?" I asked. My voice sounded accusatory.

"Oh, Arjun!" Rita smiled to herself and wiggled in her seat. "He's a very good friend of mine."

A thought flashed, and I knew they had slept together.

"Actually, he wanted to marry me," Rita said.

A cold wind smote my heart.

"He went to see my father in Cuttack."

I pictured Arjun Malik on a train journey, sad, his head bowed, and the train thundering across railway gates all the way to Cuttack. Poor man!

"And...?"

"Well, my father thought it wouldn't work out."

I gasped. "Your father, too?"

"He didn't think I could take on..." Rita sighed, "Nimmi, I'm such an artistic person."

It took me a moment to make the connection. Ah, Rita the danseuse!

"How long have you known him?"

"Maybe...a little over two years."

For god's sake, I thought. *Can't you even make decisions for yourself? You're at least pushing thirty-five even though you claim to be only twenty-seven, financially independent and you still need your father to approve your husband? It's different with me. After all, I barely know him.*

"So it's you that everyone's talking about," I said. "You're famous."

"Anyone else would have grabbed him, right?"

So why didn't you? "He has quite a reputation, I believe."

"That's just evil gossip." Rita's voice rose in defense. "Once he is married, it will be different." She narrowed her eyes. "There are other men, you know," she said. "I can introduce you."

"They're too flashy." My voice came out mournful.

"You're right," she nodded, "all except Arjun. He's the only one."

"Anyway, he's engaged now," I said triumphantly.

"I know."

"To whom?"

"I don't know," Rita shrugged.

"Arranged?" I ventured.

"Probably," Rita said. "Someone from Bombay, I think."

"Well?"

"There's someone who's interested in me…" Rita's voice faltered. "From America. They saw me, they liked me. They have investments and assets."

Ah ha! So that's what seals the deal. I didn't believe her. "What's his name?" I asked, looking Rita in the eye.

Rita stammered some improbable name.

Rita had been breaking up with lovers for as long as I had known her. From all accounts she had a string of admirers that stretched down the road. Rumor had it that when one admirer left Rita, he returned to peek into the window to see who had taken his place.

In the auto rickshaw on the way home, there were visions in my head of Rita and Arjun in bed. Vamp! I had been saved from the scaffold. For the first time, Arjun went down in my estimation. Couldn't he have picked someone better, like an environmental activist or a nuclear engineer or something?

Meanwhile, unbeknownst to me, my father was asking his best friend to scout around for suitable boys. I learned later they struck gold with an otolaryngologist from Bloomington, Indiana (an NRI, non-resident Indian) who would be stopping in India for a week prior to attending a medical conference in Japan. He wished to be married on his return from the meeting. After a few years in Bloomington, he planned to open a clinic in Delhi. Nothing negative was known about him.

That same month I graduated with my master's degree. "You could even get a doctorate from an American university," Father said. Then he left the room to make some more phone calls and check out the otolaryngologist, and on his return concluded that it would be folly to throw away such a good match.

On a quiet afternoon I met Pranab at his brother's place. He was wearing a faded green T-shirt: he was a little chubby, because of a steady diet of McDonald's burgers; I didn't like the American words he used, "picky" instead of "choosy." Afterwards, he showed us nature slides from his travels in the U.S. I earned high marks, however, because I correctly identified a bison and Old Faithful. The next morning, he sent a message: "Barkis is willing." But Pranab was no different from all the cross-eyed boys at the university, just older, better educated, and with a good practice in Bloomington. Though others would call him amiable and easygoing, I was ambivalent. But my home exploded with joy. Seeing the reluctance on my face, my father flared up. "If you refuse this man, I will have nothing more to do with your marriage. Do you hear me? Do what you want with your life." Finally, I accepted because Pranab had never asked if I could cook and even lightheartedly suggested that in a worst-case scenario we could both eat at McDonald's.

The engagement was a modest affair and passed in a blur. Other than the brother, Pranab did not have many relatives. I was relieved I had snagged a marriageable man, but, afterwards, I felt an awful headache coming.

That night, my grandmother sat on my bed, put a pinch of snuff in her nostril, clapped the excess snuff off her hands, and in a quavering voice began to tell me stories about Savitri, Damayanti and other mythological Hindu heroines who were virtuous and sacrificed everything for their husbands.

Pranab and I met twice after the engagement. During those periods, I was surprised at Pranab's ardor when he kissed me. Though the voltage and desire in my body was something new, I couldn't say I was in love.

Shortly after, I was at Kala's place in Bombay to buy a few items for my trousseau. At night I loved to see the lights on Marine Drive from the balcony overlooking the Arabian Sea. We were rolling out chapattis. "Marriage arranged by parents is the fastest way to get hitched and have a family." She pushed her hair out of her eyes. "Romance is too uncertain, *yaar*, a waste of time!"

Kala was raving about the talents of a "shadow astrologer," one who measured your shadow and read the future, and she was eager that I pay him a visit. The shadow astrologer lived in a traditional house painted blue. He was a portly man clad in a dhoti. He led me up an outside staircase with carved brackets to a sunny terrace and measured my shadow with a yardstick. He made some measurements and we entered a hall with wooden beams and columns with bird and animal motifs. He sat before an old-fashioned wooden desk on the floor and began to read from a tome.

"In her twenty-second year in the month of *Chaitra* on a Thursday, this girl met a man. The man is noble, highly intelligent and a respected man of wealth." The shadow astrologer stopped and looked at me, his eyes softening. "From the moment he set eyes on you he has been struck by passion pining for you like *yaksha* separated from his beloved. The man has very strong, ungovernable passions and desires, while the girl is innocent," he continued, reading from the tome.

I became aware that my mouth was open. Only one or two people I knew met that description. I knew the Sanskrit names of the months, the *tithis* or lunar days, and I did a quick calculation. Tears welled up; my cheeks were wet. *But why didn't you tell me?* I asked Arjun silently. The shadow astrologer continued reading but I didn't hear the rest. My head was spinning. He loved me. I wished I had known this before!

I stepped out into the crowded alley. The reading was so poetic, like a passage from the Sanskrit poet Kalidasa. Dodging traffic, I was dazed and even more in love than before.

My wedding date drew near. My father didn't believe in long engagements. One day, on an impulse, I phoned Arjun Malik. The shadow astrologer's words gave me courage. I knew he had not yet tied the knot with the Bombay girl. I dialed the number, hardly able to breathe.

"Nimmi," he said with surprise.

The words tumbled out pell-mell. I blurted out my feelings for him, that the stars indicated that we were perfect for each other, that Father was pressuring me to marry someone else, but I would marry none other than him.

He listened to me very quietly. "Do you really love me so much?" His voice was low and intimate. "Then come away with me," he said after a pause. He promised to call me back with a plan. "But, we will have to be very careful," he said. "Is there another number where you can be reached?"

A phone booth stood next to a cart selling iced water. There were two callers ahead of me, so I had to wait my turn.

"Listen to me carefully," Arjun said, his voice gentle. "Do you have a friend? Can you tell your family that you are going to visit her? But you must swear her to secrecy, in case any questions are asked. We need just three days. *Just three days.* We must keep everything secret. I'm going to be away at that time, but I can meet you at the train station in Dahod."

He gave me instructions. I resented his tone of unquestionable authority, he sounded like my father, but a younger and sexier version of my father.

I was to reserve a seat, in the ladies' first class two-tier coupe on the Frontier Mail. I should get off at Dahod. The Frontier Mail reached Dahod about one hour after midnight. The stop would be merely five minutes. There was only one platform and he would be waiting for me there. "You'll be there, won't you?" There was a nervous excitement in his voice.

"Yes," I whispered.

It was the season for weddings. One of my lady professors compared us to lemmings flying over cliffs. Kala too had gotten engaged to a man from her community. This gave me an excuse to visit Kala for I would not be able to attend her wedding.

I packed a bag with my wedding sari, a periwinkle blue Banaras silk heavy with gold thread. I wore the gold slippers with the pencil-thin heels that I had picked for my wedding reception. They made me look tall and willowy. I packed cheese sandwiches and a thermos of tea for the journey. The day before the trip I got cold feet, and wanted to call the whole thing off. Pranab in Bloomington suddenly did not seem so bad. I could get used to him. At least I felt comfortable with him—but I couldn't let Arjun down. This was the bravest thing I had ever done.

The temple bells were ringing for the evening arati at the Krishna temple. I took it as a good omen. A yellow and black taxi dropped me outside Nizamuddin station. Father was very angry at this last-minute trip. "All the relatives will be arriving," he said, but then relented because Kala was my oldest friend. More important, I was marrying the man chosen by him.

Surprisingly, I was alone in the coupe. My compartment was the last one. I wasn't afraid of traveling alone. No other passenger occupied the second berth, but a drunk was hanging out in the corridor. Even in the coupe you could smell the liquor on his breath. He claimed to be checking on a relative in the adjoining coupe. At every station I saw him on the platform picking his teeth with a safety pin and watching me.

The train moved out of the station and gathered speed. Behind the barrier at the railway crossing were trucks, bicycles, cars. At sunset, the rays of the setting sun splashed across the sky like spilled orange squash and soon the trees were a dark outline against the sky. My face looked wan and anxious when I looked in the tiny hand mirror and applied lipstick. I primped and fussed with my hair, but I could not quiet my thoughts: Arjun was a worldly man. I was too skinny, too dark, my breasts too small. I wished I was not a virgin. I was clueless about running a household. My cooking repertoire consisted of Russian salad and Greek moussaka.

The train gave a piercing wail. The landscape was covered in darkness.

I felt a flutter of terror in my belly. If only it had been Mother rather than Father who disapproved of Arjun Malik. What did I know about this man? I should have written a letter to him, something like:

Dear Arjun,

You should marry the Bombay girl that you are engaged to. I'm simply not good enough, mature enough for you. I feel as though

I am shedding my skin, totally defenseless. If this doesn't work out,
I will go mad. If you don't marry me, I'll be ruined...

Pranab would be in India any day now. My stomach twisted with
guilt. Our horoscopes had not even been matched; Father was afraid
of snafus and had omitted this step. How ironic that he would not
even consider a man whose horoscope matched so perfectly with mine.

Around two o'clock the train reached Dahod. The train halted with
a hiss of steam. The platform was lit by a single lamp. I could make out
a poster on family planning: a man and a woman with two children.
I slipped on my high heels, and stood on the footboard clutching the
duffel bag, to see and be seen better. Then I climbed down the steps
on to the concrete platform. I was surprised by the cold. I strained to
find Arjun's face. Some passengers crossed the platform, craning their
necks to look at me. Fortunately, the whiskey drinker was nowhere
around. A breeze pushed some trash on the platform. My hands felt
like ice. Shivering, I wrapped my arms around my body and waited.
The station clock read 2:07.

Then I saw him drawing on a cigarette, about twenty-five feet
away from me. He had been watching me intently from the shadows
of the trees. When he caught my eye, his teeth glistened in a smile; he
threw his cigarette away and walked towards me. I held my breath. My
father's face flashed in my mind. The flesh and blood Arjun stood on the
platform. A fissure appeared to be growing wider and wider. This was
the moment—of an irrevocable decision. I stood paralyzed, not knowing
what to do. Even though it was cold, I was perspiring. Then I whipped
around, grasped the hand grip and scrambled back up the high steps
into my compartment. My slipper fell off and rolled on to the tracks. In
a rush of adrenaline, I flung the duffel bag on the sleeper and locked
myself in the coupe.

"Wait a minute. Nimmi!" Arjun called in the dark.

Above the blood pounding in my head, I could hear footsteps
running up the platform. His eyes were searching the dark train
windows and then I heard him laugh. The bell clanged, the guard blew
the whistle. The train lurched forward. If I had never taken that scrap
of paper from my father's closet, all this would never have happened.
Wiping my wet face, I stared into the darkness, numb and ashamed, until
I fell asleep. When I woke up, the sky was light, we were approaching
Bombay. I resolved: I will return to Delhi, and marry Pranab.

The lone slipper lay sideways on the floor of the compartment, the
heel already flimsy; the sole blackened in places. I seized it and flung
it out of the moving train.

* * *

It seems treasonous to remember the past. One thing is certain, there is no escaping fate. "Pranab!" I say, a little sharply. "After all these years, you ask, 'Are you happy?' What a dumb question! Are you afraid that I am going to run away?" I ask teasingly. I put my head on his chest and hold his hand to my heart. I never want to let it go. ■

UNICORN: PROBABILITY
Minal Hajratwala

I am the needle in a bottle of hay
weaving ropes of sand & turnip's blood.

According to game theory, I am likely to exist
in a coolie's foreskin on a bottle-blue moon

at the end of the abacus.
When you catch the wind in a net,

when you win at *rouge et noir*
& devil's bones,

I will come to you with implicit eyes
& all the small hairs

of your insufficient pelt
will begin to calypso.

Under a pineapple sky
to barcarole & blues

I will feed you delicacies
of ten thousand worlds,

I will let my humours
melt into yours.

At cocklight
I will offer you this choice:

go home,
get ordinary-happy—or

join me, ease this
loneliness, disappear.

UNICORN: GEOMANCY
Minal Hajratwala

At the end of the next fancy you chase
over plains swept bright by the storm.

In a dew-slipped glade under balsamic skies
& mnemonic stars, Memory's dawn.

Through the language of faery, dragon, or snake,
the true tongue of all things.

Across the sea of your solemnest grief,
each steel wave's intimate tendrils.

Beyond the veil. Behind the waterfall that scales
the mountain whose peaks are icebergs in heaven.

In the dream you did not believe possible
yet do not, again & again, wake from.

UNICORN: HUES
Minal Hajratwala

Mirror tints, emptiness,
what the Buddha saw
breaking dawn

after his night-trials :
sylphs
with awesome
                    flaming vulvae,

childhood's fires,
pigmented threads
of water streaming
                    too late,

chartreuse hope, puce innards of
a poet's oven, holographic dream,
glitter, lint,
            shadow of August.

Look for me
beyond the gorgon's crag
in the domain of the possible
camouflaged like an assassin,
            all sacrament & rope.

FIVE MATES I AM MARRIED TO
Waqas Khwaja

Five mates I am married to
and carry on with a secret lover
devoted to each equivalently
to all together and separately
but I have neither guilt nor shame
for this or that, for one or other
nor care for those who heap blame
upon my shoulders, upon my head
curse and damn and wish me dead
some creed, I am told, permits only four
others, they say, forbid bigamy
I care for neither one nor other
nor for a hundred milkmaids who
dance to delight a god or two
my five mates I will have and keep
though share them with all most willingly
my lover too, I do not care
if she warms another's bed
she is free to go and sleep
with whomsoever she chooses to
yet when she comes to me and brings
her musky flanks, her tulip lips
her whispered breath, my spirit sings
my parched bodyscapes long dead
awaken in a thousand tiny nibs
alert to her mouth that blows on them
and all at once erupt in bloom
and there in earth's uncloistered room
sound, taste, and smell, taction, and sight
come together in a dithyramb
of unpremeditated delight

KUGHU KOHRRAY
Waqas Khwaja

Doves and horses
dumb birds and beasts
hoopoes and goats
come look, come look

pigeons and cattle
rabbits and lizards
they are all for you
run up and see

Here's a parrot with
a hole in its neck
and if you blow through it
like this, see me do it

it's a whistle as well
blow hard or blow softly
it makes a sweet sound
come try this one out

And so all these others
have no sound of their own
but only what you give them
by blowing through the hole

You give them your breath
you give them your voice
it's almost as if
they stir in your hands

Clay toys, shaped and molded
and baked in a fire
clay doves and clay horses
each one just for you

A cart and its wheels
with axle and spokes
an ox yoked to it
or a pair if you wish

There's more if you like
much more than all this
let me untie this bundle
and show you what else

Look, here, a mud oven
All ready for use
Come close, you can touch it
It won't come apart

Pots, serving trays, and saucers
clay skillets and pans
bowls, sifters, colanders
jars, dishes, and spoons

Here's a pestle, and a mortar
to grind your spices
and all that you can wish for
take your pick, or take it all

You just need a house
you just need a household
and everything to run it
is here for the asking

And when you are done
and tired of it all
you may toss these away
without worry or care

Our mother, this earth
will take them all back
and rains wash and sweep them
down rivers and creeks

Into ponds and pools
into waterholes and bogs
and again I will venture
as I have long done

Forever and a day
through seasons and years
and dredge up the loam
the pitch and the clay

And once again knead it
and mold it and sculpt it
in forms that you see
in shapes that you love

Doves and horses
dumb birds and beasts
hoopoes and goats
I bring them to you

pigeons and cattle
rabbits and lizards
they are all for you
run up and see

WE ARE OLD MEN
Waqas Khwaja

Your hand casually tapping my arm
Slapping my thigh
I will ignore it
A quiver in the bow of your lip
Your black eyes, frank and forthright
I will perceive and not notice
Later, another will say
"You came to see him today"

We are old men
Wrapped in our Siberias of loneliness
Clouded by fading memories
Entering suddenly the glare of well-lit rooms
Deafened by melodies of young voices

And it is my vanity that surfaces
All over again
I realize in despair

There are books to be read
Songs to be discovered never heard before
Unfamiliar composers, unknown singers
Movies never watched

You educate me all over again
About traversing boundaries
About defying custom and habit
Flouting rules without compunction
Putting me in touch with someone
I left behind a long while ago

It is but a game of pretend and make-believe
You have a gift to make it all seem real
But you scratch at a skeleton in skin here
And your heart will soon be restless again
Even as you seek to breathe into this frame of bones

A passing fancy that it is whole
That blood still courses through it

But it is madness of old age to believe it so
It is madness to believe again

It will all be left behind
Once life recollects itself
From the dream
Here it is but
A last rush of sap
A tremor of spring in sprig and leaf
Before exhausted branches brittle
The tree succumbs to rot
And falls

Yet, in my mind
Just for a fleeting moment
I stretch my hand to seize your arm
And clasp you to myself
As intensely as a hot full moon
Glories in his lordship for a night
Forgetting its borrowed effulgence
From a young summer sun
Whose fool he remains
Through all his phases
Of increase and diminution

While a centipede sits on my face
And slowly eats into the flesh
That remains

THE DEVELOPMENT
Ali Eteraz

Daniyal Daood put his girlfriend Mei's monthly payment in her purse and then stepped onto the patio of his brand new Monet, a three-bedroom villa in Floating City, one of the first developments in the Persian Gulf where foreigners were allowed to own land outright. A freshwater canal toothpaste green and a hundred feet across zigzagged through the development under a series of arched stucco bridges of stucco and plastic palms. The humidity had relented its sweaty headlock over the archipelago and the breeze had shifted and taken the tire smoke and chants from the village of al-Dair into the oblivious gulf. It was a very good evening to host a party, to show off his home and girlfriend, to kindle seductions.

The forty-seven-year-old Brit, who had been working as an executive in Manama since the early '90s, wore khaki shorts and a rumpled white shirt. He inspected the two wooden patio tables, adjusted the crocheted seat cushions, and checked the time to see how long everyone would take to negotiate their way out of Manama. Just before Daniyal went inside to check on Mei, his eyes turned to the big Picasso next door, the biggest of the three villa models (the midsize one was Van Gogh). The Picasso had been recently purchased by a Saudi family. He had identified them the same way he identified any other Arab in the gulf, by their license plates.

The villa had sat unoccupied since the sale; but today there was activity. The first person to come into view was a small square-faced maid with a pixie cut who entered the backyard by way of a door near the carport. She was of Southeast Asian extraction, coming in with a bag of cleaning supplies and a broom she had purchased at the Waitrose at the Lagoon. As soon as she stepped into the boundaries of the house she pulled out a white hijab from the bag and cinched it around her head with a safety pin. From the hijab Daniyal surmised that she had to be of Muslim descent—perhaps Indonesian or Filipino *moro* extraction—as the Arabs didn't force non-Muslim maids to cover. Muslim expats often had additional burdens, such as the time Daniyal's government sanctioned liquor license was revoked when a nosy bureaucrat discovered that Daniyal's father had been born in Pakistan before moving to London. Since then Daniyal had been forced to bribe an Indian from work, Ram Srikanth, to purchase all his alcohol.

The maid had made no more than two motions of her broom when a tall Saudi girl in black robes, with fake eyelashes and a red flower in her black hair, came out and pointed the maid into the house. In Daniyal's early years in the gulf he would never fail to be titillated upon seeing Saudi girls drop their veils when they entered Bahrain. It was as if he was getting a sight of something forbidden. But after years of experiencing their faces, for seeing them as they were, the lascivious had been replaced with the lethargic. The fundamental purpose of the Saudi woman was to bring more Saudis into the world, and that was good if it led to a deal for the bank, and it was bad if it meant more terrible drivers coming to Bahrain for the weekend. That was all.

With an eye at the ever-dwindling liquor trolley, Daniyal headed back inside and called for Mei.

"Sar, Ma'am upstair," said Lyn, a maid he borrowed from one of his friends at the office twice a week.

"Thank you, Lyn," he said to the youthful Filipina and watched her pour a black sauce into a pot. Lyn had arrived from the Philippines about a year ago and her accent was still thick. He hoped to rectify it over time, as he had done with Mei.

He went upstairs, straightened a pair of slippers with his feet, and then turned a crystal tray on the side-table so it could better catch the light. He went to the bedroom. Mei was not there either. He called out again.

"Guest room," came her voice.

He had forgotten that she still hadn't moved her stuff back into the bedroom after the last fight. She wanted a raise. He said he paid her too much already. She said that without her around the loneliness of being an expat would force him to run from Bahrain and that would be the end of all his money because no one would want to hire him back home. Another major point of contention between them was that exactly one-fifth of the four-thousand-dollars Daniyal gave Mei every month needed to be paid to her original residency sponsor. Mei wanted Daniyal to find a way to put her on the maid-visa allotted to him as an executive and pay for that cost. This he refused to do, not because it was beneath him to be intimate with his own maid, but because a visa was a kind of a witness, a declaration and an assumption of a relationship, much like a marriage certificate. She kept putting the forms on his desk in the study and he kept throwing them into a drawer.

Daniyal trudged up another set of stairs to the guest room and saw her from the back. She wore a black skirt and a white silk blouse. He thought back to the night at the Clipper Room Bar in the Intercontinental when he had first seen her. It had been a Wednesday night, the Saudis pouring off the Causeway at the start of their weekend. A few British businessmen drinking Guinness at the antique wooden bar discussing Bahrain's diminishing oil reserves. A couple of Saudi gentlemen reclining on black leather sofas in their white *dishdashas*, large Stella Artois glasses in hand. A smattering of male expats, known as "bachelors" in local parlance, blinked blank in the dark room, their eyes on the stage where an all-Filipino cover-band played Michael Jackson. Mei, wearing a tight black skirt, black stockings that reached mid thigh, and a white shirt with French cuffs, had been the only female in the place. Daniyal had watched her being touched and whispered and go off with a different man for weeks before he put together the proposition that had brought her into his home.

"Are you about ready?"

"Just about."

"Hurry up. I want you to open the..."

"...I said I'm not ready."

The doorbell rang and Daniyal jolted. He imagined the maid opening the door and greeting the guests with her ridiculous accent. That would reflect poorly on him. His concern was justified when he saw that the first people to arrive were Wally Johnson and his wife, Karen.

* * *

Coming to believe that the restrained stoicism with which Arabs comported themselves around foreigners was truly how they behaved, Western expats living a long time in the Persian Gulf also grew more taciturn and reserved. Some, however, became boisterous, hoping to bridge the gulf, of temperament and language, with a constant stream of exclamation, interjection and laughter. Wally was one of these people, a lawyer with a solo practice, daring to go alone into Saudi's Eastern province in search of clients that wanted to invest in Western markets, and actually getting them.

Wally was from Washington, the hard country near Deer Park, north of Spokane. He had practiced law in San Francisco for some time and left it in favor of starting a vineyard in Napa called Cleavage Hills. The picture on the label was of two wholesome American breasts and though the wine was more metallic than fruity it had done well at porn conventions and strip clubs. But after a whimsical jaunt from Turkey down to Oman, Wally had lost interest in America altogether and in 1989 settled in Bahrain, finding the locals to be the most hospitable of the various nationalities in the region. "The Bahrainis are the poorest in the gulf so they are nicer," was how he put it. In 1998 he got hitched to Karen, a twenty-year-old blonde from Kentucky who had come to Bahrain to be with her Navy husband, until he lost his leg to a rogue helicopter wing and she realized she didn't wish to be married to him, a conclusion that Wally had helped her reach by giving her a Benz.

Daniyal was an avid voyeur of Karen and Wally's relationship. He often wondered when and under what circumstances she would wander. He had been in "Boredom Friendly Bahrain"—which was a play on the "Business Friendly Bahrain" stamp that they put on your passport at the border—enough to know that expat housewives did such things.

"This is quite the place," Karen handed him a bottle of wine. He was glad to receive some fresh stuff. Ever since the protests started, the BMMI shop that sold licensed alcohol had been impossible to reach, because the Saudi soldiers that had come across the Causeway on their tanks and set up checkpoints on behalf of the Bahraini government had done so at an intersection right next to the store.

Karen sauntered. She looked at the high ceiling and the black tiled floor. "And all this is yours?"

"Yup," Wally answered. "He holds it in freehold. First time in the gulf they let non-Arabs buy land. In the past they let you buy anything else, just not the land."

"That's great. Maybe you won't ever have to go back to London." Then like a spear reaching its target she went to the shimmering canal outside. She wore just a white tank top and long white pants. Visible underneath was a dark two-piece bikini.

Wally hung back, standing in the doorway clenching a pipe with his teeth, watching Daniyal watch Karen. Then he thrust the pipe forward and wagged his finger as if he had just encountered a naughty child. Daniyal took a drag and immediately bent into a cough.

Wally walked past him. "Where is that lovely girlfriend of yours?" He saw Lyn working in the kitchen. He pulled her by the arm and turned her around. He looked at the maid and back at Daniyal. "This is not Mei. Is it? Mei did you get younger?"

Daniyal shook his head at Lyn, preventing her from responding. Then with his eyes, he gestured towards the empty maid's quarters, located underneath the stairs. She scurried over there even though it was empty and didn't belong to her.

"Mei is upstairs," Daniyal raised his voice. "Sweetie, the guests are here. They are obsessed with the canal like you said. Please put on a swimsuit. I think this house is going to become a water park."

As soon as he said the last sentence he regretted it. He had unwittingly disparaged his place, his mark of stature acquired after nearly two decades of work. This was not a piece of shit plot in a middle-class suburb somewhere outside of a forgotten British town, stuck in the purgatory between mortgage and foreclosure. It was a floating palace in an exotic country, in a place where it was largely forbidden for foreigners to own property, surrounded on one side by a development called the Dragon and on the other by a place called the Lagoon. It was a house befitting a real man, a castle for Daniyal Daood, who didn't give a shit that the sun on Her Majesty's empire had set, because he made his own empire, provided his own sun.

He took another drag of Wally's pipe and handed it back. He ushered the guests to the patio and pushed the drinks trolley. He hoped Mei would channel the version of herself from the Intercontinental. The version to make Wally raise his carved pipe.

* * *

Mei came out with her curly black hair blown dry and wild, light makeup that made her glow in the soft lighting, and a sheer lace white blouse instead of the silk one Daniyal had seen her in. She was barefoot except for an anklet she had asked Daniyal to purchase from the Gold Souq in Manama. It had been the first and only birthday gift he gave her.

Karen gave Mei a single wordless kiss to the cheek and backed away. Wally gave her a hug. Not a sideways hug but dead on, pulling her into him with his hand on her lower back.

"I do hate," Mei said in the halting way she spoke when trying to sound formal. "To inform this gathering, there have been few, cancellation."

"What? Who? Daniyal fumbled for his phone, seeing if he had missed calls. He didn't even have time to correct Mei's failure to use the plural form.

Mei wiggled her phone and sat down on Daniyal's lap. Her mannerism gave no clues to the tension over the past few days.

"I got texts. Mika and Niko live near Saar Village. They said their car had a Molotov thrown at it and now Mika is too afraid to go outside. Plus the line at the checkpoint near Burgerland is too long."

Karen huffed. "These checkpoints are a terrible thing. Illiterate Saudi soldiers. They don't even speak English. I missed my pedicure appointment twice because of them. I mean, can't they see that I don't look like one of the Shia and just let me pass?"

"The checkpoints are necessary. Just needs to be organized better. There should be two lanes at the checkpoints," Wally said. "One for expats and one for locals."

"What about Evelyn and Christian?" Daniyal asked. "They live near the base. They just need to get on the Hidd Bridge. They don't have checkpoints there."

Mei shook her head. "They said they a received a last-second invitation to go to an art gallery."

"Which art gallery survived the Saudi occupation?" Wally asked, incredulous.

"Let me ask them," Mei said.

"Also ask them who invited them," Wally added.

Daniyal stayed quiet. From a few houses to his left, just past the bend in the canal, came the sound of someone hosing down their boat after a day out in the gulf. He imagined little schools of brown guppies coming to the surface and nibbling at the salts sloshing off the skin of the craft, like when he drove through the Shia quarter near Budaiya a few years ago and the youth flung themselves towards his windows with open mouths and unblinking eyes uttering words that he could neither hear nor decipher.

"Evelyn says it is a private showing. They were invited by that banking family. I can never say the name right."

"Safrasani?"

"That's it."

Daniyal swished wine and gurgled it in his throat. Christians's cancellation irritated him, not only because he had hoped that the newly appointed VP would gossip about the villa all the way up the hierarchy of the company, but because cozying up to the Safrasani clan was quite an accomplishment. Ever since the protests had started, a number of banks and businesses had decided that they would shut down their shops in Bahrain and go to Dubai. Those that stayed, meanwhile, needed strong local backing, like the kind the Safrasanis could provide.

"I heard one of the Safrasani boys married into big money from Riyadh," Karen said.

Daniel plucked at Mei's bra strap. "Aren't the Safrasanis of Persian descent? How are they marrying into the Saudi elite?"

"Once you get to a certain level," Wally stated. "There's no Persian versus Arab. These riots and protests all fade away. Just like your bank needs the Safrasanis to stay here, the Safrasanis need the Saudis to stay relevant. It's Saudi that runs Bahrain anyway. They are the one giving oil to us. If they turn off the spigot this whole island suffocates and dies."

Wally went down into the water, knee-deep, took off his shirt, and tossed it to the side. He revealed a strong, somewhat hairy chest.

Suddenly there was a wheezing sound, like an animal dying. It reverberated along the canal. The foursome sat up.

After a few moments the noise was localized. It came from the patio of the Saudi villa Daniyal had been staring at earlier.

A ten- or twelve-year-old boy, significantly overweight, was trying to climb on the back of the maid in the hijab. He laughed and spanked her on the bottom with his right hand, as if he had a lot of practice, or seen someone do it. As she wiggled and bucked, he pulled back on her hijab and distended her neck. That was what created the choking sound they had heard.

"Jesus Christ," Wally said.

Just as it looked as if the maid's neck might snap there was a sudden reversal. The maid rolled to the side as if she was a trained fighter. She pulled the cloth from the boy's clutches. Her legs, in a scissor, locked themselves with her assailant's and brought him tumbling. She stood and kicked him until his hands came up in surrender.

Just then the sliding door to the house opened and the tall Saudi girl came out. She hit the maid on the shoulder and face, stinging slaps unreeled from some darkness where coils of power were kept. Then she guided the boy back inside the house and slammed shut the sliding door. The patio light was turned off and it left the maid in the dark.

No one said anything. The canal was quiet. It caught the lights from the various villas, but rather than flickering, swallowed them. The moon was low in the sky, so low that it didn't look much different than one of the disk style lamps on the street. The only sound was of ice clinking in glasses and water lapping against the jet-ski moored in the adjacent villa. For a brief moment Daniyal wanted the Saudi girl. The way he had always wanted land in Bahrain, the way he had wanted a home in Floating City. The want became a longing, infused with the sorrow a man experiences when he desires the impossible and simultaneously gives it up.

"Are you friendly with your neighbors?" Wally came out of the water and put his shirt back on.

"I don't know them," Daniyal replied.

"Those kids locked the maid out. You should go there and talk to the parents."

"They'll let her back in."

"We both know they won't."

"So what? It's a beautiful spring night in Bahrain. I would sleep outside."

"If you don't want to, I can do it. What are they? Bahraini? Emirati? What?"

"Saudi."

"Perfect. I'll ask them where they are from. Probably Khobar. I'll drop a few names. Clear this whole thing up."

"Since when did we start hobnobbing with the Arabs?" Daniyal replied.

"What do you mean?"

"Did some kind of peace summit between us and them take place?"

"Brother, have you forgotten where you live? What's this talk of us and them?"

"I think you've forgotten where you are. I am saying there is a way things are done around here. They leave us alone. We leave them alone. Somewhere in the middle we make money. That's the arrangement in the gulf. They provide oil; we provide the guns that guard it. They provide investment money; we provide the financial tricks that the serve it. Mutual benefit. That's all there is between the expats and the locals. Talking to them about how they deal with their servants. Not part of the deal."

"Certainly there are barriers between us," said Wally. "But we're human."

"Barriers," Daniyal said and sat up, pushing Mei off. "I'm glad you see that. The barriers are there to protect us and them both. Look, when that family bought the villa I wasn't happy but I didn't go over there and ask them if they beat their maid. But nor did they come over here and ask me, I don't know, whether I drink, or like to fornicate outside wedlock."

"Honey," Mei said. "Please, calm down."

"No really, Mei." Daniyal stood up and walked to the water's edge. "Enough is enough. I get tired of this generation of Americans trying to change everything for the better. I mean why the fuck come here if you are not going to play by the rules of the place? Your predecessors were better, Wally. Quiet guys that came in, cut the deals they needed to, and went back to Houston."

The argument was interrupted. A persistent sound began ringing up and down the canal. At first it sounded like it came from the sky, a star's lost sigh. Then they were able to focus their ears.

It was Mei that spoke up.

"The maid, she's crying."

* * *

No one could stand the mewling of the cat-woman. The party splintered and moved inside. Daniyal was the last holdout. He stayed out with his leg thrown over the side of the chair, one arm splayed over the drinks trolley, drinking gin straight, his eyes locked on the canal. He tried to inure himself against the sound through the adoption of perfect apathy. It didn't work. He came back to inhabit his body, long enough to fantasize throwing a glass at the maid and helping her go to sleep. He walked to the edge of the canal only to reach the edge and turn back around. Then he went through the sliding door and came into the living room. It was cold from the AC and bright from the chandelier. He had the bottle of wine in his hand.

Wally sat on the end of the sofa and drew out an olive from the bottom of a glass with his tongue. Karen rested her head on his lap, on her side, knees bent, watching TV. They were watching a Polish station with attractive blondes singing American pop.

"Where is Mei?" Daniyal asked.

"She went upstairs to change," Wally said.

"Wally, can you please go and check on her? Make her feel better if she's upset. I'll be back."

"Where are you going?"

"I'm going for a walk."

"Well leave the booze at least," Wally said. "You might get in trouble if someone sees you with it."

Daniyal ignored him and rushed out of the house. He only slowed down when he reached the carport and beheld a thistled vine with small pink flowers, the serpentine length supported by white threads, wrapped itself around a long wooden post. He saw a tunnel in which he was hurtling forward but falling backward at the same time. This night, which he had planned many weeks ago, long before the god damn Shia protests, as early as the moment when he first set eyes on the villa on the canal, was supposed to feel like a coronation, a recognition among the Western expats living in Bahrain that he was, more or less, equivalent to their king, their emir. And why not? He'd been here longer than any of them. Helping them through some scandal or trouble. That included Wally. How did he meet his first Saudi? It wasn't serendipity or audacity. It was Daniyal who had walked the Californian out to the Diplomatic Area and taken him to meet a Saudi working as outside counsel for a British firm. Wally owed him. All the expats owed him. Yet, never had he been able to get the recognition he deserved. Maybe it boiled down to Mei. A Filipina didn't add much to a British expat's social cache, particularly not a Brit who was infected, from his father's side, with Pakistani heritage.

Ambling and stumbling in the middle of the cobblestone street, he took a walk around the development. He went towards a cul-de-sac still under construction. He wanted to see if there had been any progress on the long promised three-palm fountain depicted in the sales brochure. The night was quiet, neither imposing nor intimate, a shadow of the day.

To his left was an inlet of the Gulf. The dusty beach-to-be, of a tan color, was still rough and rocky. Long aluminum shacks, resembling American mobile homes, sat on the edge of the beach, providing housing for the Asian laborers during the times they were kept on-site, though that practice had become rarer since the villas had filled up. No one wanted sweat-soaked and stinking Asians passing by the carports, leaving their pungency everywhere.

To Daniyal's right were some of the larger villas, with dust-covered cars bearing Qatari and Emirati license plates. The villas were dark inside, patiently waiting for their owners to come for a couple of weekends a year.

He reached the fountain. Still unfinished. The construction company had only done work on the middle fountain and just halfway. The other two palms were stumps. He shook his head and rounded the turn, headed in the opposite direction. This was what kept these people behind in the world. They never finished what they started.

The beach was now to his right. He intended on following the sidewalk all the way to security gate. But as the path curved left, in a spontaneity that only alcohol could induce, he veered off the sidewalk and walked towards the water, following the tread of tires, both trucks and four-wheelers.

He looked at the most recent track and followed it in an S shape all the way to a dirt mound sitting a construction site. Once he slipped on the deceptively gravely rock. The dust in the air was finer than he anticipated and it got into his sinus. He stopped for a moment and pulled the neck of his shirt over his nose and mouth. Turning into a thief like that he was reminded of the way the Shia protestors wrapped their shirts around their mouths when running in and out of tear gas in Karzakkan. He used to watch them from the Financial Harbor during the champagne happy hour.

When Daniyal reached the top of the mound, he saw a trampoline beneath him. It was just there, on the dusty beach. The circular frame was rusted in places, especially the joints, while the legs were splayed and bent. The coils connecting the frame to the black acrylic surface were brittle, with an entire section of eight or so having fallen to the ground. The surface was dusty but there were clear footprints suggesting recent use. He wondered who came to use this thing. Maybe the security guards at the gate came by to jump during their breaks or maybe the Asian laborers working on the endless apartment buildings found a way to entertain themselves in their off-hours.

He took a long swig of the wine and dug the base of the bottle into the sand and made his way to the trampoline. He slung himself on and rolled to the middle. The surface was aged and worn but it still retained bounce, though it made the sound of steel being shaven. He took a few test jumps and then started reaching for the sky, his hands seeking the stars, his spinning head adding to the sensation that he was flying above a world that could be left behind.

Suddenly between two villas he saw movement on a grassy embankment. It came out to street level.

He thought it was a massive house cat.

Then he realized it was the Saudi girl in black.

* * *

She made a straight line for the trampoline. He was so surprised by her appearance that his knee buckled a little and he had to stop jumping. For a long moment, accompanied only by the residual squeal of steel, the two of them looked at one another. Her expression was blank. He looked disarmingly haggard.

The stalemate was broken by a snap of her fingers. "Off," she instructed.

"We can jump together," he replied.

"Off, off," she said, snapping twice this time.

"Me," he said, "jump here," pointing to one side of the trampoline, "and you jump there. Together."

"*La*, no," she said. "You, off."

The exchange of positions happened quickly and in silence and within moments they had traded places. After her very first jump she took off her shoes and threw them to the side and then really pounded the trampoline, launching herself high and straight. Her robe billowed during descent. She wore denim underneath.

Daniyal stared at the Saudi girl as she flew, possessed by desire for her. The Safrasanis had it right. This was the talisman, the concealed power behind the wealth, the key to unlocking the mysteries of this tribal world, the way of transforming himself from just an expat who blended in with the rest of the foreigners one-day-expected-to-leave to Daniyal Daood al-Bahraini, who could never, ever, be dislodged from the space he had carved out for himself in this world, their world. If he had a Saudi girl with him there would never be a checkpoint he couldn't circumvent, never a deal he couldn't close, never a house he couldn't buy.

"What is your good name?"

She looked at him without expression. When she ascended, her legs rode imaginary bicycles.

"My name is Daniyal."

She flung off her scarf, her black hair unfurling like a sail, the abandoned cloth sighing as it plunged to a dusty death.

"Let's jump together."

"No," she pointed at him and then at the ground.

"I want to marry you," he blurted out.

She laughed.

Believing she had not understood him he used the Arabic word for spouse: "Zawja. You, me. Marry." He tied his ring fingers together for emphasis.

She shrugged and continued, with each jump rejecting further the impositions of gravity. It took a few more jumps for the robe to be hurled off. She wore a white three-fourth sleeve knee-length tunic. Her figure was full, voluptuous and curvy. Her torso was unusually long and her butt seemed to sit lower down on her legs than did Mei or Karen's. He captured every bounce of her buttocks, every ripple in her legs, measured the circumference of her hips with imaginary hands.

The desire to accompany her in a jump became the most pressing need that he had experienced in ages. He raised his right hand to get her attention and then advanced upon the trampoline, using the railing to propel himself onto the surface. His imposition left her disconcerted and she retreated without looking behind her and when she came down from her jump she fell into the gap between the frame and the surface, the place where most of the coils were missing. One foot hit the ground with a dull jamming sound, and her head smashed against the frame. She hung limp on the edge like a cloth, and then went totally still, unconscious by the look of it.

"Bloody hell," Daniyal said and stopped his momentum. The alcohol made his head spin. He clambered down to the sand and reached forward to help. But as he realized he was about touch her —a Saudi girl, a prized possession of an undoubtedly protective man—he hesitated. The taboo of the forthcoming touch stimulated him and he momentarily forgot she was injured. He looked at her lightly heaving breasts and the way her jeans creased in the place where thigh and buttocks met one another.

He remembered the way this girl had dealt with the maid, disciplined her without remorse, explicitly demonstrating her superiority. He thought of the girl's ruthlessness. Then he thought of the painful whimpering of the maid that had ruined his night. His plans to show off his house lost. His chance to demonstrate his influence to Wally gone. Like a pianist before a recital he spread his arms wide over the expanse of the girl's body. Fire wrote notes in his fingers and he prepared to compose.

No sooner had Daniyal put his digits upon the girl's body that a part of the darkness near the canal came to life. It was the maid in the white scarf. She had finished crying. She stood protectively between Daniyal and her mistress. She shoved him once, and again, and caused him to stumble. A roundhouse kick landed on the his jaw. He experienced blood. He felt teeth loosened. He felt a mewl well up in his chest and spill out from his mouth. She grabbed his mouth and looked him in the eye and whispered: "Go your home."

He brought his hand up to his face to stem the flow of blood and with the moon above and his shadow alongside he walked back to his villa.

For a brief moment, before entering the house, he stopped in the carport. One of the shoots of the vine had managed to emancipate itself from the threading and hid in the shadows to scratch him. He dabbed at the line with his middle finger and traced it all the way to his lip for a lick. His eyes turned towards the development. The canal was dark in the night. It really did look like the villas were floating, square skiffs in still ether. The yellow lights they emanated became a smoky crimson when they touched the illumination from another house.

He went upstairs and looked for the forms Mei wanted him to sign.■

A SMALL REBELLION
Chaitali Sen

L eaving New York was a trial. The cab lurched through Friday traffic to arrive at JFK long past their check-in time. Anxiously, Tania and Nasir shuffled through the slowly snaking security line and ran to their gate seconds before it closed. A large man had to get out of his aisle seat to let them in. Nasir gave Tania the window seat, but he looked over her shoulder as they flew low over the slanted skyline of Manhattan, his warm breath in her ear, and when the window was cleared of that spectacle, they both put their heads back and fell asleep. It was September now; they had been together six months, and had proven that their relationship could withstand halting conversations about destinations and airfare and scheduling. At some point each of them had been afraid to say what they really wanted, and San Francisco, for both, seemed like a compromise until they noticed how different the sky was here, how uncluttered. The whole city was lighter than what they were used to, making New York seem like an iron weight. It was to be a weeklong vacation, a holiday, something Tania had never experienced in her life. As a child in Karachi, holidays were spent with family. She had never visited an unknown city purely for pleasure and novelty.

They stayed in a hexagonal room in an old Victorian on the crest of a high hill in Pacific Heights. It had a bay window looking down over the row houses to a crescent of blue water on the horizon. In this room, they made love every morning before going out and walking until their feet were numb. At first they lumbered up the steep sidewalks, their thighs burning, the air in their lungs violently expelled until eventually their lungs opened up and their pace evened out. "This is how we're supposed to breathe," Tania said.

On Tuesday morning, after three full days in the city, they were going to drive a rental car north along the Pacific Coast Highway, but before sunrise they were startled awake by a call on Nasir's cell phone. Nasir flipped his phone open and held it up, its small screen casting a dull gray light into their eyes. The name of the caller came into focus. It was their friend Susan, who had introduced them at a dinner party back in March. At that dinner, Tania had noticed Nasir struggling to be polite to the other guests while his attention darted around the room, seeking her out. He found many opportunities to speak only to her, and of course she wouldn't have known any of that if she hadn't been watching him all evening. Weeks later, proud of her matchmaking prowess, Susan confessed that she had set them up.

When Nasir answered, Tania could hear Susan's voice. She was shouting into the phone but Tania couldn't understand the words. She tapped his wrist inquisitively. Nasir kept saying, "All right. All right." He was still half asleep. Then he said, "All right, call back when you can," and snapped his phone shut.

"I think there's been an accident," he said. "A plane crash? I couldn't understand." He leaned over and turned on the bedside lamp. It was 5:58 in the morning.

"Is she all right?"

"I think so. She said to turn on the news."

Nasir had to get up to look for the remote. He liked to watch TV before bed and last night, Tania had fallen asleep halfway through a *Seinfeld* rerun. He looked under the covers and on the floor. It had become lodged between the mattress and the wall underneath the headboard. After extricating it, with the war-weary triumph of a knight and his sword, he pointed it at the television and got back into bed.

It didn't take long to find news of the accident Susan had told him about. It was on several channels, the twin towers from various vantage points pictured against a blue sky, and black smoke billowing from the north tower. Nasir kept changing channels until he found CNN, where they were showing the same footage of black smoke pluming from the building. They said a plane had crashed into it, and the commentator wondered if there could have been a navigation error. The voice of a woman who lived in Battery Park City described what she saw, debris fluttering down like leaves and fire engines trying to get to the scene. "But the fire is so high up," Tania said. "How will they put it out?"

Nasir said, "They can't put that out. They should be evacuating. Are they evacuating? Why aren't they talking about the people in the building?" The woman in Battery Park City talked about the foot traffic on the street, how there would not have been many people walking around the base of the towers. Yet it was almost nine. People would have been going to work inside the building, and coming out of the subway underneath it. Just the other day, Tania and Nasir had come off the E train at the World Trade Center. They had walked to Battery Park and spent the afternoon there.

Suddenly the south tower also caught fire. It happened so fast even the eyewitnesses and commentator didn't understand it at first, but Tania had seen something, a swiftly moving small white object to the right of the towers. They were talking about a fuselage exploding but Tania said to Nasir, "There was a plane. Did you see it? A small one."

Nasir leaned forward, even though the plane was long gone from the picture. It was confirmed a minute later that another plane had come and hit the second tower.

Someone wondered if it was a missile attack. An aviation expert said on a clear day like this, no pilot would be relying on their navigation systems. The FBI was investigating a possible hijacking. Nasir leaned back against the headboard. "This is a disaster," he said. "Motherfuckers, this is a disaster." He picked up his cell phone and began calling people in New York. Tania could hear the three high-pitched notes that meant the calls were not going through. All circuits were busy. She didn't have a cell phone and at this moment was glad she didn't. It would have made her more frantic. All she could think about were crowds, masses of people in horizontal and vertical alignments, rushing through the streets to get to their jobs, packed into elevators to get to their floors. What was happening in the elevators, she wondered. What was happening inside the buildings? No one was talking about it.

"Maybe the landlines are working," she said softly. He looked at her in amazement. Nasir was so enamored with his technology he had forgotten about the hotel phone on their bedside table. Still he had limited success. He was only able to reach his office and have a conversation with one of his co-workers.

Their office wasn't downtown. At that time in the morning, Nasir would have been getting off the train at Columbus Circle, where he worked for a small company that specialized in medical informatics. Neither would Tania have been anywhere near the towers. She used to work for the CFO of the Guggenheim, but quit when they were about to undergo a massive procedural audit. Now she did bookkeeping for three different art galleries on the Upper East Side, jobs she had procured through personal contacts.

The Pentagon also caught fire. They showed side-by-side pictures and Nasir said again, "This is a disaster. We're at war." A headline at the bottom of the screen said *America under Attack*. Tania got out of bed to look out the window. They didn't have a view of the Transamerica Building, and anyway, Tania felt foolish, paranoid, and pulled away from the window.

After a few more minutes, the voices on the television became frantic. No one quite knew what they were seeing. They said there was a huge explosion, and then a large mushroom cloud. All Tania could see was white smoke, a cumulus cloud of it descending steadily, until it dropped out of sight, fanning out through the streets and drifting up again. The south tower was no longer visible. It appeared to be encased in smoke, or rather, it appeared as if Lower Manhattan had been lifted into the clouds. The tower, apparently, had collapsed. If someone were to tell her this was happening without her seeing it, she would have pictured something cartoonish, the building teetering from side to side before toppling over. This was not like that. This was elegant, and Tania wondered what was wrong with her, why all she could think about was the way it looked. The people on television remarked on it too. They called it extraordinary, incredible, grotesque, but that wasn't the word on Tania's mind. The word that came to her was ethereal. Now panicked voices on the screen were describing people jumping out of the windows of the top floors, jumping to their deaths or being crushed. Thousands of people were running away from the tons of steel and concrete crashing to the ground, and Tania couldn't fathom that much fear and suffering.

Nasir was staring at the screen. He looked frightened. He closed his eyes for a moment and when he opened them, he seemed to remember that she was with him. He held his hand out to her. "Maybe most of the people have gotten out," he said. "Maybe there won't be many deaths. They've only said injuries."

Tania took his hand and nodded.

"Maybe it isn't us," he added.

"Us?" she asked, but after thinking about it, she knew what he meant.

After the second tower fell, there wasn't much new information, only a long series of experts conjecturing. They had identified one of the planes, an American Airlines 767, hijacked from Boston. An FBI official mentioned Osama bin Laden and Al Qaeda. Nasir muttered, "Al Qaeda. Saudis," with a tinge of relief in his voice, and then he looked at her apologetically and said, "I'm sorry. This has ruined our vacation." She shook her head. She was almost going to say, "It isn't your fault," but that was so obvious it would have been insulting to say it.

"What do you think we should do?" she asked.

"We're supposed to check out of the room. I think we should cancel the car. I don't think we should try to rent a car today, do you?"

"No, maybe not."

"I'll go talk to the front desk."

"Should I go with you?"

He thought about it for a moment. "No, I'll just go and come back." He went into the bathroom for a while and she turned the television down. She thought about her parents in Karachi. It was midnight there. Often her parents were up late. If they had heard anything, they would have been trying to call her in New York. They would want to hear from her.

She got up and rummaged through her purse for her calling card. Then she waited for Nasir to come out of the bathroom, clean and dressed. He kissed her on the forehead and said he would be back soon, and she smiled, to let him know it was all right, that she wouldn't worry. When she was sure he was out of range, she dialed out from the hotel phone. The call went through and after two rings she heard her mother's voice, already hysterical. The news of the attacks had spread through their apartment building. "I'm fine, Amma, I'm fine," she kept repeating, but she didn't think her mother could have heard her over her own crying. Her father took the phone. He was clearly worried but able to listen.

"I'm not in New York," she said. "I'm in San Francisco, for work. I told Amma but she must have forgotten."

"Stay there for a while," her father said. "Don't go back."

"I'm here until Friday. I just wanted to tell you I'm all right. I can't stay on the phone." She was afraid of Nasir coming back, of them hearing his voice and having to lie to her parents in front of him. She didn't know which news they would have taken harder, that she was in New York surviving a terror attack, or that she was in San Francisco sharing a bed with a Muslim boy. Nasir knew she hadn't told her parents about them, of course. He hadn't told his parents either, but everything that morning was so fraught.

Her father put her mother back on the phone. She had calmed down a little, but she had something important to say. "Come home, Tania. I want to see your face."

"Not now, Amma, I have to go. I have work." She couldn't allow her mother to go on like that. Her pleas were too upsetting. Finally Tania managed to get her to hang up. The conversation left her rattled. Her hands were shaking.

She was about to get dressed and go looking for Nasir when he came through the door carrying a white paper bag. He looked more confident, stronger. "I have coffee and rolls. The manager offered us a free night. He wanted to offer his condolences."

"That was nice of him," Tania said.

"I told him we'd pay for the room. It wouldn't feel right. I went out to see what it was like. I'm sorry. I should have come back for you."

"It's all right. You weren't gone long."

"I thought you might be hungry."

She wasn't, but she was willing to be reminded of ordinary things. She got dressed while he emptied the contents of the bag on a round table next to the bay window. Outside the morning fog had evaporated and a bright sunlight had broadened over the city. They sat down and unwrapped their breakfast, buttered rolls with jam or honey. He had brought a selection, and the coffee was hot and creamy.

Nasir said, "There's a business lounge on the second floor. We can go later and send some emails." He had also bought a calling card at the corner store and had called his parents from a pay phone. He said she could use it to call her parents.

"I called my parents from here," she said. "I couldn't wait. I had a few minutes on my card."

"Mine was used up. How did they sound?"

"Hysterical. My mother is so worried."

"Mine too," he said. His family was in Hyderabad. He looked after them well but was estranged from his brother, whom Tania had never met but Nasir had described as "a bit of a fundo." His brother had been to Iran on a pilgrimage only recently, a trip Nasir had tried to talk him out of. Tania didn't really understand why, and Nasir kept saying, "It's Iran!" as if that should have explained everything. One of the few arguments they'd ever had was about how uninformed she was about politics. He had said that she was naïve, that she needed to be shrewder about the world, and he had said something that still stung when Tania thought about it. He said, "Maybe it's because your skin is fair and you have a Christian name, you have the luxury here to be ignorant about politics." He said her name then almost sneeringly —"Tania McDonald!"—with a horrible Scottish accent, even though he knew she had not an ounce of Scottish ancestry. McDonald was simply the name her great-grandfather had taken upon conversion when he was in the Frontier Corps of the British Indian Army in Baluchistan. It was the name of his commander.

"It wasn't a luxury in Pakistan," she had said, defensively, but she immediately regretted it, and he too was remorseful. "I was just teasing," he'd said, but he was very tender and penitent. And after that they were always careful to avoid the subject of their differences.

She sipped her coffee. "Do you think the flights will be running by Friday?" she asked him.

"I don't know. We'll see. It's only Tuesday now."

"I'm sure security will be very high," she said. "Maybe we should find another way home?"

He frowned. "Like what?"

"Maybe a bus or a rideshare."

"What are you worried about? Security at the airport? Because I'm a Muslim?"

"They'll do background checks, especially on foreigners, especially on Muslims. What about your brother? His trip to Iran?"

Nasir looked wounded, but he nodded. "I have to admit, that's been on my mind. I thought if I said anything, you would think I was being callous, that I was only thinking about myself."

"Of course not, I would never think that about you."

"But what can I do, Tania? I can't start living in fear. I have to go on with my life knowing I haven't done anything wrong. I have my passport, my visa. What else can I offer?"

"I'm only saying, we might need to be cautious."

He shrugged. "We'll see. For now there isn't much we can do. By Friday we'll know more."

They were quiet for a moment. The television was still on, but the voices were a steady drone now. They were beginning to repeat interviews they had already done.

"Tania," Nasir said quietly, "I appreciate you trying to see this from my point of view. I want you to know I won't let anything bad happen. You're safe with me."

"You don't have to tell me that, Nasir. I know that." She felt like crying, not only because he felt the need to reassure her, but also because he'd gotten it so wrong. And the weight of what happened in New York, what *was* happening, was finally sinking in.

She should have told him then that she didn't have her passport with her. Before the trip he had reminded her to bring it, and she had asked him why, if they were only traveling within the country. He told her again how naïve she was. She said she was afraid of it being stolen, which made him howl with laughter. "Who would want to steal a Pakistani passport?" he cried, and that was the last they spoke of it.

* * *

Later in the afternoon, they went to the business lounge to check and send out emails. Once they were confident the people they knew were at least physically unharmed, they didn't know what to do with themselves. They spent more time in their room, trying to watch the news again, but Nasir couldn't sit still and the room became unbearably small. There was no reason for them to stay cooped up in the hotel when there was no one else to check on and nothing more they could do. They decided to risk going out, and once they were out and saw so many people, they decided to go back to an Italian restaurant they had enjoyed a few nights earlier in North Beach. When they had first dined there, the restaurant had been lively but intimate. They hadn't been able to hear each other well over the clamor from the open kitchen and the rumbling conversations of the dining room, but the food and atmosphere were so stimulating they didn't have much need for conversation. The waiter had given them some ideas of what they should see in the surrounding area. He said that they absolutely could not leave California without heading north to the Point Reyes National Seashore, and if there was time, why not go to Napa? The restaurant had been such a homey and welcoming place that it seemed appropriate to seek it out now, and subconsciously, they must have both needed to go back to a place that was familiar.

On the way to the restaurant, they passed bars and cafés trying to draw people in with their doors propped open and television sets blaring, as if the events of the day were some kind of sporting match. The bars seemed full for a Tuesday night. Clearly they weren't the only ones wanting to find a world in tact. Tania wondered what their friends were doing in New York. Were they together? Were they taking care of each other? This day's memory was something she and Nasir would never be able to share with them now. She knew, because he was talking about it before they left the hotel, that it was bothering him to not be in New York, that he was letting people down somehow.

The restaurant was open, but nearly empty with only two tables occupied, one by some middle-aged women and the other by a young couple. The mood was appropriately somber. Nasir put his hand on the small of her back as they were led to their table. The other diners seemed distracted by their entrance. They stopped speaking, stopped eating, and watched Tania and Nasir take their seats. Nasir's eyes flitted over Tania as he opened his menu. He did this often, as if he were scanning her, trying to get a reading on her comfort level. She dropped her shoulders, softened her posture, and gave him a reassuring smile as she opened her menu.

After a few minutes, their server from the other night approached the table. He recognized them immediately and welcomed them back as he filled their water glasses. Remembering their conversation that night, he asked if they'd made it up to Point Reyes yet. His voice was clear and would have easily been overheard across the dining room. Nasir answered. "We were going to get on the road today, but—" He didn't need to finish. The waiter shook his head and said, "You're from New York, if I remember correctly."

"Yes," Nasir said.

"I hope your people are okay."

"Yes, thank God."

"We almost didn't open today. But I'm glad we did. I'm glad you were able to come in and take your mind off things for an hour or two."

"That's very kind of you. Thank you."

The waiter directed his concern toward Tania. "Everyone's all right. Thank you for asking," she said, thinking about how difficult his job was that evening, to be calmly sympathetic during a national crisis.

There was an awkward pause before he told them about the dinner specials. In the end, they ordered the same dishes they'd had the other night, right down to the coffee and almond cake for dessert. The two other parties finished their meals and left, and since no one else came in, Tania and Nasir had the restaurant to themselves. For a while they listened to the banter between the waiter and the hostess, and a soft clanging from the kitchen. They seemed to be cleaning up in there.

When the waiter brought them their bill, he said, "If you don't mind me saying, I still think you shouldn't leave without driving up the coast. You wouldn't regret it."

"We'd like to," Nasir said, "if we can manage it." He paid the bill, leaving a large tip and a note on the receipt—*Many thanks for your kindness*.

Out on the sidewalk, they both said they were happy they'd come. "Do you think we should still rent the car?" he asked.

"Do you want to?"

"I don't know. We don't know what these places outside the city are like."

"I'll leave it up to you, Nasir, but I'm willing." She felt a swell of panic at the idea of being stuck in San Francisco. The distraction of a road trip, even if they encountered unpleasant attitudes, was preferable to more news reports and idly waiting for a flight back to New York.

He took her hand. "Why not then? As long as we're together, we'll be all right." He held onto her hand while they walked. It wasn't something either of them usually felt comfortable doing, and after a few minutes, perhaps he felt her fingers twitch and he let go.

Back in the hotel, they watched the news again. They couldn't help it. She turned it off a little after midnight, after Nasir had already fallen asleep and her eyes were drifting closed. Even though they had done little that day, much less than usual, her body was exhausted.

But as soon as the lights were out, her mind raced and she stared into the darkness. Strangely she kept thinking about her college years in upstate New York, her reason for coming to this country. She thought about the long winters, the snow, the hills, the gray sky. It hadn't felt real. In her third year, it felt so unreal she couldn't manage to make it to her classes. She found it hard to see herself as a physical being in such an illusory place. At night she would lie awake, just like this, listing all of the things she needed to do the next day. She imagined putting on her layers of clothes, walking across campus to her classes, eating lunch at the student union, going to the library to study. These were things she had done in the past. Yet the morning would come and the tasks she had imagined, that seemed even simple as she imagined them, were impossible again. She watched the arc of the sun across her dorm room walls and got out of bed in the evenings, pretending she had gone to her classes. Before long it was the end of term. She was twenty years old. She got on a bus to New York City, thinking she might return after a short absence, a mental health break, as the Americans called it.

She slid away from Nasir, trying to achieve a gap between their bodies. Her heart was beating so hard she was afraid it would wake him.

In the morning, he moved quickly. He said he was ready to get out of the city. She'd hardly slept, but she was eager to get on the road too. She wouldn't be doing any of the driving herself. She had never learned how, and only had a state-issued non-driver's ID. All she had to do was stay awake and keep Nasir company.

* * *

As soon as they crossed the Golden Gate Bridge, they knew they'd made the right decision. They spent the morning hiking in Muir Woods, and continued driving north along the craggy coast, stopping at several points to watch the Pacific Ocean batter the rocks. They climbed large boulders and looked down onto the foaming water. The air was dry and salty and cleansing winds lashed their cheeks. It was so beautiful, so overwhelming to their senses, they felt like their wanderings were a small rebellion against all that was bitterly human. Before long they were avoiding the news altogether, finding isolated places to walk and sit and be perfectly drenched in this peace.

By Friday, air travel had not resumed and there was no flight back to New York. They decided to stay on the road and go further up the coast. One evening they were on a beach, waiting for the sunset. Lying on his back, looking up at the sky, Nasir said, "It's strange to see the sky so empty. We haven't seen a single airplane." Tania realized it was true. From her Queens apartment, right under the flight path of LaGuardia Airport, the skies would have sounded eerily quiet, but here, it could have been simply the way things were.

The waiter had been right about Point Reyes. They took a hike on a cliff high above the sea, on a trail that ran along an elk preserve. The elk grazed on tender green grass and took little notice of them. At the end of the trail, the view to the sea opened up. They could see the coastline of a small peninsula, the white waves crashing so hard they sent up a high mist. In the foreground, at a distance that was hard to gauge, there was a great ravine where it looked as if the earth had been pulled apart like a piece of meat. When they got back into the car and started driving again, Tania said, "Let's just drive forever."

Nasir squeezed her knee affectionately. "What would we live on? Air?"

They went back to San Francisco on Monday, and found out that in New York, people were already going back to their daily routines. Nasir's boss was eager for him to return, but the galleries Tania worked for were slower to start up, and hadn't even answered their phones for a week. She had left several voicemails, wondering if they would ever reopen. Eventually, one by one they called her back. They told her to take her time; there was nothing much going on at the moment. No one was buying any art right now.

They were back in the Victorian in Pacific Heights, but in a smaller room with only a view of an adjacent building. As soon as they entered the room, Nasir was irritable and restless. Tania's mood shifted as well. The dread she'd put off all week had finally caught up with her. He slept poorly that night, tossing and grunting, and in the morning, he sat up and got on the phone with the airline. He had a long, cordial, strangely flirtatious conversation with an airline representative, and before long, he had them booked on a flight to New York, with a layover in Dallas, leaving SFO at one. He hung up the phone and nudged her shoulder, thinking she was still asleep. "Tania, wake up. We have a flight. We have to go home."

"No," she said.

He nudged her again. "Wake up, Tania."

He went into the bathroom. The shower hissed and sputtered. She got up slowly and sat on the side of the bed, facing a dingy wall.

His shower ended. She heard the water running furiously from the tap into the sink, splashing against the porcelain, and the fastidious scrubbing of teeth, the door swinging open again. "Good, you're up," he said.

"Nasir, you have to cancel my ticket."

"Stop joking. There's no time." He heaved the suitcase on top of the bed, as if he were trying to catapult her off the mattress. He unzipped it.

She forced herself to stand up and face him. Many years ago, she had woven such intricate lies she hardly knew anymore what was real and what was imagined, and now she would have to untangle it all.

He was in his boxers, stretching a t-shirt over his head. There were drops of water on his stomach. When he lowered the t-shirt over his skin, the fabric soaked up the water and formed tiny wet patches.

"I'm not joking. You have to leave me here."

"Are you still afraid to get on a plane with me?" He was trying to make a joke of it until he considered it a little longer. "I think you don't want to travel with me. I think you're afraid I'll draw attention."

She shook her head. "No, Nasir, listen." She crossed her forearms in front of her stomach, bracing herself. There was nothing to do but say it in one breath. "I don't have a passport. I don't have a visa."

He tried to laugh, but at the same time, she could see him trying to work it out, thinking back on the times he had brought up concerns about his H-1, inviting her to advise him or join in with her own struggles. She never did, and he never questioned her about it. In the end, maybe it was shock, but his expression was placid. He seemed to accept something he'd already suspected.

"If they've found a way to check my documentation at the airport, they'll find out I don't have any," she said, but that point was obvious to him now.

"How could you have let that happen?"

She told him how it happened, how she had stopped going to her classes, had stopped even showing up for exams, and at the end of the semester when she had clearly failed all her classes and knew her scholarship would be withdrawn, she had gone to New York. She had thought she was prepared to go back to Pakistan and tell her parents what she'd done, but in the end, she couldn't do it. She found a way to survive. And now they were here in this situation, a man with a Muslim name on an Indian passport, a woman with a Christian name on a Pakistani passport that was long gone, simply thrown in the trash.

He covered his face and groaned, conveying his anger, frustration, and confusion all at once. Then he lowered his hands and was absolutely still, peering into his suitcase. A chill was rising through her body and she began to shiver. "You'll get through on your own, Nasir. If we're together and they stop me, what will happen to you? I'll find a different way back."

He looked up, baffled and annoyed. "Do you think I would leave you here? We got here, we can get back."

She didn't know how to tell him there wasn't a way back for them. Even if she could get back to New York, for them it was too late. If she had not lied to him from the beginning, maybe there would have been a reason for them to carry on.

"You're cold," he said. "Go and get dressed. Let me think."

He turned away from her and went to the window. She waited a moment, then hobbled past him to the bathroom, her legs stiff from the chill. In the bathroom she immediately turned on the shower and waited for the water to steam before getting in. The rays of water were needle thin and prickly, but she suffered under them for a long time. After she turned the shower off, she wrapped herself in a towel and sat on the edge of the tub. She decided she would simply not come out. She would infuriate him, and he would go.

But she didn't want to leave it like that. She brushed her teeth, combed her hair, and slipped her nightgown back on before going back out into the room. When she came out, Nasir was fully dressed with his shoes on and his suitcase ready by the door. "There's a taxi coming in ten minutes. I'm not canceling your ticket. We'll get through."

Without a word, she went to her suitcase lying at the foot of the bed, crouched down beside it and began to dress, modestly, taking her nightgown off only after her undergarments were on. She shuffled the clothes in her suitcase. As she looked for an appropriate outfit, she told him she would cancel her ticket herself.

"And then what?"

"I'll take a bus."

"Surely you can fathom the number of checkpoints there could be between here and New York. That's three thousand miles. The airport is safe. You have to get through one security line. That's it. In a few hours, we'll be home."

"I don't have a home, Nasir."

"You have a life in New York. You have a job. You have me… we were moving forward."

"But it was a lie," she said. "And you've never done this before. You don't know how to deceive people like I do. We won't get through."

She settled on a pair of jeans and a pullover sweater, realizing too late it was the same outfit she'd worn on the flight here. She was afraid it would give him the wrong impression that she was getting ready for a plane journey with him, but after she was dressed, when she looked at him, she could see his resolve had weakened.

"If this hadn't happened," he said, "how long would you have led me on before you simply stopped showing up, like you did at college? Or have you already gone, Tania? Have you been here at all?"

She didn't try to defend herself. "If we really had a future, I would have told you the truth sooner."

The bedside phone rang. He didn't pick it up, letting it clamor on like a siren. "Your taxi's here," she said.

"I'm staying with you," he said.

"No. There's no point."

"Are we not even friends now?" he argued. "Do you think I would leave a friend behind? I'll take the bus with you. I'll sit far away. At least I'll know you're all right."

"It will be a burden to me, Nasir. If you stay, it's for yourself, not for me."

The phone rang again. This time, he answered it. He said he would be down in a minute. He hung up the phone, and without looking in her direction he pulled his suitcase off the bed and opened the door. He stood there with the door open for a moment, watching her. It was easy, now, to stare at him with a cold determination. She had put up the unbreakable wall.

"You let me believe I was going to be the problem," he said. "I actually felt guilty for bringing you here, for having a Muslim name."

"You *are* guilty of that," she said.

She closed her eyes, unable to bear the sight of him another second. At last, she heard the door slam shut, followed by an immense silence. Her eyes remained closed for a long time, the silence overtaking her, and only after enough time did she open her eyes again. She went to the phone and canceled her ticket, and began a ritual of leaving. There was comfort in directing one's thoughts toward the next place, in gathering objects and navigating sequences of exits and entrances, each one holding the promise of arrival. She knew she would land somewhere. The only thing that surprised her was how confidently she knew what to do next. It had been on her mind for a week. By the time she was conscious of it, her plan was fully formed.

By the end of the morning, from the window of an express train to Los Angeles, she was again a witness to scenes of riotous beauty. She couldn't take her eyes off the hills covered with redwoods and eucalyptus, the coastline strewn with massive boulders, and the sheer rock walls rising high above the tracks. She lost track of everything—of time and distance, of the very idea of herself as a person who was born, who would die one day, who had people she loved who would also die, and this loss made her strangely euphoric.

She called Nasir from a pay phone in San Jose. When he answered, she could hear the gate announcements on his end. She didn't ask him any questions about the security line, and he didn't ask her where she was. He said he kept looking back, expecting to see her, and he was sorry for leaving her. His voice broke as he said how sorry he was. She promised him it was all right, that it was what she wanted.

"Will I see you soon?" he asked.

She didn't answer.

"It was a good vacation," he offered.

"I'll never forget it," she said, but her throat tightened and the words came out faintly. She wished she could have kissed his rough cheek one more time. He didn't know how final their parting would be. She had missed a chance, and there was nothing more to do about it now.

On his end there was a barrage of announcements. He said they were closing the gate. He had to go.

"Goodbye, Nasir."

"Goodbye, Tania…if that's even your name," he muttered, chuckling.

"It *is* my name," she said, even smiling a little herself. "Some things, I never lied about." Once, when they were lying in bed, she put his mouth against his ear and whispered "Nasir, my refuge." He couldn't have known what it meant. He couldn't have understood the truth of it.

By the time she arrived in Los Angeles that evening, all she wanted was to lie down in a dark, quiet room. She found the cheapest hotel on Wilshire Boulevard and went to bed early. She could hear people through the walls, talking and laughing with the television on.

In the morning, she checked out of her hotel and took a short taxi ride to the Consulate General of Pakistan. It was a boxy, modern building, so unlike the elegant Consulate in New York. A few years ago, in the dead of winter, she had stood shivering outside that stately gray townhouse on East 65th Street for hours before she lost her nerve. Here she went straight from the taxi to the entrance without stopping.

The waiting room was full. She had to take a numbered ticket and find a seat. There was no one else like her, no one who was alone. Everyone seemed to be part of some multigenerational group. The elderly were slumped in their seats, the naughty children played in the aisles, and middle-aged couples murmured to each other in various states of confusion. All around her, she caught bits of conversation in English and Urdu and comprehended none of it. The only thing she could follow were the numbers being called out. Yet her number was called three times before she realized it was her turn to approach the window. She rushed to her feet and pulled her suitcase to the counter. She spoke in English to a hijabi woman sitting behind the glass panel.

"I've lost my passport."

The woman was efficient, reaching immediately for the right forms. "When did you lose it?" she asked.

"A long time ago," Tania said.

The woman was still gathering forms, looking off to the side, and Tania wasn't sure if she had heard her. "I lost it a long time ago," she repeated. She didn't know what to say next. That she had to go home? That her parents were worried? That this was no way to live? That she was tired? She didn't know what she ought to say, and when the forms were handed to her, she took them without saying anything. ■

SUNDAY MORNING AT TERRETI
Meher Ali

ROADSIDE ADDA
Meher Ali

LADIES CAR
Meher Ali

LOOKING BACK
Meher Ali

RIDING THE WHITE VAN
Ro Gunetilleke

Plucked like chicken ready for boiling
hogtied, we roll at each bend
skin grazing skin, bones touching
we snap like kindling.

Pain bangles our wrists
we hear the gears churn
beneath our feet, carrying us
back to the wounded womb.

We dream of the pillowcases left
behind, gold teeth, smudged seals
on missing deeds, a whiff of
turmeric, we dream.

We won't pray
for a Divine intervention
we know
time is longer than rope.

HANDLOOM
Ro Gunetilleke

Your hands never rested.

Patterned rattan knickknacks
braided scrolled throw rugs.

You tucked away rupees each day
weaved your way over the paddies.

Your hands never tired.

Twelve hours of needlepoint—
twelve-cents an hour.
Before the crow of the engines—
riding the first trolley
over the stench of the market—
you stitched your way into
the florescent sunshine, lemon-fresh iced air,
non-stop high-speed cross-stitch singsong.

Before the gas lamps shut eyed—
you scribbled home
stories of icing topped fruitcakes
bales of brocade piled high
on moonlit sidewalks
tall tales wrapped like foam
around the Rupees.

Reaching your long arms
over the Kelani Bridge
you raised crumbling walls
brick by brick,
you laid a new roof
tile by tile,
Schoolbooks, light bills—

a few Rupees in the till
for Rosalie's dowry.
You weaved their dreams,
sixty hours a week.

I am so tired you whispered,
Rosalie had a baby girl, Cesarean
they had to pawn the cattle.
Poured your weary smile—
with ginger hot tea.

You hobbled inside the Union Hall
a dim kettle dangling—
ginger tea breath dewed on your face.

Your hands weighed a world.

A SISYPHUS STORY
Ro Gunetilleke

Sad is the man who is asked for a story
And can't come up with one
—Li-Young Lee

I won't fold it, like a leaf of parchment,
crisp creased, licked and enveloped.

I won't roll it, like an ancient scroll,
entwined, waxed and sealed.

I will crumple it, like the un-erasable thought
torn from a spiraled spine,

crumple, until the words collapse
in each other's arms, crumple, until the scars
on my palm imprint the melding pulp,

then, I will toss it over the edge,
and watch it roll and roll.

SIMMER
Ro Gunetilleke

On a monsoon night, the moon curled
into the seventh house.
You were yanked like a weed, wet and cold.
A howl filled you with dark water,
you hollered a lung full of hurt.

They said there was no cure for bad luck.
They said it was the will of the planets.
They had the time of your birth
inked on a dead scroll like a life-sentence.

You walked on the shadows two steps behind the rest.
You bathed in moonlight, humming lullabies to the lilies.

You unleashed the cumin, colored onions with saffron
cajoled the brinjal to fornicate with the tamarind.

Talk of your wicked fry splattered across the bazaar
like mustard seed on roiled oil.
Behind the kitchen curtain, unseen like the soot—
you became a legend of no one.

BX BLUES: A DANCE MANUAL FOR HEARTBREAK

Reema Rajbanshi

Prologue

This is a story, a dance, a ride in several parts. This is a story of how God saved the world, ten times in ten forms, when times got tough. This is a story of time. What the old books called Yugas, each epoch less and less graced by truth. What the regulars call train stops, each place closer or further from home. This is a manual for how to re-piece heartbreak, how to dance through wrongs, how to last a ride freighted with memory.

Introductory Dance Act

First, you must clear the stage and cast a back screen.

You, Biju, are the dokhavatar, who gestures each of the ten avatars to the stage. You, Maina, are God, who leaps into each avatar, then rests your hands into a flute by your face.

You, Biju, wear white lined with gold, a Nehru cap over your bun, and only pearls on your ears. You, Maina, wear gold silk and a blue velvet cape. A peacock feather in your loose hair and bright rings on every finger.

You, Biju and Maina, must move your hands at every chorus interval like a blooming lotus, a spinning world. You must slide your feet in a four-step slowly: keeping heel circles small, spinning on the last four-step, pressing that back-cross toe firmly.

Stop 1

Ali Baba: the train doors part. You slide to the corner seat, close your eyes to the light, to faces you'll always see and never know—Kosovar mothers with deep brows, Old World kerchiefs, black men with arms crossed, Timberlands splayed, all the riders bent over milk and bread and candles, pursed mouths guarding their own train stories.

Things are like this: you and Biju, who once roamed the city in matching brown puffy coats, are lucky if you speak once a year. You train up, the last to know of her engagement, at a dinner where she gifted you *pearls*, she laughed, *she didn't need.* Why shouldn't you gift her the mannequin you've been piecing from city trash, a mosaic that might rise and wave, *what can I sing, bhonti, to bring you back?*

Can I sing a bihu, those Oxomiya blues we danced before we could walk? Ma swathed us in gold mekhlas and we watched each other for every pentatonic stop. Can I sing a borgeet, those devotionals we clapped to every full moon? The four of us washed and seated, heads bowed as Baba rubbed brass taals, singing for salvation, for forgiveness. Can I sing the American blues you loved, fluttery notes of Si*Sé, Alicia, Mariah lifting over rain-splattered streets while you spread-eagled on your bed, hopeful in the dark?

The train heaves on to stop two—you can barely carry a note—and real people curl up around you like morning glories.

Matsya

Some of you have Noah who built the arc, some of you have King Manu, who built a boat. In that story, God himself becomes a fish to anchor the boat, to keep its two- and four-feathered-limbed sailors and the tsunamied world from dissolving. It was still the Age of 100 percent Truth, but a demon had stolen the Vedas, and without this book (lo! the power of stories!), the Age would end without the world being made anew.

So God swam deep into the ocean where the demon had buried the book, and bellied it up for readers-to-come. Then God swam, a tiny silver thing, into Manu's hands, and begged him to save his life. King Manu's compassion cradled the fish into a bowl, then a tank, then a river, then an ocean, as the little nickelback plumped into a silver-shackled barrucada of a thousand whales, who warned Manu of the coming flood in seven days.

When it was all over, God lay flopping, silvery small on the sand, gills heaving, as if saving the world had been deadlier than making it.

Dance Act I

Stage glows silver and blue, as if you were in an ocean. Cast swirls of blues and greys across the screen, to mimic currents.

You, Biju, and you, Maina, must creep in slow unison, palms atop each other, thumbs circling like fins. You must slide in the four-step time: right heel kick front, left toe back cross, right heel in place step, alternating right-left, till you reach the front of the stage.

Kneel, then slowly rise. With palms shooting up, thumbs circling fast, to indicate God swimming fast, for all our dear lives.

Stop 2

Biju, do you remember the afternoon I lost you?

It rained the way it does today—slanted torrents erasing everything till the clouds breathed five, four, three . . . and I shielded your fuzzy sleeping head on my shoulder. Boys with their puffy coats and unfettered manes hung by the closest pole, commenting on your milky rose, your delicate wrists. *I'd marry her for her cheeks*, they conferred.

I shook you—our stop—but when I dashed out the doors, you rose frantic-eyed. The train slipped off—your palms pressed to the glass— I laughed and waited till you rode back.

Your cards, when you ran onto the platform and showed me, had disintegrated into blue scraps. I could only make out two equations— $E = mc^2$ and $F = ma$—*energy and force*, you said woefully, *are the only things that made it.*

Look how Biju, a decade later, I've discovered a third: $E + F = L$, a hidden love, brash and raw and too blue to bury. How we are all the wild childs of the city, train-riding some afternoons, crush-jumping in the dark, with our frank glances, our sweet rumps, springs when merengue jiggles on car after car of tank tops and shorts, summers when we have to bust a hydrant to cool the roads down, all the goose-bumpy nights we whisper. *Yo mami, hi ma, hey bhonti, ki khobor Biju, come home, ok?*

Kurma

God becomes a tortoise in the very first race. The gods and demons had made a truce—all to churn up the nectar of immortality from the ocean of milk—but the mountain they'd turned into a churning staff began to sink. So God morphed his back into a dappled bowl, his ancient face you can't help but love rolling its eyes like, *I can't believe I have to save these kids from themselves.* The gods and demons went back to pulling each end of a snake, the mountain rebirthing the foaming pot of nectar, so that each side rushed at a taste of *Forever.*

Here's the part they never tell you: God had to shape-shift again, into the jewel-eyed-honey-pussied Mohini to lure the demons away from the other Nectar, and into Shiva the Destroyer, who had to drink up the poison that also poured forth. His was the first throat to turn blue. Even then, God couldn't stop one demon from swallowing immortality, and though he cut the demon's head, the head lives, every now and then swallowing the sun.

Dance Act II

Shadowbox power players across the back screen. Let rise a mountain, let sink the mountain, a snake's wriggle darkening the screen, the stage, the audience.

At such a moment, you Biju and Maina, stay together, from the back wing to center stage to front wing, in that simple four-step. Your hands too are basic, palms still overlapping but thumbs hidden. Swimming, sliding as shelled creatures do. But once at the front, you must split-shift, as God does.

Biju, you face front-right, and become Mohini the Temptress, cocking your hip, resting mudra-ed hand to your ample bum, cupping your back head with an arched, suggestive arm to distract the bad boys. Maina, you face front-right, and become blue-throated Shiva, kneeling and cupping your palms to catch the poison, tipping back your face to the eclipsing moon to drink in death, to save immortality for the good kids before the lights go out.

Stop 3

Don't say names, or smell Old Spice mixed with sweat, or watch that brassy face sit before you, conjuring him up. The city's *haunted* by jawlines that slope like his, by crisp white shirts unbuttoned at the top, by hands dangling from overhead holds with the same gibbon grace. Today's twin smiles at you, above his head, the ticker line flashes—12:20—and you think, déjà vu means riding with ghosts.

The afternoon your long-gone man sat by you, he said, "It's warmer over here."

"A window's open," you said, measuring the bangs that slanted his brow.

Van Gogh's wheat is what you saw, not his toothpaste smile that meant untried youth, his rum-and-Coke breath that meant bachelor ways. Art was the problem. You had to find muscle under the skin, see if yes, those anatomy lessons were right. Lie down and he'll bend his spine. Arch your neck and he'll tilt his skull. Grip his shoulder and he'll hold your waist, playing his fingerbones over all the tones of you.

Art was shit. In a painting, the subject never moved, but a human being could walk in and out the frame of your days. Art never told you: one evening, while drinking soup, he'd say, "I'm tired, this isn't working, let's be friends." Truth is: only art stays. You painted your long-gone's face on a pale blue tile, and cemented it heart-smack at the center-right of your mosaic.

Baraha

This might be the least flattering avatar of all: God the wild white boar. Oh, he was beautiful even then, but the plot twist begs the question, does God save some at the expense of others, all for Himself?

He'd turned into a long-tusked boar with shiny white spindles when Hiranyaksha, an immortal human, gathered the ball of Earth under his bicep crook and dove to the bottom of the unbreathable sea. The arrogant kid was looking to pick a fight with Vishnu, God's Preserver form, who was the only one stronger than him. So God the boar wrestled with the kid for a thousand years and, after slicing the kid's head with his disc, lifted the Earth like a dark pearl on his glistening tusks.

Thing was, Hiranyaksha had only ever become human because he had once been God's godly bodyguard and, on duty, had blocked four other gods from bothering his master's sleep. Those gods had cursed Hiranyaksha to human life but promised, when an apologetic Vishnu awoke, Hiranyaksha would be relieved when Hiranyaksha met his death at God's hands.

You tell me: what kind of reward is death for a duty done? How come Hiranyaksha never was reborn when he lost his only home? How come, for us to live, Hiranyaksha had to die?

Dance Act III

Cast, against a roiling screen of blue-and-black waves, clangs of thunder and steel, bellows of enraged bulls. Girls, charge in fast on your three-step, hands in a cowabunga sign that means tusks, by your cheeks. At the front center, close to each other, jump onto your right knee, then rise in a wave sway, as if lifting the world on your hand-tusks. Keeping your right hand up by your right cheek, grab with your left hand your string of dark costume pearls. Tug them loose, glare with squinted eyes and pouted mouth at the audience, while a hundred earths scatter and lose their way.

Stop 4

Halfway there now. Parking lot: Julian and Abe pass a blunt, watch the girls wafting by. C-town: Mr. Chakraborty walks to his Toyota, weight lifting a bag of soda, a bag of carp. Flower show: Mr. Lee jab lilies into a base, while Maribel flicks through roses for her quinceañera. Train tracks: Felicia and Eve teach Patrick double dutch, chanting, sticking gum on the ramp.

Strangers step off these streets and, for several minutes, ride with you, blank faces that'll disappear into night, that mean *home* when you're far enough away. Church ladies dozing in bright hats; brothers brushing their iPod screens; Bangladeshis clutching kids like precious cargo. You wanted them reflected in your gift, so you painted that mannequin taupe brown, laid on it a straight black wig, and cemented your map, square by square, on it. Now, you've got one tile missing, right on the face, and nothing left to say.

You too stared wordless, *bhonti*, from the mud one afternoon.

You'd run backwards from the Assamese barbeque, calling *Maina, come faster*, so that you'd be sure I was following you to the sandbox of American kids. *Plop!* your beaming moon face creased into fault lines of terror—back you fell into a mudhole.

How did this happen, you wept as you rose, arms like broken wings, *Ma will be so mad*, you pointed to the leopard print jumper she'd stitched for us.

Back at the barbeque pit, where chuckling men sipped *saa* and pointed, Ma slapped your tush. Yanked the comb through your muddy curls. Tugged on a younger kid's green shorts and shirt. You sobbed, not wanting to be a brown boy. *That's what you get,* Ma said, *for going too far.*

Even now, when your trussed-up self won't glance this way, I cannot laugh.

Bamuna

God becomes a dwarf to reclaim the three worlds from an over-powerful king. You wouldn't think revolutions work this way, would you, but in the Age of the Truth, it did. So he walked up, under his monk's umbrella, to the throne circle by guards, vixens, leashed tigers. And because it was the day of alms giving, Bali the king agreed to give whatever Bamuna's little heart desired. *Three plots of land*, Bamuna said quietly, *as large as my footsteps.* Bali laughed—austerity had clearly driven the midget mad—and said, against his counsellor's whispers, *so be it.*

And the dwarf grew—as large as the king—and grew—as large as the banyan—and grew—as large as the kingdom—and grew—till his first step covered the whole earth—*boom*—till his third step covered the heavens—*whoosh*—till, with his third and last step, he gently toe-pressed the ant-like king all the way down to hell.

Dance Act IV

Stage glows gold but, as Bamuna grows and steps one-two-three, glows red. Show an arrogant man seated on the back screen.

Walk in on your knees, taking tiny steps, gripping an imaginary handle with the left hand, forming an umbrella cover with the right hand. Standing head-bent before the audience, sweep your arms in a circle and rise, first your right leg, then your left leg. Fisting your hips, lunge forth with power: Right-one! Left-two! But on the third step, lift your right leg with the toes pointed straight down, and slowly drop your leg till the big toe touches the stage. Keep your head up, for this finale moment is an act of mercy.

Stop 5

The site of crime, the point of brilliance. You found gold carnage on the pavement, necklaces and bracelets and rings leading like Dorothy's road around the block. Fake stuff, you figured, so you grabbed what you could from looters, and melted enough for one gold arm. Your mannequin's moneymaker, holding a trowel the way you do when you're cementing one gold tile, then another.

The thing about gold tiling is, each tile shines a different spot of light, so the arm ripples to muscle when you walk around. The

Byzantines did this, used walls of gold to background dark-eyed men, to make them come alive. They knew the luster of yellow, why art should say decadent things even when it was holy.

Fifteen centuries between those walls and you, but right away those images are your own: solemn Jewish faces, formal stances of Russian and Indian immigrants, the gold and the darkness that are Bronx summer nights. The dead speak, though apparently not everyone listens.

A night like this, you found a loose train label, the number two in a big green circle. You pasted it on your mannequin's chest, for half the beats lost underground. The next night, you found a photo, you and your parents at a street fair, days before they crashed. Another two goes up beside the first. Suddenly, you can't stop, scavenging the city for what it's done. A silver scrap from the car wreck off the Major Deegan; fish scales from the Fulton Market walk; green streamers from the Saint Patty's Day parade. You paste them all, square by square, a city map exploding on your junkheap find.

Naraxingha

The only other avatar who could give Naraxingha a run for his money is Kalki, the avatar yet to come, brandishing a thunder sword and riding on a white horse, in the Kalya Yuga or Dark Age to save the people from themselves. Kalki, who might as well come now.

But what we've got is Naraxingha, who outwitted power that looks as maniacal as it does now, a Nietzschean king who thought he could out-God God. He commanded the people to worship him alone and when his son, a pure-hearted thing refused, the king prepared to kill his own blood. And because the gods/powers-that-be had blessed this king with impunity—he couldn't be killed by man or animal, day or night, on land or sea—God came at dusk, spanked that king on his human lap, and tore him open with his lion claws.

And the little brown boy, who had been put in the juvie of his age, sprang out. Vindicated, mischievous, free.

Dance Act V

The stage glows red. Cast a fire on the back screen.

Slide in sweeping arcs of the legs to the center. Pounce into wide stance, as if in a Māori haka. Raise your arms like a body shield, fingers curved into claws. Your face must go into Kali-Durga-all-the-warrior-goddesses-ever mode: eyes wide, nostrils flaring, tongue out. Breathe fire.

As you and Biju stand one-legged, do not totter, do not laugh. The audience might. This is one gesture of fear. They may even fall asleep. This is another.

Stop 6

A pink-shirted, moth-lashed Puerto Rican man lay his head by your lap once while you pretended to read. *Hola, guapa,* he said. *What big eyes you have, what a straight nose, such a pretty little pout.* Great, you thought—the words blurring before you—Little Indian Riding Hood and the Big Puerto Rican Wolf. *Please dear gods, let him get off or let me.*

The last car was no better, with a roly-poly black man sitting alone, pushing up his taped glasses. Rub-a-dub went his hand over his gray pants, his mouth open as if he couldn't breathe. Neither could you, your heart zooming with the tracks till the doors jerked wide.

You ran past the cops, their puggish Irish faces, their useless swagger round the token booth. "Whatcha readin', sweetheart?" the blonde one said. You lifted up your book, *Dada in New York,* and walked the steps backwards, away from the city's most dangerous men.

"Smart *and* pretty," the broad-shouldered one said. You slid like a criminal for the exit. "Cat got your tongue?" the blonde one said. "No habla inglés?"

Oh, you speak Englishes.

You speak Subway Ride: East Tremont, meaning Montefiore, the hospital where your father wilted like a loose balloon. Not like your mother, who lay gutted in the car, the ramp pinning her to the chair.

You speak Paramedic: *your mother died on impact, you father suffered multiple fractures and laceration of the coronary artery.*

You speak Statistics: *while the odds aren't high that your father will pull through, there's a chance, and we'll do our best to grab it.*

You speak Blog: *Mom, 9:36 a.m. Dad, 1:43 p.m. It doesn't feel real, doesn't seem fair, but it's official. I'm on my own. Another city waif.*

Paraxurama

Paraxurama was the original lumberjack, the son of a sage who'd been gifted an axe by Shiva, the Trinity's god of Destruction. Imagine this: also bearded but wearing only animal skins, holy beads, and that scintillating, bloody blade. Imagine this: his father and mother cry out that the simple things they've generously shared have been stolen by kings, after the people weep that their lives, their dignity are being looted by rich warriors—so Paraxurama rumbles out the hut with that blade.

He rampaged the subcontinent, hewing down the greedy kings, the guilty Kshatriyas with that Blade of Cold Mercy. Like they, not his parents or the people, were so much grass. And when his rage had consumed the 1 percent, he walked to the pin-prick ribbons of the Brahmaputra, stripped to his musty skin, washed each side of his blade a hundred times, then crouched like a child and wept.

Dance Act VI

Stage glows orange-and-fire, as if this were hell. Silhouettes of charging horses, of warriors clanging swords sweeps the screen.

Both of you, Biju and Maina, get to be horse and rider and God. You get to bend your arms into an L—left palm under right elbow—and chop that ax. Right arm back—drop left. Right arm back—drop right. Chop with every four-step, charging forward through the hot air of greed to the cool, watching people. At the front of the stage, you turn to mirror each other, spinning on your left foot.

Lift that right knee, raise back that ax, and shake your mane, widen your eyes. Crash down that foot, smash down that ax, till your forearms cross, bruising your twin's stiff hand, red to blue.

Stop 7

Onto stop seven now, the homestretch before the home parkway. You step between the cars yourself and watch your life unfurl before you: the PS 87 playground where you first chased boys . . . the ninety-nine-cent store where you bought your underwear . . . the halal grocery where you rented your Bollywood fix.

Breakneck—it hurtles away—dark cubes shrinking behind you.

You rush onto the one green stretch of your life, the Bronx Zoo, where fee-free Wednesdays you studied another kind of wild. Bony cheetahs sprinted like Park Avenue divas chasing a cab. An alpha bear splashed among his fur-lined ladies like some shoulder-wiggling rapper. Groundhogs, like all the immigrants you've ever known peeped in and out of tunneled dens, for any shadow that might swoop down and eat them.

Except the groundhogs you grew up with are gone. Your parents sleep with the fishes, the house they plastered sold to Chinese brothers whose hummer bumper sticker reads, Free Tibet. Mr. Gianni the painter neighbor's vanished, his body found rotting by the cops under a carpet of newspaper that detailed every life but his. The kids you learned the alphabet and algebra with—Nathan Bello, Clarice Williams, Leila Lopez—are laughing, baby-raising, hustling on some Bronx block.

Who between us, Biju, has strayed furthest from the fold? Whoring for art, who has worn pearls bought by those spared life's saltwater, had caviar with veal-eaters who pleasure themselves like swine? Who has dared to be God, turning herself into the token posh folk use when they want a purgatory tour of the Bronx? Which of us, Biju, will call this free trade and which will ask *how* if this was our life, our body, our line?

Rama

They say Rama was the perfect husband, friend, king. They say power politics cast him from Ayodhya, his kingdom by birth, into the jungle, where he lived for fourteen years as an ascetic. They say it was a darkening time—Treta Yuga, when the world was only three-fourths truthful—when another king, Ravana of Lanka, would steal his wife, Sita. This is how the saga of the Ramayana with its demons and gods and their spinning discs and magic came to be: the subcontinental war over Helen of the East.

Except Sita and Ravana never slept together—something Dravidian Pride points out—and of course, Rama won. Only with the help of monkey-men and Hanuman (my favorite, he of the endless jokes, he who did not know his own strength till push-came-to-shove) and his true-blue bro, Lakshman, Rama killed Ravana, freed Sita, and returned to Ayodhya where the people lamp-lit the kingdom in the first Diwali.

But I'd add, Rama made Sita take a purity test. He didn't believe she, who'd been abducted by a strange man to another country, could be blameless. He *shamed* her, she who'd had his twin boys by then, who'd been careful all along. So once she proved herself to his suspicious ass, she pulled a Medea and asked the earth to swallow her and her children whole. The earth, remembering all things, opened her bosom and took the outcasts in.

Dance Act VII

Stage glows green, to indicate you have entered a forest. Cast the repeated silhouettes of birds and deer scattering across the screen. You are Rama the exile, Rama the hunter, Rama who has lost everything, including his queen.

So you must patter up fast—no easy walk here—to the front-right of the stage, and place your right hand to your forehead, to indicate you are looking. Place your left hand to your ear to indicate you are listening. Shimmy your neck. Then patter back diagonally to your starting point. Bend to one knee, directly facing the audience. Stretch out your left hand as if you were gripping a bow. Reach back to your right shoulder with your right hand, as if drawing an arrow from a quiver. Set your arrow for one beat. Draw your arrow back for three, arms taut. Let the arrow fly, opening your hands to sudden starfish, lifting your chin to the undoubted victory of good.

Stop 8

Sudden halt, when you first fell in love at sixteen, with a stranger ten years older.

The city's like that: seducing you in the seconds it takes to walk from that subway car to this one. A stroll, really, the way he eased into the rattling dark between cars, watching the city pass him by. A slump, into the seat across you, thumbing through the ghetto murders and penthouse divorces of the Daily News, biceps shivering like tawny faces. Spelled right over the right orb, in green curling script that read like Assamese, was a Bengali woman's name. Petite, sweet: Meena.

The next thirty minutes, you imagined her drawing those strange lines for him before he etched them on himself, them walking skinny arm in sturdy arm to the neighborhood parlor, themselves the exhibit, his wearing that wifebeater to display her claim to the world.

"You an artist?" he asked, nodding at your open book. *Indian Art From the Mughals On.*

With one finger, he paused your turning, and traced the dome of the Taj Mahal. "You know a couple's buried there? The world's greatest love souvenir is a tomb."

You *didn't* know, or what to say, so you read aloud, "Legend has it the emperor cut off the architect's hands. The masterpiece couldn't be repeated."

"Says a lot about power," the stranger said. "Be careful no one does that to you."

"Yeah, right," you said, and watched that arm swing into night, some Indian woman's name inscribed on it.

The city's like that: in one night, you fall for someone else's man, you admire a dead woman's shrine, you memorize all the ways love makes art around you. *Ay que linda*, you used to hear folks say about things you never saw until now.

Krishna

Krishna was loverboy-playaman-magician number one. First, there was the trick of his birth: he avoided getting killed by a king who'd locked his mother, the king's own sister, in jail. (The gods had known, and told the king, his nephew would one day kill and conquer him.)

In the village where he'd been whisked to, he played so many tricks on the people for the people—saving them from demons even as he stole everyone's backyard cream—that he came to be called the child of *Leela*, a magic that exceeds words.

As a young man so dark and beautiful he is always painted blue, playing the flute, a peacock's feather in his long hair, he stole every milkmaid's skirt and heart. You see why anyone grown up praying to him would have a playa pattern? Why the real saving isn't how he did kill the king and free his mother, or abduct Rukmini, an Assamese princess, but not Radha his married love, or counsel Arjuna through war against his own brothers in *The Mahabharata*? These were heroics less than the leela of love, when he set up mirrors at midnight in the village fields, so that he might be everywhere at once, so that every milkmaid would think she was his, but all the while, he was with RadhaRadhaRadha, the beloved he abandoned but whom the people remember for the people as his greatest love of all.

Dance Act VIII

Stage shimmers red and blue, as if this were the gasping whirlpool of a heart. But rising along the back screen are silhouettes of trees, women, and those terribly vain, cruel, mesmerizing peacocks.

You, Biju, are the heartbreaker god, with his flowering hands, his one leg suggestively crossed over his delicate ankle, that single blue-and-green eye of a feather locked in his hair.

You, Maina, are Radha, dervishing about him, head cast up in ecstasy, pausing now and then by his side to clasp your palms to your heart, to blossom them in a whorl into a flute by your lips. The song you cannot help singing, you poor, wild, un/lucky thing.

Stop 9

One a.m., and fifteen hours till the wedding. Till you find a face for your mannequin.

You and Biju, trained to scout for knives and kisses in a three-mile radius, know: faces are stories, petals hiding their seeds, the masks we wear, that we become. But your face, Maina, neither east nor west, neither street nor fine, leads where?

Once upon a time, Biju would've known, but roots hacked, you're half a tree. When you tramp up icy subway steps without her skipping gait, you're half a leg. When you skate over black-iced pavement with snow mounds you'd traversed hands-held, you're half an arm. When you run your numb fingers over bare brick and hedges, their sparkly Braille edges read *there is no good gift anymore.*

Still, you nurse your four-limbed doll in this penultimate moment. You think of slapping a glass oval on the face, something like: *dear viewer, see thyself in me.* Then you think, your patrons may be unknowing, but they're not stupid. You think of filigreeing glass in the space between the tiles, but your patrons are paying to see the work done on you, not them.

You cradle your mannequin alone in the emptied-out car, your hands throbbing as if you've got no choice but to find someone to pass on the brush, let another you finish your baby's face, sign the cheekbones in broad-tipped black marker, *I was here.*

Buddha

They say Buddha was a tubby peacemaker, sitting free of suffering under a wide-armed boddhi tree. Out here, far from the tree, they forget: he was a prince with no need whatsoever to look out the window, much less see the princeless begging there. Yet he looked, he saw, he left. After wandering and wisening up at thirty-five years, he founded a new fucking religion, but the real catch was this. Not the freedom from suffering stuff, but one of the roots of it, freedom from that dirtiest of words: caste.

'Cause when Buddha closed his eyes, he began to see the whole lotus-mud thing was true. You couldn't have those living at the top without feeding off the bottom, and the bottom was really the source of all that is, untouchable though it might seem. Fragrant, full petaled, an endless fire like the sun's.

Dance Act IX

Cast the trembling carcass shadow of a banyan across the stage, the walls, even the audience.

You, Biju and Maina, must saunter in like royalty—robed in silk and costume jewelry—but halfway to the stage, you must face each other. As if enacting two mirrors, remove your pink and gold studs and pearls, then your silk robes, till you are wearing only your cotton kurtas.

In slow, sweeping three steps together, heel-step-cross to the stage front. Half-squat and open your palms as if reading a book. Leave one palm-leaf up to receive. Lift one hand in the pointer-to-thumb mudra to the heart to give.

Stop 10

Open Sesame: train doors part. A newborn day, and the dividers lining the platform are signed. Tags and tags of *name*-loves-*name*, crack-is-wack-*name*, stay-in-school-*name*, *name*-was-here. They've signed the station, they've claimed the street, they've written *we are the BX, remember this.*

Climb the green stairs and sing that Oxomiya spiritual your grandma sang: *gase gase pate dheele / phulo re xorai / he ramoram / phulo re xorai / phulo re xorai.* Round the curve of quiet houses and sing to the willows hunched over the buckled intersection: *gase gase pate dheele / tree by tree you pick.* Sing to the sunflowers someone has planted, by whim, in the rectangle across their fenced front: *phulo re xorai he ramoram / blooms to adorn this xorai, Lord.* Sing across the dank subway pass, where the pigeons nest, warble, and die: *phulo re xorai / a xorai of blooms.* Sing to the concrete squares between the bodega and the synagogue, between childhood and survivalhood, to the faces you will always see and never know: *phulo re xorai / a xorai of blooms.*

You will rub a washcloth down your mannequin's arm of gold. You will let others write themselves on its spare earthen face. You will invite all your ghosts to circle your body displayed. Home? Not yet, ma, but you've pressed your talon to the station wall for some other city kid to read: *my heart got danced out here.* ■

TOGETHERNESS
Faisal Mohyuddin

> *We were together, I forget the rest.*
> —Walt Whitman

Sometimes forgetfulness is not the reason
we forget, nor is it necessary to say [I forgot]
when something was forgotten. Instead,

we must mirror our faces up to the May sky
and find within its blue depths our own
inner selves looking down upon us, vessels

filled with togetherness and love, and the kind
of gratitude that needs not be spoken,
not when the next morning, after a night

of quiet rain, the world is glazed over with
the newness of newfound things, like a joke
understood long after the telling, which,

even now as you think about it on the train,
makes you chuckle, makes the traveler
beside you wish he'd picked a different place

to sit. No, don't blame forgetfulness, not
when what we keepsake away in our hearts
are the things really worth remembering,

when the remembering of these happens,
not in great bursts of noise, but in the smiles
we smile while deeply immersed in sleep.

BEING IN TOUCH
Faisal Mohyuddin

Good morning. I have just returned from North Carolina.
I spent a week with my friend after Wildacres. I am now
meeting my brothers in Wisconsin to spread my mother's
ashes. I'll be in touch when I return. Blessings,
—Dora Robinson

Afterwards, I imagine the dust
of her life, each a touch of her being,
lingering on your fingertips,
wafting up into the sun-filled room
as you type off a quick note,
each mote a moment she spent alone
in her rocking chair, remembering.
Her favorite stories were yours.
Binge-drinking while cloistered
at that Chicago convent, blaming
the teargas and not the pain
when you cried during the riots
of '68. She told the world about
how you'd outwitted Daley all the way
to Texas only to find yourself
face-to-face with the Devil himself.
Even as a girl, you asked her impossible
questions about God and good
and giddiness, about the differences
between right and righteousness.
Her quiet smiles were her most honest
answers. You've left some of her
unfinished prayers on the laptop keys,
her being in touch. When the next
person sits there to write—perhaps
it will be one of your brothers,
or an old friend still alive in Wisconsin—
he will feel her papery skin there,
think of the way her cheeks glowed
in winter. If when your plane touches

down in Austin, the place feels
unfamiliar, and you finger away a tear
rising up from the past like a ghost,
think of how she will remain
on your face, a shimmer more holy
than mere resemblance, a holiness
made tactile with remembrance.

ZINNIAS. HOW. FOREVERNESS.
Faisal Mohyuddin

Zinnias, dahlias, peonies all pluck from the sweet
air of those faraway spring days another breathless
yearning for warmer things. We dream of golden
angles of sun, silver scribbles of rain, the thronging
noise of the earth waking again in soggy greenness.

How is it, then, that despite this longing, we find
inside each waking moment a blissful stillness
nuanced by frolic and coo? This bright, beautiful boy
anchors every goodness, his wonder gracing ours.

Foreverness is the only way to measure love, is
another wisdom he gifts, is a daily bread to give life
its blazing awe. So we set ourselves awhirl in joy,
sing fire into these slow, snow-filled February days,
and let his enchanted ways wrap our hearts with
light, three buds readying to burst into music.

LOST EARRING
Faisal Mohyuddin

Someone put it on my desk. Is it yours?
—Julie Ann Carroll

With its
creamy gray
head
and that
shimmering
hickey of
light,
it looks
like a tadpole
lost, tiny
tail wriggling
in search
of its perch:
a lobe,
somewhere,
hanging
unadorned,
forlorn,
not
an ear
to it, but
a home.

RUSSELL EMBRACES HIS CALLING NAME
Mahmud Rahman

H ad he not been born and named with extraordinary promise? How many times had his father reminded him that he had been named after a Nobel laureate in literature?

He could still remember the last time. A year after his mother died, his father's health began to break down. Russell regretted that he had not had the foresight to ask his mother about her life before she passed away. He had never imagined she would leave so soon, before he had even turned thirty. But he was not going to allow his father to depart without sharing his stories. When asked, Zainul was delighted. Unstoppable.

"When you shouted the first cry of your life," Zainul had started, "it had just been two years after the English Raj folded up their Union Jack and left us. Once the jewel of their crown, now we were a butchers' festival." He looked out at the far edge of the back compound, his eyes darting up to the mango tree that wore an explosion of golden blossoms.

"The massacres broke out the year before Partition. I was still in Kolkata, the last month I would stay there. The city's name now carried the stench of blood. I could not stay. Could you have?"

He didn't stop for a reply. "Sir Cyril Radcliffe—who was he but some mere lawyer? He dashed in from London, broke up a land he knew nothing about, handing a district here to India, another one there to Pakistan, and when he suffered a bout of loose stools, he quickened the end of his mission." Zainul, appearing in his son's eyes as a gray, skeletal man, chuckled. "That bit about the soft belly you wouldn't know from history books. I learned about that from a poem by W. H. Auden. Know who he was?"

"I've heard the name," Russell replied.

"You can't call yourself a writer until you read him. Why, I almost named you Auden. But it just didn't sound right in Bangla."

"I'm happy with the name you chose for me."

"We returned, and though there would be riots here—after all we were living in the old neighborhoods that were the scene of much violence—we weren't personally affected. Of course not. We were from the majority here. But we knew neighbors who hastily disposed of their possessions and fled with whatever they could carry on train and steamer.

"On the day Pakistan came into being—Azadi some called it," he leaned forward in the cane chair on the back veranda and spat out into the grass, "most of our neighbors in Kalta Bazaar hoisted the white crescent on green flag and distributed sweets. I stayed in that entire day, I refused to allow any of those sweets, contaminated by blood, entry into the house."

Russell asked, "What did Maa do?"

Zainul thought for a minute and replied. "I don't remember her disagreeing. She just wanted the killing-cutting to end." He smiled at some memory, a thin wan smile.

"You were talking about the time I was born."

"Yes. The story about how you were named. You sure I haven't told you this before?"

"Not all the details." He had heard the story many times before, but he didn't mind hearing it again. Each time there would be some new memory. Or perhaps an embellishment. Whichever the case, it only made the story worth giving ear to.

"When you were born, my Nana, my only living grandparent, claimed the right to name you. Just as he had your sister." He stopped and his eyes went moist.

Russell had an older sister, but she was taken away in an epidemic of typhoid before she turned eight. He had some hazy memories of her from childhood, recalling thick, curly tresses and her methodical style of play, each step determined, spelled out, commented on afterwards. Although he was her only playmate, her words seemed to be directed at herself, to some private soul inside her.

"What happened then?"

"The old man sent a fellow, some nephew of his, to carry the name on a scrap of paper on the long journey from the village in Jhalokathi. The boy had never gone beyond the ghat, but now he took the steamer to Narayanganj, the train to Fulbaria, and showed up at our door. Unfortunately he got caught in the rain along the way and the piece of paper got wet and we couldn't make out the words. We had to trust what he told us. He was terrified, asked for forgiveness over and over again—but all he really wanted was to make sure we would not tell Nana. He didn't have to worry. The old man died soon after. So who can tell if your name Zafar Ahmed came from the old man or the nephew?" Zainul laughed. "Do you care?"

Russell laughed as well. "Who knows, the man might have been inspired by the name of some rickshawallah or the kitchen boy on the steamer."

"I was more concerned about your other name anyway."

"You told me that many times."

"Do you want to listen or what?"

"Yes."

"When I was a student in Kolkata I spent a fair amount of time traipsing the book stands along Chowringhee. I found myself quite taken by the writings of Bertrand Russell. I gave up cigarettes for two months just so I could acquire a precious used copy of *Skeptical Essays*. It would stay on my bookshelf until the termites digested it. You remember the book, right?"

He nodded.

"When the riots broke out and others chanted from the Qur'an or the Gita, I memorized a quote from that book and repeated it to my friends every time I met them. Later I had the quote printed at a press and framed it."

Russell remembered the framed quote that hung over the father's desk. It would have collected a layer of grime and dust like the other framed photos on the walls, but Zainul insisted on wiping it clean every morning.

He now recited, *"Religion is based primarily on fear and mainly upon fear. It is partly the terror of the unknown and partly the wish to feel that you have a kind of elder brother who will stand by you in all your troubles and disputes. Fear is the basis of the whole thing—fear of the mysterious, fear of defeat, fear of death. Fear is the parent of cruelty, and therefore it is no wonder cruelty and religion have gone hand in hand. A good world needs knowledge, kindliness, and courage."*

"What did your friends say?"

"Them? They thought I had totally gone bonkers! Two urged me to pray for wisdom, one said I would go straight into the fires of Hell. One of them also said Bertrand Russell was a dog because he had lost faith in the workers' paradise, the Soviet Union. Bengalis—you put two of them at a tea stall and you can be guaranteed at least three opinions. When I asked them to refute Russell's logic, they failed. I was vindicated. So while Nana seized the right to give you your good name, I made sure I would assign you your calling name."

"What did Maa think?"

He paused. "I don't remember her minding." He continued, "And when Lord Russell won the Nobel Prize for Literature—was it the same year or the year after?—I felt vindicated again. This time it was I who distributed sweets to our neighbors. Though they didn't understand the occasion or the true nature of the man who was being honored, sweets were sweets. They greedily accepted."

"How did Maa react?"

"I had to explain to her what the Nobel signified. She did wonder what an honor from one distant cold country given to a stranger in another cold country should have to do with our son's name. But then I asked her, what about the boy's formal name? Didn't that too come from a distant country? A desert land, almost unfit for humans?"

"What did she say to that?"

"She did the '*touba touba*' thing, looked to the heavens for forgiveness. What else?" He stopped. Once again, he looked up at the blossoms on the mango tree. "I wonder how many will last after the first storm. No matter, there will still be some left over for you to indulge your craving for green mango. You got that from your mother. She loved that so. She could never understand that I couldn't stand that sour taste, no matter how much salt and chili paste you dunked it in. I once saw her buy some off a vendor in the street. I warned her, you're bound to get sick."

"Did she?"

"No. That was always a surprise. An iron stomach." He patted his stomach, paused, and looked at his son. "We never really talked about the religious stuff. I let her be who she was, she let me be who I was. But now and then, after she started praying in late life, I could see she prayed extra long after some remark I'd made." He laughed through wet eyes. He wiped his eyes and said, "Have a cigarette?"

"Me?"

"Yes, you. You don't think I know you have a pack lying around?"

"You shouldn't smoke."

"Just get me one. I'm going to die soon, I might as well have a drag of pleasure before I go."

Russell went to his room and returned with a single cigarette. He didn't smoke often, but he always kept a pack for those occasions when he was in the company of friends. It helped loosen tongues.

"She happily grew to call you Russell."

He had trouble lighting the cigarette. The match kept going out. Russell would have helped, but he let his father have this moment of independence.

"So did everyone else. The name caused no great controversy. I was almost disappointed. But it was nothing. After all, other good Muslim boys were being named after hardcore atheists like Lenin. Others who were not so lucky to get exalted names like you had to make do with fruit and vegetable names. Or girlish names like Bonny and Shelly." He blew a smoke ring into the air, then watched it climb upwards until it dissolved.

"You know when it comes to nicknames, our culture is very

broadminded. Whether you were Hindu or Muslim, maybe Christian too, you found calling names from the bounties offered by nature, the Raj, or Soviet Russia. The three greatest affinities of Bengalis in those times. What, are you happy with Russell? Or would you have preferred Auden?"

"Russell was a good choice."

"Not Aloo?"

"The best choice you could have made."

"Some other vegetable, maybe? Potol?" Zainul burst into a full-throated laugh. And he began to cough hard, leaning over, spittle dribbling from his mouth.

Russell got up, touched the old man's back, rubbed it up and down. His fingers glided over what felt like a fragile structure of bones. He resisted admonishing his father about smoking. But when the partially smoked cigarette dropped from the father's hand, Russell put his foot out and stubbed the cigarette with a vehemence that surprised him. He would miss his father.

"Drink some water." He raised a glass to his father's mouth. "You should go in and rest now. We'll talk again."

After he put his father to bed, Russell retreated into his own room. The cigarette pack lying open on his desk, he pulled one out and lit it. He promised himself this would be the last one. He glared at the pack with hatred. It would take a few more years before he'd give up the habit altogether. Dipika kept at him until he did.

* * *

Other than a few sketchy details, his father did not know the rest of the story about his name. The story resumed around the time when Russell had become old enough to discover that while soaping himself while bathing, his penis would get hard and if he tugged at it, there was a pleasurable feeling and some thick fluid would emerge with a consistency different than the lather. Shy of water until then, Russell began to take two showers a day. Sometimes even three. By this time Russell had also discovered dirty magazines and pulp fiction with naughty bits. He began to raid his father's stash of books. The old man didn't keep any locked up in the almirah like some other fathers, but until now Russell had not felt much curiosity about his father's collection. They consisted mostly of unappealing looking old paperbacks that had been half eaten by termites and silverfish. But now he discovered Havelock Ellis, solving the mystery of that odd fluid that came into his hands, and also John Cleland and Frank Harris, which only led to more emissions. Then he stumbled upon the Bertrand Russell collection. To the old copy from Kolkata, Zainul had added an entire series of the new Unwin paperbacks bought in the 1960s from New Market.

Until this moment Russell had not given much thought to his namesake or his own nickname. It had led to no great pride or lament. He pitied his classmates who had the kinds of names that led them to become the butt of cutting jokes. Now he rolled his name around his mouth and felt that Russell had a strong, virile sound to it, along with a softness at the same time. He quite liked the mix.

As he paged through the Russell books, he too found a quote that excited him, but it was from a different place in the Englishman's writings. From the commentaries on marriage and morals, the teenager was blown away by the suggestion that sex between unmarried men and women was not immoral if they loved one another, and that curiosity about sex was not a human frailty but a positive thing. Shame he had not bothered about much, but after reading this he lost any sense of it where sex was concerned. Guilt over his bathroom pastimes also beat a retreat.

When it came time for Russell to sit for his high school matriculation exams, he took the initiative to correct the official records at his school and added Russell to his formal name. He typed up a letter and forged his father's signature. He needn't have. When the matric certificate came bearing the new name, Zainul felt a rush of pride that the boy had had the courage, no doubt inspired by his namesake, to make this an act all on his own. Even his mother did not complain. The fact that his results put him in the first division, with letters, probably explained her acquiescence. She must have also accepted that times were changing. Little did his parents know that with their indulgence they were opening the doors to entire new generations of Bangladeshi youth who would attach a local brand to their names derived from Arabic, Persian, Sanskrit or Portuguese. Now you could open the newspapers and see names like Keramat Ali Lichu or Michael Gomes Polash.

It came as a surprise to Russell when he started writing stories at sixteen—he had shown no such proclivities earlier. But he had been a voracious reader and readers do sometimes toy with questions like "what if?" and "could I?" The encounter with Bertrand Russell, launched by his father, reaffirmed by Russell, did contribute to the eventuality that when he began to write, one of his first stories included a sexual tryst between two teenagers, the boy a high school student, the girl already matric pass. They were neighbors and the relationship was consensual, exploratory, involved no promises of marriage, and there was no hint of either party being consumed by heartbreak or guilt afterwards. More to the point, fate did not reserve a nasty fate for the two—or the woman in particular—for their transgression of traditional rules. It was all treated quite matter-of-factly.

Old Bertie's words had not been the only spur behind this story. Russell had read a Bangla novel that had enraged him. He wrote his story as a direct response to that plot in which every female character who fell in love met a tragic end. Pretending to be a celebration of love, Russell felt such a book was hostile to the concept, designed to wean their young readers away from dangerous thoughts.

That was the larger explanation Russell would tell of what inspired that first story. In his own mind, he knew that there was another piece to the puzzle that he had tried to suppress beneath profundities. Truth be confronted, there was a flesh-and-blood inspiration behind the story. Wasn't it always the case with adolescent would-be writers? Russell often made eye contact with a neighbor girl who lived three houses down the road. But just as he was trying to screw up his courage to mouth a word to her, working towards the notion of even slipping her a note, she disappeared. The father had been transferred and they moved to a distant town.

He had shown the story to Azad, who was then helping out at a newspaper. He suggested Russell let him show it to the editor of their literature page. When it came time to choose a name for the author of the story, they decided together that he would become more memorable if he simply used the single name Russell. Like Shankar from Kolkata. The newspaper accepted the story but the editor asked for his full name and published the story under Zafar Ahmed. He also censored the one sentence that had made the sexual relationship explicit. The other sentence that suggested it had stayed.

When he saw the printed version of his story, Russell's eyes kept returning to the disappointment of that truncated name. He felt as if the editor had cheated him in some large, unfair manner. The name above the story felt alien to him. He had come up with fourteen paranoid theories of the reasons behind the editor's choice when it finally hit him: he was now a published writer! At sixteen, and not on the page for children's stories.

That thrill led him to write a second story, then a third. Eagerly he waited for the next one to be published, but the newspaper ignored his submissions. The editor confided in Azad that he didn't want to give the boy a big head. One was sufficient for encouragement, the boy needed to have a sense of proportion where writing belonged in his life, publishing a second one would set him on the road to ruin. Russell was not about to be brushed aside. He thought larger, and in his mind consumed by hurt feelings, a book was born. He was going to show them all what it was possible to do with diligence, determination, and sacrifice. ∎

FROM THE TEMPLE DELILAH PREDICTS THE GAZA FIRE
Kazim Ali

Seconds after the sky does open but not in rain
The equation for a bomb's trajectory must be known
so laughter has pride of place in this home

I touch myself to remind myself the world is there
in the dark but you cannot know geometry's shame
When it taps the roof and the walls shake and

The body is forced to choose what it loses
your body made redundant your claim
on the land irrelevant and anyhow undocumented

In the ancient text I sheer his hair
and he pulls down the temple
but in the meantime in one moment

the approaching shriek,
the amputated landscape
then utter sudden nothing—

LIGHT HOUSE
Kazim Ali

Shining over the dark harbor
lonely and unchurched

Robin whose ship sank in the storm
Names her son Faro

We built our way by current and star
To fathom is the ruin of dusk and depth

FALCON
Kazim Ali

His life then lifted
Just for a moment then
Plummeted down

Sky to beach,
white wings unfurl
Useless but beautiful

Bird of dust thrust landward
And learn through life in the body
Of a man

what it means
To be flawed
A follower fallen

His brother the falcon flew
On a silver boat chasing the storm
While he stayed dumbly home

CALLING THE COPS
Tara Dorabji

I can't stop the cops from coming. I keep calling the cops. The cops keep shooting kids. I can't stop the cops from coming.

It's still dark outside when I dial 911. The dispatcher says, "Ma'am, what is his ethnicity?"

"He's a person of color."

"Ma'am, is he Latino or Black."

I pause. One hundred and two Black people were killed by police in 2015.

"It's dark out," I say. My head clouds with the racist texts written by San Francisco Police officers. One of the cops is Asian and came under investigation for allegedly raping a woman. The texts, released by the media, include:

Niggers should be spayed.

I am leaving it like it is, painting KKK on the sides and calling it a day!

White power.

Cross burning lowers blood pressure! I did the test myself!

The 911 dispatcher says, "Please answer the question. Ma'am, is he Latino or Black?"

I am a woman alone in my house. A man is on my doorstep, refusing to leave.

Last year, over one thousand civilians were murdered by police in America. Black people are killed by police at twice the rate as White people.

I cannot open my door to this man, ringing my doorbell, shaking on my stoop, grinding his teeth, his eyes searching for something, his fingers scratching into skin. I give thanks that my daughters are with their dad.

"He's a young, Black man on my doorstep. Please, don't shoot him," I say.

I am alone in my house.

I go over to the door and peer through the peephole. He cranes toward me, trying to get in. His arms shake as he scratches his neck. I hold my breath, hoping he will go. Fear prickles up my spine.

He knows someone is on the other side of the door.

Just weeks back, another man lurked outside my back door, drunken and wanting. I was praying outside with my daughters. When he kept leering at us, I went inside and closed my curtains and blinds even though it was morning. I told my girls to get away from the windows. I waited. An hour later, he was still peering in my window, eyes searching for me.

I did not yet know that a woman was just found murdered in the park. I did not yet know how drunk he was. I was so tired. I balled up and cried. He was Brown. He hid in the bushes and watched me.

I am sickened by the irony that I can find comfort in calling the cops that ultimately my skin, though Brown, is still light enough to protect me from being shot.

I yelled at my daughters to get away from the windows. I called my neighbor because I was so damn tired of calling the cops.

My neighbor called the cops. The cops took pictures of the guy grizzled and drunk in the bushes on the hill above my bedroom.

I am utterly broken by my need for armed men to save me from hungry men.

Now, a man rings the bell at my front door. He refuses to leave. I call my boyfriend and he answers even though it isn't six a.m. He gets ready for work when it is still dark outside.

"Hey," I say. "Some guy is ringing my doorbell, hanging out on my porch, and he won't go away."

"How long has it been?" My boyfriend asks.

"Five to ten minutes. I turned on the light, but he wouldn't go away."

"Call the cops, then call me back," my boyfriend says.

"Are you sure?"

"Yeah, call me back."

I already called the cops three times in the last few weeks. They keep coming to my house, whether I call them or not.

My son's dad called the cops, the first time they came. Our son was sixteen and a 5150. They came more times than I want to remember that winter of 2012. They were young, round-faced men of color. I kept trying not to cry. I didn't cry. I remember that. They kept their guns hidden and were social workers—maybe one of them hugged me, realizing that I had no idea what to do when my boy walked out. That was the winter after we split up. I learned to answer the doors to cops and they didn't shoot me. They kept their eyes cast down unable to see me broken. An invisible badge of privilege passed back and forth between us on my doorstep. A momentary glimpse of what a peace officer could be if they weren't armed and human. If there weren't an epidemic of young men of color being slaughtered. If skin color and class didn't matter.

That same winter, undercover cops pulled over my kids' dad with our twins in his black, paint faded and scratched Honda Civic. He parked at New Life Grocery on Bernal Hill. An unmarked vehicle rolled up behind him and the cops jumped out surrounding the car, guns drawn on my daughters in boosters—their father unforgivably Brown. One itchy finger and my daughters could be dead. One flinch. They were blocks away from where Alex Nieto was murdered by cops while eating dinner a few years later.

But instead of firing, one of the cops recognized my ex. They'd been to his house after he'd called about our son.

"We have the wrong guy. I know this guy," the cop said. "Your car matched the description of a stolen car."

My daughters cried in the backseat. The guns were lowered. They were four years old.

A few weeks later that same winter, the cops came by my house again. My daughters were home. I stepped outside to answer questions about their brother, who had run away.

My daughter stood at the window crying, watching me talk to the cops. When I came back in she said, "I got so scared, Mommy. I thought they'd shoot you like they did Oscar Grant."

Still, I keep calling the cops. The cops keep coming.

Why do peace officers carry guns? Suppose we armed teachers?

The other night, I kept hearing this child screaming. My neighbors, three generations in one house, were fighting in the street. I watched from my window. There was yelling and cursing. The little girl was hysterical in the car. The mother hit her father who put her in a headlock.

"Don't touch me; let me go," she was screaming. They were throwing down. He was three times her size. I called the cops. If it's that bad on the street, it is usually worse in the house.

Bettie Jones was "accidently" killed by cops in Chicago, who responded to a domestic dispute at her neighbors. She opened her door to the cops to tell them where to go and was killed.

When a man hits a woman, I call the cops. When men beat on my door in the middle of the night, I call the cops. When a man has a mental break on my doorstep just before dawn breaks, I pause before calling the cops. When a man hides drunken in the bushes, watching me pray on a Sunday morning, I find someone to call the cops for me.

The morning after I called the cops on my neighbors, my friend videotaped an Oakland police officer murdering a man on the street after he hit a cop with a bicycle chain. No one was allowed to go near him as his blood soaked into the concrete. He died alone in the street, his hand outstretched.

The cops keep coming to my house, even when I'm not home.
Last summer, my boyfriend was sleeping in my bed, waiting for me
to come home. He heard the garage open and assumed it was me, but
there were male voices. He wondered if I were bringing someone home
with me. *Seriously?!* He then thought that the travelling nurse staying
downstairs must be bringing someone home. Loud feet clomped up the
stairs and a semiautomatic weapon entered my room aimed at him half
naked under my covers.

"SF Police, is there anyone in here?"

"Yes, don't shoot." My boyfriend was White, even in the dark.

"Is this your house?"

"No it's my girlfriend's."

And they left like a bad dream. The woman staying downstairs
called the cops because she heard noises upstairs and my car wasn't in
the garage. They came in riot gear. Weapons aimed.

I came home and found my boyfriend in the dark. His flesh warm
against mine. My man was still alive.

He lives. He is White. Unlike Keith Childress, Bettie Jones, Kevin
Matthews, Leroy Browning, Roy Nelson, Miguel Espinal, Nathaniel
Pickett, Tiara Thomas, Cornelius Brown, Chandra Weaver, Jamar
Clark, Richard Perkins, Stephen Tooson, Michael Lee Marshall, Alonzo
Smith—unarmed Black people all murdered by police in just two months.

I wait for the cops and watch the young, Black man outside my house.
He has gone to my neighbor's doorstep. He is yelling and pounding on
their door. I keep my cell phone near for when the cops come, so I can
videotape, just in case.

The first time I called the cops this summer, I heard noises downstairs.
This was after the travelling nurse had moved on. I was home with my
daughters. It was 1 a.m. I kept trying to rationalize the noises away.
I turned off the light and slid into the cotton of my sheets.

Then, I heard the thumping against my front door. There were
men yelling and banging on my front door. I've dreamt this dream a
thousand times—intruders trying to break in. They were coming for me.
I called 911. The dispatcher told me to look out the peephole in my front
door and see who was banging on it. I didn't want to go near the door.
It was shaking. Would they break it? Would they shoot me through it?
I imagined the glass of the window shattering around me. There was a
spotlight on my house. I was under attack.

I called my boyfriend. "Hey, can you talk me through something?"

The pounding on the door increased. I didn't want to go near it. He
convinced me to look out the window at the front of the house. Just to
see what the light was. See what was going on.

Finally, I looked out the window. It was the cops. I just called the cops on the cops. *I called the cops on the cops.*

I kept my boyfriend on the line when I went outside.

I stepped out the door in my robe and in the second they saw me, the home invasion dissipated. My skin coated me like a balm. We were not at war anymore.

One look at me and the light went off and everyone was calm. I am fortunate. The bullets didn't fly. The guns came down, not up, when I opened the door.

"Ma'am, you left your garage open," the cop said.

I blinked in confusion. The cops were banging on my door.

"Why didn't you open the door, ma'am? Your neighbors called the police. They saw the garage door open and got scared."

"Why didn't you just ring the doorbell?" I asked. Why would I ever open the door to armed men banging on my door in the middle of the night?

I shut the garage door. My daughter had left it open. We went to sleep. She will tell the story. Cops pull guns on her. Cops bang on our door in the middle of the night. Cops look for her brother when he goes missing. Cops come when her father and brother fight.

Cops take her on field trips.

These nature hikes are designed to build up community relationships since so many Brown kids are killed by cops in our neighborhood. These hikes with the cops pushed the kids and built endurance. The cops wore guns and taught outdoor education. I guess some teachers are armed. They passed around handcuffs and batons for show and tell. They let each child ask a question. My daughter came home and told me that she asked a question.

I asked policia Karl if he'd ever been against the police, but that's not the question I really wanted to ask. I wanted to ask, "Who killed Alex Nieto?"

Alex Nieto was twenty-eight years old when he was shot on Bernal Hill. At the time, he was on a full scholarship at City College. A community worker, watching the sunset and eating dinner before work when a dog walker called the cops on someone Brown. The cops came. Fifty-nine shots were fired by Sergeant Jason Sawyer (then lieutenant), Officer Roger Morse, Officer Richard Schiff, and Officer Nathan Chew.

My daughters met Alex Nieto's uncle. My daughters met Oscar Grant's grandmother. Twenty-two-year-old Oscar Grant was shot unarmed on New Year's Day at the Fruitvale BART station. When my daughters heard that their *tia*'s son was shot sixteen times in the back in the Bayview last week, my daughter asked, "Did the police shoot him?"

Twenty-six-year-old Mario Woods was shot dead by the police in

Bayview, leaving thirty-six casings on the ground and his new uniform unworn for the UPS job he would've started the next day. Most of the twenty gunshot wounds were in his back.

These are the stories from our neighborhood that get swallowed by an epidemic. Researchers at the Harvard School of Public Health are calling on public health agencies to acknowledge police killings as a public health issue—not just a criminal justice one.

It takes less than a breath to flip from social worker to soldier when armed on the streets.

The cop arrives on my block and the young man is shaking on my neighbor's steps. I step out on the porch to be visible, to witness if needed. I am a hypocrite, calling the cops to be my savior and ready to be the savior for the guy I called the cops on.

The cop asks him, "What are you doing?"

The young man keeps clawing at his neck. "I'm looking for my mom. There she is." He points to me.

We are too close in age for him to be my boy. I hope my son never ends up broken on some stranger's doorstep.

The cop has his social worker hat on. He doesn't take out his weapon. He asks the young man to leave. He tells him that I am not his mom.

I am grateful for the cop who moves him along. I lock my door. My kids come home. They are eight. I don't tell them what happened. It is only a small moment. We can't live in fear.

They are old enough to unlock the door and go outside by themselves. ∎

AS IF
S. Afzal Haider

First of all:
I am afraid all my fears are fears of the heart. Fear of being unloved, unwanted, undesired. The lonely are brave. Lonely I am. Brave I am not. But in the end what does it matter.

The solitude of the heart continues. Day after day, night after night, I remain sad and feel all alone. And there is, it seems, no end in sight. Yes, I can easily think about terminating my own life, but beyond a fleeting thought, that is one option I will never seriously consider or exercise. That is not my style. I cannot swim, so I wouldn't jump into a wild river and drown. I'm afraid of heights, therefore it would be difficult for me to jump down from a high-rise, and besides, I hate the sight of blood on a sidewalk. I'm totally against gun violence, I don't believe in shooting in the head to kill anyone, including myself. One who could kill oneself is a brave soul, I'm not that courageous. I could go on, but the point is I am not frightened and I will dare to face my life by not running away from it. I must die of old age, feeble, frail, immobile, preferably in my sleep. I wouldn't mind, when I'm old, if my plane were to crash, but that doesn't seem fair. Most passenger plane crashes kill more than one individual. What's the sense of including men and women lusting for life. The unfortunate pilots, the humble flight attendants, why bring them down to fullfil the death wish of one old man.

"If we can do anything to make your flight more enjoyable, please do not hesitate to ask."

"Yes. How about a fuck, a blow job." That would make this flight more pleasurable.

So the simple point of this chatter, the monologue between us is this: Why, oh why, am I so full of gloom?

Yes, drinking helps, yes smoking marijuana eases the pain. I'm a kind, good person, a good friend and probably a decent husband. Not good, not bad, just decent. Definitely fair. Nothing works. When it rains, and it rains a lot, there is darkness, no light. The sun is millions of light-years away.

* * *

I had another bad day yesterday. Not a bad hair day, not a bad attitude day, not a bad weather day, not a gust of bad wind day. A day of asking the serious question of should I live today and if I do, why? Inside all this obvious misery, it all sucks. I'm resourceful, I enjoy good movies, good meals and good sex, and most of the time I get to have all three. I'm not deprived of anything and I deny myself very little. So. As they say, living well is the best revenge. I live well with all that I can afford, and I can afford a lot, all that is essential and necessary. And in my vengence I can live, that may be beyond all that's superfluous and dispensable. But still, why am I sad more often than I need to be?

* * *

One week after the death of my father, in Pakistan, I packed for the return trip home. Into my carry-on bag I put the portrait of my mother that Baba had painted when she was a young woman as well as an unfinished self-portrait of Baba. I took two of his books, a biography of Mohammed and a volume of poetry of Ghalib, also his silver betel tin and his diary from 1930 to 1937, a thick black leather-bound notebook with his name engraved on it in fading gold capital letters. My nonstop flight from Karachi to Amsterdam made an emergency stop in Cairo to fix a plumbing problem; the toilets wouldn't flush.

After more than four hours' delay, my plane landed at Schiphol Airport. The speakers played the Beatles' "Good Day Sunshine." It was raining in Amsterdam—I had missed my Amsterdam-to-Chicago connecting flight. There wouldn't be another until the next day. I didn't care; there was no rush, my father was no longer dying. From the airport I booked a room at Hotel Museumzicht, on Jan Luykenstraat. I had stayed there before, great location, a quiet street, two blocks from the Rijksmuseum.

In a night's journey I had traveled from 118 degrees Fahrenheit in Karachi to 54 degrees Fahrenheit in Amsterdam, not counting the temperature at the Cairo airport. I took a train to Central Station and a cab to my hotel. Leaves were green, the flower market on Singel was busy. Amsterdam is a city with a beauty mark that both adds to it and takes something away. Indians have a tradition, they put a black dot on a beautiful face to ward off an evil eye.

* * *

After a short nap at my hotel, I had lunch and went to Rijksmuseum. Following that, I walked around the canals and got lost and asked a drunken artist with a long unkempt beard, puffing a pipe, with brown burn holes in his red velour jacket, for directions. "Americans have not produced a single great composer," said the drunken artist. "And Americans have not produced a great artist," he insisted. All I wanted were the directions to Hotel Museumzicht, on Jan Luykenstraat. I was not interested in an intellectual discussion. I was an American by default, born in India. My family moved to Karachi and I came to America to study—as a naturalized citizen I was both offended by and extremely defensive of Americans and American ways. It is a good country—an easy country to live in. More fair than equal, but good. Yes, it lacks culture, art, and compared to the rest of the world, has a shorter history after we destroyed the ways of the Native Americans, and not to mention, for me it is a source of shame, the slavery of black people of African origin and the continued destruction of that population, black lives don't matter. It is simply unforgivable.

It seemed like only yesterday that I watched the Million Man March on TV. African Americans with issues of real life, and real live situations gathered together to acknowledge that predicament, the plight and the straits that comes with being black. Among the thousands, millions of those African American faces, the men of color on the TV, I tried to find my face. I tried to find myself. I wasn't there.

Still, with the drunken artist I was more a critic than critical, simple, not necessarily simplistic. I argued for American architecture, mostly modern and mostly in New York, Chicago and San Francisco. The American artists, musicians, filmmakers, scientists and whatnot. But there was no point to make with a drunk artist who thought Americans had not produced a single great composer or artist. I found my way back to my hotel.

Get to it, Mo. We all know you are a desperate soul. And doomed as well.

I sat in Caffe Esprit, near Universiteit van Amsterdam. Across the street, the red sign of the Lone Star Cafe burned brightly on a cloudy day, young men and women walked around—a book market was in progress on the sidewalk . . . alone. Alone by choice, "alone by choosing" was a concept that some men subscribed to, believing that they could always find company if they so wanted. The reality was that they were lonely people, they lacked social graces, were incapable of making small talk or profound statements. They acted overconfident, smug to cover their ineptness and clumsiness.

I am one of those. Someone once asked me, Do you have children? Yes. A boy and a boy and both are good boys. I love my boys and they love me. Unlike girls, boys need to work on being good, because boys are not naturally good, I know, I was one, once upon a boy. Girls are inherently good—good by nature, good in deeds. I sat there, drinking dark ale, and a woman with red roses, all open and blossoming in full—like her open radiant face—walked by.

Nothing gets taken. In the early evening, next door to Hotel Agora on Singel, they were playing Chicago Blues in Amsterdam.

"Is there any Chicago connection?" I asked the attractive woman sitting at the entrance. "Yes, our percussionist, Terry White, who also sings, he is from Chicago," she told me with a grateful, beautiful smile, moving her head left to right.

"Do you love me as much as I love you?" I wanted to ask. I walked in, sat down at the bar, and ordered a Heineken. Terry did sing well. "I'm going to move, way out of town"—I already have.

The band took a break. After long applause the band members mingled with the audience—"You were great," I told Terry White the percussionist, the lead singer.

"I'm good," said Terry White, confident, self-assured. A black man in his early fifties and with a balding head, he sang with a hat on. Terry White had class, flare, a style. "Whereabout in Chicago did you live?"

"Fifty-Seventh and Woodlawn."

"I live in Chicago," I volunteered.

"You do?" responded Terry White. He walked away.

I was alone again, and that was fine. Had I offended Terry in some way, I wondered. Maybe this guy was running from the law or a bad marriage or divorce and he didn't want to meet another tourist from back home, I reflected.

At my hotel I closed an adjoining hallway door on the index finger of my right hand. After absorbing the initial excruciating pain, I examined it under a lamp. The skin was not punctured, blood was not gushing out, but there was a Rorschach pattern spreading under the nail and a purple swelling, a blister, on the fingertip. Unlike my mother, who had long, thin fingers, I had my father's hands with short stubby fingers. Hands, I regretfully reminded myself, that would never bowl for a national team in a test cricket match nor pitch for the New York Yankees. I asked for a Band-Aid at the front desk. They directed me to the hotel bar. The Dutch are so practical, I reflected, carrying my sore finger in my left hand as though it were a small crippled bird. Antiseptic and mood elevator both available in one convenient location.

Behind the bar stood a stunning maid, spellbinding enough to make me forget my throbbing finger and move it to different location. She wore tight black jeans and a loose-fitting black silk blouse. Around her waist was a short red cotton apron. She was watching world soccer. Holland versus West Germany, on a television mounted on a pole. There was nobody at the bar. With her dark, curly hair, large brown eyes and tanned skin, she reminded me of an old girlfriend, Tara Khan. I asked her for a Band-Aid.

"Are you Indian?" she asked, handing a plastic strip across the bar.

"No," I answered soberly. "I'm a cowboy."

She ignored my attempt at humor, her eyes on the soccer game again.

I sat down on a bar stool across from her, watching the game in the mirror behind her.

"My grandfather was Indian. A sailor," she volunteered. "He jumped ship in Holland when he was nineteen and married my grandmother when he was twenty-one."

"Until last night I was in Wonderland," I said. "Now, I'm only Alice."

"What was that?" she asked.

"Nothing," I said. "That was a private conversation."

On TV, the game stopped; someone had committed a foul.

Looking at me appraisingly, she said, "My name is Rita. Can I get you anything?" Her smile completely did me in. She had full red lips, and even, dazzlingly white teeth.

Anything I want is a generous offer, I wanted to say. I wanted to bury my face in her bosom, spill out my life story. I became conscious of my finger throbbing again. "A shot of Bokma and a St. Pauli Girl, dark," I said, smiling back.

"My grandpa took me to India once, Bijnor," she continued, pouring my drink. "I was four or five; he was an old man. All I remember now are spices, shades of yellow, green and red and animated conversations in languages I couldn't understand. He died a few years later. We never went back."

I'm returning to America after missing my father's funeral in Karachi, I wanted to say, but I said nothing. The soccer game on TV started again. We both watched.

"I play soccer," she said. "I love the game."

I looked at her standing in front of me and I saw her in the mirror. She was slim and petite; she had a perfect body for the game. I pictured her in knickers and knee socks, kicking the ball and I was ready to tell her that I was captain of my high school cricket team when another man walked in, someone she seemed to know well. I sat watching soccer, sipping my drink and listening to Rita and the other man talk. Apparently he was an Englishman, a captain on a cruise boat, and he had an apartment in the city. I responded only briefly when they tried to draw me into their conversation. Before I finished my drink, he asked Rita if she would join him for dinner when her shift was over.

I had been planning to ask her out to dinner myself! I wanted to scream. Lovely Rita looked away from the TV toward me for a brief moment. I stood up, gulped my drink and looked at the cruise-ship captain sitting a few stools away. I rubbed my thumb over the Band-Aid. I thanked Rita and left.

* * *

The next morning I woke up hungry. Sitting in a three-windowed breakfast nook, overlooking the very Rijksmuseum, I ate my breakfast, a hard-boiled egg, muesli, a banana, coffee and orange juice. Contemplating the life and, for the lack of better words, the passing away of my father, and a good father, an art master. He supplemented his income by painting the portraits of famous people as well as common folk: a Gandhi for Mohan Das, a Jinnah for Mohammed Ali and someone's beloved late mother.

Baba's paintings were precise, accurate in all important details, intolerant of any variation. Baba took pride in painting portraits and nature that looked like photographs. "Van Gogh spent too much time being madly in love and not enough time in fine-tuning and promoting his craft," Baba used to say.

Unlike Van Gogh, Baba knew how to sell his paintings. He had a robust freelance business. His clients commissioned him to paint just about everything—book and magazine covers, monograms, logos, trademarks. Baba calligraphed the first and possibly still-in-use logo for Pakistan International Airlines; he also created art for the label of Tibet Beauty Cream. I know that sometimes he was commissioned to paint pornographic postcards that I used to peek at as works in progress with much pleasure when he was not around.

But before he became respectable and well regarded. Soon after the partition of India, our family arrived in Karachi, Pakistan, as refugees. I was eight years old. Times were hard. Baba was commissioned to paint a peacock, the trademark for a local fabric mill. Baba stayed up late nights after his day job as an art master. Using watercolors, he created the image of a magnificent male peafowl, featuring a crested head, with upright plumes and a large, greatly elongated, loosely webbed tail with oscillated spots, ready to spread and hold up in courtship, like a luminous, dazzling fan. He painted it on an 8½-by-11 sheet in brilliant iridescent hues of blue, green and brown watercolors, against a sky-blue background. He scribed "Peacock Fabric Mills" in elegant bold black capital letters across the bottom. Finally it was done.

It was Friday afternoon, a half day at school. I answered the doorbell to our ground floor apartment. Dressed in a light-green cotton suit, a yellow tie and dark sunglasses, Mr. Chaman, the general manager of Peacock Cotton Mills, had arrived to pick up his trademark. Mr. Chaman stood beside his motor scooter, which he had parked on the sidewalk. He declined to come in. "I must leave in less than three minutes," he told me to tell Baba. The trademark peacock, wrapped in transparent paper, was all ready to go. Baba brought it outside to show Mr. Chaman; I followed.

It was a hot and muggy day. The open sewer by the sidewalk in front of our apartment building overflowed from a heavy rain earlier that morning and from too many ritual baths taken by Friday afternoon worshipers living in their shacks on the sidewalks.

Baba handed the trademark bird to Mr. Chaman, who stood on the wet sidewalk. Mr. Chaman examined the work, still wrapped in transparent paper, without removing his sunglasses. From his expression I could tell that something was not right. He lifted his sunglasses and set them above his forehead, roughly unwrapped the painting and crushed the wrapping into a ball. He gave the bird a close look, shaking his head in disapproval. "But this peacock is not dancing!" he scowled.

"I was commissioned to paint a male peafowl with a crested head, with upright brown plumes and a large tail with brilliantly colored blue and green spots, and I did just that," said Baba. "There was no instruction that it had to be a dancing peacock."

Mr. Chaman, a short pudgy man, strutted around his motor scooter. "But this peacock is not dancing," he repeated. "We wanted a proud male peafowl, holding up its brilliant iridescent tail in a courtship fan!" he contended.

My father was a man of quick wit and a savage debater. "If you want a peacock-feather fan you can buy it for four annas at the old market," said Baba. "Now, if you would like for me to paint a dancing peacock holding its tail up in a courtship fan, I'll do it for half the price after I'm paid in full for the artwork I've already completed."

"No. That is out of question, totally unacceptable," said Mr. Chaman indignantly, tossing the ball of wrapping paper into the open sewer. "I'm not going to pay a counterfeit penny for this bird."

Baba, a stout man of five feet ten with a muscular body, moved closer to Mr. Chaman and placed his right hand on Mr. Chaman's shoulder, very close to his necktied collar. "In that case," said Baba with much confidence, "I'll take whatever action I deem necessary to collect my wages."

Baba was not a man of empty words and he had little tolerance for empty heads. When we lived in India, he used to exercise every day, lifting weights, doing sit-ups, push-ups. He was in impressive physical form, quite the specimen of solid matter. He shaved his skin smooth to have a body of flat, even and single color.

"I didn't know I was dealing with a hooligan," said Mr. Chaman, reaching for his wallet.

"And I didn't know I was dealing with a swindler," said Baba, loosening his grip unapologetically.

Mr. Chaman handed Baba two crisp, newly minted twenty-rupee notes with the face of Mohammed Ali Jinnah on them. He looked at the trademark bird one more time and then tore it into four pieces, then eight, and threw it into the sewer. It floated for a moment, its blue, green and brown pigments bleeding into the dirty water before it was swept away in the murky current.

Baba, who still held the two twenty-rupee notes in his hand, tore them into tiny little pieces and tossed them like confetti into the running sewage. Mr. Chaman placed his sunglasses back over his eyes, kick-started his Vespa and scooted away, splashing dirty water on his trousers.

When I think of it now, it was the perfect zero-sum game.

First of all: My father is dead and gone now.

Life is a cell in hell with and without memory. I carry my baggage from my room at Hotel Museumzicht, pay my dues at the front desk and leave for the airport to fly home. ■

A STREET MUSICIAN
Syed Ishaq Haider

HARVEST
Syed Ishaq Haider

A BEGGAR
Syed Ishaq Haider

A CAMEL CART DRIVER
Syed Ishaq Haider

ANJALI'S MOTHER
Moazzam Sheikh

N amastay ji. How are you? Please come, come, come. Oh I am good, okay, not bad. Thank you ji. Sit please, sit, sit. Grateful for coming you. Here, this way. Yes, the weather good today, bohat accha, the sun out, shining little little. How is everyone in your family? I have not seen your wife lately. Is she good? Wah ji, I see. Have your daughter graduate from Santa Crude now? Aha good, and your son? Good, then. Yes, yes, everyone fine in my family also, thanking Bhagwan, I mean God, same thing, sure, sure. His blessing very important, but you know old age tough rough at old people, sometime very hard, very unfair. My mother not well, falling down two times while doing small things in the house. No need to take your shoes off. Everyone telling her Amma tell us what you want but my mother stubborn, very stubborn sometime, but now I am far away I understand why she want to do her work by herself. People are wrong thinking it is pride or brain turning into porridge, no Robert Saheb, you will understand this, it is not pride or bad weak brain. It is good to move, stay active, that is what Amma want. Me too here, in a foreign country. I am sorry if I am taking very much of your time. Thank you for your time and kindness. I am very very worry. I am lucky our family know you. You are like a second father to Anjali but she is very crazy these days. Don't know what to do, how to handle her. She very reebellion. Things no too good here and back in India things okay, but older relatives I worry. Especially since I am so far away I feel helpless and sad and sometimes I cry but Anjali no care anymore. You tell me why good children turn out bad. Is it fast food? She is a good girl but don't know what wrong with her head since past year. So I am asking to you for help. She listen to you. Yes, yes, take off your coat. I'll hang it.

You know how difficult life for us sometime, but now only most times. Anjali's father leave us, why? I don't know, my mind don't understand. A good man he is, but now doing bad things by not coming back. I come here because of him. Back in India everyone happy. Sunil go to Amreeka, a relative help him get visa. He first go to England to stay with his cousin sister, then from there to Chicago, then here in San Francisco. He like it very much, used to send pictures with his friends all happy and everyone smiling, other men from India like him working hard missing their family shamily. Let me be honest with you, Robert Saheb, I did not want to come because I like what I had, family and friends and neighbors. Everyday someone coming to see you, coming to borrow onion or salt. In hard times I can depend on others. I love my in-laws very much, the whole family love me, treat me like their own daughter. Now my mother-in-law is been diagnosed with cancer one year ago and my heart is broke because I cannot be there for her. All because of this man who has abandoned us for no good reason. If I did not to worry about my girl I will pack right now and hurry back. But what to do and that is why I want to speak with you. Thank you for your time. I know you are a busy person and must be with your own worries. But will repay you for your kindness. No, no, I am no embracing you. It is the true you like family. Yes, thank you, I will make some tea.

You know Anjali since she was this small. I still remember how shy she was when you called her and asked her name. She was mute hiding behind my leg. She was so good for all these years but now she has sprout wings, Robert ji, and flying from one bad company to another bad company, and even I have studied enough English in India to learn in my class that man is known by accompany he keep. So if she hanging out with good for nothing boys how can she come out good. I am not worry about myself and at this point I don't care what her father's family will say. I am worry about her. She is a very good girl with a very good brain and heart. She help me out in the house and take care of many things outside like if there is any office paperwork like when I was hospitalized, she take care of everything, talk with the nurse, fight the doctor, bring medicine, social worker and everything else. Now I don't even see her for weeks and she is losing weight. Last time I saw her I ask Anjali are you not getting enough sleep or have you reading late late night? My daughter telling me Amma don't worry. I am not a baby. I tried not to be possess by temper but I cannot control and said you will always be my baby. How can you leave your own mother who has no one in this country. You don't call, you don't come home, is that what children do to their parents? She gets annoyed so fast like a speedy train and tells me to my face Amma that's why I don't come home because you're always nagging. I am American Amma. So I say American no worry about their parents? Give me some space and she used the eff word. My ears did not stop burning for days. My own child using the eff word in front of her own mother! Even Sunil never use cuss word. Heartless children. I said Anjali shame on you for using bad language in front of your mother. In India you will get a spanking. She said Amma this is not India. I said Beta but we are Indian Americans, immigrants. We are not on tourist visas here. We came with the help of our family. They suffered so your father can go to Europe and Amreeka. When he went away, your family took care of me. Don't forget you were born in Delhi in your dada and dadi's house. You did not see your papa till we came here. You were two years old by then. How can you remember the times you had fever and everyone in the family stayed up at nights! Your father and I still have to send money to your grandparents every month. What if I die tomorrow?

I have a hard time believing that my own flesh and blood can one day become so unkind, Robert Saheb, this is what she said, Amma but you don't have to send any money. You don't owe others anything. You can spend that money on you instead. Go take a vacation. She said other silly things which I cannot repeat in front of you or others. I have no idea how shameless children can be here. I am sure your children are not like her. So I had to explain to her that even if I never see my family again it does not break the bond and it is not the money, it is the thought. I do not owe. If I am not here, I will help my family in other ways. This is what the relatives who don't have money do. Who do you think remembers to give medicine to your dadi? Who do you think takes your nani to the hospital for her chemo? Who do you think cooks for her? Who do you think give help to me when I was pregnant with you? So just because one family member moves away the problems of life stop? Who goes and fetches electrician when the electric fuse is gone, gone? I send money because that is the only way I have to help out. And I don't send money because I have to but because she is your dadi and your nani. You have their blood. It is a moral obligation.

She tells me Amma I understand but she understand nothing. She is young and fallen into bad, bad company and hangs out with other children who only think for themselves. I pray to Bhagwan she is not eating any drugs or drinking tobacco. She says she is spending time with guitar and drum people, given up school. She is telling me she is working in a cafe. Is that why we came to Amreeka so you can work in a cafe selling chai and pastry? I did not say but wanted to My darling we can move back to India and you can make chai for your dadijan ten times a day if you want. While she is surrounded by all kinds of friends I sit home alone waiting for her and cursing my luck and wondering what got into Sunil's head. What kind of a man leave his wife and daughter for someone else? I am not a whore. I am his wife. You have to treat me with respect. How can he forget the sacrifices I have made for him and his family. He only remember his sacrifice. Nobody deny that. I always tell Sunil, Sunil, you are a brave person, a good obedient son, I admire that you married because that is what your parents wanted, but he and I already know each other and like each other and we are lucky that both our parents give us their blessings. So what more can you ask from Bhagwan. Bhagwan is not a businessman. I tell him don't be ungrateful. I am not a bazaari woman. Don't treat me like them. Don't make me do things a decent man will not make his true wife do. Sometimes very chee chee. I always treat him with love and respect. Did I not always treat him with respect? Has anyone heard me using loud voice when talking to him? So why did he insist I drink alcohol with him? I don't drink alcohol. No one drinks in our family. Anyway, I cannot want to bother you about Anjali's father. I am here to talk to you about Anjali. Can you help me? Can you help me get Anjali back and back to her good behavior days? I am believing you can. Yes, yes, she will listen to you. You are real Amreekan, American, sorry.

Ah, all these years, she was like sister to me. Every time Sunil act bad or lacking in fairness to me with his words, Anjali was creeped up to me, wiping my tears, holding me in her embrace, patting my cheek with one hand as if she is mother and I daughter, "Amma, don't worry. Papa doesn't mean it. Papa will change. Don't feel sad, Amma, I am here, look!" And looking at her melting my heart. Looking at each other smiled she and I and then laughed and another day passed. Another night passed. Curse the mother's heart! Now I am all alone and where is she? Wasting her days with loafers from all around the world. I even tell her, Anjali, I am not old fashion. I know you are an American girl, not born but raised here. I cannot expect you to be like your cousins in India. If you like someone I don't mind. Stay at home. He can visit you at your home. I like company too. Tell your friends to come whenever they want. If I am home I will cook for them. They sit all day in the living room and talk and play guitar or watch movies. I don't mind. Who am I? Yes, yes, Robert ji, I am crying. What to do? So I said to her, my child, I will understand if you are in love with someone or have a boyfriend, whatever, I know it is not her fault, it is a different culture and I have to accept it when I accept a new country and make it my home. All your friends are like my children too. Why not! But I tell her, girl, just be respecting fully of your home, your mother. If not your mother, then at least your grandparents. Every week they ask me about Anjali. On the phone it is always Anjali Anjali Anjali. As if I don't exist. No, no, I am not saying they don't love me. Oh, thank you, Robert Saheb, no, that's fine, thank you. I will just use this to wipe my eyes. I should not cry in front of you, but speaking with you has opened so many wounds. Thank you for listening to a wounded mother. So speaking with Sunil's father, it is all: What is Anjali doing these days? How is her college going? Tell her to call her Dadi ji. Tell her this, tell her that. And when I tell him Baba, I want to come back. Your daughter-in-law is tired and alone, he raises such a storm. My mother-in-law backs him up too, saying, Anjali's mother, have some common sense. Who's been putting all that straw inside your skull? It is all for Anjali's future. You must stay there so she can get good education. Why come back to India? What's here? We can always speak on the phone. Over here we are miserable. Corruption, no electricity, pollution, bad hospitals, bad doctors, broken roads. Only cricket cricket cricket. You want to come back to watch cricket? Okay, we'll tape it for you and mail it so you can watch it with Anjali. I feel like a cow that gives dollars instead of milk. The money I sent helps out a lot of people and I cannot just walk away. I can visit them but I cannot leave Anjali behind. Anything can happen to her, and if I am not here when she needs me, how will I show my face to the world? And if something happens to me there and I cannot come back for sometime. Will Anjali leave her friends and come and take care her of poor mother? Somehow I doubt it, yes, yes, the tears again. I will take your handkerchief this time. Thank you, you are very kind. When was the last time when even Anjali held my hand!

The reason I am speaking to you now is that perhaps if you speak to her and tell her, explain to her it is not good to abandon your old mother. Thank you, but that is now how I meant. Yes, you are right. I am only in my forties, but Sunil and Anjali have put on extra years on me. I feel old, abandoned. I used to think I was lucky. Please tell me if my word put burden on you. I will stop. Thank you to be so very kind. You are not human. You are an angel, Robber ji. No, I cannot simply call you Robber. I know, how you feel, but it again that culture thing, so hard to break. Okay I will try. What was I saying? My brain has finished. Oh yes that when I was young I used to think I was a very lucky girl. A very lucky girl despite being poor compared with our relatives. You know my father died when I was nine years old. I was number three child, two older brothers. I miss them so much. So because of pitaji's sudden death Amesh, my barre bhayya, had to drop out from college and start working. He became the father of the house. Chotte bhayya, Kamlesh went as far as FA, then my mamaji—mama is a mother's brother, Robber ji, sorry, Robert ji—can I get you one more cup of chai? Please do let me know. You are not a guest. You are like a relative. So my mamaji got chotte bhayya a job driving rickshaw. Barre bhayya refused to get married despite Amma's pleading. We lived in a neighborhood called Chiragh Dilli in Delhi where all kinds of people lived and we got help from many family friends and relatives. That is why I say we were lucky. After pitaji's death we can have fallen on very hard times. But life was not too bad. I was in high school. My younger brother felt in bad company. He became a friend with another boy in our neighborhood whose father was an actor, only small roles in television dramas and theater also. My brother was always more artist than the two of us. After his work he went to watch rehearsals and staying away from home. Amma even slapped him a few times, but eventually she gave in when he said, Look, Amma, I can be famous some day. I want to act. Please let me. And Amma relented. After thirty-some years he is still acting small roles raising his own small family. He lives nearby, so that is a blessing. His wife is good, only she is a Muslim, a daughter of his friend's father's friend. But Amma does not mind. Barre bhayya was cross for a while but soon he said who is he to stop anyone from doing what they want to do. I always liked her, but soon I was married and moved to my in-laws and so did not get to know her very much. So my two nephews, Sameer and Vazeer, are being raised both as Hindu and Muslim. I don't like that. I told my sister-in-law, this is not good for the boys. Choose one thing. Otherwise that will confuse your children. And how will you feel if because of that confusion the boys or one of them grows up not believing in Bhagwan or Allah, then what will you do? She laughed. It is no laughing matter, or is it, Robert? Maybe, you are right. It is her life, their lives. Yes, it is weird to be crying one minute and laughing another. Your kindness is making me like that only. It was funny to watch my younger brother in a TV drama last year as Anjali and I sat down after dinner. He had a small role. He is playing the father of a young girl and he is on his deathbed. I shout to Anjali, look that is your chotte mamaji and suddenly I am crying, yes, just like I am crying right now. Only what to do? Only my own brother pretending to die. It broke my heart and if I did not have Anjali with me here I will have packed my things and fly back to India. Because I don't know if Kamlesh is dying in real life or no. He looked very weak and perhaps that's why the director chose the poor man for the role of a poor man. I felt helpless, but I thought I will always have Anjali.

You may be thinking these Indians are so sentimental and melodramatic but you are right, we are. Many I know are. Our movies are like that too. After I watched my brother dying I cannot get out of my mind a scene from a picture I was as a child. Raj Kapoor joining a circus as a clown like his father used to be who is dead and that is why his mother never wanted his son to be a clown because his father fell during circus and died. So the mother finds out and creeps into the circus to watch her son jumping around, so the scene that made all of us cry during and after the picture is that the mother watches Raj Kapoor fall and as the son fall he sees his mother in the sitting crowd and he know the mother is dead, her heart stopped seeing her son fall but only there is a net that stop the son from dying but before she dying she didn't know the net will save the son, so Raj Kapoor crying and crying Ma, Ma, Ma, and everyone one laughing thinking the clown doing a clown drama. So if you think we Indians melodramatic, we are but what to do. I cannot change myself. The worry part is natural come to me. I wish I were different.

Sometimes the thought of leaving Anjali to her fate coming in my mind. Sometimes the yearning to be close to my family is too strong, especially when it rains here and the only thing people say here is either they love the rain or they don't love the rain. What a thing to say! That is it. Back in India the rain is totally another thing. The first thunderclap followed by the downpour wakes everybody up. When I was a girl I used climb to the rooftop with my girlfriends and dance and sing in the rain pretending I was in a movie while the boys were playing cricket and running around shouting. Some boy would always be watching us soaked in rain from his rooftop also getting soaked acting like a hero. And we jumped and danced without abandon, pretending not to notice the young boy in love with us. Those were such innocent days. My Amma often made pakoras. Yes, you are right, those jaggedy little pieces, the yellow dumplings which they serve at restaurants. Do you like them? Oh good, I can make them for you some day. So, yes, some mornings I wake up and tell myself, Jyoti, time to pack your things and move back. Don't ruin your old age in this cold place. Your daughter and your husband if they love you they will come and find you. Then I make my chai and get ready to go to work and on the way I think about how I will live even a week without Anjali. I say to myself, Jyoti, what if your girl wake up one morning and feeling all bad for how neglectful she has been to her mother decides to apologize and move back with me but I am in India. What will Anjali do? That breaks my heart all over again. Robert, I now realize I made a big mistake staying here. I should have moved back with my girl. Anjali will have been a very different girl. She could not have run away like this abandoning her own poor mother. You know, Robert, my own pitaji ran away from home when he was a teenager. My grandmother and my mother have told me that story so many times and every time I think about it I cannot stop laughing. He used to live in a village then. My dadaji was school teacher in the village primary school, a follower of Gandhi. My father heard there was circus taking place nearby, outside few miles from Allahabad. One evening he went there with his friends and liked it so much that he ran away with them few days later. My Dadaji had to take a leave from school and go look for him, his only son.

I have four aunts, all younger than him. So the son had to come back. They found out from the other two boys who also wanted to run away but cold feet got them at the end, that pitaji had eloped with the circus. Dadaji took his bicycle with him and after four days of running around returned with pitaji, looking haggard and shamefaced, a rope tied around his neck. Yes, Robert, it is okay to laugh. Dadaji had zeroed in on the circus which had pitched its tent near Mirzapur. When dadaji pounced on his son, pitaji was feeding animals. "Ullu ke patthay, feeding animals but no care for your own family?" saying that dadaji give pitaji a thrashing he never forgot. From that day on, my father became the best son anyone can ever have. Pitaji used to say that dadaji did him a big favor by teaching him how to be a caring person and not a selfish person. After dada and dadiji passed away, my father made sure that his three remaining sisters got education and then married off before he thought of settling in his own nest to drop his own eggs. My eldest aunt, mausi Kela, used to tell me that when bapuji gave bhaiya the spanking, a girl rushed to his defense, but her elders in the circus restrained her. She told me that my grandfather heard that girl's shrieks in his dreams and that woke him up sometimes. Spanking embarrassed pitaji so much that he never can face the young woman again. But sometimes I tell myself that was not fair to pitaji. It is very true that he became a better man to society, although he never got to follow his heart. I am differing. I don't want to be strict and harsh with Anjali. I want her to follow her heart, not just the selfish part of her heart. Am I wrong?

As you say, I will tell you now. Both Sunil and I come from Arya Samaj background. We don't believe in cast and consider all human beings equal in the eyes of all gods and goddesses. It is not that I am against her spending her time with people from backgrounds different than ours. My great-grandfather was from the Punjab. Who knows what the truth is but I am from a pundit family and my elders have served the Mughlas, the Marathas, even the Sikhs, and it was during the British Raj that my great-grandfather left his job with the English hearing the call of Arya Samaj and settled in Gujrat. There he married the daughter of an Arya Samaj teacher. My dadaji and his sisters and brothers were all born there. My dadaji used to tell me that he had heard from his father that in fact we were from Kashmir and might have been related to India's first prime minister Pandit Nehru. My father's family name is Nehra. You can see the similarity. Nehru ji actually appeared in my dream just smiling. My dadaji also gave up the opportunity to work better jobs in a big city. He was a bright student and can have gone to England for bigger studies, but began following

Gandhiji when he returned to his motherland from Africa. And that is why he took a job teaching poor children in a small village near Allahabad. He also took part in the Salt March of 1930 for whole two months. On his return he fell ill. When Gandhiji surprised him with a visit, there was a young woman with him who take care of dadaji and made him recover. They fell in love with each other. I wish someone had made a film about it. Gandhiji officiated their wedding in the village. Thank you, Robert, for your kindness. Hai Ram, your hands are so warm and soft and look at mine they are so rough because here I am toiling away my days working in the kitchen of an Indian restaurant where I am just a dumb immigrant who can be treated like a cow. Every once in a while someone will touch me down here or up here, but I pretend nothing happened. All for Anjali's sake. What hurts even more is how Anjali too think like the people I work with. She think I am some country bumpkin, some old fashion mother trapped in her old fashion view of the world. So she had decided to discard her mother because Anjali is a modern girl and her mother is a relic from the past. Does she even know who Nehru is? Today's children only. Yes, I am crying again, and, yes, you may hold my hand, Robert. I am thanking you for asking. Thank you. I miss Sunil and Anjali so much, no shoulder to cry on.

Ah, deep breath always helps. I do it often. So my pitaji decided to move to the city after his Amma became ill seriously and there was no medical help nearby. That is when he told everyone he had enough. Our family, he said, sacrificed enough for India. British had left and the poor were still suffering. He thought it was going to be more effective to fight corruption in the cities where the rich people eats, walks and sleeps without caring for the poor. But he remained Arya Samaj both in his heart and actions. My dadaji has passed away. Job took pitaji to Calcutta. He took his mother along, and there he became involved with the Naxalite movement, writing pamphlets and going to small villages and talking to peasants. When Amma pleaded with him to stop this revolutionary nonsense, he realized the danger he was exposing his old mother to. But then he got involved with the Hindu Bengali refugees from East Pakistan. That is when he met my mother. So I am little Kashmiri, little Punjabi, and little Bengali, although I was born in New Delhi. My Amma's family used to own many many acres of land growing rice and other things. One of the great-grandfathers had once saved the life of a white man during an uprising. After the uprising was broken, the white officer whose life my ancestor had saved, gave him all that land of the area. My pitaji used to tease Amma that her ancestor had become a Thakur only then. But with time they lost most of the land and by the time my Amma was born, they were only Thakur in name, having lost most of the land to creditors and squatters. Then came the partition of India and my Amma's family decided to not leave East Pakistan and paid a huge price because when the trouble started in nineteen seventy and seventy-one, they had no choice but to leave. They felt their lives were not safe in the land of their ancestors anymore. They came to India penniless. If they had left during partition, they will have claimed some property left by Muslims who migrated to East Pakistan. Why is life so messy, tell me, Robert? Thanks for listening to my nonstop chatter. No, I don't mind. You are a good person. More chai? Biscuits?

So pitaji met Amma at a refugee center and he told grandmother that he wanted to marry a refugee. While dadiji had hoped to find a better match for pitaji, she had an instant liking when she saw Amma. There is a funny story. Dadi had heard that many Bengali girls of Hindu background take music lessons, and when Amma came to visit, my dadiji asked her if she can sing. She said she can and then she sang a Bengali song from a Pakistani film, a very melodious tune sung by a very famous singer Mehdi Hassan. So as you know my pitaji died young, but he will ask Amma on many occasions to sing that very song and it cheered everyone in our house. One can see such love in their eyes when she sang *dhako jotona noyono du haate*. But she continued to sing that song after his death making her three children sad. I often bursted into tears. Very much like right now. Robert, I am so sorry I don't know when and how my head came so close to your chest, no, no I don't mind, Robert. I am a human too. What am I to do? Where am I to go for one penny's worth of compassion when my own husband and daughter have left me? Oh Bhagwan, your heart is beating like a hammer, so is mine!

So Amma continued to sing *dhako jotona noyono du haate* and my elder brother would get irritated, pleading Amma to stop but she did not stop, saying, son, his memory should not make us sad, only happy. He was a wonderful person wasn't he? Barre bhayya also did not like the fact that we were singing a song by a Pakistani singer whose people had wreaked so much misery on Amma and her family. My younger brother argued with barre bhayya that it is not Mehdi Hassan's fault. Chotte bhayya pointed out that people all over India were falling in love with Mehdi Hassan. Almost every household that had a tape recorder had at least one tape of his Urdu songs. Oh I should also tell you that it was this cassette player business that brought Sunil and me close to each other. Sunil's father owned a tailor shop in our neighborhood, and one day as my Amma and I went to the shop to leave our pieces of cloth for stitching I saw Sunil sitting in the back in one dark corner with a recorder like a body split open for operation under a small lamp. As we spoke with his father and Amma scolded me about why I wanted my shirt to be like one worn by Parveen Babi in *Majboor* I suddenly asked Sunil if he can also fixed up our tape recorder. As he is suddenly looking up at me, my heart is beating like a scooter sputtering so fast just like it is now because Amma is stunned at my un-girl audacious behavior. Though I used to be known for a vicious temper when I was small, I was very shy outside the house. Sunil mumbled he can look at it and I thanked him for saying those words and that was the end of it. At school when I told my close friends that I managed to speak to a young man, a total stranger, who looked like Amitabh and that too in mother's presence, my kite went up in my circle of friends. The news spreaded like water spilling on floor. One of the girls went home and bragged about me in front of her mother, who confronted my mother one day in the vegetable market and told her about it as if forewarning, and so when two weeks later someone knocked on our door, my heart stopped to find Sunil there fulfilling his promise to take a look at the tape recorder. Amma did not like it but she cannot stop Sunil from entering our living room.

He later told me he can have fixed up the recorder in one hour; instead he stretched it to a whole month. Fixing it a little, then leaving with a promise to come back with a part he will have to purchase from a market where they sold used parts. Amma and my brothers understood something was going on between us, so Amma asked Sunil's father one day if the boy had already been engaged to someone. And then one thing led to another, but what tied our match that my father-in-law is an Arya Samajvadi. So there were no caste issue and class issue to speak of. We were married within a year. Before we got married, Sunil used to come over and play chess with my brothers or just hang around and listen to music on our tape recorder. He used to bring a new cassette with him to share with us. Amma was worried that Sunil was not very seriously looking for a job. But he had told me that there is nothing for him in India. I tried to reason with him, but he was stubborn as a dog's tail about going overseas. His friends had put all sorts of ideas in his head about golden opportunities awaiting him in countries like Spain and England. Then he met someone who could get him the English visa for a big sum of money. His parents were poor and had no money to support his fantasies, but my brothers and my Amma's brothers came up with some money and my Amma sold what little jewelry she had given me as part of my dowry and off Sunil went. He got a tourist visa because Indian cricket team was going to

England for matches and Sunil had played some first-class cricket, just a level before becoming totally professional where you can make lots of money. Disillusioned with India, many men his age wanted to go and try their luck in the Middle East, Japan, Singapore, Europe and Amreeka, I mean America. I cannot argue with him those days. It was like a demon had coming to inside his head. He saw only one solution to his financial problems. When I tried to reason with him, he said he was doing it for everyone's happiness. Robert, do you think I am happy now?

So when he got to England, instead of watching matches he worked twelve or more hours every day thanks to the connections his cousin had. He wrote letters almost every other day and such lovely, romantic letters. I cried for hours. I worried about his health. What good is money if you get sick in a foreign land and there is no one to look after you? Now as I have already told you I am not religious, but then for his sake I began going to a nearby temple and praying. He had a friend in California who managed to put Sunil in touch with someone who can help him cross into America from the Mexican side if he paid a certain amount. That person got him the Mexican visa as well. I prayed for his safety. If he died in Mexico, I will not know if he were alive or dying. Then things moved so fast that I began to believe that my instinct was wrong. That what I valued in India, my friends, relatives, the support system, all that I did not want to give up was due to my selfishness. Within weeks he had crossed safely into Arizona and from there to California. He worked all kinds of jobs, from farm worker to cab driver to delivery person to security guard and he missed me, his family but above all his daughter whom he had not seen. And one day he showed up at his parents' house with a green card in his pocket. Those few days he spent with us were good as everybody we knew came to congratulate him as he had made it in harsher climate despite all odds. He went back and had both me and Anjali fly to San Francisco in six months. Everything seemed like a miracle. In my eyes, Sunil cannot do anything wrong I thought.

Robert, my heart broke when I climbed up the plane thinking when will I see my family, friends and neighbors again. But once the plane took off excitement to be with Sunil and meet new people creeped up in me. Sunil was happy, very happy, like a little boy who is excited to get new toys. He showed us around. I cannot believe he had a car, a mustard-color Volkswagen but with rabbit printed on it. He showed us all the places he thought his wife should see. Some of his friends, mostly from Pakistan and India, invited us over, but mostly they came to our house to hang around after work. Anjali was well taken care of by so many uncles. I don't trust men so I will not leave Anjali for too long with any of them. I trust you, Robert, of course, otherwise I will not be sitting with you like this. But they all helped out playing with her, talking with her in Hindi and even Punjabi while I cooked. At the age of five Anjali chattered away so well in Hindi. She was really my only best friend now. But he became irritable and sullen when I told Sunil that I don't like that your friends show up like our house is some kind of a hotel where they can get free meal and chai and sit and drink and play card with no regards to our privacy and look what kind of effect this will have on your daughter. Within a year I had started to feel suffocated in a free country. I had no friends. I was more educated than Sunil but I did not want to make an issue of this. I had thought I could find work, perhaps go to school in the evening, but nothing can happen without Sunil's help. He was just too busy and tired with working long shifts as a security guard at an electronics store and various downtown buildings. He had no motivation left to go back to school either. Sometimes he worked night shifts as well. I asked him a few times if that is what he is wanting to do for the rest of his life and he always always coming up with some scheme in his head which never making any sense to me. So I told myself, Anjali's mother, have patience, have trust in your husband because you know he will come through as he already has or else how come you are in America enjoying good and modern life. All because of Sunil. He is your devta, your god!

Life got better when Anjali started kindergarten and Sunil began driving a cab. Suddenly we had more money, but again he was working long hours and keeping the same company and I am the cook for his friends who were coming over without calling first. I stopped complaining as long as they did not make too much noise and Anjali can sleep on time. I told myself, Anjali's mother, be thankful. You have no friends. It's a blessing that these men come over and give your apartment some noise and music. I wish some of them had their wives with them so I can have friends from my own culture. I found it so hard to make friends with other women here. Hi and hello, that's all. No one walked up to me to ask, Hi, how are you? Will you like to be my friend? No, too private, too polite. That's how I have lived here for so many years. I can have been happy if I felt Sunil was there for me, but it was I was there only for just few things. You know him, he was always shy, but he used to hold me, talk to me, we used to go out, meet our relatives, and go to parks before he left India. I cannot tell my family or his family how lonely I was and how Sunil was treating me like a servant. I keep telling myself he'll get better, things will change once Anjali is a bit older. But he became a withdraw and quiet. His friends also changed. Those who came over to eat at our place were now mostly cab drivers and you will not believe, Robert, what dirty jokes and gossips they shared with each other with no sense of shame for being loud enough to be heard by me. I told him, Sunil, change your job, do something else. But what to do the money was good and our family needed our help. Then his leg started hurting from driving for long hours. He was bedridden for over a month. Is there anything I did not do to make him get better? And you know how he paid me back for my dedication! He blamed me for his shooting pain in his leg. I am so embarrassed to even tell you what he said. But I cannot keep things inside anymore. Yes, the tears. Let them come. It's all right. Let me cry a bit. Can you believe he said that his leg got hurt because I will not let him have any rest at night, that I am always asking him for some man and woman time. All this talk about me bugging him at night after I heard him and this other no-good-for-anything friend talk about how they had sex with someone who was riding their cab. It does not matter whether they are only lying to each other. It is the way they think and enjoy fantasy. Hai Ram, how good men turn into sour milk is beyond me! Is a wife have no right to his husband's time? Is she only there to cook and iron clothes and clean and open her legs when his highness is hard and in the right mood because he is the one who brings food to our table? I am sorry about my unclean language, but I have holded all of this in my heart for too many years. I have suffered so much for so many years that when Sunil finally left us for another woman it did not really matter, though it hurt. He was around and he helped out with Anjali's school and other things. Anjali was big and was growing into a responsible girl. It was hard when one of us got sick, but we managed. I thought we will always have each other. Now I cannot believe she is disappearing. I am breaking like a plate made of china and she is not there to hold me together. Yes, yes, I realize you are here, and thank you again for this comfort. But I need Anjali and only you can bring her back. She must listen to you. You are American friend of our family. She will pay attention to you. You tell her you work for police also. Yes, yes, I am joking for a change.

Please tell her, Anjali, your mother is alone. She is missing. She is needing. She is needing your company and your love and your touch. Please tell her, you are all she has in this country. Tell her, I have no other relative or friends here. Please remind her that she is from a decent family and tell her that she is an educating girl who should know better than to hang out with the wastrels and ruffians. She must not waste the effort of her parents and her relatives who made her father's overseas journey possible. How quickly the children forget. They retain no memory of the hardship their parents has endured. Does she remember how many nights I stayed awake when she fell ill year after year? Does she understand how I agonized over when children at her middle school called her names, racist names? Robert ji, she does not have to remember when I threatened to take my own life if the bullying at the school did not stop. Sunil cannot care a bit. I cared. Come flu, come cold, I sat up all night right by her pillow making sure my baby is getting better. And look now that my baby is all grown up and strong and smart, she has left her mother to her own devices. Yes, mother is a superman, she can take care of herself, get sick and go to the doctor on her own. What if I take a fall? What if I burn myself cooking? What if I have a cramp in my back and cannot get out of bed? But no, we are all for ourselves. Please ask her if she has any clue to what happens when people find out that you are alone with no one to come to your help? Robert, please do not take it personally, but world is full hyenas always sniffing someone's weakness, someone being left alone. Ask her if she knows why I left my previous job for the Indian restaurant? She was young but not too young to not have thought about it. Sunil had been gone for a year, left us for that woman though he did not tell us that, but you know rumor fly. His own friends told me, in the guise of showing sympathy, they wanted to end up in my bedroom. His close friends! Can you believe, Robert? The ones I had been letting spend time under my roof and cooking chai and food for them as uninvited guests. The ones who addressed me as didi and aunty and bhabhi, all hoping to score, how shameless!

Perhaps I should have thought differently. I can have taught Sunil a lesson by taking up with one of his friends. Who does not need company, companionship, when your own husband abandons you. Maybe I am just old-fashion and only I am to blame for not changing my fate, just sitting with my hands in my lap. Now even my own daughter has left me. If I have taken in one of his friends, mean people will not have seen me as alone and weak. Mean people like my manager who forced himself on me, forced his three hundred pounds on me and I cannot escape from under his weight till he has had his lust taken care of. It does not matter that I am crying, begging, begging for mercy, his eyes are closed. He has acting to be dead, can you believe that? All I can do then was to pray to Bhagwan that the bastard haramzadah will not kill me after he is done with. No, Robert, you don't need to cry. I am strong. I survived. Here, take the handkerchief you gave me. I survived because all the time I am thinking I have to live for Anjali. I have to be strong so she can go on to have a better future. I was grateful to God the manager let me go. I quit the job, but I cannot tell anyone. The manager apologized the next day but I cannot look him in the eye because I know he is lying. Who can I have told then? Sunil was not here. I cannot tell Anjali as she was too young to understand what happened to her poor mother. Working with my own people, people from India and Pakistan is not any different. Whenever one can say a lusty joke or touch my behind or arms, they do it as if they are coming out of their mother's vagina. I am sorry. Others, younger women who work there, are not safe either. I can feel their eyes upon me like hyenas even when they are talking to me like we are one big family in the kitchen and dish washing room, but I know their eyes are watching me to detect my loneliness and weakness. Who knows when one of them will pounce on me. I am so afraid when I am working alone in the kitchen before the restaurant opens. What to do, Robert? Only why do women have to feel abandoned and weak and lonely? Why another woman, my own daughter not understand this? Can you explain all of this to her? Will she listen to you when she does not listen to me?

No need to weep. Tell her I understand she needs friends. Who does not need friends? I need friends too. I will never stop her from having friends. Friends are important, friends are good. Even bad friends are good sometimes. My feeling of losing friends when I moved here because of Sunil was greater than losing my relatives. But one does not abandon parents because of friends. I choose to stay in Amreeka not because of Anjali but because my relatives advise me to, so Anjali has a better shot at getting educating, but also because the money I send makes my relatives' lives more manageable. One does not abandon family, especially parents. What if I die in my sleep tonight! How will it take Anjali to find out? Robert, I still cannot forget about that young girl who had epilepsy who died while taking a shower. She was getting ready to go to have dinner with her friend. Her friend was a good friend. Even then she waited a whole day to get worried. She called police and they found her dead in her bathtub. Robert, what kind of living is this in your country with so much comfort, so much money and jobs but no one to be around for a sick person to take shower? What if Anjali is sick? Will her roommates do something? Or call me? She says Amma, I am an adult. But just because you become an adult does mean your mother's heart has turned into a rotten mango? I cannot sleep when the thought of something happening to her the way it happened to me enters my head. She so badly wanted to visit her grandparents and I began saving money for our tickets. And then suddenly my princess does not want to go. She spouts so much rubbish about India it is hard to believe she is the same Anjali. Can you believe she says Amma, India is just a very long open-air toilet. What filth her friends put inside her head. I don't know, Robert, what to do! I am sorry I have spoken like a train derailing. I have taken up so much of your time and even made you cry. I am so sorry. You are very kind. Please give my love to your daughter and my regards to your wife. I should have your family over for dinner some day. Please call Anjali and tell her to at least call me every day. If not every day, then every few days. I will be forever grateful to you. Here is your coat. You are so very kind. Bhagwan is my witness I am telling you the truth. No easy life for me, I have to go to work now. ■

A BOY TAUGHT ME HOW TO KISS A GIRL

Ifti Nasim

Playing cricket was praying
Five times at once.
Every evening after
We all gathered in the school ground
Like a different set of animals
Around the watering hole
In Serengeti.
Some playing hockey
Some football
Some doing nothing, reading, watching
Some predators.
We both were sweating rather drenching.
We jumped in the swimming pool.
My fear of water and drowning came over me.
He knew.
He held my arm and waist and made me swim.
Coming back home at dusk
He looked around.
Under a mango tree
He held my face in his palms
And put his lips on mine.
Fragrance of freshly dropped rain on hot earth
Surged in my palate
I was tasting cloud.
"That's how you kiss a girl."
He whispered in my ear.

NOTES ON CONTRIBUTORS

VIDHU AGGARWAL was born in Ranchi, India, and grew up in the southern U.S. A Kundiman Fellow, she is the founding editor of *SPECS*. Her work has recently appeared in *Boston Review*, *VIDA*, *As[I]Am*, and the *Missing Slate*. Her book of poems *The Trouble with Humpadori* (2016) received the Editor's Choice Prize from the (Great) Indian Poetry Collective. She teaches transnational studies and poetry at Rollins College.

KAZIM ALI'S many books of poetry, fiction and essays include the poetry collection *Sky Ward* and the essay collection *Resident Alien*. His book of short stories *Uncle Sharif's Life in Music* was released in 2016.

MEHER ALI recently completed her bachelors in history, with a focus on modern South Asia, from Brown University. During her undergraduate career, she was involved with the Brown-India Initiative, the Ivy Film Festival, and the Brown Journal of History. She spent the last year in Kolkata, India, conducting an oral history project as a Fulbright research scholar. Her other interests include creative writing, film, and classical Indian dance, and she plans to pursue a PhD in South Asian history.

NEELANJANA BANERJEE'S writing has appeared in *Prairie Schooner*, *PANK*, *World Literature Today* and many other places. She is the managing editor of Kaya Press and teaches with writing workshops Los Angeles.

NADIA CHANEY is a poet, performer, visual artist and extreme manicurist. She is a first-generation Indo-Canadian born in Saskatoon, grown up in Ottawa, matured in Vancouver and currently living in Montreal, all of which she recognizes as the traditional territory of Indigenous people who are its rightful stewards. For more, visit: www.nadiachaney.com.

SAYANTANI DASGUPTA, born in Calcutta and raised in New Delhi, is the author of *Fire Girl: Essays on India, America, and the In-Between* and the chapbook *The House of Nails: Memories of a New Delhi Childhood*. Her essays and stories have appeared in the *Rumpus, Phoebe,* and *Gulf Stream,* among other magazines and literary journals. She teaches at the University of Idaho and edits nonfiction for *Crab Creek Review*. To learn more, visit www.sdasgupta.com.

TARA DORABJI is a writer, strategist at Youth Speaks, mother, and radio journalist at KPFA. Her work is published or forthcoming in *Al Jazeera, TAYO Literary Magazine, Huizache, Good Girls Marry Doctors* (Aunt Lute 2016), *So Glad They Told Me* (HerStories Project Press 2016), *Nothing but the Truth So Help Me God: All the Women in My Family Sing* (2017 edited by Deborah Santana), Center for Asian American Media, *MUTHA Magazine,* and *Midwifery Today*. She is working on novels, set in Kashmir and Livermore. Her projects can be viewed at www.dorabji.com.

ALI ETERAZ is the author of the novel *Native Believer* (Akashic), a *New York Times Book Review* Editors' Choice selection. Previously he wrote the coming-of-age memoir *Children of Dust* (HarperCollins), featured on NPR and PBS. He received the 3 Quarks Daily Prize in Arts & Literature judged by Mohsin Hamid and served as a consultant to the artist Jenny Holzer on a permanent art installation in Qatar. He has lived in the Dominican Republic, Pakistan, the Persian Gulf, and Alabama.

SAADIA FARUQI is a Pakistani American writer of fiction and nonfiction and the author of the short story collection *Brick Walls: Tales of Hope & Courage from Pakistan*. She is editor-in-chief of *Blue Minaret,* a magazine for Muslim art, poetry and prose. Her short stories have been published in several literary journals and magazines such as *Catch & Release, On the Rusk, In-flight* and the *Great American Literary Magazine*.

MALA GAONKAR was born in St. Louis and grew up in Bangalore. She currently lives in London and is collaborating with the musician David Byrne on a theatrical neuroscience project called Theater of the Mind. A workshop version of this, Neurosociety, is on at Pace Gallery's Menlo Park outpost. Gaonkar is on the board of the Tate Museum and recently set up a public health social enterprise called Surgo.

MADHUSHREE GHOSH works in cancer diagnostics in San Diego and is a New Delhi transplant. Her work has been published or a finalist in *Zoetrope, Glimmer Train, Origins, Hippocampus Magazine, Serious Eats @ Medium, Sirenuse Journal, Del Sol Review, OneGlobe Citizen,* the *Scofield* and others. A *Garnet News* contributor, a *Panorama: The Journal of Intelligent Travel* contributing writer and an Oakley Hall scholar, her award-winning plays have been performed at Actors Alliance of San Diego festivals. She is currently working on a collection of essays, *Chittaranjan Park Tales,* based on her childhood in 1970s and 1980s India and her current focus on oncology, and her memoir, *214 Days of Silence.*

RO GUNETILLEKE was born in Sri Lanka and lives writes and creates photographs in downtown Los Angeles, California. His poems and short stories have appeared in *Catamaran Literary Reader, Muse India, Malpais Review, Indivisible: An anthology of South Asian American Poetry,* and *Poetic Diversity.* His photo projects have been exhibited at the Los Angeles Center of Photography, Arena 1 Gallery, and the Perfect Exposure Gallery.

S. AFZAL HAIDER continues to resist all attempts at self-definition. His short stories and essays have been published in a variety of literary magazines. Oxford University Press, Milkweed Editions, Penguin Books, Pearson, and Longman Literature have anthologized his writings. He is author of the novel *To Be With Her* (Weavers Press). When not working on his own writing, he keeps busy as one of the senior editors of *Chicago Quarterly Review.*

SYED ISHAQ HAIDER was an art teacher and an artist of reknown. He painted portraits of the rich and famous as well as of ordinary people. He also authored a Drawing Book Series for middle school children. He died in 1986 in Karachi, Pakistan.

MINAL HAJRATWALA is the author of the award-winning epic *Leaving India: My Family's Journey from Five Villages to Five Continents* (2009), which was called "incomparable" by Alice Walker and "searingly honest" by the *Washington Post,* and editor of *Out! Stories from the New Queer India* (2013). Her latest book is *Bountiful Instructions for Enlightenment,* published by the (Great) Indian Poetry Collective, a collective of which she is a cofounder. She graduated from Stanford University, was a fellow at Columbia University, and was a 2011 Fulbright-Nehru Senior Scholar. As a writing coach, she loves helping people give voice to untold stories through the Write Like a Unicorn portal. Her

Granta essay "A Brief Guide to Gender in India" was named one of the ten best pieces of writing on the web for 2015 by the Golden Giraffes.

SONIAH KAMAL is a Pushcart Prize–nominated essayist, fiction writer and literary journalist. Her debut novel, *An Isolated Incident*, was a finalist for the Townsend Prize for Fiction, was short-listed for the Karachi Literature Festival–Embassy of France Prize, and is an Amazon Rising Star pick. Her work is in the *New York Times*, the *Guardian*, *Catapult*, *BuzzFeed*, *Atlanta Journal-Constitution*, the *Huffington Post*, *Literary Hub*, the *Rumpus*, the *Normal School*, *ArtsATL* and more. Her essays and short stories are included in *The Best Asian Short Stories* and award-winning anthologies. She is a Paul Bowles Fiction Fellow at Georgia State University where she serves as assistant fiction editor for *Five Points: A Journal of Literature and Art*. She was born in Pakistan, grew up in England and Saudi Arabia and lives in the U.S. with her partner, their three children and their dog. www.soniahkamal.com.

KIRUN KAPUR is the winner of the Arts & Letters Rumi Prize in Poetry and the Antivenom Poetry Award for her first book, *Visiting Indira Gandhi's Palmist*. She is director of the New England arts program the Tannery Series and serves as poetry editor at the *Drum Literary Magazine*.

MAYA KHOSLA has written *Web of Water* (nonfiction), *Keel Bone* (poems), and essays including "Tapping the Fire, Turning the Steam: Securing the Future with Geothermal Energy" and "Notes from the Field." Awards from Save Our Seas Foundation have supported her writing about climate change and other impacts on sea turtles. She has won awards from Bear Star Press, Flyway, and Poets & Writers. Her screenwriting efforts include narratives for *Shifting Undercurrents* and *Village of Dust, City of Water*, award-winning documentary films. She is currently working on a film about post-fire habitats in the Sierra Nevada and Cascades entitled *Searching for Gold Spot: The Wild after Wildfire*, with support from the Audubon Society, Patagonia, Fund for Wild Nature, and Environment Now. "Fire Works," a short excerpt and trailer of the film project, can be found at www.conbio.org/publications/scb-news-blog/fire-works.

SWATI KHURANA was born in New Delhi, raised in the Hudson Valley, and now lives in the Bronx. She has been published in the *New York Times*, *Guernica*, the *Offing*, the *Rumpus*, and elsewhere. Her art has been shown at the Brooklyn Museum, Bronx Museum of the Arts, and Queens Museum (New York City); DUMBO Arts Festival (New York City); Chatterjee & Lal (Mumbai); Museo de Arte y Deseño Contemporáneo (Costa Rica); ScalaMata Gallery (53rd Venice Biennial); and Zachęta National Gallery of Art (Warsaw). Her collaborative project *Unsuitable Girls* with Anjali Bhargava was in the Smithsonian's *Beyond Bollywood* exhibition. She has received awards from the Jerome Foundation, Bronx Council on the Arts, Cooper Union, and Center for Book Arts. A graduate of Hunter College's MFA fiction program and Kundiman Fellow, she was a founding member of SAWCC (South Asian Women's Creative Collective). In 2017, she will be working on her novel *The No.1 Printshop of Lahore* through the Center for Fiction's Emerging Writers and Vermont Studio Center's Grace Paley Fiction Fellowships.

WAQAS KHWAJA is a professor of English at Agnes Scott College, has a PhD in English from Emory University and teaches courses in postcolonial literature, British Romanticism, nineteenth-century poetry and prose, and creative writing. He has published three collections of poetry, *No One Waits for the Train, Miriam's Lament and other poems*, and *Six Geese from a Tomb at Medum*, as well as a literary travelogue, *Writers and Landscapes*, and edited a number of anthologies of Pakistani literature. He was translation editor and contributing translator for *Modern Poetry of Pakistan* (Dalkey 2011) and has guest edited special issues on Pakistani literature and poetry for the *Journal of Commonwealth and Postcolonial Studies* and *Atlanta Review*. His articles, poems, and translations have appeared in U.S., Pakistani, European, and Far Eastern publications, literary journals, and anthologies.

ANU KUMAR is a recent graduate of the MFA in Writing Program from the Vermont College of Fine Arts. She lives in Maryland with her family. She has written for older and younger readers alike. Her most recent works are *Across the Seven Seas: Travelers Tales from India* (middle grade, Hachette India) and *The Girl Who Ran Away in a Washing Machine and Other Stories* (Kitaab).

ADITI MACHADO is from Bangalore, India. She is the author of the chapbook *Route: Marienbad* (Further Other Book Works 2016) and the poetry collection *Some Beheadings* (Nightboat Books, forthcoming in 2017). Her translation of Farid Tali's *Prosopopoeia* will appear from Action Books in 2016. Her poetry, translations, and criticism have appeared in *VOLT*, *FOLDER*, the *Capilano Review*, the *Chicago Review*, *World Literature Today*, and elsewhere.

AMIT MAJMUDAR is a widely published poet, novelist, and essayist. He is the first poet laureate of Ohio and a diagnostic nuclear radiologist. His latest poetry collection is *Dothead* (Knopf 2016).

SHIKHA MALAVIYA is a South Asian poet and writer. She is cofounder of the (Great) Indian Poetry Collective, a mentorship model press dedicated to new voices from India and the Indian diaspora. She has been a featured TEDx speaker and AWP mentor and has been nominated for the Pushcart Prize. She will serve as the poet laureate of San Ramon, California, from 2016 to 2018. Her book of poems is *Geography of Tongues*.

ZAFAR MALIK is an artist, Director of Publications and Dean for Development and University Relations at East-West University in Chicago. He is also Managing Editor of East-West University's Center for Policy and Future Studies journal *East-West Affairs*. Prior to moving to Chicago in 2000, he was based in London, England and was the Art Director of *Arts & The Islamic World*, a quarterly journal. He has a studio at the Noyes Cultural Arts Center in Evanston where he paints regularly. Artist Statement: Since childhood, I've been fascinated by patterns and shapes. There's something mystical about the natural relationship and juxtaposition of quite diverse and seemingly random elements that appeals to me. The infinite variety of color, texture, contour, and spatial organization of the natural world inform my aesthetics. I am also acutely aware of the same random pattern of my own existence—attachment, separation, longing, loss, adjustment and compromise. In my work I simply attempt to understand and relate to this profound dichotomy, harmony and balance.

VIKAS MENON is a poet, playwright and songwriter. He was a 2015 Emerging Poets Fellow at Poets House and his poems have been featured in numerous publications, including *Indivisible: An Anthology of Contemporary South Asian American Poetry* and *The HarperCollins Book of English Poetry*. He was a cowriter and cocreator of the augmented reality comic book, *Priya's Shakti* (www.priyashakti.com), an innovative social impact multimedia project that helps illuminate attitudes towards gender-based violence. The project was nominated as a Gender Equality Champion by UN Women and the series is currently supported by the World Bank. He is a cowriter of the shadow play *Feathers of Fire*, which premiered at BAM (Brooklyn Academy of Music) in February 2016 and is currently touring the country. His other plays have received readings at or have been produced by Pratidhwani, Ruffled Feathers Theater, Ingenue Theatre and the Classical Theatre of Harlem. He was a Keynote Speaker at CantoMundo 2011 and is an Advisory Board member of Kundiman, which is dedicated to the creation and cultivation of Asian American literature. He received his MFA (poetry) from Brooklyn College and his MA in literature from St. Louis University.

FAISAL MOHYUDDIN teaches English at Highland Park High School in suburban Chicago, is a recent fellow in the U.S. Department of State's Teachers for Global Classrooms program, and received an MFA in fiction writing from Columbia College Chicago in 2015. His writing has appeared in *Prairie Schooner*, *Narrative*, *Poet Lore*, *Atlanta Review*, *RHINO*, *Crab Orchard Review*, *the minnesota review*, *Indivisible: An Anthology of Contemporary South Asian American Poetry*, and elsewhere. Also a visual artist, he lives in Chicago with his wife and son.

DIPIKA MUKHERJEE'S two poetry collections include *The Third Glass of Wine* (Writers Workshop 2015) and *The Palimpsest of Exile* (Rubicon Press 2009). She is contributing editor for *Jaggery* and curates an Asian American reading series in Chicago. Her debut novel was long-listed for the Man Asian Literary Prize as an unpublished manuscript, then published as *Thunder Demons* (Gyaana Books 2011) and *Ode to Broken Things* (Repeater Books 2016, distributed by Penguin/Random House). The unpublished manuscript of her second novel won the Virginia Prize for Fiction and was published as *Shambala Junction* by Aurora Metro Books (2016). She won the Gayatri GaMarsh Award for Literary Excellence (2015) and the Platform Flash Fiction Prize (2009). Her short story collection is *Rules of Desire* (Fixi Novo 2015) and her edited anthologies on Southeast Asian fiction include *Champion Fellas* (Word Works 2016), *Silverfish New Writing 6* (Silverfish Books 2006) and *The Merlion and Hibiscus* (Penguin 2002).

SOMNATH MUKHERJI is a social activist working with marginalized communities of India. He works with *adivasi* (indigenous) communities in eastern and central India, gender variant groups and many others working for economic, environmental and gender justice. He was trained as electrical engineer but started working full-time on social issues since 2007. He writes fiction and nonfiction, both of which are informed by the perspectives of the poor and marginalized. He lives in Boston with his wife and daughter and spends a few months every year in India with the communities.

NAYOMI MUNAWEERA'S debut novel, *Island of a Thousand Mirrors*, was long-listed for the Man Asia Literary Prize and the International Dublin Literary Award. It was short-listed for the DSC Prize for South Asian Literature and the Northern California Book Award in Fiction. It won the Commonwealth Regional Prize for Asia. The *Huffington Post* raved, "Munaweera's prose is visceral and indelible, devastatingly beautiful—reminiscent of the glorious writings of Louise Erdrich, Amy Tan, and Alice Walker, who also find ways to truth-tell through fiction." The *New York Times Book Review* called the novel "incandescent." The book was the Target Book Club selection for January 2016. Her second novel, *What Lies Between Us*, was hailed as one of the most exciting literary releases of 2016 from venues ranging from *BuzzFeed* to *Elle* magazine. Her nonfiction and short fiction are also widely published. www.nayomimunaweera.com.

SHABNAM NADIYA is a writer and translator from Bangladesh. She completed her MFA from the Iowa Writers' Workshop in 2012. Currently she is working on her collection of stories titled *Pye Dogs and Magic Men: Stories* and a translation of Shaheen Akhtar's novel *Beloved Rongomala*. Her work has appeared in *Flash Fiction International* (W. W. Norton), *Law and Disorder: Stories of Conflict and Crime* (Main Street Rag), *One World* (New Internationalist) and journals such as *Five Chapters*, Amazon's *Day One*, *Wasafiri*, *Words without Borders*, *Copper Nickel*, *Gulf Coast* and *Arsenic Lobster*. Her work can be found at www.shabnamnadiya.com.

SHIVANI NARANG is a second-generation South Asian American womxn attending the University of California, Berkeley. She is the 2016 Bay Area Youth Speaks Grand Slam Champion, is a part of UC Berkeley's slam organization CalSLAM, and is director of the South Asian, Southwest Asian, and North African (SSWANA) coalition at UC Berkeley. She writes for purposes of collective healing to individual, community, and generational trauma. Her writing is grounded in resistance to forces of silence that have affected her own life, the womxn in her family, and her community. She writes for self-preservation, to allow herself space to breathe and process, to voice particular pieces of her experiences so we can celebrate the intricacies of this *zindagi*. She loves reading, sharing books, writing, running, sharing art, drinking chai, listening to music, going to Vik's Chaat, and spending time with family and friends. She is constantly low-key figuring and refiguring her life out.

IFTI NASIM was a Pakistani-American poet and civil rights activist living in Chicago before his death in 2011. Mr. Nasim wrote in English, Urdu and Punjabi. One of his books was banned in Pakistan, where he received death threats from religious groups for his outspoken support of gay rights, both in his writing and in his political work. He earned numerous prizes and accolades, including an honorary doctorate in literature from the World Peace Academy in Delaware and induction into the Chicago Gay and Lesbian Hall of Fame.

SOPHIA NAZ is an Asian American writer, artist, filmmaker and practitioner of Kayakalpa. She was born in Karachi in 1964 and has lived in the U.S. since 1988. She writes in both Urdu and English and her poetry has been translated into Bengali as well. Her writing has been anthologized worldwide, in both print and online journals including *Poetry International Rotterdam*, the *Adirondack Review*, *DailyO*, *BlazeVOX*, *Cactus Heart*, *Askew Poetry Journal*, *Bank-Heavy Press*, *Spilled Ink*, *Lantern Journal*, *Convergence*, *Antiphon*, the *Sunflower Collective*, *Antiserious*, the *Ghazal Page* and many other publications. *Peripheries*, her debut collection of poetry, came out in September 2015. Links to her published works can be found on her site: www.trancelucence.net. She blogs at www.rootsandwings.tumblr.com.

TONI NEALIE is the author of *The Miles Between Me*, an essay collection about borders, homeland, dispersal, heritage and family, published by Curbside Splendor. Her essays have appeared in *Guernica*, *Hobart*, the *Offing*, the *Rumpus*, *Entropy*, the *Prague Revue* and elsewhere. Her essay "The Displeasure of the Table" was nominated for a Pushcart Prize. Originally from New Zealand, where she worked in journalism, politics and public relations, she holds an MFA from Columbia College Chicago. She currently teaches and writes in Chicago, where she is literary editor of *Newcity* and coeditor of the *Sunday Rumpus*.

MAHMUD RAHMAN was born in Dhaka (in then East Pakistan) and came of age in the late sixties leading up to the creation of Bangladesh. During the 1971 Bangladesh Liberation War, he was a refugee in Calcutta. Since then he has lived in Boston, Detroit, Providence and Oakland. He has worked as a factory worker, data entry operator, community organizer and database support techie. He is the author of a collection *Killing the Water* and his translation of Mahmudul Haque's *Kalo Barof* was released in January 2012 by HarperCollins India. His novel *The Fiction Factory* is currently seeking publication.

REEMA RAJBANSHI is a creative and critical writer, residing in California and raised in the Bronx. She is interested in troubling "purity" of form and in collaging sounds/silences/herstories. Her short fiction has appeared in *Blackbird, Confrontation, So to Speak,* and *Southwest Review,* among others, and has been nominated for the Pushcart Prize and awarded the 2015 Maurice Prize. She is currently working on a travel memoir and conducting doctoral research in India and Brazil.

ROSHNI RUSTOMJI-KERNS has lived, studied and worked in India, Pakistan, Lebanon, Mexico and the U.S. She is the coeditor of *Blood Into Ink: South Asian and Middle Eastern Women Write War* and the editor of *Living In America: Poetry and Fiction by South Asian American Writers* and *Encounters: People of Asian Descent in the Americas.* Her short stories and essays have appeared in journals and anthologies in the U.S., Canada, Pakistan, India and Mexico. Her novel *The Braided Tongue* was published in 2003. Her novella *The Great American Movie Script* was published in 2015.

CHAITALI SEN is the author of *The Pathless Sky,* published by Europa Editions in 2015. Born in India and raised in New York and Pennsylvania, she currently lives in Austin, Texas with her husband and stepson. Her short stories, reviews, and essays have appeared in *New England Review, New Ohio Review, Colorado Review,* the *Aerogram,* the *Los Angeles Review of Books,* and other journals. She is a graduate of the Hunter College MFA program in fiction.

MOAZZAM SHEIKH writes and translates fiction, with two collections, *The Idol Lover and Other Stories of Pakistan* and *Cafe Le Whore and Other Stories,* to his credit. He is also the editor of *Letter From India: Contemporary Short Stories From Pakistan* (Penguin). His translations of Intizar Husain were published in India as *Intizar Husain Stories* (Katha). He currently works as a librarian at San Francisco Public Library and lecturer at City College of San Francisco, where he lives with his wife and two sons.

RAVIBALA SHENOY was born in India and lived in Germany and France before settling in Illinois. Her fiction and nonfiction have appeared in *Sugar Mule, India Currents,* the *Copperfield Review,* and *Cooper Street Journal,* among others. She is a retired librarian.

RANBIR SINGH SIDHU is the author of the novel *Deep Singh Blue* (Unnamed Press/HarperCollins India) and the story collection *Good Indian Girls* (Soft Skull/HarperCollins India). A novella, *Object*

Lessons (in 12 Sides w/Afterglow), was published late in 2016 by Run/ Off Editions. He is a winner of a Pushcart Prize and a New York Foundation for the Arts Fellowship, and his stories have appeared in *Conjunctions*, the *Georgia Review*, *Fence*, *Zyzzyva*, the *Missouri Review*, *Other Voices*, the *Happy Hypocrite*, the *Literary Review*, *Alaska Quarterly Review* and other journals and anthologies. He lives on the island of Crete.

PIREENI SUNDARALINGAM was born in Sri Lanka and is coeditor of *Indivisible: An Anthology of Contemporary South Asian American Poetry* (University of Arkansas Press 2010), winner of the 2011 Northern California Book Award and PEN Oakland/Josephine Miles Award. Her poetry has been published in over twenty literary journals including the *American Poetry Review* and *Ploughshares*, featured in anthologies such as Amnesty's *101 Poems for Human Rights*, and translated into five languages. Literary awards include a San Francisco Arts Commission Award and fellowships from PEN and the Berlin Academy of Arts. She is currently completing a poetry manuscript exploring her memories of the Sri Lankan Civil War.

SADIA UQAILI is the Founder of Explore Their Stories, Inc. a program dedicated to discovering, documenting, preserving and sharing the extraordinary in our everyday lives. She believes that art is the best language to build bridges and to find the finest in our communities. Sadia is committed to archiving and sharing our global culture and heritage, forge connections, foster empathy, educate, inspire, empower and ensure understanding and awareness now and for our future generations. She is an artist, educator and a curator, an arts administration executive who leads teams of filmmakers, creative writers, musicians, visual artists and actors to produce outstanding art programs. Sadia specializes in collections, curated multimedia large-scale art events including film screenings, poetry readings, theater and art. Her teams create engaging corporate and healthcare environments with museum quality art installations and creative arts workshops for high-performance teams. She is an accomplished curator of international exhibits, a visual artist, and a printmaker. Sadia was recently the Chief Program Officer at Snow City Arts, specializing in developing fine arts educational programs at four leading pediatric hospitals in Chicago. Sadia Uqaili has served on several juries for film screenings and festivals. The most recent is the 2015 Chicago South Asian Film Festival. Her work has been exhibited internationally, in Chicago, Karachi, Kuala Lumpur, Singapore, Phoenix, and Quebec.

SACHIN WAIKAR'S award-winning writing appears in national magazines and journals including *Esquire*, Amazon's *Day One*, *Drunken Boat*, *South Asian Review*, *Highlights*, *Parents*, *Kahani*, and several published anthologies. His screenwriting has placed in HBO/Miramax's Project Greenlight and been nominated for an ABC/Disney Talent Development Grant. As a freelance writer, he writes for businesses, universities, and individuals. Before turning to writing, he worked as a business strategy consultant for McKinsey & Company and a Beverly Hills psychologist. A member of Phi Beta Kappa, he earned a BA in psychology with honors and distinction from Stanford University and a PhD in clinical psychology from the University of California, Los Angeles. He lives in Evanston, Illinois with his family.

TANU MEHROTRA WAKEFIELD holds a BA in English from Wellesley College, an MA in English from Tulane University, and an MFA in Poetry from San Francisco State University. She works in communications at the Stanford Humanities Center. Her poems have been published in numerous journals and have also appeared in *Indivisible: An Anthology of Contemporary South Asian Poetry*. She is the inaugural poet laureate of Belmont, California. She lives there with her husband, daughters, and beloved pet rat.

LAURA WILLIAMS is an artist and designer living in North Carolina. You can see more of her work at laura-williams.com.

ANAPHORA LITERARY PRESS
Publisher of fiction, poetry and non-fiction
anaphoraliterary.com

PENNSYLVANIA LITERARY JOURNAL

ISSN#: 2151-3066; 6X9", $15/iss: is a printed journal that runs critical essays, book-reviews, short stories, interviews, photographs, art, and poetry. Also available from EBSCO and ProQuest. One PLJ article won the 2015 CCCC Lavender Rhetoric Award for Excellence in Queer Scholarship. PLJ published *New York Times* bestselling and major award-winning writers such as Larry Niven, Mary Jo Putney, Bob Van Laerhoven and Geraldine Brooks.

DISTRIBUTION:
• In full-text on EBSCO Academic Complete and ProQuest databases.
• On sale as single issues on Amazon, Barnes and Noble.
• YBP/ Coutts distribution
• Annual Subscription: $45: shipping included, 3 issues/ year. No extra fees with electronic or paper checks. 4% for PayPal and 3% for SquareUp.
• Free excerpts of reviews and interviews with best-sellers are publicly available on the Anaphora website.

CINEMATIC CODES REVIEW

ISSN 2473-3385 (print); ISSN 2473-3377 (online); 6X9", $15/iss: features work in all visual genres, especially those with moving pictures, be they music videos, feature films, documentaries, photography, or just about any other mode or genre of art that does not fall into the realm of "literature."

Unsolicited submissions to both journals (scholarship, reviews, interviews) and for Anaphora books are **always warmly welcomed** at director@anaphoraliterary. com, Anna Faktorovich, PhD.

PACIFICA
LITERARY
REVIEW

Call

for

Poetry

Prose

and

Art

Submissions

2017

PacificaReview.com

Writing that
moves you.

University of Nebraska | 110 Andrews Hall, PO BOX 880334
Lincoln NE 68588 | 402-472-0911 | **prairieschooner.unl.edu**

PRAIRIESCHOONER Now accepting
electronic submissions

SUNDAY SALON CHICAGO

IS A READING SERIES THAT TAKES PLACE
EVERY OTHER MONTH

STIMULATING, OUTSTANDING, AND OPEN TO ALL FOR OVER TEN
YEARS, THE SALON SERIES HAS BROUGHT NEW YORK CITY,
NAIROBI, MIAMI AND CHICAGO OVER TEN YEARS OF
WORD-POWER MAKING PRESENT OUR BEST LOCAL AND
NATIONAL WRITERS.

PLEASE JOIN US!

WE MEET AT
RIVERVIEW TAVERN, 1958 W. ROSCOE IN CHICAGO
FROM **7PM TO 8PM**

COME EARLY IF YOU'D LIKE TO EAT,
DRINK YOUR FAVORITE DRINKS,
MAKE NEW FRIENDS

ENJOY THE READINGS

OUR EXCELLENT EVENTS ARE ALWAYS FREE!

FIND OUR CALENDAR AT **http://www.sundaysalon.com** or
SUNDAY SALON CHICAGO FACEBOOK page.

MUNRO
CAMPAGNA

ARTIST REPRESENTATIVES

410 SOUTH MICHIGAN AVENUE
SUITE 439
CHICAGO, ILLINOIS 60605
+1 312 560 9638
SMUNRO@MUNROCAMPAGNA.COM
WWW.MUNROCAMPAGNA.COM

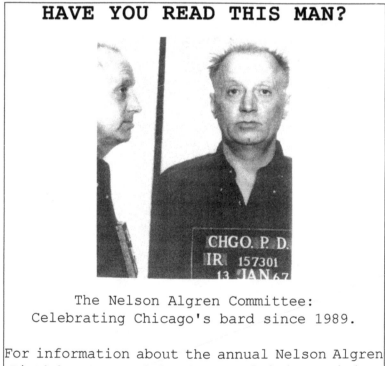

Bedeviled

a novella by Pat Matsueda

Resonant and true to place, Pat Matsueda's mesmerizing novella offers a glimpse into the unraveling of one man's life, along with a close look at a Hawaiʻi few outsiders know.

Phyllis Gray Young
Author of *Sea Home*

Bedeviled asks essential questions: How do we process hurt? How do we forgive wrongdoing? And how do we heal, with—or without—the support of our families? Through her carefully crafted characters, Matsueda makes these philosophical questions powerfully real.

Kristiana Kahakauwila
Author of *This is Paradise: Stories*

Matsueda explores addiction's roots in abuse and loneliness, and demonstrates how confronting pain—and making oneself vulnerable to love—can be a way to freedom.

Shawna Yang Ryan
Author of *Green Island*

Bedeviled is a beautiful metaphor, surprising, riveting, and honest. Within its pages, Internet porn and the floating world seem made for each other, and are grounded in the human heart. The prose is spare and searching; the overall effect is luminous.

Robert Shapard
Coeditor of *Flash Fiction International*

Told with charity, clarity, and insight, this story of an unassuming Everyman who has tried—and failed—to "lead his life by the book" is a compelling and touching read. I loved Bedeviled and hope it finds a wide readership.

Molly Giles
Author of *All the Wrong Places*

A sensitive, gutsy novel.

Alexander Mawyer
Editor of *The Contemporary Pacific*

A PUBLICATION FROM

Mānoa Books
manoafoundation.org

El León Literary Arts
elleonliteraryarts.org

BEDEVILED
can be found at
createspace.com
amazon.com

$15 • ISBN 978-0-9799504-0-7

DISCOVER MĀNOA

STORY IS A VAGABOND

Guest-edited by Alok Bhalla, Asif Farrukhi, and Nishat Zaidi

One of Pakistan's most loved writers, Intizar Husain published seven volumes of short stories, four novels, and a novella, as well as travelogues, memoirs, and critical essays. *Story Is a Vagabond* is the first collection in English to show the breadth of his innovative and compassionate work. Images by Imran Qureshi.

BRIGHT AS AN AUTUMN MOON

Translated by Andrew Schelling

Worshipful love for Krishna comes to life in these fifty erotic Sanskrit verses written from the fourth to the twelfth centuries. Beautifully rendered into English by American poet and Sanskrit scholar Andrew Schelling, each translation is accompanied by the original Sanskrit, as well as a transliteration, glossary, and commentary. Included are reproductions of eighteenth-century Deccani miniature paintings.

ANDHA YUG

Translated by Alok Bhalla

One of the notable plays of post-Independence India, Dharamvir Bharati's *Andha Yug* is set on the last day of the Mahabharata war. The play explores what happens when individuals succumb to the cruelty and cynicism of a blind, dispirited age and lose their capacity for moral action, reconciliation, and goodness. Introduction by Alok Bhalla. Illustrated in color.

2017 SMITHSONIAN ASIAN AMERICAN LITERATURE FESTIVAL

JULY 27-29, 2017
WASHINGTON, DC
AT THE SMITHSONIAN,
LIBRARY OF CONGRESS, AND
GEORGE WASHINGTON UNIVERSITY

COME FOR READINGS, MENTORING, SALONS,
INTERACTIVE WORKSHOPS AND MAKER SPACES, POP-UP
LIBRARIES, AND THE LAUNCH OF A NEW ASIAN AMERICAN
POETRY ISSUE OF POETRY MAGAZINE!

SPONSORED BY:

Kaya

KUNDIMAN

✳ Smithsonian Asian Pacific American Center

POETRY
FOUNDATION

ALONG WITH THE LIBRARY OF CONGRESS POETRY AND
LITERATURE CENTER, AALR, AND POETRY MAGAZINE

*T*wo "Indians," one Native American and the other South Asian Parsi meet in the sixties in Berkeley, and in their friendship and extended families, old and new worlds meet. But as we always suspected, the old world was also always new and the new world of course old, and the making of "American" is as confusing as "Indian." Spanning a period from war to war -- Vietnam to Chiapas, Mexico, friendships and stories intertwine with the controversies of race and history, by turns tragic and comic, heartbreak tempered by hilarity. In this great very American script, the politics of dreams meet the dreams of politics. It is a mismatching and yet a tender reconciliation.

- Karen Yamashita

- **Pub Date:2/15/2016**
- **ISBN 978-0-984-37768-8**

Price: $ 14.50

Weavers Press Presents

Small Press Distribution

BLUE
A NOVEL
RANBIR SINGH SIDHU

david lida
ONE
LIFE
a novel

J.M. SERVIN
TRANSLATED BY
ANTHONY SEIDMAN

ARCADE
DREW NELLINS SMITH

A NOVEL
YEAR
OF THE
GOOSE
CARLY J. HALLMAN

THE
BORDER
OF
PARADISE
A NOVEL
ESME WEIJUN WANG

Florence
in Ecstasy
a novel
Jessie Chaffee

HENRIETTA
ROSE-INNES
NINEVEH
A NOVEL

Rebecca Entel
Fingerprints
of Previous

The
Annie
Year
A NOVEL
STEPHANIE WILBUR ASH

THE a novel
SHOOTING
James Boice

Cutting edge contemporary literature
from the U.S. and around the world.

un named
press